The Greening of Business
in Developing Countries

Zed Titles on Transnational Corporations

Zed Books publishes extensively on globalization and modern capitalism. An increasing number of its titles focus specifically on the workings of transnational corporations.

Sharon Beder, *Selling the Work Ethic: From Puritan Pulpit to Corporate PR*

Walden Bello, Nicola Bullard and Kamal Malhotra (eds), *Global Finance: New Thinking on Regulating Speculative Capital Markets*

Ricardo Carrere and Larry Lohmann (eds), *Pulping the South: Industrial Tree Plantations and the World Paper Economy*

John Madeley, *Big Business, Poor Peoples: The Impact of Transnational Corporations on the World's Poor*

Hans-Peter Martin and Harald Schumann, *The Global Trap: Globalization and the Assault on Prosperity and Democracy*

Judith Richter, *The Regulation of Corporations: Business Behaviour, Codes of Conduct and Citizen Action*

Amory Starr, *Naming the Enemy: Anti-Corporate Social Movements Confront Globalization?*

Keith Suter, *Curbing Corporate Power: How to Control Giant Corporations*

Peter Utting (ed.), *The Greening of Business in Developing Countries: Rhetoric, Reality and Prospects*

David Woodward, *The Next Crisis? Foreign Direct and Equity Investment in Developing Countries*

For full details of this list and Zed's other subject and general catalogues, please write to: The Marketing Department, Zed Books, 7 Cynthia Street, London N1 9JF, UK or email Sales@zedbooks.demon.co.uk

Visit our website at: www.zedbooks.demon.co.uk

About UNRISD

The United Nations Research Institute for Social Development (UNRISD) is an autonomous agency engaging in multidisciplinary research on the social dimensions of contemporary problems affecting development. Its work is guided by the conviction that, for effective development policies to be formulated, an understanding of the social and political context is crucial. The Institute attempts to provide governments, development agencies, grassroots organizations and scholars with a better understanding of how development policies and processes of economic, social and environmental change affect different social groups. Working through an extensive network of national research centres, UNRISD aims to promote original research and strengthen research capacity in developing countries.

Current research programmes include: Civil Society and Social Movements; Democracy, Governance and Human Rights; Identities, Conflict and Cohesion; Social Policy and Development; and Technology and Society. A list of UNRISD's free and priced publications can be obtained by contacting the Reference Centre.

UNRISD, Palais des Nations,
1211 Geneva 10, Switzerland
Phone: (41 22) 917 3020
Fax: (41 22) 917 0650
E-mail: info@unrisd.org
Web: www.unrisd.org

The Greening of Business in Developing Countries

Rhetoric, Reality and Prospects

Edited by
PETER UTTING

Zed Books
LONDON & NEW YORK

in association with

UNRISD
UNITED NATIONS
RESEARCH INSTITUTE
FOR SOCIAL DEVELOPMENT

The Greening of Business in Developing Countries was first published in 2002 by
Zed Books Ltd, 7 Cynthia Street, London N1 9JF, UK and
Room 400, 175 Fifth Avenue, New York, NY 10010, USA

On behalf of the United Nations Research Institute for Social Development
(UNRISD), Palais des Nations, 1211 Geneva 10, Switzerland

Distributed in the USA exclusively by Palgrave, a division of
St Martin's Press, LLC, 175 Fifth Avenue, New York, NY 10010, USA.

Cover designed by Andrew Corbett
Set in 10/11 pt Bembo
by Long House, Cumbria, UK
Printed and bound in Malaysia

A catalogue record for this book
is available from the British Library

US CIP has been applied for

ISBN   Hb 1 84277 088 8
       Pb 1 84277 089 6

Contents

Boxes, Figures and Tables

Acknowledgements

The essays which make up this collection originated under the auspices of an international research programme on Business Responsibility for Sustainable Development that was sponsored by the United Nations Research Institute for Social Development (UNRISD) and supported financially by the Agency for Development and Co-operation of the Swiss Government and the MacArthur Foundation. Funding for the project was also provided by the Institute's core budget which is supported by voluntary contributions from the governments of Denmark, Finland, Mexico, the Netherlands, Norway, Sweden and Switzerland.

I am grateful to the *Universidad Nacional* in Costa Rica, and in particular to Antonieta Camacho and Olman Segura, for having organized the international workshop which brought together most of the writers who contributed to this volume.

I would like to thank Harris Gleckman, Gabrielle Koehler, David Levy, David Murphy, Yusuf Bangura, Solon Barraclough and David Westendorff, as well as four anonymous reviewers, for their insightful comments on various draft chapters. I am most grateful to Erika Drucker, Jenifer Freedman, and Kelly O'Neill for editorial assistance; Anita Tombez and Christine Vuilleumier for secretarial support; and Renato Alva and Virginia Rodríguez for research assistance.

Peter Utting

Notes on Contributors

David Barkin is Professor of Economics at the Metropolitan University in Mexico City. His current work involves analysis of the impact of international economic integration on the environment and on economic opportunities for communities in Latin America. Among his books are *Distorted Development: Mexico in the World Economy* and *Wealth, Poverty and Sustainable Development*.

Jem Bendell is a researcher, writer and consultant on business and sustainable social development. He worked on forest certification issues while at the World Wide Fund For Nature-UK, and contributed to the establishment of the new Marine Stewardship Council. He is co-author of *In the Company of Partners: Business, Environmental Groups and Sustainable Development Post-Rio* and editor of *Terms for Endearment: Business, NGOs and Sustainable Development*.

María Antonieta Camacho Soto is a professor at the School of Planning and Social Promotion, Universidad Nacional, Costa Rica, where she coordinates a multidisciplinary action-research programme (CAMBIOS). She is co-author of a forthcoming methodological series issued by CAMBIOS and a forthcoming book on participatory issues and case studies about the environmental policy-making processes in Costa Rica.

Ricardo Carrere is a project coordinator at the Instituto del Tercer Mundo in Uruguay. He is also the international coordinator of the World Rainforest Movement, which aims to protect tropical forests and the peoples which inhabit them. Since 1988, he has conducted research and international and national campaigns on both native forests and commercial tree plantations. His publications include *Pulping the South: Industrial Tree Plantations and the World Paper Economy* (co-authored with Larry Lohmann) and *Forestry Geopolitics and Sustainable Development: An Overview and the Case of Uruguay*.

Emily Fintel served as Programme Assistant at the Instituto Centroamericano de

Administración de Empresas (INCAE) and Executive Assistant to the Dean until March 1999. She holds a Bachelor of Science degree from Cornell University and also studied at the Universidad de Costa Rica.

Jonathon Hanks teaches at the International Institute of Industrial Environmental Economics at Lund University, Sweden. Previously he was Group Environmental Adviser at AECI Ltd in South Africa. He also served as the South African representative to the Subcommittee on Environmental Auditing of the International Standardization Organization (ISO), and participated in various environmental policy initiatives on behalf of AECI and the South African Chemical and Allied Industries Association.

Michael Hansen is an assistant professor at the Copenhagen Business School (CBS). He previously worked at the United Nations Centre on Transnational Corporations and is currently coordinating a joint CBS–UNCTAD project that considers cross-border environmental management of European TNCs with affiliates in South East Asia. He has published several articles and chapters of books and is co-editor of *International Trade Regulation, National Development Strategies and the Environment*.

David Murphy is Senior Researcher at the New Academy of Business, specializing in the fields of sustainable development and corporate social responsibility. In recent years he has undertaken assignments for several international organizations. Prior to his arrival in the United Kingdom, he worked for Canadian University Service Overseas (CUSO) in both West Africa and Canada. He is co-author of *In Company of Partners: Business, Environmental Groups and Sustainable Development Post-Rio*.

Martin Perry was an associate professor at the National University of Singapore where he taught environmental aspects of geography and public policy until 2001. He is co-author of *Singapore: A Developmental City State*, and has acted as a consultant to the Singapore Ministry of Trade and Industry. He now works as a senior research analyst for the Department of Labour in Wellington, New Zealand.

Lawrence Pratt is Associate Director of the Latin American Center for Competitiveness and Sustainable Development at INCAE, in Alajuela, Costa Rica, and teaches environmental strategy and environmental policy in INCAE's Masters Degree programmes. Prior to 1996 he was Senior Policy Analyst and Director of Training Programmes at the Environmental Law Institute in Washington, DC.

Silvia Rodríguez Cervantes is a professor at the School of Environmental Sciences, Universidad Nacional, Costa Rica. She leads the Biodiversity and Social Actors Project and recently coordinated the commission formed by the National Assembly of Costa Rica to draft the biodiversity law. She has written several articles on sustainable development, biodiversity, bioprospecting and patenting rights, and is co-author of an award-winning book on forestry policies in Costa Rica.

Sanjeev Singh is a PhD scholar in the Department of Geography, National University of Singapore, undertaking research on voluntary environmental initiatives in South East Asia.

Peter Utting is a project coordinator at the United Nations Research Institute for Social Development (UNRISD) in Geneva. In recent years he has directed research projects on the politics of environmental protection in developing countries and on business responsibility for sustainable development. He is co-editor of *States of Disarray: The Social Effects of Globalization*, editor of *Forest Policy and Politics in the Philippines* and the author of several books, including *Trees, People and Power*.

Richard Welford is Professor of Corporate Environmental Management at the University of Huddersfield, Director of the Centre for Corporate Environmental Management, and Professor of Sustainable Management at the Norwegian School of Management. He is the editor of the international journal *Business Strategy and the Environment* and co-editor of *Business and the Environment* and *Corporate Environmental Management*. Among his books is *Hijacking Environmentalism: Corporate Responses to Sustainable Development*.

Abbreviations

ABECEL	Brazilian Association of Cellulose Exporters
AESF	American Electroplaters and Surface Finishers
AFL-CIO	The American Federation of Labour
AGAPAN	Associaçao Gaúcha de Proteção do Ambiente Natural
AMCEL	Amapá Florestal e Celulose SA
AMHSA	Steelmaking Division of GAN
APC	Association for Progressive Communications
ASEAN	Association of South East Asian Nations
BAT	Best available technology
BCSD	Business Council for Sustainable Development
BECC	Border Environmental Cooperation Commission
BFI	Browning-Ferris Industries
BGMEA	Bangladesh Garment Manufacturers and Exporters Association
BLCC	Bunyad Literacy Community Council
BNDES	Brazilian National Economic and Social Development Bank
BOD	Biochemical oxygen demand
BP	British Petroleum
BS 7750	a national environmental standard of the BSI
CAIA	Chemical & Allied Industries Association (South Africa)
CAMBIOS	Cambio Social, Biodiversidad y Sustentabilidad del Desarrollo
CANACINTRA	National Association of Manufacturing Industry
CANACO	National Trade Association
CBS	Copenhagen Business School
CCE	Business Coordinating Center
CDDH	Centro de Defesa dos Direitos Humanos
CEC	Commission for Environmental Cooperation
CEFIC	European Chemical Industry Council
CENIBRA	Celulose Nipo-Brasileira SA
CEO	Chief Executive Officer
CEP	Council on Economic Priorities
CEPAL	Comisión Económica para América Latina y el Caribe (Economic Commission for Latin America and the Caribbean–ECLAC)
CEPDES	Center of Political Economy for Sustainable Development
CEPEDES	Centro de Estudos e Pesquisas para o Desenvolvimento do Extremo Sul da Bahia
CERES	Coalition for Environmentally Responsible Economies and Societies
CESPEDES	The Center for Private Sector Studies for Sustainable Development

CFCs	Chlorofluorocarbons
CFE	Federal Electricity Commission
CIEN	Clearinghouse for Eco-efficiency for Business
CIMI	Conselho Indigenista Misionario
CO_2	Carbon dioxide
CONCAWE	Conservation of Clean Air and Water Western Europe
CONIECO	The National Council of Ecological Industrialists
CONNEP	Consultative National Environmental Policy Process
COPs	Conferences of the Parties
CSIR	Council for Scientific and Industrial Research
CUSO	Canadian University Service Overseas
DAC	Development Assistance Committee
DANCED	Danish Co-operation for Environment & Development
DDT	Dichloro-diphenyl-trichloroethane (insecticide)
DEAT	Department of Environmental Affairs and Tourism
DESD	Department of Economic and Social Development (United Nations, New York)
DIY	Do It Yourself
DME	Department of Minerals and Energy
DWAF	Department of Water Affairs and Forestry
ECOSOC	Economic and Social Council
ECTG	Executive Commission of the Tupinikim and Guarani
EDF	Environmental Defense Fund
EEA	European Environmental Agency
EHS	Environment, health and safety
EIA	Environmental Impact Assessment
EMAS	European Eco-Management and Audit Scheme
EMBRAPA	Brazilian Agricultural Research Company
EMS	Environmental management systems
EPA	Environmental Protection Agency, US
ESCAP	Economic and Social Commission for Asia and the Pacific
EU	European Union
EVF	Environmental Value Fund
FAO	Food and Agriculture Organization (United Nations)
FASE	Federação de Orgãos para Asistência Social e Educacional
FDI	Foreign direct investment
FIDE	Fideicomiso para el Ahorro de Energía (Trust Fund for Energy Savings)
FIFA	Fédération Internationale de Football Association
FoE	Friends of the Earth
FSC	Forest Stewardship Council
FUDENA	Foundation for the Defense of Nature, Venezuela
G77	Group of 77 developing countries
GAN	Grupo Acerero del Norte
GATT	General Agreement on Tariffs and Trade
GBN	green business networks
GEAR	Growth, Employment and Redistribution strategy
GEMI	Global Environmental Management Initiative
HIID	Harvard Institute for International Development
IBAMA	Instituto Brasileiro do Meio Ambiente e dos Recursos Naturais Renováveis (Brazil)
IBASE	Instituto Brasileiro de Análises Sociais e Econômicas
ICC	International Chamber of Commerce
IEF	Industry Environmental Forum of South Africa
IFBWW	International Federation of Building and Wood Workers

IFC	International Finance Corporation
IFU	Industrialization Fund for Developing Countries
IIED	International Institute for the Environment and Development
ILO	International Labour Organization
ILRF	International Labor Rights Fund
IMF	International Monetary Fund
INBio	The National Biodiversity Institute
INCAE	Instituto Centroamericano de Administración de Empresas
INE	National Institute of Ecology
IOC	International Olympic Committee
IPEC	International Program for the Elimination of Child Labour
IPN	National Polytechnic Institute
IRRC	Investor Responsibility Research Centre
ISO	International Standardization Organization
ITESM	Technological Institute of Monterrey
ITTA	International Tropical Timber Agreement
ITTO	International Tropical Timber Organization
IUBS	International Union of Biological Sciences
IUCN	World Conservation Union
JATAN	Japan Tropical Forest Action Network
KPMG	International Firm of Chartered Accountants & Business Advisors
LCA	Life-cycle analysis
LDC	Less developed country
MAI	Multilateral Agreement on Investment
MBI	Market-based instrument
MICC	Malaysian International Chamber of Commerce
MIGA	Multilateral Investment Guarantee Agreement
MINAE	Ministerio de Ambiente y Energía
MIRENEM	Ministerio de Recursos Naturales, Energía y Minas
MOSOP	Movement for the Survival of the Ogoni People
MSC	Marine Stewardship Council
NADBank	North American Development Bank
NAFTA	North American Free Trade Agreement
NEF	New Economics Foundation
NEPP	National Environmental Policy Plan
NGO	Non-governmental organization
NIEO	New International Economic Order
NIMBY	Not in my backyard
NNPC	National Nigerian Petrol Company
ODA	Official development assistance
OECD	Organization for Economic Cooperation and Development
OPEC	Organization of Petroleum Exporting Countries
PACSA	Packaging Council of South Africa
PAN-USA	Pesticide Action Network
PAP	People's Action Party (Singapore)
P&PA	Paper and Packaging Analyst (periodical)
PBM	Pakistan Bait-ul-Mal
PCB	Polychlorinated biphenyl
PPI	Pulp and Paper International (periodical)
PR	Public relations
PROFEPA	Office of the Federal Attorney for Environmental Protection
PRTR	Pollution Release and Transfer Register
PVC	Polyvinyl chloride (type of plastic)
R&D	Research and development

RAFI	Rural Advancement Foundation International
RAG	Rainforest Action Group
RAP	Red Ambiental Peruana
RAPAM	Red de Acción Sobre Plaguicidas y Alternativas en México
Red Mocaf	Mexican Network of Peasant Forestry Communities
RSA	Republic of South Africa
SA	South African
SACOB	South African Chamber of Commerce
SCCI	Sialkot Chamber of Commerce and Industry
SCIC	Singapore Chemical Industry Council
SCF	Save the Children Fund
SEDUE	Ministry of Ecology and Urban Development
SEMARNAP	Secretariat of Environment, Natural Resources and Fishing
SGMA	Sporting Goods Manufacturers Association
SGS	Société Générale de Surveillance
SICA	Soccer Industry Council of America
SINAC	National System of Conservation Areas
SINADES	The National System of Sustainable Development
SINTICEL	Pulp Industry Workers' Union
SITRAP	Agricultural Plantation Workers' Union
SKEPHI	Indonesian Forest Conservation Network
SME	Small and medium-sized enterprise
SPI	Indian Protection Service
TNC	Transnational corporation
TRI (polluter)	Toxics Release Inventory, US
TRIMs	Trade-related investment measures
TRIPs	Trade-related aspects of intellectual property rights
UK	United Kingdom
UN	United Nations
UNA	Universidad Nacional (Costa Rica)
UNCED	United Nations Conference on Environment and Development
UNCSD	United Nations Commission on Sustainable Development
UNCTAD	United Nations Conference on Trade and Development
UNCTC	United Nations Centre on Transnational Corporations
UNDP	United Nations Development Programme
UNEP	United Nations Environment Programme
UNESCO	United Nations Educational, Scientific and Cultural Organization
UNICEF	United Nations Children's Fund
UNIDO	United Nations Industrial Development Organization
UNITAR	United Nations Institute for Training and Research
UNPO	Unrepresented Nations and Peoples Organization
UNRISD	United Nations Research Institute for Social Development
US	United States
USA	United States of America
USAID	United States Agency for International Development
WBCSD	World Business Council for Sustainable Development
WBCSD-LA	World Business Council for Sustainable Development – Latin America
WCC	World Council of Churches
WCED	World Commission on Environment and Development
WFSGI	World Federation of the Sporting Goods Industry
WHO	World Health Organization
WICE	World Industrial Council for the Environment
WTO	World Trade Organization
WWF	World Wide Fund For Nature

INTRODUCTION

Towards Corporate
Environmental Responsibility?

PETER UTTING

So-called 'development' during the past 50 years has been closely associated with environmental degradation, much of it caused directly or indirectly by big business. In developing countries, as elsewhere, logging and mining enterprises, pulp and paper mills, agribusiness, oil and chemical companies, and many other industries and enterprises have wreaked havoc with large areas of tropical forests, marine and coastal resources, fresh water sources, agricultural land and the urban environment.

The Earth Summit in 1992 called on the world's governments, business, international development agencies and non-governmental organizations (NGOs) to work together to minimize the trade-off between economic growth and environmental protection. The Rio Declaration urged the business community to support a precautionary approach to environmental challenges, undertake initiatives to promote greater environmental responsibility and encourage the development and diffusion of environmentally friendly technologies (Annan, 1999). An important sector of the business community, led by a small group of very large transnational corporations (TNCs), explicitly acknowledged the need for firms to clean up their act and take a more proactive role in promoting environmental protection and sustainable development.[1] Through publications such as *Changing Course* (Schmid-heiny, 1992), this sector called for a rethinking of corporate strategy in relation to natural resource use and management, and proffered a solution in the shape and form of 'eco-efficiency'.[2] The confrontational politics of earlier decades, which had pitted a pro-regulation and redistributive lobby against TNCs, lost momentum as governments, business and multilateral organizations alike, as well as an increasing number of NGOs, embraced ideas of 'partnership' and 'co-regulation' in which different actors or 'stakeholders'[3] would work together to find ways of minimizing the environmental cost of economic growth and modernization. The hands-on, regulatory role of the state ceded ground to 'corporate self-regulation' and 'voluntary initiatives'[4] as the best approach for promoting the adoption of instruments and processes associated with corporate environmental responsibility, such as codes of conduct, environmental policies and management systems (EMS), the use of energy-efficient and cleaner technology, recycling, life-cycle analysis[5] and environmental certification, labelling, reporting and audits.

In some of the richer countries of the world, a combination of government regulations, civil society pressures, technological innovations and market conditions has encouraged some sectors of business to act in a more environmentally responsible way. What is far less clear is the extent to which the greening of business is catching on in developing countries, and whether or not an institutional and political framework conducive to corporate environmental responsibility is being constructed.

Processes associated with globalization indicate that whereas the global reach and influence of TNCs has increased considerably in recent decades, the power of certain institutions that might regulate business activities, notably those associated with the nation state and trade unions, is weak or declining in many countries of 'the South' (UNRISD, 1995). NGOs and civil society movements have become more active but their demands and priorities are not necessarily those related to corporate accountability. In the context of this changing balance of forces, how are developing countries expected to deal with and minimize the environmental damage associated with business practices?

What we know about these questions is extremely superficial, with 'knowledge' often falling into one of two camps. One believes that business in the South will follow in the footsteps of business in the North, gradually improving environmental management systems, and doing so largely via corporate self-regulation and voluntary initiatives. Foreign direct investment (FDI) and TNCs are often singled out as important conduits for environmental management reform, given their capacity to diffuse cleaner technologies and impose higher standards throughout supply chains. The other is highly sceptical of corporate rhetoric associated with environmental responsibility, often labelling it as 'greenwash' and claiming that changes in environmental management systems and eco-efficiency do little, if anything, to alter 'business as usual'.

Debates on the Greening of Business

Such positions reflect, to some extent, different theoretical positions regarding the environmental problematic and appropriate solutions. Mainstream policies for dealing with environmental problems and, in particular, initiatives and interventions associated with the greening of business, are increasingly associated with 'ecological modernization' (Dryzek, 1997; Dryzek and Schlosberg, 1998). This involves an approach that emphasizes technological and managerial innovations to improve the efficiency of resource use, and so-called 'win-win', as opposed to zero-sum scenarios, where both environmental and economic benefits can be attained simultaneously (Hajer, 1995). Ecological modernization generally 'assumes that existing political, economic, and social institutions can internalise care for the environment' (*ibid.*: 25).

A strong element of 'technological determinism' characterizes the ecological modernization perspective (Benton, 1994): technical 'fixes', it is assumed, can go a long way towards solving environmental problems. Some observers also argue that, historically, industry inevitably 'moves in the right direction' of minimizing factor inputs per unit of output, 'primarily driven by economics and continuous technological change' (Grübler, 1994). According to this latter position, the history of industrial capitalism can be divided into different phases, each of which is associated with sets of technological and institutional innovations which have different environmental effects. For some observers we are presently in the midst of another transition that involves a shift from 'mass production and consumption' to one – speculatively labelled 'total quality' (Socolow *et al.*, 1994: 20) – in which companies adopt a systems or life-cycle approach that attempts to reduce or eliminate the use of certain inputs; minimize air emissions, liquid and solid waste; design for energy efficiency and recycle both during manufacture and after use (Graedel, 1994: 34–5). Hawken *et al.* (1999) suggest we are on the eve of a new era of natural capitalism characterized by radically increased resource productivity, massive reductions in waste and toxicity achieved through closed-loop cycles of materials use, a service economy in which goods are increasingly leased rather than sold, and reinvestment in sustaining, restoring and expanding stocks of natural capital.

Ecological modernization emphasizes not only the role of technological and economic factors but also changes occurring in corporate culture. This is reflected in the increasing adherence to the concept of

> product stewardship [which] recognizes that organizations involved in the production of a product share a responsibility for the product's environmental effects with other organizations in the supply chain and with consumers of the product. Product stewardship is increasingly replacing the traditional perception among industrial managers that the environment is an 'economic externality' and that environmental issues are the organizational domain of the company's Health, Safety, and Environment group. (Roome, 1998b: 4)

CEOs and managers are seen to be increasingly responsive to environmental and stakeholder concerns, partly in response to ethical considerations. According to Smart:

> In response to this new awareness, the sensitive corporation will come to see that its self-interest is best served by a new approach. That managers also perceive it as 'the right thing to do' will give them a personal, as well as a corporate, incentive to proceed along a path in which newly crafted policies are followed by changes in organization, behaviour, and attitude, eventually resulting in implanting an environmental ethic throughout the workforce. (Smart, 1992: 6)

This new corporate culture is also characterized by the fact that companies are becoming more proactive rather than defensive. Instead of simply complying with legislation, they move 'beyond compliance' (Smart, 1992) and become more a 'policy-maker, not a policy-taker' (Socolow, 1994: 12). Business, it is assumed, can take the lead and need not be dictated to by government. So-called 'corporate self-regulation' and 'voluntary initiatives', as opposed to 'command and control' regulation, are seen as the appropriate way of promoting environmentally responsible business.

Business, then, is seen to be moving from simply remedying environmental problems through *ad hoc* solutions to preventing them through a more holistic or systemic approach (Hajer, 1995; von Moltke *et al.*, 1998). Others have referred to this evolution in terms of a shift from 'environmental protection' to 'resource management' (Colby, 1989). Whereas the former recognizes the need to repair or set limits on harmful industrial activity as a means to minimize environmental problems that constrain the process of economic growth, the latter emphasizes the long-term sustainability of resource use, the interdependence of human activity and the environment, and the need to facilitate ecological functions while simultaneously taking advantage of them (Hoffman and Ehrenfeld, 1998: 60–1; Colby, 1989). Whereas the former position is associated with environmental management, the latter is associated more with sustainable development.

The concept of sustainable development involves far more than environmental protection. Core elements of the concept, as popularized by the World Commission on Environment and Development, also include meeting people's needs and intra- as well as inter-generational equity (WCED, 1987). What it would take to attain these goals is, of course, open to debate but a strategy that carries the sustainable development label would need to be multi-faceted, embracing economic, social, environmental, political and cultural dimensions. It has been suggested that any company that is serious about contributing to sustainable development would have to demonstrate progress in several areas (Welford *et al.*, 1998), including environmental performance, the empowerment of employees, economic performance, employment generation and conditions, ethics, equity and education. Also important is 'a measurement framework based on the idea of continuous improvement; and a process of sustainable development dialogue that involves two-way communications between firms and their stakeholders' (*ibid.*, 1998).

While there are an increasing number of companies in the North that are engaged in environmental management, very few companies have attempted to adopt the more comprehensive strategy associated with sustainable development. As companies come to interact, however, with a broader range of stakeholder interests – for example, through partnerships with NGOs – and as environmental values pervade corporate cultures, some argue that certain sectors of business may be evolving towards the resource management perspective and philosophy (Hoffman and Ehrenfeld, 1998; Schmidheiny *et al.*, 1997). The fact that some companies (such as those involved in the United Nations Global Compact)[6] and business associations (such as the World Business Council for Sustainable Development – WBCSD), which previously emphasized eco-efficiency, are now engaging more actively with issues of corporate social responsibility (Holme and Watts, 2000) could be regarded as evidence of this shift.

While recognizing that the pace and location of change is still very uneven, the WBCSD suggests that various changes in corporate policy and practice point to a 'paradigm shift', which presumably will enable business to overcome what Schmidheiny referred to as 'the inertia of the present destructive course, and [the need] to create a new momentum towards sustainable development' (Schmidheiny, 1992). The constituent elements of this shift involve a change from:

- seeing only costs and difficulties in the concept of sustainable development to seeing savings and opportunities;
- end-of-pipe approaches to pollution to the use of cleaner, more efficient technology throughout entire production systems;
- linear, 'through-put' thinking and approaches to systems and recycling approaches;
- seeing environment and social issues as responsibilities only for technical departments or experts to seeing these issues as company-wide responsibilities;
- a starting premise of confidentiality to one of openness and transparency;
- narrow lobbying to more open discussion with stakeholders. (Schmidheiny *et al.* 1997: 9)

This dynamic is thought by many observers to be relatively strong in the advanced industrialized countries (Dryzek, 1997; Cairncross, 1995; DeSimone and Popoff, 1997; Smart, 1992; Socolow *et al.*, 1994), and is expected to spread to developing countries (UNCTAD, 1999; Flaherty and Rappaport, 1997; Watts and Holme, 1997). Changes in the international division of labour during the past three decades associated with the emergence of 'newly industrialized countries', the export orientation of developing economies, the rapid increase in foreign direct investment since the 1980s and related patterns of technology transfer provide the contexts and conditions in which the greening of business can extend to the South (UNCTAD, 1999). It is generally considered that large Northern corporations (both TNCs and giant retailers) are taking the lead in adopting or promoting technological and managerial innovations in affiliates and other companies involved in their supply chains. According the Flaherty and Rappaport, these lead companies 'seek greater uniformity in process, production and product standards' and recognize the considerable competitive advantages to be gained from having a company or product image associated with environmental and social responsibility (Flaherty and Rappaport, 1997). Their activities are being encouraged, supported and publicized by certain industry and business associations such as the International Chamber of Commerce (ICC) and the WBCSD, as well as the United Nations and specific agencies such as the International Labour Organization (ILO), the United Nations Environment Programme (UNEP) and the World Bank.

Both the substantive and geographical dimensions of corporate responsibility, then, appear to be widening, and environmental management reforms are assuming a more systemic character at the level of the firm. The driving forces underpinning such changes, however, are thought to be essentially technological, managerial, economic and cultural. There is little, if any, suggestion that the fundamental character of modern economic, political and social life – reflected in certain types of consumption patterns, the concentration of economic power in large corporations, and sharp inequalities in power and levels of living – must change.

The critics of corporate environmentalism – those, referred to earlier, who dismiss the greening of business as 'greenwash' or see it as essentially 'business as usual' – tend to be associated with so-called 'radical' perspectives and philosophies, including, for example, 'eco-development', 'deep ecology', 'ecosocialism' and 'political ecology'. While the concerns, diagnosis, prognosis and solutions associated with these positions may vary considerably, there is a common concern that the solution to the world's environmental and developmental problems rests not simply with reducing the intensity of resource use, waste and pollution but with transforming the nature of the dominant models of production and consumption that characterize modern industrial society.

The greenwash critics see the greening of business as essentially a public relations exercise or disinformation that attempts to portray an image of corporate responsiveness to environmental and social concerns when in fact companies continue to seriously degrade the environment, the livelihoods and quality of life of certain groups in society (Greer and Bruno, 1996). TNCs are generally singled out as major culprits in this regard. These and other critics charge that the dominant approach to the greening of business amounts to 'business as usual' (Welford, 1997). It is centred on eco-efficiency, which simply 'adds an environmental dimension to the mainstream development path and reinforces the growth paradigm' and consumption patterns that constitute the root cause of the environmental crisis *(ibid.)*.

Whereas the proponents of ecological modernization see considerable potential for a fairly vigorous process of corporate greening driven by technological innovation and win-win opportunities, the critics highlight the fact that certain features of the international economic order and globalization, notably those associated with competition, deregulation, the free movement of goods and capital, and the globalization of consumer culture, are putting pressure on firms to lower costs and standards, particularly in developing countries. Furthermore, structural adjustment programmes which encourage the 'downsizing' of the state are weakening the capacities of governments in many developing countries to shape national development processes and to regulate and monitor corporate activities. Under such conditions, progress towards corporate environmental responsibility is neither inevitable nor evolutionary. While the critics of corporate environmentalism may propose different policy recommendations and approaches, these generally involve fundamental changes in economic policy and accounting systems, the scale of production units, as well as in power relations, with civil society, governmental and international regulatory pressures playing an important role.

Some critics have adopted a perspective which sees increasing corporate responsiveness to environmental and social concerns as a reality but one which is fundamentally political in nature (Levy, 1997; Murphy and Bendell, 1997). According to Levy: 'The view taken here is that capitalism is resilient and adaptive; corporations will accommodate the environmental challenge through compromise and cooption, ameliorating their environmental impact sufficiently to blunt serious challenge to their hegemonic position' (1997:131). To the extent that environmental, consumer, human rights and other activist groups organize and mobilize and constitute a 'corporate accountability movement' (Broad and Cavanagh, 1999), there is considerable scope for promoting corporate environmental responsibility. Certain features associated with globalization, such as transnational activism and networking, as well as the rise of 'consumer politics', suggest that big business will increasingly come under the spotlight and will be forced to reform its policies and practices in both the North and South (O'Neill, 1999; Murphy and Bendell, 1997).[7] Elements of this approach are now being adopted by mainstream organizations. The World Bank, for example, has recently highlighted the importance of 'informal regulation' – various forms of pressure from NGOs and community groups – as an important driver of corporate environmental responsibility. Such pressures, coupled with market-based instruments, are seen as constituting 'a new model for pollution control in developing countries', which is preferred to the traditional 'command and control' model (World Bank, 2000: 3).

About This Book

To what extent is the greening of business a reality in the South, what are its implications for sustainable development and what might be done to scale up and deepen corporate environmentalism in the developing countries? It is these questions that are addressed in this book. What emerges is a critique suggesting that not only has change been extremely piecemeal but that the nature of change is fraught with contradictions from the perspective of sustainable development. The considerable gap that separates corporate rhetoric and practice would appear to lend weight to the proponents of 'greenwash'. Various chapters reveal, however, that there are some fairly strong economic, political and structural forces in place which are encouraging greater responsiveness on the part of some sectors of big business to environmental and stakeholder concerns. As such the greening of business amounts to far more than window-dressing or a public relations exercise. What needs to be questioned is not so much whether the greening of business will extend to the South but the scope of that change and its quality in terms of environmental impacts and the promotion of sustainable development. Certain types of policy approaches, pressures and partnerships that might facilitate the scaling up and deepening of environmental management reform and corporate sustainability strategies are therefore considered.

The chapters are organized in two main parts. The first – 'The Environmental Record of the Private Sector: Large Corporations and Domestic Firms' – considers whether there has been a significant shift from 'business as usual' to corporate environmental responsibility. In Chapter 1, David Barkin provides an overview and assessment of the greening of business in Mexico. He reveals that many firms are taking steps to improve environmental management and that various institutions – private, public and regional – are now in place which are stimulating private sector responses in the field of corporate environmentalism. This scenario of incipient but positive change is contradicted, however, by other trends associated with the dominant economic strategy that is being pursued in the country. This strategy has encouraged investment in highly polluting industrial activities and the location of firms in urban areas with weak infrastructure, planning systems and fiscal regimes. The author also questions the content of corporate environmentalism, suggesting that it has focused much too narrowly on technical 'end-of-pipe' solutions to reduce waste streams rather than more thorough-going restructuring to improve community health and safety and the quality of life more generally.

In Chapter 2, Lawrence Pratt and Emily Fintel assess the state of corporate environmentalism in Central America. They present the preliminary results of a survey of leading firms in Costa Rica and El Salvador carried out by the Instituto Centroamericano de Administración de Empresas (INCAE), a regional business school, in association with the Harvard Institute for International Development. This study reveals that relatively few firms are seriously engaged in taking responsibility for the environmental impact of their operations. Firms with greater international involvement were found to perform better in terms of environmental responsibility. The authors also identify the principle drivers of corporate policy reform: company image and government regulation. They go on to identify key institutional and policy contexts that account for the limited response of business, emphasizing confusing and weak legislation and a range of disincentives generated by fiscal and financial policies.

In Chapter 3, Silvia Rodríguez and Antonieta Camacho take to task one of the reputed 'success stories' in the field of corporate environmentalism in developing countries – the bioprospecting partnership between the large US pharmaceutical company, Merck and Co., and the Costa Rican NGO, INBio. They contrast the economic, environmental and developmental claims that have been made concerning this agreement and the reality of resource flows and the distribution of costs and benefits among various stakeholders. The arguments they put forward challenge the conventional wisdom that bioprospecting constitutes a 'win–win' situation where all stakeholders stand to benefit. They show that the contribution of Merck to conservation and development in Costa Rica has been fairly minimal. They also cast doubt on the idea that such an agreement will eventually yield successful commercial products and handsome royalty revenues for Costa Rican institutions. Whereas the Merck–INBio agreement is often held up as a 'model' to be replicated elsewhere, they show how it developed within a context quite specific to Costa Rica, which is unlikely to be found elsewhere. The authors suggest that certain stakeholders, notably indigenous groups and local communities, continue to be excluded from existing or future benefits associated with this agreement and that greater participation of actors is needed to negotiate environmental and social responsibilities.

In Chapter 4, Ricardo Carrere scratches the surface of another well-publicized 'success story' – the case of the Brazilian pulp and paper company, Aracruz Cellulose. He also considers the response of four other leading firms in this sector in Brazil. He shows that the major corporations, forced to respond to stricter environmental legislation and, in particular, to various forms of social pressures, have mitigated some of their worst practices. The analysis reveals, however, that in spite of their environmental discourse and policies, all five corporations continue to have a damaging environmental and social impact in the areas where they operate. It is clear from this analysis that different stakeholders, in particular workers and indigenous peoples, have very different perspectives on whether or not these companies are promoting 'sustainable development'. The author argues that it is extremely difficult for the logic of a large-scale, profit-oriented company to be compatible with the logic of sustainable development. Such companies, however, are very adept at mobilizing a publicity machine to suggest otherwise.

In Chapter 5, Martin Perry and Sanjeev Singh examine efforts to promote corporate environmental responsibility in Singapore and Malaysia. They report the results of surveys carried out to assess the extent and type of voluntary environmental action among foreign-owned TNCs and the influences that motivate improvements in environmental management. In both countries they find that most respondents have adopted a range of voluntary initiatives, but that substantial activity is limited to a small number of organizations. The types of initiatives adopted and the factors influencing firm behaviour vary significantly in both countries. They question the assumption that ISO 14001 certification[8] is an important indicator of business commitment to environmental improvement, as well as the notion that voluntary approaches constitute an effective alternative to government regulation.

Part II of this volume – 'Promoting Corporate Environmental Responsibility: Mechanisms and Strategies' – considers the debates and initiatives surrounding the question of what types of regulatory regimes, policy instruments, partnerships and pressures are promoting or might facilitate corporate environmental responsibility. Five chapters examine the role and potential of different policy frameworks and 'civil regulation', involving closer relationships between business and civil society organizations.

In Chapter 6, Richard Welford questions the assumptions that (1) significant reform is taking place, and that (2) globalization is conducive to reform. He also questions the way the concept of sustainable development has been used by sectors of the business community, which tend to equate it narrowly with environmental and economic concerns and often ignore the social, ethical and political dimensions. Whilst recognizing that there are many opportunities for improving environmental management, he analyses in particular the constraints and barriers that impede progress. Few corporations, he argues, have recognized the gravity of the environmental and social crises to which they have contributed. The dominant approach which corporations have adopted to address environmental problems, namely eco-efficiency, is not promoting the types of reforms in business strategy that would be consistent with sustainable development. Business has, however, been fairly effective in controlling the global environmental agenda and weakening alternative visions and approaches to development and conservation. The chapter ends by presenting a broad policy framework and identifying specific policy instruments which might promote meaningful change in corporate environmental and social performance.

Highlighting the growing importance of TNCs in the global economy and in shaping the development prospects of many developing countries, Michael Hansen considers, in Chapter 7, the arguments for and against establishing environmental rules specifically targeting TNCs. On balance, he argues, international standards should be adopted. Such norms are warranted to (1) mitigate the adverse environmental impacts of TNC activity on host economies; (2) compensate for regulatory failure at the national and international levels; and (3) enhance the positive contribution of TNCs to environmental upgrading and capacity building in developing countries. After considering various ways in which such standards could be designed, the case is made for including minimum environmental standards in a multilateral agreement on investment while leaving the pursuit of best environmental technology and management practice to business self-regulation and to voluntary and incentive-based initiatives.

In Chapter 8, Jonathon Hanks explores the potential for shifting greater responsibility for environmental protection from the public to the private sector through 'co-regulation'. In view of the poor record of enforcement of environmental laws in many developing countries and the positive experience in several industrialized countries with innovative forms of environmental regulation, he argues the case for 'negotiated agreements'. This chapter also points out, however, the limits not only to voluntary agreements themselves but also to replicating in developing countries policy instruments developed in and for the very different contexts of the Organization for Economic Cooperation and Development (OECD). By referring to the case of South Africa, the author outlines the potential and limits of co-regulation in developing country contexts.

Much of the debate on how best to regulate business activities has focused on so-called 'command and control' measures versus self-regulatory initiatives. In chapters 9 and 10, David Murphy and Jem Bendell suggest the need to recognize that a new actor – other than government and business – has emerged which is playing an increasingly influential role in promoting corporate environmental and social responsibility. This actor is associated with 'civil society', and constituted in particular by NGOs and consumer movements. Chapter 9 presents three in-depth case studies, involving the timber, oil and sporting goods industries, which reveal different modalities of partnership and pressure. Chapter 10 develops a theory of 'civil regulation' to explain how corporations are being regulated in the context of globalization. The chapter highlights the role of Northern NGOs and consumers in this new regulatory wave and suggests that stronger alliances between Northern and Southern NGOs will need to develop if the legitimacy of civil regulation is not to be undermined. The emerging model of international certification, controlled by bodies such as the forest and marine stewardship councils, is, they argue, likely to be extended to other industrial sectors and will constitute a new system of 'global private regulation'.

In the concluding chapter, the present author examines both the limits and prospects of corporate environmentalism in the South. Following a review of the limits of corporate greening which have emerged in the preceding chapters, the chapter goes on to consider its potential by analysing both the major economic, political and structural forces that are driving this phenomenon and its implications for sustainable development. The conclusion reached is that various developments, associated with the way in which power in democratic and 'civil' societies is contested and the restructuring of global production, may indeed be encouraging some sectors of the business community in developing countries to take various initiatives associated with corporate environmentalism. For this reason, it is argued, environmental management reform should be seen as more than a response to so-called 'win–win' opportunities or a reaction to 'civil society' pressure. Rather, certain political, technological and economic conditions have coalesced which encourage sectors of the business community, notably some TNCs, to take a lead in promoting corporate environmentalism. The global reach and structures of organization and influence associated with TNCs mean that this process will inevitably spread to the South. This process, however, confronts various limits which suggest that, in the absence of stronger forms of regulation and more concerted civil society pressure, corporate environmental management will remain a fairly minimalist and uneven affair – one that is perhaps more conducive to economic growth and the legitimization of big business than sustainable development.

One of the problems with this field of inquiry is not only the ideological and polarized nature of much of the debate, but also the lack of reliable data and analysis. The evidence surrounding changes in corporate environmental policy, practice and performance is often highly anecdotal. There is a tendency to focus narrowly on one particular corporate activity, which is often portrayed as either highly positive or negative when, in fact, it may constitute a relatively insignificant component of a corporation's relation to natural resources and the environment. Much of the analysis has also become repetitive, with the same cases of 'best' or 'bad' practice being recycled in the literature.

Given the limited research that has been conducted on issues of corporate environmental responsibility in developing countries, it is in fact extremely difficult to assess the content, scale and prospects of the greening of business phenomenon in the South. Any analysis, at this stage, must be based on very partial evidence. This usually means drawing upon various sources of information, which may include theoretical thinking about globalization and the changing nature of capitalism and their implications for firm behaviour; reviews and analysis of environmental legislation and government policies and regulations which target or affect business practices; surveys of firms which attempt to identify both what it is that motivates companies to improve environmental management and what steps they are taking; official data on the number of firms which have been environmentally certified; and case studies of specific company initiatives, practices and performance.

The 11 chapters in this volume draw on varying combinations of these sources. The papers which make up this book were prepared under a research programme of the United Nations Research Institute for Social Development (UNRISD). The programme 'Business Responsibility for Sustainable Development' aims to understand better the potential and limits of corporate environmental and social responsibility, as well as the mix of policies, market conditions, institutional settings, pressures, partnerships and alliances that encourage business to act in a more responsible way. Under this programme two international workshops were held in Costa Rica and Switzerland in 1997 and 2000. These meetings brought together Northern and Southern researchers, as well as representatives of international organizations and the business and NGO communities. Most of the chapters in this volume are based on draft papers that were presented at these workshops.

Reflecting the mix of participants at the workshops, the chapters are written by researchers from a range of disciplines and with varying institutional affiliations. They include economists, sociologists, geographers, and environmental and forestry engineers. Several are also environmental and human rights activists and environmental advisers to business. Most of the chapters consider the experience of big business, mainly transnational corporations; they do not deal in any depth with small and medium-sized enterprises (SMEs). Furthermore, attention is focused mainly on national or sectoral developments in Latin America, notably, Central America, Mexico and Brazil, although certain chapters also refer to country experiences in Africa and Asia. The case studies included are not meant to be representative of 'the South' but they do involve countries that are highly integrated in the world economic system. As such they are relevant for testing the assumption, referred to above, that globalization, foreign direct investment and transnational corporations are conducive to the greening of business in developing countries.

Notes

1 The Business Council for Sustainable Development (BCSD) played a particularly prominent role in influencing the process sponsored by the United Nations Conference on Environment and Development (UNCED). The promotion of improved standards of corporate environmental management was taken a step further in 1993 when the International Chamber of Commerce (ICC) formed the World Industry Council for the Environment (WICE). In January 1995 the BCSD and WICE merged to form the World Business Council for Sustainable Development (WBCSD). By early 1999 the WBCSD membership included 127 large corporations.

2 Eco-efficiency has been defined by Schmidheiny and the WBCSD as 'a process of adding ever more value while steadily decreasing resource use, waste, and pollution' (Schmidheiny and Zorraquín, 1996: 5).

3 The term 'stakeholder' was defined by Freeman as 'any group or individual who can affect or is affected by the achievement of the organization's objectives' (1984: 46). Given the extremely broad nature of this definition and the fact that in reality only some stakeholders are taken into account, attention has focused on those who have legitimate (moral, legal and property-based) claims on an organization. More recently, Mitchell *et al.* have also highlighted the importance of power in stakeholder–manager relations, arguing that the power and urgency of claims are also crucial in determining which claims managers respond to (Mitchell, Agle and Wood, 1997).

4 The term 'voluntary initiatives' encompasses a wide range of initiatives which go beyond existing environmental laws and legislation. They may be unilaterally developed by industry, designed and run by government, jointly developed by government and industry, or developed and run by non-governmental organizations (UNEP, 1998).

5 Life-cycle analysis examines the environmental impact of a particular product or service throughout all the stages associated with its production, marketing and disposal.

6 On 26 July 2000 the United Nations formally launched the Global Compact, which encourages business leaders to adhere to nine principles related to human rights, labour standards and environmental protection, and to put these principles into practice via voluntary initiatives.

7 Certain proponents of ecological modernization theory also recognize an important role for civil society organizations and movements in promoting corporate environmental responsibility. In contrast to the 'radical' critics, however, they generally argue that there is no longer a need for confrontational tactics – change can be achieved through dialogue and collaboration.

8 Various authors in this volume refer to ISO 14000 or 14001 certification. The ISO 14000 series is a set of standards on environmental management established by the International Standardization Organization. This is an international association of national standard-setting bodies. One of the standards within the ISO 14000 series is ISO 14001, which outlines the requirements for an environmental management system that may be audited.

References

Annan, K. (1999), 'A Compact for the New Century', address to the World Economic Forum, Davos, 31 January. www.un.org/partners/business/davos.htm

Benton, T. (1994), 'Biology and Social Theory in the Environment Debate', in M. Redclift and T. Benton (eds.), *Social Theory and the Global Environment*, Routledge, London.

Cairncross, F. (1995), *Green Inc.: Guide to Business and the Environment*, Earthscan, London.

Colby, M. (1989), *The Evolution of Paradigms of Environmental Management in Development*, Working Papers 313, Strategic Planning and Review Department, The World Bank, Washington DC.

DeSimone, L. and F. Popoff (1997), *Eco-efficiency: The Business Link to Sustainable Development*, MIT Press, Cambridge, Mass.

Dryzek, J. (1997), *The Politics of the Earth: Environmental Discourses*, Oxford University Press, Oxford.

Dryzek, J. and D. Schlosberg (1998), *Debating the Earth: The Environmental Politics Reader*, Oxford University Press, Oxford.

Flaherty, M. and A. Rappaport (1997), *Corporate Environmentalism: From Rhetoric to Results*, paper presented at UNRISD/UNA workshop on 'Business Responsibility for Environmental Protection in Developing Countries', Heredia, Costa Rica, 22–24 September.

Freeman, R. (1984), *Strategic Management. A Stakeholder Approach*, Pitman, Boston.

Graedel, T. (1994), 'Industrial Ecology: Definition and Implementation', in Socolow *et al.*, *op. cit.*

Greer, J. and K. Bruno (1996), *Greenwash: The Reality Behind Corporate Environmentalism*, Third World Network, Penang.

Grübler, A. (1994), 'Industrialization as a Historical Phenomenon', in Socolow *et al.*, *op. cit.*

Hajer, M. (1995), *The Politics of Environmental Discourse: Ecological Modernization and the Policy Process*, Clarendon Press, Oxford.

Hawken, P., A. Lovins and H. Lovins (1999), *Natural Capitalism: The Next Industrial Revolution*, Earthscan, London.

Hoffman, A. and J. Ehrenfeld (1998), 'Corporate Environmentalism, Sustainability, and Management Studies', in N. Roome (ed.), *op. cit.*

Holme, R. and P. Watts (2000), *Corporate Social Responsibility: Making Good Business Sense*, World Business Council for Sustainable Development, Geneva.

Korten, D. (1995), *When Corporations Rule the World*, Kumarian Press, West Hartford; Berrett-Koehler Publishers, San Francisco.

Levy, D. (1997), 'Environmental Management as Political Sustainability', *Organization & Environment*, 10 (2), June, 126–47.

Mitchell, R., B. Agle and D. Wood (1997), 'Toward a Theory of Stakeholder Indentification and Salience: Defining the Principle of Who and What Really Counts', *The Academy of Management Review*, 22 (4), 853–86.

Murphy, D. and J. Bendell (1997), *In the Company of Partners: Business Environmental Groups and Sustainable Development Post-Rio*, The Policy Press, Bristol.

O'Connor, J. (1998), *Natural Causes: Essays in Ecological Marxism*, The Guilford Press, New York.

O'Neill, K., (1999), *Internetworking for Social Change: Keeping the Spotlight on Corporate Responsibility*, Discussion Paper No. 111, UNRISD, Geneva.

Roome, N. (ed.) (1998a), *Sustainability Strategies for Industry: The Future of Corporate Practice*, Island Press, Washington DC.

—— (1998b), 'Introduction: Sustainable Development in the Industrial Firm', in N. Roome, *op. cit.*

—— (1998c), 'Conclusion: Implications for Management Practice, Education, and Research', in N. Roome, *op. cit.*

Schmidheiny, S. (1992), *Changing Course: A Global Business Perspective on Development and the Environment*, MIT Press, Cambridge, Mass.

—— and F. Zorraquín with WBCSD (1996), *Financing Change: The Financial Community, Eco-Efficiency, and Sustainable Development*, MIT Press, Cambridge, Mass.

——, R. Chase and L. DeSimone (1997), *Signals of Change: Business Progress Towards Sustainable Development*, World Business Council for Sustainable Development, Geneva.

Smart, B. (1992), *Beyond Compliance. A New Industry View of the Environment*, World Resources Institute, Washington DC.

Socolow, R. (1994), 'Six Perspectives from Industrial Ecology' in Socolow *et al.*, *op. cit.*

——, C. Andrews, F. Berkhout and V. Thomas (eds.) (1994), *Industrial Ecology and Global Change*, Cambridge University Press, Cambridge.

UNCTAD (1999), *World Investment Report 1999: Foreign Direct Investment and the Challenge of Development*, United Nations, Geneva.

UNDP (1998), *Human Development Report 1998*, Oxford University Press, Oxford.

UNEP (1998), 'Voluntary Initiatives for Responsible Entrepreneurship: A Question and Answer Guide', *Industry and Environment*, 21 (1–2), January–June, 4–9.

UNRISD (1995), *States of Disarray: The Social Effects of Globalization*, UNRISD/Earthscan, Geneva.

von Moltke, K *et al.* (1998), *Global Product Chains: Northern Consumers, Southern Producers and Sustainability*, Environment and Trade 15, United Nations Environment Programme, Geneva.

Watts, P. and Lord Holme (1997), *Corporate Social Responsibility: Meeting Changing Expectations*, World Business Council for Sustainable Development, Geneva.

Welford, R. (1997), *Hijacking Environmentalism: Corporate Responses to Sustainable Development*, Earthscan, London.

——, W. Young and B. Ytterhus (1998), 'Toward Sustainable Production and Consumption: A Conceptual Framework', in N. Roome, *op. cit.*

WCED (1987), *Our Common Future*, Oxford University Press, Oxford/New York.

World Bank (2000), *Greening Industry: New Roles for Communities, Markets and Governments*, Oxford University Press, Oxford/New York.

PART I

The Environmental Record of the Private Sector

Large Corporations and Domestic Firms

1

The Greening of Business in Mexico

DAVID BARKIN

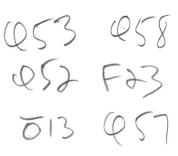

Introduction

The advent of environmental consciousness in the business community in Mexico is relatively new. As institutions were reshaped in the mid-1980s, pressures on the environment intensified. The economy rapidly opened to the global market, and local institutions responded to the demands of international capital, inducing a dramatic increase in foreign investment. Trade barriers and tariff rates fell, destroying protected sectors serving the domestic market and stimulating export-driven producers. The growth in international trade and investment along with the rising dominance of unregulated markets provoked a vigorous debate about their effects on the environment: defenders of the process like Bhagwati (1993) argued that specialization and competition would lead to the development and adoption of cleaner and more productive technologies with enormous gains to all participants, while nay-sayers like Daly (1993) voiced concern about the impact of unrestrained capital movements. Environmental non-governmental organizations (NGOs) went further, predicting tremendous damage to the environment exacerbated by the effects of the heightened social polarization (Barkin, 1998). The debate was 'Mexicanized' as the large environmental NGOs in the United States sought out sympathetic supporters in nascent local environmental groups who might spark opposition to the proposed free-trade agreement (Barkin, 1994; Mumme, 1993).[1] Although the environmental movement was strengthened as a result, the pace of opening to the global market did not slow and Mexico entered the North American Free Trade Area in 1994.

With a change in administration in 1994, the Mexican Ministry of Ecology and Urban Development (SEDUE) was transformed into the Secretariat of Environment, Natural Resources and Fishing (SEMARNAP). A quasi-independent National Institute of Ecology (INE) was also created, as a centre for reflection on policy formulation and an apparatus for its implementation. These developments reflected a belated official recognition of the need to strengthen institutional capabilities in the face of growing challenges to the environment, which were presented by a more permissive investment climate, increased demands for natural resources and deteriorating quality of the environment. Two particularly glaring problems were influential in galvanizing public opinion and spurring governmental action: (1) unaddressed severe air pollution problems in the Mexico City

17

metropolitan area; and (2) international attention focused on the environmental crisis in communities on both sides of Mexico's northern border with the United States.

These pressures were institutionalized with the signing of the environmental side agreement of the North American Free Trade Agreement (NAFTA) in 1993. This protocol provided for the creation of a trilateral Commission for Environmental Cooperation (CEC), to be headed by the ministers of the agencies charged with overseeing environmental affairs in Canada, the United States and Mexico. The Commission was to handle complaints from grassroots organizations about the impact of the integration process. The new body was granted independent investigative authority to determine whether environmental legislation in the member countries was being adequately enforced. In addition to being empowered to conduct investigations in response to citizen complaints about violations of local norms, the CEC has initiated its own studies of the overall impact of integration on environmental conditions in general.

At the same time, the Border Environmental Cooperation Commission (BECC) was created. The BECC and its funding agency, the North American Development Bank (NADBank) are not formally part of NAFTA. They were created to promote and help finance infrastructure along the US border and were designed to convince sceptics to support the trade pact, since the infrastructural improvements would mitigate any potential environmental degradation associated with NAFTA's promised economic development (Varady *et al.*, 1996).

In this political climate, an important segment of the Mexican business community realized the importance of forging its own political capability in the area of the environment. In the various business chambers (manufacturing – CANACINTRA; commerce – CANACO), environmental commissions were created to counter social sector critiques and attempt to pre-empt initiatives by domestic and international environmental NGOs. By focusing on their own agendas, and participating collectively in public and legislative discussions of environmental initiatives, these commissions aim to provide a 'greener' image of business and to forestall further public regulation of private sector activities. The government warmly received these moves, which came as it was attempting to reduce official intervention in the economy and promote the use of administrative and market mechanisms to induce the private sector to behave more responsibly in its use of resources. This chapter analyses private sector programmes aimed at reducing the negative impacts of production on the environment. The following types of initiatives and impacts are considered: (1) institution building; (2) private sector responses to environmental concerns; (3) local programmes resulting from global policies by transnational corporations; and (4) the environmental impact of economic change.[2]

Institution Building: Developing Relations between the Private and Public Sectors

The private sector developed a concerted programme of institution building to confront the challenges posed by demands for environmental responsibility. This activity was initially motivated by the concern of a small group within the Mexican business community to improve its environmental image. This coincided with Schmidheiny's initiative to create the Business Council for Sustainable Development (BCSD) in the years leading up to the 1992 United Nations Conference on Environment and Development in Rio de Janeiro. His book, *Changing Course: A Global Business Perspective on Business and the Environment* (1992), was a clarion call to the private sector; it also served as a warning that if there was not a better process of self-regulation and certification leading to a greater degree of environmental responsibility, general public dissatisfaction with deteriorating environmental conditions would lead to much stricter regulation. The book was translated almost immediately in Mexico and published by the government-owned publishing house, Fondo de Cultura Económica.

A Latin American chapter of the BCSD was founded in Mexico just after the Rio conference. In 1993, a unique binational chapter was also formed. Originally based in western Texas, for industries working exclusively in the border region around the Gulf of Mexico, this chapter has since expanded its area of influence to encompass the whole of the Gulf region, including forest products industries on the Yucatán peninsula. Shortly thereafter (in 1995), the BCSD was merged with the International Chamber of Commerce's environmental arm to form the World Business Council for Sustainable Development (WBCSD); as part of this process the two regional chapters became part of the BCSD–Latin America, which in turn became the Latin American chapter of the WBCSD in 1997. In 1995, both were located in Monterrey, Mexico, with close institutional ties to the Technological Institute of Monterrey (ITESM), a private university enjoying strong support from the business community in northern Mexico (WBCSD–LA Web page); the Mexico chapter is now located in Mexico City. With strong backing from US interests and the Mexican government, the BCSD–LA was active in the 1996 Summit of the Americas, where it counteracted Mexican grassroots participation.

The National Council of Ecological Industrialists (CONIECO) was created in 1992 as an organization of manufacturers and resellers of products that can help clean up environmental problems, reduce waste streams, or provide other environmental services. It describes itself as a group of 'industrialists in a variety of areas … who have joined forces to face the challenge involved in the fight for ecological preservation' (Rozenberg, 1997). CONIECO's founder and director, Carlos Sandoval, maintains a high profile in the private sector, promoting his constituency's interests with trade fairs that offer the opportunity to inform potential clients of new technologies and equipment for controlling various sources of contamination and for remedial programmes. In 1997, its fifth annual congress emphasized responses to environmental audits, a mechanism used by governmental agencies to stimulate a process of self-regulation and compliance among industrialists. Such audits are of increasing importance for environmental certification and in order to participate in bidding for government contracts. As at most meetings of industrialists, this congress was also an important venue for the display and demonstration of recent advances in industrial equipment; and speakers included high-level Mexican officials describing their plans for cooperation with the private sector, officials from international organizations, and private sector experts offering suggestions for projects in environmental engineering and protection.

Another private sector organization, the Center for Private Sector Studies for Sustainable Development (CESPEDES), emerged in 1994. As part of the elite Business Coordinating Center (CCE), it is becoming a vehicle to promote private sector initiatives to protect and enhance the environment. Representing Mexico's most powerful financial and industrial groups, it was conceived as a mechanism to anticipate regulatory initiatives and perhaps even to become the implementing organization. Although it started with a decidedly academic focus, the appointment of the former director of the INE, Gabriel Quadri de la Torre, as its executive director in late 1997 signalled the business community's readiness to take a more active role in promoting research and training at the enterprise level. During his first six months in office, Quadri became an outspoken critic, focusing on the absence of a clear government policy to confront the numerous existing environmental challenges and the ineffectiveness of the people charged with resolving these problems.

In another initiative, supported by the United Nations Industrial Development Organization (UNIDO) and based at the National Polytechnic Institute (IPN), international assistance is being channelled to create a new capacity for responsible environmental management of production processes. The Mexican Center for Clean Production forms part of a global network organized to promote industrial research and training. This Center, with assistance from the United Nations and the Center for Clean Production located at the University of Massachusetts, Lowell, promoted a first round of studies in the metal plating industry (galvanoplasty). This research demonstrated the cost effectiveness of minor but significant changes in process and technology that would promote a more benign effect of these industries on their local environment. A business seminar was held to give broad exposure to this work, but further lines of study have not yet been defined.

The CEC (based in Montreal) has also begun to play an important role in guiding private initiatives towards greater environment responsibility. One dramatic example is its response to a complaint arising from the massive killing of migratory ducks near a dam in central Mexico. A special investigative team examined work processes and made recommendations that pointed the way towards significant and cost-effective changes in the tanning activities associated with the shoe industry in Leon, Guanajuato. As a result of the CEC's findings, and with its support, important changes were promptly introduced into production and effluent recovery processes of the larger enterprises. This case is important because it lent credibility to the CEC, an institution that raised serious suspicions within the business community from the time it was established. By going beyond the expected pattern of convening meetings with expert consultants, producer representatives, environmental NGOs and bureaucracies in NAFTA member countries to work with both small and large industrial groups, the CEC effectively demonstrated its willingness to transform potential areas of conflict into avenues for constructive environmental improvement. Furthermore, as we shall see below, this applied research project pointed the way for similar initiatives in other segments of the corporate community.

The BECC and NADBank have successfully initiated a dialogue about environmental problems along the border between the United States and Mexico among all stakeholders. Traditional mainstream actors have been forced to share their platforms with social groups, NGOs and local governments. This novelty is giving new visibility and attracting increasing attention to the serious environmental problems and concerns that were formerly denied or neglected. Although recognition and discussion are not tantamount to solution, new resources are available and greater authority is now lent to the opinions of environmental experts. While these institutions are only charged with evaluating proposals and financing public infrastructure for water and sewage, the consultative and evaluative mechanisms offer support to local and national authorities attempting to ensure that the private sector plays its part in complying with the regulatory framework.[3]

Private Sector Responses to Environmental Concerns

Mexican enterprises are guiding their efforts to improve environmental quality in a number of different directions. Perhaps the most important thrust of their collective action is a multifaceted attempt to gain credibility and build capacity for corporate self-regulation, both as an acceptable method for compliance with environmental norms and as an alternative to government regulation and bureaucratic enforcement of rules. They are carefully negotiating a new relationship between the private and public sectors with the aim of avoiding conflicts between the public sector mandate of establishing a normative framework for regulation and the private sector's objective of assuming responsibility for compliance.

The drive for capacity building is being orchestrated by the Mexican and Latin American chapters of the WBCSD. In Mexico, these developments have been strengthened by the direct participation of the ITESM. Through its Center of Political Economy for Sustainable Development (CEPDES), it created a Clearing-house for Eco-efficiency for Business (CIEN Web site), an institution charged with collecting and disseminating information on environmentally friendly technologies and state-of-the-art practices. Its research functions are designed to complement corporate initiatives, adapting eco-efficiency information to the conditions and environment of a developing country, and serving as an important bridge between the larger enterprises that are capable of confronting the challenges of responsible production on their own and the small and medium-sized firms that require outside support (Farrera Athie, 1997). After the powerful CCE endowed CESPEDES with the capacity and resources to fund research, conduct training and serve as a liaison with national and international governmental and non-governmental organizations, the business community was in a position to take leadership in the field; with a new director, the CCE has strengthened its ability to influence governmental policy directly in the area of environmental regulation (Moncada, 1997; WBCSD–LA Web page).

This political strategy for creating an organizational capacity was particularly effective in that it defined a specific approach to environmental responsibility. A wide-ranging debate on the subject was pre-empted, with the analysis limited to a narrow definition of the production process itself, and its generation of waste streams within the work centre. This contrasted sharply with the attempts by grass-roots community groups, labour unions and health sector workers to expand the analysis to include the impact of production processes on national and local resource use, environmental conditions, workplace health and safety, and community health in its broadest sense. Issues relating to the 'viability' of prevailing wages or the adequacy of the existing regulatory framework were successfully shunted aside. The business community also attempted to shape fiscal policy to shift as much of the cost as possible for adopting an environmentally responsible policy to the public sector.

An important step in the effort to legitimize self-regulation is the local implementation of international procedures for environmental certification. The largest corporations are focusing on achieving certification under the procedures of the International Organization for Standardization (ISO 14000), as part of a broader programme to include environmental factors in their overall drive to reduce costs. There is a great deal of scope for improvement, given a long history of inexpensive energy and unfettered access to resources that contributed to their squandering and the irresponsible handling of residual products and other waste matter. By the end of 1998, only a handful of corporations had successfully qualified: among Mexican-owned firms, two had been certified: parts of the Altos Hornos de Mexico (steel making) division of the Grupo Acerero del Norte (GAN), and the Nhumo (black tar for the rubber industry) division of the Grupo Girsa-Desc. Other corporations are moving rapidly in this direction, and every environmental consulting firm in

Mexico appears to be engaged in working with one or more clients to achieve certification.

Most investments in the industrial sector are directed towards reducing the regulated contaminants through end-of-pipe technology that reduces effluent streams and emissions – primarily in scrubbers in smokestacks and vapour recuperation systems. Such technology is now mandatory in an ever-increasing number of industrial sectors. Investments are being encouraged and partially financed by tax incentives that allow for the accelerated depreciation of such equipment. The members of CONIECO report considerable increase in investment as a result of this effort. These stimuli account for the vast majority of investment, together with other measures to raise efficiency through a more careful use of inputs of raw materials and energy sources. Redesign of production processes themselves to improve efficiency and worker productivity as well as make the products themselves more environmentally benign (source reduction) has still not been considered in Mexico.

From the government's side, the Office of the Federal Attorney for Environmental Protection (PROFEPA) initiated an ambitious programme to encourage self-compliance. This programme enables qualifying companies to use the label 'clean industry' in their consumer advertising and international marketing; it also certifies them as having complied with official standards for environmental protection in industrial categories. At the end of 1997, 86 companies (115 plants) were certified as being in compliance with a broad set of standards for eco-efficiency (see Appendix 1); another 26 plants (7 additional companies) had been certified by mid-1998. As might be expected, the companies most able to qualify are the larger corporations, especially subsidiaries of international firms, with easiest access to capital markets, technology and know-how, as well as the institutional capacity to undertake the training and investments required for incorporating these innovations in an increasingly competitive market. The concentration among the larger plants is clear from the data in Appendix 2 (Dasgupta et al., 1997; Tapia Naranjo and Pichs, 1997).[4] The programme, established in 1992, has assumed greater importance since 1996 when PROFEPA started encouraging firms to participate voluntarily as a way of avoiding the more cumbersome environmental audit process involved in programmed or surprise inspections by government officials. The list of participant firms is quite impressive, including a wide variety of national and transnational corporations. PROFEPA's certification of state petroleum, electricity and railroad enterprises, however, has led analysts to raise serious questions about the process, since there are continuing complaints from citizens' and workers' groups throughout the country of environmental abuses by all three companies (Procuraduría Federal del Medio Ambiente, 1998).

Two other significant initiatives being undertaken at the producer level, with coordination within the private sector, are: (1) energy savings through audits and changes in equipment; and (2) technological evaluations and the implantation of a international certification for organic and/or sustainable production in agriculture and forestry. The energy savings programme is run by the Trust Fund for Energy Savings (FIDE) within the Federal Electricity Commission (CFE). It works with individual enterprises in both the public and private sectors to reduce total energy consumption, placing emphasis on the problems of peak versus non-peak usage, and the integration of more efficient motors and sources of lighting. It has access to some loan funds to finance technological and equipment changes; such loans are reimbursed through scheduled payments added to the electricity bill. The cost of the investment should be offset by energy savings. Long-term savings are often considerable. Although progress has been slow, this programme appears to be an effective if modest way of implementing a meaningful plan for reducing energy consumption. The programme has been particularly effective among larger firms and public institutions.

International certification for the quality of primary production is gaining importance among certain groups of producers. This effort is directed primarily at coffee, fruit and vegetables, and forestry products. The struggle to develop local standards consistent with international criteria, and the development of credible local certifying mechanisms and institutions, have involved complex negotiations between local organizations and international certifying bodies. At present, there are at least 76 enterprises engaged in organic agriculture in many states (22 of 32) (Gómez Tovar, 1996). Almost half (35) export organically grown coffee, for which an important market has developed in Europe. Most of these producers are coalitions of peasant communities that help finance production, maintain quality, and negotiate with buyers. Through the 'good offices' of European organizations, this business now involves several hundred million dollars of exports and the partnership guarantees that some international credit is available directly to the producers. Most of the remaining producers of organically grown agricultural products are concentrated in spices, honey, fruit and vegetables. Perhaps the most significant of these are the peasant producers of Baja California Sur, who are organized in a number of cooperatives. This is the result of an initiative by a group of entrepreneurs in the United States who saw an opportunity to supply their US market with fresh, organic spices. They took advantage of the excellent local conditions and an air transportation infrastructure to develop long-term marketing arrangements. Their first efforts involved contract farming, and since then the arrangement has evolved into a local partnership with foreign distributors.

An incipient initiative is that of the Mexican network of peasant forestry communities (Red Mocaf), which is developing an ambitious programme that will enable it to qualify for certification under the international standards for sustainability associated with the international Forest Stewardship Council and the Smart Wood Program. Like organic produce certification, this effort involves designing production processes that ensure the long-term viability of the forests from which timber resources are extracted; the criteria involve not simply quantitative aspects related to sustainable harvests, but also a broader vision of the viability of the participating communities that depend on the forests for their livelihoods (Madrid, 1998). While most of the communities in the programme are poor, the volume that they harvest and the potential for future growth are such that the Red Mocaf is expected to become a major exporter of wood products within the next five years, with turnover amounting to hundreds of millions of dollars annually. This is in sharp contrast to the official government forest development programme, which is based on subsidies for corporate management of plantation forms of single-species production on peasant lands; in addition to the serious environmental questions that the single-species strategy raises, the corporate approach is being questioned because it will not generate sufficient employment or income to permit the communities to survive in their traditional regions.

A review of various business practices with relation to the environment reveals a significant number of conflicts and examples of 'greenwashing' throughout Mexico. The number and variety of these cases were sufficiently striking to warrant brief comment. The problem of pesticide production and use is of great concern throughout the world. In Mexico, a large number of pesticides used to be readily available that were not certified as safe by the phytosanitary authorities; in fact, several chemicals produced in the country or imported for agricultural use were explicitly banned by the authorities. In one particularly egregious case, Galecron, produced by Ciba-Geigy, was sold in large quantities in Mexico's northern states for use in cotton fields; it was also sold to intermediaries who delivered it to US farmers unable to purchase the chemical legally themselves. Local investigative reporters and academic studies identified the problem after high rates of poisoning were observed in the region. Energetic protests in Mexico, supported by the Pesticide Action Network (PAN–USA), were successful in stopping this abusive practice. Today, its Mexican counterpart, the Red de Acción sobre Plaguicidas y Alternativas en México (RAPAM), plays a growing, constructive role in documenting the present situation and organizing public campaigns to ensure a more responsible use of agrochemicals.

With privatization and economic integration, however, the problem of agrochemical abuse has evolved. In 1992, a Mexican firm, Velsipol, purchased the government's fertilizer and pesticide company, Fertimex. In 1996, it was acquired by a German chemical company, Tekchem, and continues to produce DDT for the campaign against malaria, and to export it to other countries, although it will be slowly withdrawn from use during the next decade. The company also produces Parathion, which is still authorized for use in Mexico in spite of being widely prohibited around the world (Bejarano, 1997; *La Jornada Ecológica*, 1998b).

Today, the principal problem of pesticide abuse in Mexico and elsewhere has changed. Many chemical companies now boast that they are protecting the environment, and contributing to a sustainable form of agriculture, by selling products that are biodegradable. Genetically engineered seeds, designed to resist the toxic effects of chemicals intended to eliminate other growth, are the latest development. Such misrepresentation is very troubling, but serious problems and abuse from a previous era still persist: 32 pesticides, widely prohibited elsewhere because of their toxicity, are legally used in Mexico; only ten have a restricted status. In 1990, the Pan American Health Organization estimated that there were 13,000 serious poisonings from agrochemicals in Mexico, leading to more than 700 deaths per year; the National Epidemiological System is still plagued by under-reporting and misdiagnosis (Cedillo, 1996). A law on phytosanitary control, enacted in 1994, and a national programme promulgated with the principal objective of promoting agro-exports and controlling 'plagues of economic importance' compound the problem. Together they eliminate the requirement to report poisonings to the agricultural authorities, transferring this function to the health system, which itself is overwhelmed with many other responsibilities. In contrast, the CEC is taking an active role in promoting 'the good handling of chemical substances' by developing an action plan to reduce emissions and risks of toxic, persistent and biocumulative substances in all three countries. The working group is focusing on PCBs, DDT, chlordane and mercury, with the heaviest commitments being placed on Mexico.

University studies continue to report unacceptable levels of agrochemical and heavy metal residues in samples of milk collected from major brands (Prado *et al.*, 1998). In spite of the prohibition on the use of organochlorates imposed more than a decade ago, unacceptable levels are still found in cow's milk and fatty tissue. When questioned about a February 1998 study, the bottling companies responded that they had no ability to control the practices of contract managers of the dairy herds or to deal with the above limit concentrations of these substances in the aquifers of major dairy producing regions, especially the former cotton-producing area of La Laguna, the source of a substantial proportion of all milk delivered to Mexico City. The government has become intransigent on this issue, with officials responding unofficially that if they were to take action, the country would be without more than one-half of present milk supplies, further aggravating already serious supply problems.

When questioned about the quality of water discharges into an urban waterway in central Mexico from a major paper plant owned by the Kimberly Clark paper company (recently merged with Scott), managers responded that water quality was well within official norms and that the sulphurous odour that was being emitted was 'quite normal' (interview with author, November 1997). They went on to add that the company was voluntarily undertaking sizeable additional investments to upgrade the plant, but that there were limits to what could be done, given the depressed international prices of paper products and the low productivity in the plant, a consequence of antiquated equipment that was brought in from plants in other countries.

In spite of regulations prohibiting the use of urban sewage for irrigation of fruit and vegetable production, neither the infrastructure nor the funds exist to reverse this practice in many parts of the country. This is a particularly serious problem in those areas where the sewage system was deliberately designed to flow into areas specifically designed for such produce. In one highly publicized case, sewage water is channelled into an area where strawberries are cultivated for export. Field workers and their families have settled in a zone where the same waste matter has invaded the aquifer. They are acutely aware of this problem, but unfortunately even their efforts to reduce their exposure to contamination by trucking in drinking water are to no avail, because the nearby springs from which they buy these supplies are similarly polluted (Lemus, 1995; Barkin and Lemus, 1997).

The Mitsubishi Corporation, co-operator (with the Mexican government as majority owner) of a large solar evaporator for salt production on the Pacific Coast in Baja California, has proposed a three-fold expansion of this operation that would have a direct impact on the biosphere reserve of El Vizcaíno. While international opposition has been strong, the joint venture has effectively purchased local support, generously contracting with the local university to produce the environ-mental impact assessment (in October 1997). Faculty members were told in no uncertain terms that any questioning of this very lucrative arrangement would not be tolerated, and those with doubts were excluded from the review process. The proposed facility not only threatens a calving area of the protected grey whale and the reserve, but, just as importantly, it also endangers the fishing communities in the area by requiring the development of roads, industrial plants, service industries and housing for people who would be attracted to the region by the employment possibilities. It would also intensify conflicts over natural resources associated with land tenure, scarce water and the fishing areas themselves (Crawford, 1998).

This case is notable because Mitsubishi has taken a high-profile and seemingly responsible position on the issue. In 1995, it took out an advertisement in the *New York Times*, extolling the virtues of the project and promising to 'proceed only if the project is environmentally sound and can be so sustained over the long term' (27 June 1995, p. A9). The company took the offensive once again in the autumn of 1997, with full-page newspaper advertisements announcing the award of a contract to the state university in cooperation with the prestigious Scripps Institution of Oceanography to conduct a second environmental impact assessment (the first one was rejected by the Mexican authorities). The proposed expansion is to provide inputs of the very highest quality for industrial processes, especially chlorine plants. So troublesome are these corporate activities that numerous NGOs have specifically targeted the salt project for its environmental threats. In the spring of 1998, Corporate Watch awarded its quarterly Greenwash Award to Mitsubishi for the brazen way in which it obfuscates the complex issues involved in the management of such a facility (Karliner, 1997; see also the Corporate Watch website: http://www.igc.apc.org/trac/greenwash/mitsubishi.html).[5]

An alternative development proposal (being discussed at the Universidad Autónoma de Baja California Sur) for the region has not received a hearing by regional authorities. The programme focuses on improving the productivity of the existing solar evaporators and of the local fisheries, along with building an ecotourist programme and efforts to strengthen the local community. This course of action would involve a different scale of development, which would favour a local resource management programme over an export-driven scheme in which the local residents and the region itself would be transformed and the communities threatened, as has occurred in many other locations in Mexico.

An 'ecotourism' theme park, constructed on the southern coast of Quintana Roo, involved the dynamiting of natural wells (*cenotes*) of natural and religious value and in direct contravention of numerous local and national regulations. The theme park also contains numerous exhibits and facilities that violate local laws and international treaties with regard to the management of a natural environment and the care, capture and maintenance of endangered species, such as giant marine turtles. Another tourist development programme in the region, carried out by the Spanish Melia consortium, threatens beaching areas for giant marine turtles. And a domestic developer (Hotel Cid) is seeking to build near the few remaining mangrove swamps on the Yucatán peninsula. A March 1998 decision to approve two large hotel developments on the 'Mayan Riviera' confirms that the concerns of the local population, environmentalists and experts in local development are well founded: large-scale private developmental interests are prevailing over the more creative proposals offered by groups seeking balance between economics and the environment. The rhythm of development is intensifying, for the state's governor ends his term in office in 1999 and is attempting to leave his mark on the region (his activities are also a source of personal profit).[6] Perhaps even more serious, in the long run, is the direct threat that this development represents to the viability of the remaining Mayan communities, whose very existence is threatened by the expansion of tourism. No effective effort is being made to involve these communities, as has been suggested by the numerous independent consultants who have evaluated the process. If current trends persist, these people will be forced to abandon their way of life, and we will all lose the extraordinary fount of knowledge about the management of natural resource systems in the region which has underpinned the survival of the indigenous communities.

On the Pacific Coast, the mega-resort of Huatulco is facing a crisis due to water shortage, but has the opportunity to resolve the problem creatively. The aquifer that was supposed to supply 24 luxury hotels has proved inadequate to the task, because of excessive withdrawals by the first few hotels that were completed. In this case a local environmental organization has proposed mobilizing the surrounding communities to collaborate in a large-scale and long-term project for resource management, thereby increasing permanently available water supplies while dramatically improving conditions for the 10,000 people in the nearby communities. The foresight of a local entrepreneur, and the systematic efforts to build bridges of communication and mutual respect among stakeholders in the region are making this unusual effort possible (Barkin and Paillés, 1998).

One of the leading sponsors of the CESPEDES, the GAN, has taken decisive moves to sharpen its 'green' image of corporate responsibility. GAN has been one of the first to qualify for ISO 14000 status in Mexico, and has taken a leadership role in transforming the CESPEDES into a more active participant in the private sector drive for environmental responsibility. It has assumed an even more high-profile position by sponsoring the cleaning of some of Mexico City's most important public monuments. But after presuming that GAN was committed to improving environmental conditions in its plants, and offering unrestricted access to a university group anxious to train professionals in worker health and safety under real-world conditions, the vice-president in charge of this area was apparently overruled at the highest level, and all further communication was suspended. The academic analysts involved believe that this reluctance to permit scrutiny of claims of progress in environmental and worker health reflects the large gulf between standards of progress as determined by procedures established by the institutions of self-regulation, on one hand, and, on the other, objective progress as might be defined by internationally defined indicators of environmental impacts in the workplace and community (interview with author, December 1997).

As a result of the substantial climatic alterations induced by El Niño in 1998, Mexico suffered a large number of persistent fires throughout its territory. Fragile ecosystems were destroyed and massive quantities of smoke caused respiratory problems for millions. Environmental crisis also affected the southern part of the United States where, in several states, air quality emergencies were declared, leading to serious impairment of activities and heavy economic losses. The United States sent several million dollars' worth of material and technical assistance to combat the conflagrations. The experience revealed once again that, discourse aside, environmental authorities are still not developing contingency plans for such disasters. And the private sector has chosen to remain on the sidelines, criticizing inadequate bureaucracies rather than facing up to the serious structural problems created by the cutbacks in government spending for rural development and environmental protection that has decimated the communities best equipped to deal with such problems, through regular programmes of informed soil and water management (*La Jornada Ecológica*, 1998a). Even more troubling, there is ample evidence to suggest that many of the fires were deliberately set as a result of local conflicts over land tenure or as part of an effort by powerful local interests to prepare the way for development projects opposed by local communities (Barkin and García, 1998).

The Local Programmes of Transnational Corporations and International Agencies

Growing demands for environmental responsibility have produced an outpouring of materials from the internationalized corporate sector to demonstrate its sincerity. One of the most striking examples of such efforts is the highly visible programme of the American Chamber of Commerce in Mexico to document the activities of its members. In spring 1997, it conducted a mail survey among them, asking about the impact of NAFTA; three of the questions related to practices in the area of the environment and in health and safety matters. Of the 217 firms responding to the mail survey, 123 indicated having made investments (on average, of about US$200,000 per respondent) in new technologies for improving environmental practices. Almost two thirds (136) had implemented new health and safety measures since 1994, including changes in the work process, new guidelines for industrial safety, better techniques for handling wastes, on-the-job training, and the install-ation of new safety equipment. Finally, 84 firms indicated that they had implemented new labour practices, including the general upgrading of health and safety conditions, productivity bonuses and other incentives, new training pro-grammes for personal development, sensitivity training, and renegotiating collective bargaining agreements (American Chamber of Commerce, 1997).

Corporate support for the efforts by UNIDO and the CEC to implement programmes for environmental remediation in certain industries has increased as studies demonstrated their value in reducing direct production costs and improving the quality of products. In fact, findings have been so convincing that the demand has mushroomed for experts to apply the same methodology in specific settings. Not satisfied with restricting the recommendations to the firms covered by the international studies, the ITESM is promoting the broader application of the findings in other firms and industries. Private initiatives in this area are also being announced by local consulting firms as well as by private international organi-zations, both corporate and university-based.

Perhaps the area of greatest international interest is in the industries that supply environmental equipment and provide environmental services. Many transnational firms are installing such equipment in their Mexican plants as part of a global programme to improve performance and reduce effluent streams. As a result of these programmes and other initiatives associated with self-regulation and the 'clean industry' programme, most of Mexico's largest firms are vigorously pursuing strategies to install a wide variety of equipment to reduce their production of toxic wastes and recover effluents for reuse, sale or appropriate disposal.

The market for environmental services in Mexico is just beginning to develop. Subsidiaries of Waste Management Inc. and Browning-Ferris Industries (BFI) account for a significant share of this market, having successfully bid for numerous municipal waste disposal contracts and installed at least two important toxic waste collection and processing plants. Solid waste disposal is still an important field of contention in Mexico, because of a lack of consensus about the best way to organize the provision of such services, their ownership, and the regulatory procedures. As a result, much of the competition among international firms includes proposals for the design and organization of privatized services. Problems of implementation are compounded by the lack of expertise in local government, the very limited budgets for these services, and the lack of a tradition of charging fees for such services. In present practice, limited local budgets for garbage collection services are sup-plemented by 'tips' paid to the collection teams and the income generated by separation and resale of recyclable materials. These 'other' sources of income have proved so significant that the garbage workers' unions, the scavengers' associations, and the politicians associated with these groups have strongly opposed most campaigns by government for privatization.

The development and management of toxic waste processing facilities has been even more contentious, with groups organizing around typical NIMBY ('not in my back yard') interests at the local level. The federal government has offered no leadership in developing a national policy for handling toxic waste streams, including contagious hospital and biological products, which are still generally handled as just another category of solid waste. In a few notable cases, where public disclosure has created particularly embarrassing situations for government firms (PVCs in the case of electrical transformers, spent radioactive fuel near a nuclear power plant, or petroleum by-products) or private chemical companies, no adequate solution has emerged. One of the most serious of the unresolved waste issues is that of the spent fuel rods used in the nuclear power plant at Laguna Verde, Veracruz. The power company (Federal Electricity Commission or CFE) remains intransigent, assuring doubters that there are no health hazards involved with the plant or with the present storage procedures (in deep water holding tanks), in spite of numerous medical problems among the workers and studies of radioactivity at the site.

In the area of water management, including processing, distribution and disposal, a similar situation prevails. It is only with the installation of huge water treatment plants in the Mexico City metropolitan area, at a cost of more than US$1 billion, that people are beginning to realize the cost of this aspect of modern urban life. In some smaller metropolitan areas local conflicts have emerged over the management and design of water and sewage authorities, which are required to become self-financing. Until recently, there has been no outside investment or interest in this service, but with the institutional changes brought on by NAFTA, in particular the requirement of national treatment of investors from the other member states, there has been greater discussion of these matters in industry circles. Most of this interest has been in the northern border regions, where some international financing is available from NADBank for installation and upgrading of infrastructure and for the reorganization of water authorities; international bidding for equipment and management has virtually excluded Mexican firms from the competition in these cases.

The Environmental Impact of Structural Adjustment and International Integration

One of the greatest environmental challenges for policy makers in Mexico is the changing structure of production and the regional redeployment of activities and people. In the new economic model, emphasis is being placed on export pro-duction. As part of this move away from stimulating production for the domestic market, politicians have placed their faith in the investment initiatives of international capital and the ready availability of inexpensive labour and natural resources, including energy. Mexican leaders consider these advantages crucial to the country's ability to attract new investment. They are hoping to transform the country into a productive platform for foreign firms seeking access to markets in the United States and Canada.

This change in emphasis was extraordinarily successful in stimulating the growth of *maquiladoras* (assembly plants for export production) in the northern border region, and more recently in other parts of the country. Over the past 15 years, employment has grown more than fourfold to about one million people, or about one quarter of the industrial labour force. Most assembly plants are distributed among some 18 border regions, with more than half of them concentrated in only four cities. In spite of this growth, however, the *maquiladoras* still only employ about 3 per cent of the Mexican working population of about 33 million, fewer than the number of young people entering the labour force each year.

This dramatic increase in industrial assembly plants led to a number of problems in the border region, especially as concerns the environment. Although there is little hard data on contamination resulting from these industries, case studies suggest profound impacts in the whole region (Balcazar *et al.*, 1995; Moure-Eraso *et al.*, 1994, 1997). And environmental problems are intensifying, in part, because the fiscal regime in the region virtually exempts the plants from any local taxes that might be used to finance infrastructure for a rapidly growing population, to confront the severe water shortage in this arid area, or the lack of any publicly owned water treatment plants. Problems are further compounded by a widespread flouting of environmental laws and regulations by companies on both sides of the border: toxic wastes are regularly shipped into Mexico from the United States, in direct contravention of law, and effluents generated in Mexico from imported raw materials are not separated and re-exported to their country of origin, as stipulated in the La Paz Agreement of 1983.[7] But more importantly, in spite of improving governmental capacity to supervise implementation of the existing regulatory framework, industrial growth is simply outstripping the region's carrying capacity.

The emergence of the border region as a principal locus of production and as a trans-shipment point for the rapidly growing trade among the NAFTA countries has significantly increased the volume of vehicular traffic. To accommodate the growing demands, new border crossing points, along with the needed infrastructure (roads, bridges, administrative processing centres, and so on), are being built. The problem of increased traffic in urban areas is aggravated by the lack of housing for new workers, who are paid wages too low to be able to afford anything that might be supplied by the private sector. Makeshift sheds and shanty towns are springing up without even minimal public services. Privately supplied collective transport services quickly respond to growing demand in every Mexican border town but are devoid of official regulation, with disastrous impacts on the environment and tragic consequences when the inevitable accidents occur. Unfettered growth is raising levels of air pollution and noticeably reducing the quality of life in border communities (*La Jornada Ecológica*, 1998c). Other related problems include an unusually high incidence of birth defects, which often makes for spectacular headlines (as in the case of a rash of anencephalic births) and the growing problems of drug trafficking and consumption. Political violence and personal insecurity are also fixtures of everyday life, and kidnapping and assassination incidents are increasingly common. But even the horror and repulsion caused by the serial rape and murder of almost 200 young *maquiladora* workers over the past three years in Ciudad Juarez seems insufficient to arouse the local Chamber of Commerce or the authorities to take strong measures to control the situation.

A less apparent but potentially more serious problem, in the long run, is the changing 'pollution intensity' of the border export industries. Using international coefficients for 1987 to measure the contaminating effect of different industrial branches, we detected a tendency towards a slightly more contaminating productive structure.[8] Thus, contamination in the border region is intensifying not only because of the impact of economic growth, but also because some of the new plants generate more toxic waste than those that formerly settled in the region. Although the results are still preliminary, they show a clear tendency towards a greater concentration of growth in the *maquiladora* sector in industries with higher pollution intensities. On the basis of these results, and similar studies in other parts of the country (see Ten Kate, 1993), it seems that the particular pattern of growth in Mexico is leading to the expansion of industries which have more negative effects in terms of contamination than was the case in the past.

Analyses of the energy and water intensity of Mexican exports show similar results. It is striking that unlike most of Mexican industry, where the energy intensity of production has declined with productive modernization and techno-logical innovation, the number of kilowatt hours per million dollars of exports has actually risen substantially over the past 10 years (Constantino, 1996). Similarly, examination of the changing structure of agricultural production toward exports demonstrates that the new higher-valued crops require more water. Present policies that grossly underprice water are causing scarcities of basic food grains in many parts of the country, while stimulating the planting of crops that use more water along with agrochemicals (Diaz Coutiño, 1999). In a related vein, a detailed analysis of the dramatic but short-lived increase in international maize prices in 1994 demonstrates how large-scale livestock interests in northern Mexico created an environmental problem for personal gain. As prices of calves fell because of the rise in feed costs, they halted the export of live calves that were fattened in feedlots in Texas and Oklahoma (a practice going back more than one hundred years) and put their animals out to pasture in Mexico. The increased demand for water by the 1.5 million animals that were not sold contributed to a severe water shortage in Mexico that was conveniently, but erroneously, attributed to a drought during the 1995–6 agricultural season. The ranchers were able to divert water from industrial and agricultural uses, thereby shifting heavy economic losses to other groups and reaping spectacular speculative gains, in spite of some cattle deaths during the seasonal dry spells (Barkin and Constantino, 1997).

But globalization is not only causing problems for the northern border region. It is radically changing the regional distribution of activity in Mexico and, in the process, causing environmental damage in the new centres of productive growth.[9] In contrast to past eras, large manufacturing firms no longer choose to locate in the Mexico City metropolitan area or in the neighbouring cities of Toluca, Cuernavaca or Puebla. Instead, new industrial centres have been established in the northern cities of Aguascalientes (where Nissan moved operations from Cuernavaca), in Silao and Ramos Arizpe (where General Motors transferred production formerly in the capital), and in Hermosillo (where Ford built a brand new plant). Guadalajara fancies itself another Silicon Valley as well as a textile centre. Monterrey continues to grow as a result of the international alliances forged by the companies traditionally based there.

Problems on the border, like those mentioned above, are inducing many entrepreneurs to disperse their new assembly operations further south. Although still limited to a few dozen examples, small factories employing several hundred people can now be found in rural communities throughout central Mexico, as well as in intermediate cities. While this new pattern of productive expansion is cele-brated by policy makers, a more careful examination of the process reveals that employment growth is limited and that the leading industries are actually causing a net drain on foreign exchange in spite of being heavy exporters. This results from the fact that a high proportion of their machinery and parts must be imported, as well as remittances for licences, royalties and profits. Furthermore, in virtually every area where new industries are being installed, there are reports of conflicts over access to water and the siting of solid waste disposal and sewage systems, while traffic congestion and pollution become major sources of complaint. State and local governments do not have the resources to finance new infrastructure, nor do they possess the administrative and technical capabilities to meet these challenges. Central government authorities are not prepared to support them. There is no effective urban planning process, even as the influx of new workers and managers is unleashing speculative movements in land prices that are forcing many people into shanty towns and marginal housing as rents rise in their old neighbourhoods.

Although the new firms are undoubtedly using cleaner and more productive technologies than were characteristic of the old industrial plant, environmental pressures are increasing. The sheer increase in the volume of production, the requirements for transport of burgeoning volumes of imports for production and exports of finished goods, and the demands for water and energy are creating many environmental problems.[10] No satisfactory solution has been developed for solid waste collection and processing or disposal; sewage systems are virtually non-existent, and many of those that have been built use technologies that are too costly to operate. In the workplaces themselves, there is ample evidence of an increase in the intensity of work, with a consequent growth in occupational health problems. Many of these problems are not yet documented because data are highly unreliable. However, workers comment that they are being offered cash payments in lieu of reporting workplace accidents, since the workers' compensation system changed over to a risk-weighted premium system for employers' insurance payments (Lemus, 1999).

In the Mexico City area, environmental conditions continue to deteriorate in spite of the slower rate of industrial growth. During the past decade, the government moved many of the most contaminating industries from the valley and placed limits on private automobile use, but these steps have been insufficient to deal with air pollution; air quality rarely meets even the lax standards of the Mexican system. Supplying the demand for water requires going as far away as 500 kilometres to a river basin 1,000 metres below Mexico City that is beginning to provoke protests from the people in the regions whose communities and economies are threatened. With globalization, Mexico City is being transformed into a true global city (Sassen, 1995), as the stock exchange, banks, and international financial and real estate service firms replace factories in the urban centre. Modern shopping malls are being built to serve a small elite, the real beneficiaries of the new economic model, while Mexico City's working classes are left to fend for themselves, with an inadequate transportation system and rising personal insecurity compounding the problems caused by a deteriorating environment.

The greatest environmental problem, however, is poverty itself. The new economic model is increasing social polarization, as formal employment in stable jobs declines and part-time jobs, contract labour and other less secure forms of work proliferate. Self-employment, street vending, service work (including domestic work and those self-taught plumbers, painters and electricians who ply their trades on street corners) and other forms of 'informal sector' activity are a last resort for those who cannot find adequate alternatives elsewhere. But with low incomes and several people in each family working, there is little time and no money to devote to the basic tasks of environmental management that were an essential part of community life in the past, such as maintaining water canals clear of debris, assuring the stability of small terraces, or planting trees. Although the public sector is generally expected to assume these responsibilities today, it is unable to do so because of dwindling revenues and pressures to support economic expansion. The collective labour practices common among rural communities in the past – building and maintaining community infrastructure such as roads, canals, schools and other public works – have been severely undermined by the desperate need to leave the community to earn basic (infra)subsistence wages.

With the privatization of many public firms and the transfer of public responsibilities to the corporate sector throughout the country, local governments and community organizations are just beginning to understand the problems of incorporating 'externalities' into the negotiation process with individual enterprises. Among the issues that are still to be struggled over is the problem of defining how urban open spaces can be created, protected and maintained. The task of assigning responsibility for the clean-up of problems left from decades of mismanagement and lack of regulations seems virtually intractable. On top of all this, however, is the growing problem of an economic model that is unable to create sufficient quality jobs, while an ever increasing number of people are being prevented from strengthening their traditional forms of subsistence.

Conclusion

An analysis of the greening of business in Mexico necessarily produces a complex scenario of advances and retreats. As in the rest of the world, with greater information about the effects of industrial production, and increased concern for the quality of the environment, more public pressure is being placed on business for responsibility. In return, markets require greater consideration of these effects and reward some of the participants handsomely. On the other hand, the increased volume of production, the trend towards more production for international trade, and the changing composition of output all conspire to intensify pollution while shifting towards greater use of scare natural resources in countries like Mexico. Aggravating the problem is the accelerating tendency towards regional concentration with its associated ills of urbanization.

The heightened visibility of corporate campaigns to publicize their individual and collective efforts for environmental responsibility is a direct response to citizens' demands for greater regulation. In Mexico, the impressive process of private institutional development to forestall public sector action has been warmly welcomed by a government committed to restraining its intervention in the economy. While there have been some notably successful new partnerships, and important advances in the dissemination and application of viable technological remedies for some particularly egregious examples of industrial contamination, the overall quality of the environment is deteriorating as a result of the present strategy of development with the ensuing pattern of social polarization.[11]

Corporate programmes for self-regulation have created the impression of important advances. The marketplace and consumer demands are playing an important role in creating opportunities for producers to behave responsibly while increasing their profitability. This is particularly true of products whose environmentally benign qualities can be readily identified and marketed, as in the case of organically grown produce and environmental services, like ecotourism. Inevitably, there is an element of confusion in the process of informing and educating the public, and in cultivating new demands, but some Mexican producers have clearly embarked upon ambitious programmes to take advantage of this trend. Given the present-day conditions of heightened international competition, however, it is likely that some players will choose the less costly route of 'greenwashing' in place of genuine environmental responsibility. It is the difficult task of an informed environmental and consumer movement to insist that corporate efforts to promote environmental responsibility are more effective.

Notes

1 At this early point, the international environmental movement had an important impact on the policy debate in Mexico because it explicitly sought out local counterparts, or even created new Mexican organizations to ensure consideration of its concerns.

2 These results are the product of my research into environmental efforts in the corporate sector (Barkin, 1997 and research in process) as well as that of others (such as Domínguez, 1996) participating in a programme coordinated by Rhys Jenkins in the UK (1998).

3 For a critical evaluation of the BECC, see Sprouse and Mumme, 1997.

4 Scholars in Argentina, Brazil, Mexico and Malaysia, examining the question of corporate activities in the area of environmental performance, have come to similar conclusions (Jenkins, 1998; Domínguez, 1996).

5 The literature about this matter is readily available on the Internet. Mitsubishi has created a Web site (http://www.bajasalt.com/) to air its position; the executive vice-president and general counsel for Mitsubishi International published an article in the *San Diego Union-Tribune* (Brumm, 1998) reiterating the official position. The Natural Resources Defense Council prepared a briefing book (http://www.nrdc.org/camp/ cagray.html) on the importance of the lagoon for protecting the whale. The Corporate Watch Web site has links to all parties to support its claims against the corporation (http://www.igc.apc.org/trac/greenwash/ mitsubishi.html); their page includes an analysis of the corporate position by an environmental lawyer, Mark Spalding, of the Center for US–Mexican Studies at the University of California at San Diego (Spalding and Saldaña, 1998).

6 At the end of his term, the governor was under indictment for drug-related crimes and money laundering through various properties along the Maya Riviera; he was also a fugitive.

7 Agreement Between the United States of America and the United Mexican States on Cooperation for the Protection and Improvement of the Environment in the Border Area (14 August 1983). The text of the agreement may be found in United States Department of State, Treaties and Other International Acts Series, Number 10827, US Government Printing Office, Washington, DC.

8 By isolating the impact of increasing contamination due to economic growth, we were able to identify the effect of changing industrial composition in generating various vectors of pollutants.

9 A more complete examination of some of the environmental consequences of structural adjustment and international integration can be found in a report prepared for the World Resources Institute (Barkin, 1997).

10 The impacts of rising production on the environment and worker health and safety in existing industrial plants are explored in Lemus, 1999.

11 For more on the relationship between the quality of the environment and social polarization, see Barkin, 1998.

References

American Chamber of Commerce (1997), *Midiendo el Exito del TLCAN*, American Chamber of Commerce, Mexico City.

Balcazar, Hector, Catalina Denman and Francisco Lara (1995), 'Factors Associated with Work-related Accidents and Sickness among Maquiladora Workers: The Case of Nogales, Sonora, Mexico', *International Journal of Health Services*, 25 (3), 489–502.

Barkin, David (1998), *Wealth, Poverty and Sustainable Development*, Editorial Jus and Centro de Ecología y Desarrollo, Mexico City.

—— (1997), 'International Financial Flows and the Environment: The Effect of Financial Globalization on the Prospects for Sustainable Development in Mexico', working paper,

International Financial Flows and the Environment Project, World Resources Institute, http://www.wri.org/iffe/ pdf/Barkin.pdf.

—— (1994), 'Las organizaciones no-gubernamentales ambientalistas en el foro internacional' in A. Glender and V. Lichtinger (eds.), *La Diplomacia Ambiental: México y la Conferencia de las Naciones Unidas sobre Medio Ambiente y Desarrollo*, Secretaría de Relaciones Exteriores y Fondo de Cultura Económica, Mexico City.

—— and Roberto Constantino (1997), 'La construcción social de la sequía', in C. Pérez and C. Rozo (eds.), *Continuismo y Alernativas en la Política Económica*, Departamento de Producción Económica, Universidad Autónoma Metropolitana, Xochimilco, Mexico City, pp. 69–94.

—— and Miguel Angel García (1998), 'The Social Construction of Deforestation in Mexico: A Case Study of the 1998 Fires in the Chimalapas Rain Forest', http://www.igc.org/bionet/.

—— and Blanca E. Lemus Ruiz (1997), 'La modernización rural y la calidad de la vida: Propuesta para el desarrollo colectivo frente a la ofensiva neo-liberal', in G. López Castro (ed.), *Sociedad y Medio Ambiente en México*, El Colegio de Michoacán, Zamora, México.

—— and Carlos Paillés (1998), 'Water as an Instrument for Sustainable Regional Development', *Arid Lands Newsletter*, 44 (November). http://ag.arizona.edu/OALS/ ALN/aln44/barkin final.html

Bejarano, Fernando (1997), 'Los efectos de la política neoliberal en la regulación estatal del uso de plaguicidas y la participación ciudadana en México', in L. Gomero and E. Rosenthal (eds.), *Plaguicidas en América Latina. Participación ciudadana en políticas para reducir el uso de plaguicidas*, Red de Acción de Plaguicidas y sus Alternativas para América Latina (RAPAL), Lima, Peru.

Bhagwati, Jagdish (1993), 'The Case for Free Trade', *Scientific American*, 269 (November), 42–44.

Brumm, James E. (1998), 'A Better Life for People – and Whales', *San Diego Union-Tribune*, 19 April, p. G-3. http://www.bajasalt.com/

Cedillo, Leonor (1996), 'Plaguicidas y salud ocupacional' in O. Rivera Serrano and G. Ponciano Rodríguez (eds.), *La situación ambiental en México*, Programa Universitario del Medio Ambiente, UNAM, México.

CIEN, Web page at http://www.mty.itesm.mx/dcic/centros/cepdes/cien

Constantino Toto, Roberto (1996), 'Ambiente, tecnología e instituciones: El reto de un nuevo orden competitivo', *Comercio Exterior*, 46 (10) (October), 774–84.

Crawford, Leslie (1998), 'Mexican Salt Waters Run Deep', *Financial Times*, 2–3 May, p. xxiv.

Daly, Herman (1993), 'The Perils of Free Trade', *Scientific American*, 269 (November), 50–2.

Dasgupta, Susmita, H. Hettige and David Wheeler (1997), 'What Improves Environmental Performance? Evidence from Mexican Industry', Working Paper Series 1877, World Bank Development Research Group, Washington, DC.

Díaz Coutiño, Reynol (1999), *Apropiación mundial de recursos naturales y humanos: El caso de la agricultura de exportación del estado de Sinaloa*, unpublished PhD dissertation, Instituto Tecnológico de Oaxaca, Mexico.

Domínguez, Lilia (1996), 'Determinantes del comportamiento empresarial hacia la preservación del ambiente', UNAM, México.

Farrera Athie, Humberto (1997), 'Panorama de la tecnología limpia en México', Centro de Información par la Ecoeficiency de los Negocios, ITESM, Monterrey, México.

Gómez Tovar, Laura (1996), 'La agricultura orgánica de México: Una opción viable para los agricultores de escasos recursos', Master's thesis, Department of Agricultural Economics, Universidad Autónoma de Chapingo.

Jenkins, Rhys (1998), 'Industrialization, Trade and Pollution in Latin America: A Review of the Issues', paper presented at the meeting of the Latin American Studies Association, Chicago, September.

Karliner, Joshua (1997), *The Corporate Planet: Ecology and Politics in the Age of Globalization*, Sierra Club Books, San Francisco.

La Jornada Ecológica (1998a), 'El Fuego: Elemento purificador o factor de la devastación? Una reflexión sobre los incendios forestales' (special issue, July).

La Jornada Ecológica (1998b), 'Plaguicidas' (special issue, October).

La Jornada Ecológica (1998c), 'Guerra Ambiental en la Frontera Norte' (special issue, December).

Lemus, Blanca E. (1995), 'El uso de aguas negras para el riego y su impacto sobre el medio ambiente y la salud pública', in I. Restrepo (ed.), *Agua y Derechos Humanos*, Comisión Nacional de Derechos Humanos, México.

—— (1999), 'Bitter Sweetness: The Health Impact of Privatization in a Sugar Mill in Mexico', unpublished PhD dissertation, University of Massachusetts, Lowell.

Madrid, Sergio (1998), 'The Forest Resources Control Process by Indigenous Communities of the Northern Sierra of Oaxaca, Mexico', paper presented at the VII annual conference of the International Association for the Study of Common Property, 'Crossing Boundaries', Vancouver, Canada, 10–14 June.

Moncada, Gerardo (1997), 'CESPEDES: La congregación de voluntades', *Manufactura*, 4 (30) (December), 29–33.

Moure-Eraso, Rafael, Meg Wilcox, Laura Punnett, L. Copeland and Charles Levenstein (1994), 'Back to the Future: Sweatshop Conditions in the Mexico–US Border. I. Community Health Impact of Maquiladora Industrial Activity', *American Journal of Industrial Medicine*, 25 (3), 311–24.

Moure-Eraso, Rafael, Meg Wilcox, Laura Punnett, Leslie MacDonald and Charles Levenstein (1997), 'Back to the Future: Sweatshop Conditions in the Mexico–US Border. II. Occupational Health Impact of Maquiladora Industrial Activity', *American Journal of Industrial Medicine*, 31 (5), 587–99.

Mumme, Stephen (1993), 'Environmentalists, NAFTA, and North American Environmental Management', *Journal of Environment and Development*, 2 (1).

Prado, G. *et al.* (1998), 'Residuos de plaguicidas organocloradas en leches pasteurizadas comerciales en la Ciudad de México', *Archivos de Medicina Veterinaria* (Valdivia, Chile), 30 (1), 55–6.

Procuraduría Federal del Medio Ambiente, Secretaría de Medio Ambiente, Recursos Naturales y Pesca (1998), Web page. http://www.profepa.semarnap.gob.mx

Rozenberg, Dino (1997), 'La industria de pinta de limpio', *Manufactura*, 4 (30) (December), 8–28.

Sassen, Saskia (1995), *Cities in a World Economy*, Pine Forge Press, Thousand Oaks, Ca.

Schmidheiny, Stephan (1992), *Changing Course: A Global Business Perspective on Business and the Environment*, MIT Press, Cambridge.

Spalding, Mark and Lori Saldaña (1998), 'San Ignacio Lagoon Has Value Beyond the Sum of Its Parts', *San Diego Union-Tribune*, 6 May. (Also available at: http://www.netconnection.com/lsaldana/bajawhales.html)

Sprouse, Terry and Stephen Mumme (1997), 'Beyond BECC: Envisioning Needed Institutional Reforms for Environmental Protection on the US–Mexico Border', paper presented at the Meeting of the Association of Borderlands Scholars, Western Social Science Association Annual Meeting, Albuquerque, New Mexico, 23–26 April.

Tapia Naranjo, Alfredo and Ramón Pichs (1997), 'Empersas innovadoras en la esfera de la protección ambiental', in L. Corona Treviño (ed.), *Cien Empresas Innovadoras en México*, UNAM and Miguel Angel Porrua, México.

Ten Kate, Adrian (1993), *Industrial Development and the Environment in Mexico*, World Bank Working Paper WPS 1125, World Bank, Washington, DC.

World Bank (1997), 'Mexico Air Pollution Intensities: Estimates of Air Pollution Load per Employee for Plants in Mexico'. New Ideas in Pollution Regulation, World Bank. http://www.worldbank.org/nipr/data/ mexico

Varady, Robert G., David Colnic, Robert Merideth and Terry Sprouse (1996), 'The US–Mexican Border Environmental Cooperation Commission: Collected Perspectives on the First Two Years', *Journal of Borderlands Studies*, XI (2).

World Business Council for Sustainable Development–Latin America, Web page. http://www.wbcsd/Regional/regionla.htm or http://www.wbcsdla.org.mx

Appendix 1

Office of the Federal Attorney for Environmental Protection:
Firms Certified Under the 'Clean Industries' Programme (1997)

1 3M México, S.A. (P.D.F.)
2 Adydsa del Sureste, S.A.
3 Aga Gas, S.A. (P.Guadalajara)
4 Agronitrogenados, S.A.
5 Alambrados y Circuitos Eléctricos, S.A. (P.V)
6 Alambrados y Circuitos Eléctricos, S.A. (P.VII)
7 Albright and Wilson Troy de México, S.A. (Complejo Industrial Pajaritos)
8 Alcoholes Desnaturalizados y Diluentes, S.A. (P.Tlalnepantla)
9 Bayer de México, S.A. (P.Ecatepec)
10 Carplastic, S.A. (P.Hermosillo)
11 Celanese Mexicana, S.A. (Complejo Cangrejera)
12 Celanese Mexicana, S.A. (Complejo Cosoleacaque)
13 Celanese Mexicana, S.A. (P.Celaya)
14 Celanese Mexicana, S.A. (Terminal Marítima Coatzacoalcos)
15 Cementos Anáhuac, S.A. (P.Barrientos)
16 Cementos Guadalajara, S.A. (P.Guadalajara)
17 Cementos Mexicanos, S.A. (P.Torreon)
18 Cerillos y Fósforos La Imperial, S.A.
19 Cervecería Cuauhtémoc-Moctezuma, S.A. (P.Monterrey)
20 Cervecería Cuauhtémoc-Moctezuma, S.A. (P.Orizaba)
21 Cervecería Cuauhtémoc-Moctezuma, S.A. (P.Tecate)
22 Cervecería Cuauhtémoc-Moctezuma, S.A. (P.Toluca)
23 Cervecería del Pacífico, S.A.
24 Cía. Cerillera La Central, S.A.
25 Cía. Mexicana de Terminales, S.A.
26 Ciba Especialidades Químicas México, S.A. (P.Atotonilquillo)
27 Ciba Especialidades Químicas México, S.A. (P.Puebla)
28 Ciba Farmacéutica, S.A. (P.Tlalpan Norte)
29 Cloro de Tehuantepec, S.A.
30 Colgate Palmolive, S.A. (P.D.F.)
31 Compañia Nestle, S.A. (P.Xalapa)
32 Crisoba Industrial, S.A. (P.Morelia)
33 Curtidos Toluca, S.A.

34 Cyanamid de México, S.A. (P.Tlalpan)
35 DELPHI Ensamble de Cubiertas Automotrices, S.A. (P.Parral)
36 DELPHI Vestiduras Fronterizas, S.A. (P.Juárez)
37 DELPHI Vestiduras Fronterizas, S.A. (P.Río Bravo)
38 Detonadores Estrella, S.A.
39 Dow Química Mexicana, S.A. (P.Tlalnepantla)
40 Dow Química Mexicana, S.A. (P. Tlaxcala)
41 Dupont México, S.A. (P.Lerma)
42 Federal Mogul, S.A.
43 Fenoquimia, S.A. (P.Cosoleacaque)
44 Fertilizantes Guadalajara, S.A.
45 Gates Rubber de México, S.A. (P.Toluca)
46 Glicoles Mexicanos, S.A.
47 Grasas Vegetales, S.A.
48 Grupo Industrial N.K.S., S.A.
49 Industria Química del Istmo, S.A. (Complejo Industrial Pajaritos)
50 Industrias Cydsa Bayer, S.A. (Complejo Industrial Pajaritos)
51 Industrias Resistol, S.A. (P.Coatzacoalcos)
52 Industrias Texel, S.A.
53 Insecticidas de Occidente, S.A.
54 Insecticidas Nacionales Corey, S.A.
55 Kimex, S.A.
56 Koblenz Eléctrica, S.A.
57 Kodak de México, S.A. (P.Guadalajara)
58 Masterpak, S.A. (P.Celorey)
59 Masterpak, S.A. (P.Propirey)
60 Masterpak, S.A. (P.Reyprint)
61 Nueva Fábrica Nacional de Vidrio, S.A.
62 Nylon de México, S.A.
63 Operadora Metamex, S.A.
64 Orozco Polaris, S.A. (Marina Aqua Ray)
65 Papelera del Nevado, S.A.
66 Pavillion, S.A.
67 Pemex Petroquímica Centro Embarcador Pajaritos
68 Pemex Refinación Centro de Transportación Terrestre de Cadereyta
69 Pemex Refinación Centro de Transportación Terrestre de Cd. Madero

70 Pemex Refinación Ductos Norte Cd. Madero

71 Pemex Refinación Refinería Ing. Antonio Dovali Jaime, Salina Cruz, Oax.

72 Pemex Refinación Terminal de Almacenamiento y Distribución, Cd. Madero

73 Pemex Refinación Terminal de Almacenamiento y Distribución, Nuevo Laredo

74 Pemex Refinación Terminal Marítima de Cd. Madero

75 Pennwalt, S.A. (P.Santa Clara)

76 Petroquímica Cosoleacaque, S.A.

77 Petroquímica La Cangrejera, S.A.

78 Petroquímica Morelos, S.A.

79 Petroquímica Pennwalt, S.A. (P.Coatzacoalcos)

80 Pinturas y Barnices Calette, S.A.

81 Polaquimia, S.A.

82 Polimeros de México, S.A. (P.Tlaxcala)

83 Procter & Gamble de México, S.A. (P.Talismán)

84 Procter & Gamble de México, S.A. (P.Vallejo)

85 Productos de Consumo Resistol, S.A. (P.Vallejo)

86 Productos Pelikan, S.A.

87 Productos Químicos Coin, S.A.

88 Productos Químicos Naturales, S.A.

89 Pyosa, S.A. (P.1 y 2)

90 Química Hoechst de México, S.A. (P.Santa Clara)

91 Química Lucava, S.A.

92 Quimobasicos, S.A.

93 Reichhold Química de México, S.A.

94 Reind Química, S.A.

95 Residuos Industriales Multiquim, S.A.

96 Resirene, S.A.

97 Rexcel, S.A. (P.Química Lerma)

98 Río Bravo Eléctricos, S.A. (P.I)

99 Río Bravo Eléctricos, S.A. (P.IV)

100 Río Bravo Eléctricos, S.A. (P.V)

101 Río Bravo Eléctricos, S.A. (P.VII)

102 Río Bravo Eléctricos, S.A. (P.IX)

103 Río Bravo Eléctricos, S.A. (P.X)

104 Río Bravo Eléctricos, S.A. (P.X-A)

105 Sales del Istmo, S.A.

106 Schneider Eléctric México, S.A. (P.D.F.)

107 Servicios Minerometalúrgicos de Occidente, S.A.

108 Síntesis Orgánicas, S.A. (P.Puebla)

109 Sistemas Eléctricos y Conmutadores, S.A.

110 Stepan de México, S.A.

111 Tecniquimia Mexicana, S.A.

112 Tetraetilo de México, S.A. (Complejo Industrial Pajaritos)

113 Univex, S.A. (P.Salamanca)

114 Vidriera Toluca, S.A.

115 Viniles de Acuna, S.A.

Appendix 2

Office of the Federal Attorney for Environmental Protection:
Environmental Audits (1992-3/1998)

Firm	In Process	Completed	Total
1 Grupo Cementos Mexicanos	0	19	19
2 Ferrocarriles Nacionales de México '	0	54	54
3 Grupo Peñoles	0	14	14
4 General Motors	0	50	50
5 Pemex	23	133	156
6 Comisión Federal de Electricidad	0	30	30
7 Ford Motors	0	12	12
8 Asa	5	24	29
* 9 Others	28	197	225
*10 Procuraduría Federal de Protección al Ambiente	0	315	315
TOTALS	56	848	904

Source: PROFEPA, Undersecretariat of Environmental Audits
* Letters of Commitment; in other cases, formal agreements

Negotiated	349	In process	338
Fulfilled	177	TOTAL	864

Of the 848 environmental audits completed, 864 action plans have been drawn up:

Summary of Environmental Audits by States (1992-3/1998)

State	In process	Completed	Total
Aguascalientes	0	14	14
Baja California	1	37	38
Baja California Sur	1	7	8
Campeche	0	5	5
Chiapas	0	11	11
Chihuahua	2	66	68
Coahuila	3	58	61
Colima	0	9	9
Distrito Federal	1	32	33
Durango	7	15	22
Guanajuato	0	25	25
Guerrero	0	6	6
Hidalgo	0	22	22
Jalisco	1	34	35
México	1	95	96
Michoacán	1	22	23
Morelos	1	18	19
Nayarit	0	1	1
Nuevo León	2	43	45
Oaxaca	0	18	18

State	In process	Completed	Total
Puebla	4	33	37
Querétaro	4	15	19
Quintana Roo	1	4	5
San Luis Potosí	1	21	22
Sinaloa	0	22	22
Sonora	2	15	17
Tabasco	9	42	51
Tamaulipas	3	37	40
Tlaxcala	1	29	30
Veracruz	7	71	78
Yucatán	1	8	9
Zacatecas	2	7	9
Various states*	0	6	6
TOTALS	56	848	904

Source: PROFEPA, Undersecretariat of Environmental Audits

* Environmental Audits to the right of way of PEMEX

2

Environmental Management as an Indicator of Business Responsibility in Central America

LAWRENCE PRATT AND EMILY D. FINTEL

M14 Q58
F23 Q57
Q52013

Introduction

After decades of political conflict and relative economic isolation, Central America has only recently begun to experience the government restructuring, technological innovation and economic trends which characterize the increasingly competitive globalized environment of the 1990s. As several countries of the region enter periods of true political stability for the first time in years, they must simultaneously initiate a long and difficult process of transition and adaptation. Many Central American businesses are taking the first steps to renovate their operations, from their productive capacity to their corporate images. Central America remains well behind the industrialized world in many aspects of what is considered 'modern' corporate and market behaviour. In their efforts to become more competitive, businesses are finding that they must focus industrial restructuring strategies on areas such as technology, quality management and control, production efficiency and marketing (Doryan, 1991: 23–4). While there are some noteworthy exceptions, many Central American businesses also need to restructure their efforts where business responsibility for the environment is concerned.

The environmental responsibility of business is a concept which has only recently begun to be recognized and understood in Central America. Anecdotal evidence suggests that an increasing number of firms are taking steps to improve their environmental performance. It has been extremely difficult, however, to gauge with any degree of accuracy the extent of this trend and what, precisely, are the types of measures which companies are adopting.

The actual measures taken by firms to improve environmental performance are certainly one strong indicator of business responsibility. The Latin American Center for Competitiveness and Sustainable Development (INCAE), with the cooperation of the Harvard Institute for International Development (HIID), conducted a study of approximately 500 leading Central American businesses. The study survey inquired about a number of business-related variables and opinions. One section focused on the environmental efforts of these firms. Results from the two countries for which we have collected data thus far, Costa Rica and El Salvador, show that a remarkably small percentage of firms are engaged in improving environmental performance. Even in areas known to improve financial as well as environmental outcomes, performance is weak. In a more detailed study of Central American

41

industry behaviour, INCAE researchers are beginning to discover factors which potentially contribute to this neglect of environmental performance.

Referring to the preliminary results of this survey, this chapter assesses the emerging phenomenon of corporate environmental responsibility in Central America, identifying both the scale of business efforts to improve their environmental record and some of the measures that are being taken. The discussion below is divided into two main parts. The first identifies some of the methodological problems of assessing corporate environmental responsibility in the region and presents the initial survey findings related to Costa Rica and El Salvador. Part 2 discusses possible reasons why businesses are not acting in what would seem to be the environmental, financial and competitive best interests of private enterprise in the region.

The Survey

Background and methodology

Evaluating the current levels of environmental responsibility in the region is an arduous task. Using traditional methods for assessing corporate environmental responsibility is problematic because of the difficulty in determining the standard against which company-level behaviour should be measured. For example, weak environmental legislation, lack of specific regulations and frequently conflicting legal mandates make inferring responsibility from company-level commitment and ability to comply with appropriate environmental legislation nearly impossible. Measuring current versus optimal levels of pollution and other environmental impacts can also be misleading. Having conformed to a model of import substitution for several decades, many businesses have generally less efficient production methods than those found in industrialized countries (Katz, 1984: 299–300). Finally, self-declared responsibility often lacks validity as well, given the general lack of understanding with regard to environmental issues.

Another possible means of assessing the level of business responsibility in Central American firms is to observe how businesses are thinking about and acting on their own environmental performance. Since business responsibility with regard to the environment is fundamentally a management decision, assessing the type and scope of management activity would seem a meaningful place to begin. Regardless of a firm's stated commitment to the environment, the programmes and procedures actually implemented are what will ultimately reveal whether the company has a serious intention or ability to influence environmental performance. Variables such as the existence of environmental plans, programmes to reduce raw material use and minimize waste, and employee training go much further in determining environmental responsibility than a stated or advertised 'environmental position' or other typical measures. For this reason we expect that the level of reported management activities on environmental performance will be a good proxy for determining current levels of environmental responsibility in Central America.

INCAE, with the cooperation of HIID, conducted a survey of approximately 500 leading Central American businesses. One hundred leading firms in each of five Central American countries (El Salvador, Costa Rica, Nicaragua, Honduras and Guatemala) were presented with a business attitudes survey which seeks to establish a basic understanding of the current state of Central American business. The survey collected data on a variety of variables which include capital formation, infrastructure needs, and opinions of leaders on government relations, among others. The data discussed below were collected from May to July 1997, and are derived from the section of the survey which focuses on the environmental efforts of the various businesses. The objective of the environmental portion of the survey is to gather baseline information on the activities currently being undertaken by Central American businesses regarding the environment. This effort provides the first real quantitative insight into business environmental performance in the region.

Although data are being collected for each of five Central American nations, only Costa Rica and El Salvador will be discussed here. These countries present particularly interesting cases within the region, primarily because one would expect their levels of awareness and business response to be elevated in comparison with the other countries. Costa Rica's experience with protected areas and nature-based tourism has led to a higher level of awareness of the need to protect natural resources. In El Salvador, severe environmental degradation has heightened the awareness of all sectors of society. El Salvador's new Ministry of Environment and Natural Resources reports that several hundred newspaper and magazine articles regarding environmental issues were being published each month in 1997 (Araujo, 1997). Given the absence of the aforementioned conditions in the other countries, expected levels of environmental action in Nicaragua, Guatemala, and Honduras would be significantly lower than in El Salvador and Costa Rica. It is important to note as well that only leading firms in each of the countries were surveyed. This would naturally lead one to expect a lower general level of environmental performance in each country than that reported by the leading firms.

Survey results and findings

The survey, combined with information gathered in other INCAE research, provides a preliminary understanding of the environmental profile of Central American businesses. The study depicts a worrying though seemingly improving state of affairs. The number of firms that are engaged in efforts to take responsibility for their environmental impact is small. However, regional trends, particularly the globalization of Central American business, are likely to lead to increases in levels of environmental performance and responsibility.

Of the businesses polled, 62 per cent in Costa Rica and 48 per cent in El Salvador claim to have written plans to reduce environmental impact. However, a more in-depth look at the data indicates inflated numbers in the case of Costa Rica. Although nearly two thirds of those polled responded affirmatively to having a written environmental plan, the details reported in Table 2.1 are more revealing. Only 36 per cent of businesses surveyed claimed to have written procedures for handling environmental concerns; only 33 per cent had written environmental policies; and only 29 per cent claimed to have emergency response plans. Still, 40 per cent reported having company procedures to comply with current environmental laws.

This highlights concerns about self-identification inherent in survey research; analysis of survey results must incorporate into its assumptions the interviewee's natural tendency to respond in accordance with social, cultural, legal, and political norms. It is not in a firm's best interests to maintain operational practices which may tarnish its image in both local and international markets. As stated above, actions may be far more indicative in determining true levels of environmental responsibility than company-stated outlooks or policies.

With regard to the kind of written plan deployed by companies, the three most popular responses in both countries were plans for solid waste management, liquid

Table 2.1
Survey Findings: Policies, Plans and Procedures

	Costa Rica	El Salvador
Question	N: 101	N: 105
Written procedures regarding relevant environmental situations	35.6%	21.0%
Written environmental policy, including the company's environmental commitment	32.7%	23.8%
Procedures to ensure compliance with current environmental laws	39.6%	31.4%
Clear plans and procedures to face environmental emergencies	28.7%	20.0%
Procedures to identify the main environmental issues related to the company's activity	23.8%	25.7%
Environmental plan with goals and objectives	20.8%	17.1%
Does not have any	34.7%	22.9%
Did not answer	2.0%	

discharge control, and energy conservation (see Table 2.5). Interestingly, in spite of increased global attention to air pollution issues, plans for air pollution control received significantly lower responses for both Costa Rica and El Salvador: 43 and 36 per cent respectively. This behaviour can be explained in part by looking at the different motivating factors cited by firms in the development of and changes to their environmental plans.

The reasons stated by firms for adopting or changing existing environmental plans indicated that the strongest motivators were image and reputation of the company and government regulations (see Table 2.2). It is interesting to note in this instance the connection between these two main drivers. To a large extent, a positive corporate image is associated with ethical, socially responsible behaviour. Clearly, a large component of such behaviour is compliance with government laws and regulations. Community concerns, parent company requirements, and the desire for productivity gains also scored high, while customer demand and product differentiation did not. This implies that companies in both countries see relatively little environmental demand in the marketplace.

Although government regulations were cited as a prime motivator for companies, actual knowledge of environmental legislation was discouraging. In Costa Rica, 25 per cent of respondents claimed not to be familiar with current laws and regulations relevant to their business operations. In El Salvador, this figure was 29 per cent. Even those who claim not to be aware of laws and regulations, however, seem to be concerned about the safety and well-being of their employees. An impressive 97 per cent of Costa Rican respondents and 82 per cent of Salvadoran ones reported that they train their workers in occupational health and safety.

Table 2.2
Survey Findings: Causes of the Changes in the Environmental Plan

	Costa Rica	El Salvador
Question	N: 63	N: 50
Consumer demand	19.0%	10.0%
Product differentiation	20.6%	6.0%
Government regulations	63.5%	46.0%
Higher efficiency of production processes	58.7%	42.0%
Community awareness	46.0%	44.0%
Image/reputation of the company	76.2%	58.0%
Headquarters guidelines	46.0%	36.0%
ISO 14000 and international norms	1.6%	4.0%
Other causes	8.0%	4.0%
Did not answer		14.0%

The responses presented in this survey indicate that involvement of firms in environmental actions is surprisingly limited and is thereby a great cause for concern. Clearly, companies that do not currently have programmes in place to understand and manage their environmental impact are not near any relevant level of 'responsibility' for their environmental impact.

The parent company hypothesis

INCAE and HIID sought to support a hypothesis of positive association between environmental action and international involvement of the firm. Based on a similar study conducted in Mexico, it was expected that firms which have significant international capital participation and which consider themselves exporters would have more environmental policies, plans and procedures than domestic firms selling to domestic markets.

The survey in Mexico, which was conducted in early 1996 by the Lexington Environmental Management Group, found that environmental performance was more closely associated with some form of participation in the international arena than it was with size, profitability or other attributes (Lexington Environmental Management Group, 1996: VI-14–VI-6). A strong 'parent company effect', which assumes that leading local firms implement programmes consistent with home-country corporate directives, would have been expected on the basis of the Lexington Group's findings.

A breakdown of the data by the source of the firms' capital reveals a certain level of truth to this hypothesis (see Table 2.3). In the international firm category, any respondent who identified his or her firm as deriving 30 per cent or more of its capital formation from self-reported international sources has been included. Interestingly, the source of capital was not associated with much, if any, increased

Table 2.3
Survey Findings: Policies, Plans and Procedures, by Local and International Firms

Question	Costa Rica			El Salvador	
	Local N: 52	International N: 38	Did not Answer N: 11	Local N: 80	International N: 25
Written procedures regarding relevant environmental situations	28.8%	44.7%	36.4%	17.5%	32.0%
Written environmental policy, including the company's environmental commitment	26.9%	39.4%	36.4%	16.3%	48.0%
Procedures to ensure compliance with current environmental laws	36.5%	44.7%	36.4%	28.8%	40.0%
Clear plans and procedures to face environmental emergencies	19.2%	26.9%	45.5%	16.3%	32.0%
Procedures to identify the main environmental issues related to the company's activity	*	*	*	*	*
Environmental plan with goals and objectives	21.2%	18.4%	36.4%	22.5%	36.0%
Does not have any	44.2%	21.1%	18.2%	12.5%	32.0%
Did not answer	3.8%	26.3%	18.2%	28.8%	4.0%*

*insufficient data.

environmental action. However, it is important to note that the survey did not attempt to identify sources of international capital. Controlling for capital might have shown a distinction in performance between industrial country international investment and developing country international investment.

Table 2.4
Survey Findings: Plan to Reduce Environmental Impacts

Question	Costa Rica			El Salvador		
	N: 73 Local	N: 23 Export	N: 5 Mixed	N: 32 Local	N: 4 Export	N: 64 International
Written plan to reduce environmental impacts	58.9%	73.9%	60.0%	46.9%	25.0%	50.0%

Table 2.5
Survey Findings: Type of Plan

Question	Costa Rica			El Salvador		
	N: 43 Local	N: 17 Export	N: 3 Mixed	N: 15 Local	N: 1 Export	N: 32 International
Energy saving	58.1%	70.6%		40.0%	100.0%	43.8%
Air pollution control	41.9%	52.9%		20.0%		37.5%
Liquid discharge control	60.5%	76.5%	66.7%	53.3%	100.0%	68.8%
Solid waste management	67.4%	76.5%	33.3%	66.7%	100.0%	68.8%
Workers' exposure to toxic materials control	53.5%	52.9%	33.3%	20.0%		40.6%
Other actions	6.9%					
Did not answer						21.9%

The truth of the hypothesis must be derived from a more in-depth look at the sales data. Categorized by sales orientation, whether the companies' products are exported or are sold only locally, the data indicate a strong relationship between being an exporter and the existence of environmental management programmes. Significant findings include that 74 per cent of Costa Rican exporters claimed to have written plans, compared to 59 per cent for non-exporters (see Table 2.4). The data from El Salvador did not show this pattern, but this is perhaps attributable to the very low number of self-identified exporters in that country's sample. Furthermore, 43.5 per cent of Costa Rican exporters claimed to have 'a specific environmental plan with goals and objectives', compared to only 15.5 per cent of firms dedicated to local markets (see Table 2.6). Similarly, El Salvador showed a much higher percentage of exporters with a specific environmental plan (25 per cent to 9 per cent, although the problem with the small sample size remains).

As mentioned previously, a relatively high percentage of firms overall claimed not to know of or be in compliance with relevant environmental laws (25 per cent of Costa Rican and 29 per cent of El Salvadoran respondents). This figure remained consistent across export and domestic firms. However, when asked about motivators for the change of environmental plans, 35 per cent of Costa Rican exporters cited consumer demand, compared with only 14 per cent of local firms (see Table 2.7). Furthermore, 71 per cent of exporters noted community concerns as a motivator, compared with only 33 per cent of local firms.

Table 2.6
Survey Findings: Policies, Plans and Procedures, by Firms' Sales Orientation

Question	Costa Rica			El Salvador		
	N: 73 Local	N: 23 Export	N: 5 Mixed	N: 32 Local	N: 4 Export	N: 64 International
Written procedures regarding relevant environmental situations	34.2%	47.8%		15.6%		25.0%
Written environmental policy including the company's environmental commitment	31.5%	39.1%	20.0%	21.9%	25.0%	25.0%
Procedures to ensure compliance with current environmental laws	43.8%	30.4%	20.0%	34.4%	50.0%	29.7%
Clear plans and procedures to face environmental emergencies	34.2%	17.4%		15.6%	25.0%	20.3%
Procedures to identify the main environmental issues related to the company's activity	21.9%	26.1%	40.0%	28.1%		26.6%
Environmental plan with goals and objectives	15.5%	43.5%		9.4%	25.0%	20.3%
Does not have any	39.7%	21.7%	20.0%	34.4%	25.0%	18.8%
Did not answer		4.3%	20.0%			

There was also a strong 'parent company effect' which became more visible in this data sort. A strong 65 per cent of Costa Rican exporters claimed 'headquarters guidelines' as a motivator, compared with only 40 per cent for local firms. Following this pattern, the responses yielded 100 per cent versus 27 per cent for El Salvador. Such significant differences between domestic and internationally oriented firms indicate that these two groups face distinct sets of pressures, opportunities and other stimuli which may be influencing their behaviour in different ways.

Table 2.7
Survey Findings: Causes of the Changes in the Environmental Plan, by Firms' Sales Orientation

Question	Costa Rica			El Salvador		
	N: 43 Local	N: 17 Export	N: 3 Mixed	N: 15 Local	N: 1 Export	N: 32 Mixed
Consumer demand	14.0%	35.3%				12.5%
Product differentiation	20.9%	23.5%		6.7%		3.1%
Government regulations	55.8%	82.4%	66.7%	33.3%		50.0%
Higher efficiency of production processes	58.1%	64.7%	33.3%	46.7%	100.0%	37.5%
Community awareness	32.6%	70.6%	66.7%	53.3%		37.5%
Image/reputation of the company	72.1%	88.2%	66.7%	60.0%		53.1%
Headquarters guidelines	39.5%	64.7%	33.3%	26.7%	100.0%	37.5%
ISO 14000 and international norms	2.3%			6.7%	100.0%	
Other causes	9.3%		33.3%			6.2%
Did not answer						21.9%

Analytical Framework

In order to fully understand the significance and implications of these findings, diligent attention must be given to the potential causes and factors which influence such behaviour. Through a discussion of the information and policy issues, economic conditions, legislation and regulations, fiscal policies, financial practices and corporate structures, the following sections of this chapter will seek a better understanding of the findings presented in the survey.

Information and policy issues

Under-performance and under-investment characterize the activities of most Central American businesses. In economic terms, the assumption would be for companies to improve environmental performance to the extent that it is in their self-interest to do so. Holding this to be true, it must then be asked why Central American companies seem to perceive such a low level of self-interest. Increased profitability is certainly a top company priority, and reductions in energy, water, and raw material consumption are nearly always guaranteed to provide impressive financial returns. (For a number of specific examples, see von Weizsäcker et al., 1997). However, only 59 per cent of Costa Rican respondents and 44 per cent of Salvadoran respondents claimed to have programmes to reduce energy consumption. Other potential incentives include strategic or image-related goals such as corporate goodwill, market expectations and green imaging, which only a handful of Central American companies have begun to consider.

The surprisingly little effort placed on reductions in these high-profit areas suggests a broad set of information and policy problems. The ongoing industry-level research being conducted by INCAE is examining the reasons for this under-investment and under-performance. The research seeks to ascertain whether such behaviour is a result of lack of information on the economic value of sound environmental management, or whether it stems from institutional structures which discourage or reduce a more socially desirable level of environmental performance.

The evidence suggests that it is a combination of both factors. There is a troubling shortage of information in the region on environmental responsibility, environmental management and other relevant topics. However, this information shortage only aggravates a more complicated situation. Institutional structures in the region – laws, policies, and practices in many parts of society – make it extremely difficult for firms to see or realize benefits in environmental responsibility and performance. Even with perfect information and awareness, such structures are often so powerful that relative improvement in business performance would still be limited.

With regard to information, there is little Spanish language material (original or in translation) and very few organizations are involved in disseminating materials on environmental performance, environmental management or other relevant topics. A few organizations in the region, particularly trade associations, are developing technical extension programmes in environmental management. In fact, nearly all of the principal chambers of commerce in Central America have established environmental offices. However, these pioneering efforts cannot service the entire region's need for information, and they tend to focus primarily on waste reduction and corporate image issues. Furthermore, there is little or no effort on environmental strategy, management, responsibility or best practices. Information efforts are likely to remain only marginally effective until more strategically focused programmes emerge.

More troubling than the lack of information is the current status of 'rules of the game' and their effect on environmental performance. INCAE's research on fifteen industries determined that firms operate in an atmosphere which makes business unlikely to focus on environmental issues (Pratt, 1998). The findings indicate serious problems in a variety of institutional structures which are leading to the sub-optimal environmental behaviour and performance of Central American business. Difficulties arise in the economic conditions, legal systems, fiscal policies (tax, tariff, subsidy), financial practices and corporate structures. Below are examples of some institutional obstacles which give an indication of the severity of problems with regard to business responsibility.

Economic conditions

First and possibly foremost, a lack of general economic stability in the region leads to a shorter-term outlook in business planning and financing. This short-term outlook results in either a complete lack of concern or in heavy economic discounting of future effects. The resulting high interest rates and short lending terms impede serious long-term investment, including investment in cleaner, more efficient technologies.

With interest rates in the region hovering between 15 and 40 per cent in real terms and long-term credit (more than one to two years) severely limited or unavailable, many 'common sense' investments that lower environmental impact are priced out of reach. There is little incentive to be concerned about regeneration of a forest or severe soil erosion if a company's planning horizon is only two to five years. With that horizon, there is nothing irrational about treating forest and soil resources as non-renewable and applying mining-style techniques. The micro-level problems are seen clearly in efficiency questions. Energy and waste reduction programmes that are typically in the 15 to 30 per cent return range are usually ignored because of cost of capital. These conditions annul the incentives present in an internationally competitive market, and thereby allow more damaging production techniques and wasteful practices to continue.

Legislation and regulation

Because of poor design and lack of political will, environmental laws and regula-tions are often ineffective in bringing about changes in business environmental plans. In recent years there has been an increase in the number of environmental laws and international assistance in regulatory development and enforcement. Although environmental laws in the region represent increased attention on the part of governments and are generally associated with responsible, ethical business practices, they do not appear to have any significant effect in changing the behaviour of businesses. A closer look at the laws themselves and the institutions in which they operate yields a better understanding of this pattern.

If the fundamental objective of environmental legislation is to protect the natural environment, why does it so often fail? INCAE's research on fifteen Central American industries points to a combination of factors and characteristics. First, environmental laws in the region generally fail to focus on the business activities that are most harmful to the environment. Operational activities such as hazardous waste management, water consumption and energy use remain largely unaddressed by legal systems throughout Central America (Pratt, 1998).

Where laws do exist, such as for water discharge, they are generally unenforced for one or more reasons. First, many of the laws do not set parameters and regulations for implementation. Generally speaking, laws tend to be far-ranging yet cover similar issues, thereby complicating the possibility for specific applications. Another potential pitfall is the frequent lack of staff and resources available to enforce laws and the few regulations which have been set. Yet a third challenge to the effectiveness of environmental legislation is its potential conflict with other laws or regulations. For example, INCAE's research thus far has found only one success-ful pollution control programme in the region, a programme which ironically has achieved its results in violation of standing laws. The Costa Rican coffee industry has adopted a strategy to reduce its water pollution load to 80 per cent of 1995 levels through a series of innovative agreements and investment in clean technologies (Morera, 1996: 4–5).

Even where the above conditions do not exist, laws often lack sufficient clarity. Ambiguity is extremely difficult to avoid in environmental legislation, where decisions involve putting dollar figures on invaluable natural resources and where legal plans must be translated into fair, enforceable regulations. This is further exacerbated by the fact that communication between various government institu-tions is often limited.

A general lack of sensitivity, awareness, and understanding of environmental issues by public sector employees has also contributed to the above state of affairs. Likewise, a lack of knowledge and participation by the various groups and busi-nesses affected by environmental legislation completes the loop, thereby seriously hindering the ability of legislation to improve overall environmental performance

(Harner, 1997:17–18). However, such a discussion must recognize that Costa Rica is in the process of evaluating and restructuring its environmental control functions (Chacón, 1997: 9).

It is easy to see how such drawbacks and limitations of environmental legislative measures would allow for extreme disregard of the environment by businesses. One illustrative example is the importation and use of pesticides in Costa Rica. Despite laws which on paper severely restrict pesticides banned elsewhere in the world, such as DDT, aldochlor, paraquat and methyl parathion, Costa Rica is the largest importer of pesticides per agricultural worker in Central America, with an average of 38 kg per agricultural worker imported throughout the 1980s (Conejo, 1996: 58). These quantities make Costa Rica's pesticide use equivalent to ten times the world average (in use per km squared) (Conejo, 1996: 58). Although their use is severely restricted by Costa Rican law, we were able to purchase all of the above products (except for DDT) for self-proclaimed 'home garden use' at several different hardware and agriculture supply stores in the San José metropolitan area. DDT was available by special order. Aldochlor and paraquat were on special promotion in one chain of stores. With the purchase of a second bottle, the customer was entered in a raffle for an all-expenses paid trip to Mexico!

In El Salvador, where 90 per cent of the country's superficial water supply suffers from contamination, a similarly distressing situation exists (Madrigal and Mauri, 1997: 5). Agro-industry, through the use of pesticides for crops, is considered to be the primary activity responsible for this disturbing situation (Requena and Myton, 1991: 19). Among other potential hazards, the use of pesticides also has also been found to cause reproductive defects and other health impairments. In El Salvador, approximately 50 per cent of the population works in the agriculture sector and thereby finds itself routinely exposed to such chemicals. These effects of the use of pesticides would seem to demand more regulation and control of their use by the Salvadoran government.

Just as in Costa Rica, laws to regulate the discharge of agricultural byproducts into rivers do exist. The Irrigation Law of 1970 was invoked to regulate the conservation and distribution of water; the 1988 Health Code was drawn up to work towards the creation of programmes to ensure potable water and to purify contaminated water sources; and the Regulation of Water Quality of 1988 was developed to control and reduce further contamination of the country's water. While each of these legislative measures was instituted with positive intentions, they failed to set forth specific parameters for El Salvador's different industries. Furthermore, the legislation was not accompanied by effective enforcement measures (Pérez, 1997: 14).

What these two examples show is that the role played by environmental legislation in actually protecting the environment will not be sufficient to preserve these countries' natural resources in the future. In many cases the laws which have been enacted are largely disregarded, and these breaches receive very little attention from the government or the society as a whole. In order to change the current state of affairs, it would seem that Central American businesses and industry need to find ways to provide incentives for 'good' behaviour and procedures for holding offenders accountable.

Fiscal Policies

Fiscal policies can often influence environmental and social responsibility greatly, both positively and negatively. In Central America, tariffs, subsidies, and taxes have long since played prominent and often controversial roles in influencing industrial behaviour. With regard to their effects on the environmental responsibility of business, fiscal policies appear to perpetuate an industrial lack of efficiency and to encourage the exploitation of natural resources (Pratt, 1998). For example, the tariffs placed on imported technology (including 'green' and high-efficiency technology) have slowed the adoption of more efficient and less polluting technology by businesses. Such tariffs on imported equipment hover around 20 per cent in both El Salvador and Costa Rica (*AmericaEconomía*, 1997: 21–5). Because the taxable basis includes freight and insurance costs, these tariffs understate the cost of importation. In addition, the staggering transaction costs (permits, forms, security storage, and tax stamps) mask the true costs associated with importing such products.

Another vexing characteristic of fiscal policy relates to both direct and indirect subsidies for land, water, and electricity. Such subsidies more often than not lead to undervalued use of these resources (for examples, see de Moor, 1997). Ubiquitous land and water subsidies encourage expansion of extensive agriculture and other activities not capable of paying full cost for their inputs. A final element which needs attention in this regard relates to corporate tax systems. In Central America such systems are largely based on tariff assets and equity rather than income. This results in tax disadvantages for investment in new, clean, efficient technology because purchasing new equipment increases the taxable asset base.

Fiscal policies appear to be having a strong negative effect on the promotion of sustainable development and competitiveness of the Central American countries. This is principally because the entire concept of competitiveness has been misconstrued in the realm of fiscal support policies. Generally, fiscal objectives are based on maintaining continually lower costs, not on developing higher value and greater productivity. Such policies often distort market realities and thus allow firms to operate at suboptimal production levels while maintaining virtually fixed profit levels. The result is that Central Americans pay three times for their productive output. First, they pay the price for goods out of their pockets. They are then charged the price of inefficient production for which they must compensate with their tax dollars. Finally, even if less directly or in the longer term, they pay the price of environmental damage caused by industries which have been given indirect incentives to damage the environment.

Financial practices

INCAE's research has found that many current financial practices and policies hinder sustainable development and competitiveness in Central America. Because the financial systems being utilized have been designed to promote government objectives in agricultural and industrial production, they cannot effectively facilitate capital nor correctly evaluate risk. Instead, they often endorse the suboptimal use of resources, inhibit the use of technological innovation and promote environmentally unsustainable behaviour (Pratt, 1998).

Agriculture is one sector in which financing policies seriously impede sustainable development and competitiveness. Historically, most of agricultural financing comes from national banks. While during past periods of political instability bank practices found their justification in ensuring food supply, this rationale is becoming less relevant. Regional stabilization and increased competitiveness on a global scale are requiring a new approach to financial practices in the region. With the system as it now stands, agricultural loan practices, consisting of 'technical packages' for agriculture loans, promote unsound and frequently dangerous practices. As a condition of their loans, farmers must adhere to specific technical recommend-ations made by the banks. These technical packages are frequently outdated and rarely reflect current agronomic practices. In Costa Rica, loan conditions also often encourage the inappropriate use of agrochemicals in crop production. Some of the pesticides, fertilizers, and other such products specified by the banks are prohibited by Costa Rican law (Harner, 1997: 20). Such policies rarely consider specific crop and climate information which can lead to agricultural innovation in the region (Pratt, 1998). An interesting area for future investigation would be the effect that these banking practices have on the development of new products.

Another point of concern is that current financial practices hinder the adoption of environmental improvements and innovations. First of all, loans are not granted on the basis of financial merit in many cases; rather, funding is reserved for certain traditional and non-traditional products. This approach favours old products and methods by making them artificially cheaper to produce than products utilizing more innovative methods. Furthermore, pollution control and prevention equip-ment is typically charged higher interest rates. Lending policies in many of the countries, particularly in the national banks, consider pollution prevention and control equipment 'non-productive assets' which means they are assessed an interest rate 'surcharge' of several percentage points (Pratt, 1998).

When seen in their true light, the financial systems in Central America seem to be doing very little to promote sustainable development and the environmental responsibility of business. Because such systems fail to evaluate financing projects on their true feasibility and merit, they end up promoting out of date, unsustainable practice at the expense of more environmentally sound production methods.

Corporate structures

The fact that domestically oriented firms are not addressing environmental performance aggressively can be understood better in the context of the corporate history of Central America. Domestic firms tend to fall into two major categories. The first group consists of the larger firms which have traditionally benefited from monopoly conditions, protection from high tariffs, and favourable market regula-tions. The second category includes smaller firms ranging from micro to medium-sized businesses.

These two types of companies can be characterized by two distinct operating environments. In general, protected markets and managed competition have allowed companies to pay less attention to efficiency, technological innovation, cost reduction, and rational use of energy and consumables (Velázquez, 1988: 74). Companies still under protection, principally larger domestic firms with secure local markets, have little incentive to change operating practices. Profits are frequently guaranteed by economic, legal and commercial structures. For these firms, environmental performance is merely one of many areas which could be improved, along with productivity, marketing and strategy, among others.

The micro, small and medium-sized firms, a huge percentage of total Central American business, operate on the margins of economic viability and do not generally participate in the tax, financial and other societal systems. Financing is scarce or non-existent for most of these firms, and the business planning horizons are extremely short, given the high risk of operations. The companies recognize the need for reduction of energy consumption and waste, but frequently lack the knowledge and financial liquidity to realize potential gains (Jiménez, 1997).

In either operating environment, improvement is unlikely to be initiated unless external forces act upon the firm, and this type of external pressure is unlikely to evolve in Central America until capital markets develop. Currently Central American companies tend to be family enterprises or owned by a small number of individuals. The fact that companies are not publicly traded (in stock or other markets) may prevent concerns of disparate interests from being discussed and addressed. These firms seem to note very little interest and demand from customers, shareholders, government and parent companies with regard to environmental responsibility. Their multinational counterparts, however, are witnessing increased demand in this regard. For the smaller firms, the low levels of concern appear to be attributable to lack of information, general unavailability of appropriate investment capital to improve performance, and the absence of customer or government pressure.

The higher levels of performance among international firms may be attributed to several factors. As mentioned above, there appears to be an important influence contributed by the 'parent company effect', though at this time it is difficult to discern the association between international capital and export orientation. It is interesting to note, however, that companies with multinational affiliations – usually with North American or European parent companies – generally have greater and more varied expertise and face different external pressures. Parent company policies, customer and shareholder expectations and company image are among the pressures that lead to higher levels of environmental performance (Savage *et al.*, 1991: 61–2). In addition, these companies contribute knowledge and experience in environmental management learned in their more demanding home markets. Export firms appear to be responding to stronger customer and stakeholder demand; they are being forced to operate in the arena of heightened international competition.

Given these new observations, the principal objective of future policy research on regional environmental performance will be to determine what institutional incentives and disincentives exist that positively or negatively influence company-level initiative on environmental affairs. In spite of the obstacles discussed above, internationalization of the private and public sectors in the region is likely to have a strong positive impact on business environmental performance in the coming years. Furthermore, increased internationalization in capital formation, and in markets at home and abroad, is likely to bring with it greater levels of parent company pressure and expertise, and to increase consumer-driven demand for environmentally sound products and processes. Government efforts to harmonize environmental protection with the levels required for future hemispheric trade integration are also likely to promote greater response to regulatory drivers.

Conclusion

The findings and analysis presented here provide a preliminary understanding of the complexities of business responsibility in Central America. This study opens the door to more in-depth research on the associations between attributes of industries, the institutional conditions under which they operate and their environmental performance. Further analysis will also attempt to link the institutional structures more clearly to specific behaviour among the region's industries. Some general questions have been answered; yet others still must be addressed.

The research conducted thus far indicates an alarmingly low level of business responsibility among leading firms with regard to the environment. Legislation and regulations are in place, but they are often so confusing and weak that they do little to improve the actual performance of firms. Further, fiscal and financial policies remaining from decades of import substitution are clearly providing direct and indirect incentives to perform in environmentally irresponsible ways.

Central America, however, finds itself in the midst of transition. Economic liberalization, governmental restructuring and a myriad of other changes are drastically shifting the current state of affairs. With regard to business responsibility for the environment, much could change. Only continued observation and research will provide the understanding and lucid analysis necessary to generate solutions for the future.

References

AmericaEconomía magazine (1997), 'Especial Comercio Exterior 1997'.

Araujo Padilla, Miguel (1997), Minister of Environment and Natural Resources, interview by Lawrence Pratt, 10 September 1997, San Salvador.

Chacón, Carlos (1997), 'Aspectos Relacionados con las Políticas Públicas y la Sostenibilidad de 5 Actividades Económicas en Costa Rica: Turismo, Forestal, Piña, Café y Palmito', analysis prepared exclusively for INCAE by its environmental lawyer and consultant, San José.

Conejo, Carlos, Rafael Díaz, Edgar Furst, Eduardo Gitli and Leiner Vargas (1996), 'Comercio y Medio Ambiente: El Caso de Costa Rica', Centro Internacional en Política Económica para el Desarrollo Sostenible, San José.

de Moor, A. P. G. (1997), 'Perverse Incentives.' Earth Council, San José.

Doryan, Eduardo (1991/2), 'Para Entender la Reconversión Industrial', *Revista INCAE* 5 (2), 13–29.

Harner, Claudia (1997), *Sustainability Analysis of the Coffee Industry in Costa Rica*, Latin American Center for Competitiveness and Sustainable Development (INCAE), Alajuela.

Jiménez, Luis Diego (1997), EcoIngresos, interview by Lawrence Pratt, San José.

Katz, Jorge M. (1984), 'Tecnología y Desarrollo Económico; una Visión Panorámica de Los Resultados de Recientes Investigaciones', in Moshé Syrquín and Simón Teitel (eds.), *Comercio, Estabilidad, Tecnología y Equidad en América Latina*, Banco Interamericano de Desarrollo, Washington, DC, pp. 283–316.

Lexington Environmental Management Group (1996), 'Industrial Environmental Management in Mexico: Report on a Survey', prepared by the Lexington Group for the World Bank.

Madrigal Cordero, Patricia and Carolina Mauri Carabaguíaz (1997), 'Diagnóstico de Las Regulaciones Jurídicas Existentes en El Salvador en Materia de Desechos Sólidos, Agua y Aire', forthcoming in *Estudio de Diseno y Factibilidad del Programa para la Descontaminación de Areas Críticas en El Salvador, Banco Interamericano de Desarrollo*, Interamerican Development Bank.

Morera, Rolando Vasquez (1996), 'Descontaminación de las Aguas Residuales en el Beneficiado del Café en Costa Rica', ICAFE, San José.

Pérez, José Manuel (1997), 'Análisis de la Sostenibilidad de la Industria Azucarera en El Salvador', Centro Latinoamericano para la Competitividad y el Desarrollo Sostenible (INCAE), Alajuela.

Pratt, Lawrence (1998), *The Role of Central American Institutional Structures in the Environmental Performance of Select Initiatives*, forthcoming.

Requena, L. Fernando and Becky A. Myton (1991), 'Contaminación de Agua de Superficie y Subterránea en Cuencas Seleccionadas del Suroeste de El Salvador', WASH Informe de Campo No. 354, Environmental Health Project, USAID, Washington, DC.

Savage, Grant T., Timothy W. Nix, Carlton J. Whitehead and John D. Blair (1991), 'Strategies for Assessing and Managing Organizational Stakeholders', *Academy of Management Executive*, 5 (2), 61–74, Texas.

UNCTAD (1996), *Trade and Development Report, 1996,* report by the secretariat of the United Nations Conference on Trade and Development, United Nations, New York and Geneva.

Velázquez, José Luis (1988), 'Los Empresarios y el Cambio', *Revista INCAE,* 2 (2), 73–8.

von Weizsäcker, Ernst, Amory B. Lovins and L. Hunter Lovins (1997), *Factor Four, Doubling Wealth – Halving Resource Use,* Earthscan Publications Limited, London, chapters 1–3.

Bioprospecting in (Costa Rica)

Facing New Dimensions
of Social and Environmental Responsibility

SILVIA RODRÍGUEZ and MARIA ANTONIETA CAMACHO

Introduction

A positive outcome of the global environmental movement of the past decade has been the growing awareness of the vulnerability of the biosphere and of the role of human beings in causing environmental degradation. In relation to natural resource use, there is increasing recognition of the need for new ethical standards and methods of economic valuation which transcend the short-term, self-centred, profit-maximizing orientation of free market economics. In short, we are engaged in a process of reassessing our responsibilities and rights.

In this chapter we examine the activities of a specific sector of the business community whose actions are closely associated with renewable natural resources and conservation in developing countries, namely pharmaceutical companies engaged in biodiversity prospecting.[1] More specifically, we look at the role of Merck & Co., the large US company, which had annual sales of $US24 billion and research and development (R & D) expenditures of $1.7 billion in 1997 (Merck & Co., 1998).

In response to innovations in biotechnology and the growth of demand for genetic materials and chemical components, many Northern pharmaceutical companies have become actively involved in bioprospecting since the late 1980s. By the early 1990s, companies with bioprospecting interests in developing countries included Glaxo Group Research, Inverni della Beffa, Merck & Co., Novartis, Pharmagenesis, Phytopharmaceuticals, Rhone-Poulenc Rorer, Shaman Pharmaceuticals, Syntex Laboratories and Upjohn Co. (Reid *et al.*, 1993: 8–13).

In Costa Rica, the agreements and partnerships entered into for bioprospecting and research are becoming more diverse as well as increasing in sheer numbers. This is partly the result of the fact that the country is unique in having approximately 4 per cent of all terrestrial living species which exist in the world and one quarter of its territory in protected areas (Gámez *et al.*, 1993: 53).

By examining the experience of Costa Rica, our objective is to reflect on the state of this novel activity during the first half of the 1990s. Much has been written about the partnership between Merck & Co. and the large Costa Rican environmental NGO, INBio; in fact it quickly acquired international status as a model for joint implementation in the field of bioprospecting and for North–South coopera-tion for sustainable development. In this chapter we will consider whether such a partnership is producing the type of economic and conservation outcomes originally envisaged. We will also identify some of the key institutional conditions that have favoured such a partnership and the development of bioprospecting in Costa Rica.[2]

Through this analysis we wish to contribute to the global debate on corporate environmental responsibility by presenting a number of ideas and arguments which question the role of bioprospecting as a tool for conservation and sustainable development in Third World countries with high levels of biological diversity. In particular, we are critical of the 'win–win' rhetoric surrounding bioprospecting in general and the INBio–Merck partnership in particular, where there is a tendency to assume that all the relevant actors or 'stakeholders' benefit – including govern-ment, companies, NGOs and local communities. Our analysis suggests that, in practice, benefits accrue to very specific stakeholders and are quite limited.

More specifically, the chapter raises six concerns. First, relatively few resources associated with bioprospecting have been channelled towards conservation. Second, bioprospecting is taking place under rapidly changing and uncertain conditions, and often involves 'hard' or sophisticated technologies which may be of limited value for developing countries. The complexity of bioprospecting and its long-term and slow results greatly complicate the process of adding value to raw materials. Moreover, certain estimates regarding financial returns from the royalties on future products appear exaggerated. Third, the process of negotiating benefits with the multiple social actors associated with access to biodiversity resources is flawed, given the failure to include local providers of so-called 'traditional' or 'indigenous' knowledge which may contribute to the process of identifying properties of plants, trees and animals in tropical forests. Fourth, the much-heralded advance payment made by Merck to INBio had little to do with corporate benevolence or environmental responsibility but was fundamentally the 'price' for good quality samples. Fifth, bioprospecting is contributing to a worrying trend associated with the privatization of protected areas, traditionally considered part of the public domain and national heritage. Finally, although the INBio–Merck agreement is often held up as a model to be replicated in other countries, such replication may prove extremely difficult, given that the agreement was shaped by – and negotiated in – a specific country context where particular institutions and core competencies exist. While there are many other bioprospecting experiences, they do not conform exactly to the INBio–Merck model.

In the first part of the chapter we look at the context in which the concept and activity of bioprospecting have gained currency. Next, we examine the INBio–Merck accord and recount briefly the expectations associated with it in 1991, when the contract was signed. We then identify some of the limitations, challenges and outcomes facing bioprospecting at present, and confront this situation with the expectations. Finally, we consider if there are ways in which it might be made more ethically responsible, economically viable, socially just and ecologically sustainable.

The Concept and Activity of Bioprospecting

At the beginning of the 1970s it was argued that conserving tropical forests was important in order to take advantage of their incalculable potential for providing the leads necessary to develop medicines for what were incurable illnesses. Nearly two decades later, however, this argument was still grounded more in theory than practice.

At the end of the 1980s Thomas Eisner, an entomologist at Cornell University, stated that basic support was needed if biodiversity prospecting was to realize its potential.

How was this to be achieved? Eisner imagined the case of a tropical country which, in association with one of the large pharmaceutical companies, would systematically screen and characterize the country's native species in search of compounds that contain characteristics potentially useful in the development of medicines. The company would have immediate access to the riches of the tropical forest[3] and the host country would receive payment for providing access to natural products and adding some value to extracts of plants and animals.

This economic incentive would in itself help in conserving forests. For the initial exploration activities, Eisner created the term 'chemical prospecting', drawing on other existing terms such as mining or petroleum prospecting (Lyons, 1991). Later this term became 'bioprospecting'[4] when the search for leads for the development of commercial products widened to include not only the chemical but also the genetic properties of plants, animals and micro-organisms.

While aspects of bioprospecting have been carried out since prehistoric times, we should be clear that Eisner's conception went well beyond the search for natural products for human use. He tried to incorporate the idea of a sophisticated and modern partnership[5] between a highly industrialized company and a tropical country in which incentives would be provided and profits shared with the country concerned. In this way it would be possible to support tropical ecosystem conservation efforts *in situ*.

Chemical prospecting, as Eisner conceived of it, was put into practice with the signing of the agreement between INBio and Merck & Co. in September 1991 – for which Eisner served as the broker (Lyons, 1991: 27).[6] The pioneering nature of this agreement is evident from the fact that it was finalized prior to the signing of the Convention on Biological Diversity at the Earth Summit in 1992. While the term 'bioprospecting' was not used in the Convention itself, it quickly gained prominence in the different Conferences of the Parties (COPs), which are the subsequent negotiations of the signatory countries on the implementation of the Convention, and the INBio–Merck agreement was held up by many as a model.

One important outcome of the Convention related to ownership rights of the elements and components of biodiversity. These were no longer regarded as 'the patrimony of humanity'. Rather, the Convention reinforced each nation's sovereign rights over its resources according to its laws and policies. This approach strongly supported Eisner's ideas: transnational corporations using genetic and biochemical resources would be obligated to sign formal agreements with the countries where they sourced their raw materials and information, and establish rules and regulations for the equitable sharing of benefits.

The National Biodiversity Institute (INBio)

At the beginning of the 1990s there were high hopes that bioprospecting would make an important contribution to conservation and development in Costa Rica. These hopes derived not only from the technical and economic potential of bioprospecting but also from the country's favourable 'enabling environment' associated with legal, cultural and political aspects, as well as environmental policy and awareness. INBio began to take shape with the institutional changes in the public sector that occurred during the latter half of the 1980s. At this time environmental aspects were more strongly incorporated into national development policies and a new Ministry of Natural Resources, Energy and Mines (MIRENEM) was established at the beginning of the Arias Administration (1986–90), funded partly by debt-for-nature swaps. An office dealing with biodiversity issues began to operate within the ministry in 1987, with a mandate to design a new development strategy for wildland and conservation areas. The idea of a programme for the integrated management of biodiversity soon emerged. This led to the establishment of a private institute by an *ad hoc* commission. According to INBio's director, in a context where government budgets were being cut, only a private organization would have the agility and capacity to mobilize resources (Sánchez, 1992: 5-A, citing Rodrígo Gámez).

At the end of 1989 INBio was legally constituted as a non-profit private association in the public interest. It could by law receive funds and donations and was tax-exempt. In 1992 MIRENEM and INBio signed a cooperative agreement which established mechanisms for collaboration and the transfer of resources and benefits (Sittenfeld and Gámez, 1993: 86–9).

In a relatively short time INBio received resources, principally from private foundations and international organizations, to acquire land, construct buildings and train personnel to perform its principal objectives – establishing an inventory of the country's biodiversity, guaranteeing the conservation of extracts and samples, and facilitating user access to the biodiversity information of wildland areas. Such tasks, it was believed, would support conservation through the use of scientific knowledge in the management of protected areas, by enhancing institutional capacity, and promoting 'biological literacy' as well as strengthening the ecological dimension in land use planning (Gámez and Gauld, 1996; INBio, 1996; Sittenfeld *et al.*, 1996).

INBio's work was organized in various areas or divisions. These included:

- Inventory: this entity is responsible for taxonomic classification, collecting and cataloguing of species and establishing collections. Thirty biodiversity stations were set up in the country with approximately 50 parataxonomists;
- Biodiversity prospecting: working in conjunction with companies and researchers, this division plays a crucial role in demonstrating the economic and research value of biodiversity (for example, chemical prospecting, exploring for tropical forest aromas and fragrances, and searches for enzymes with industrial applications and substances with insecticidal, antiviral and antibacterial activity);
- Information: dissemination of some information and knowledge transfer using a modern computerized data base;
- Social management area: INBio is also working to promote public education on biological diversity and increase 'bio-literacy' through this area;
- Administrative and financial support unit.

The distribution of the overall budget of INBio in 1996 (INBio, 1996: 56) indicates that the largest expenditures were concentrated in inventory activities (34 per cent of the total) and biodiversity prospecting (22 per cent). Special programmes, located mainly in the Guanacaste Conservation Area in the north-west of the country, accounted for 14 per cent. Information systems received slightly more (8 per cent) than the social management programme (7 per cent), which was initiated more recently. Finally, administrative costs accounted for 15 per cent of the total budget.

Table 3.1 presents budgetary data for the 1991–7 period. It is important to note, however, that such aggregated figures tend to differ from one source to another. According to estimates provided by INBio's bioprospecting director (personal interview, 1997), INBio's division of bioprospecting and research disbursed nearly $2.3 million for research, conservation and institutional strengthening between 1991 and the beginning of 1997.

Table 3.1

Estimated Direct Contributions Made by Bioprospecting and Research Division of INBio (US$; 1991—January/March 1997)

Contributions and payments to:	1991— 1993	1994	1995	1996	Jan—Mar 1997	TOTAL	%
MINAE	110,040	43,400	66,670	51,092	23,531	294,733	13
SINAC	86,102	203,135	153,555	192,035	30,394	665,221	29
Public universities	460,409	126,006	46,962	31,265	7,522	672,164	30
Other groups at INBio	228,161	92,830	118,292	172,591	19,834	631,708	28
TOTAL	884,712	465,371	385,479	446,983	81,281	2,263,826	100

The INBio—Merck Agreement

High hopes and expectations

Both in Costa Rica and internationally the INBio—Merck partnership received considerable acclaim and publicity, given the various benefits that were associated with it. The original agreement laid the basis for institutional changes that were needed to facilitate bioprospecting – changes associated with joint implementation and the privatization of public sector responsibility for environmental protection. Through this agreement, INBio would provide the company with the chemical extracts of plants, insects and micro-organisms from within the National System of Conservation Areas (SINAC) of Costa Rica.

The press releases announcing the signing of the INBio—Merck agreement were many and disseminated worldwide. These were followed by innumerable articles in journals and books, the majority of which were optimistic about the outcomes of the agreements, especially the potential benefits derived from the advance payment by Merck of $1,135,000 (Laird, 1993: 110, citing Sittenfeld, 1992). More measured opinions, or ones which voiced scepticism with regard to the time and costs involved before a marketable product would be produced, were relatively few.

For Costa Rica and Merck different types of benefits were typically identified. In the economic sphere the country would receive benefits from two sources: one would be the advance payment and the other would be the royalties from commercial products eventually developed on the basis of samples and information provided by INBio.

The advance payment or 'up front money' would support a two-year programme of research, sampling and initial screening activities. It also included $120,000 for training of Costa Rican scientists and $100,000 for immediate use by MIRENEM in the conservation of public protected areas. In addition, the agreement established that out of the royalties eventually given by Merck to INBio, if and when a commercially viable product was developed, 50 per cent would be paid to the environment ministry for conservation activities and 50 per cent to INBio. The precise figure of the eventual royalties given by Merck to INBio was not officially disclosed, although various observers note that it is likely to be in the 1 to 5 per cent range (Gámez et al., 1993: 75; Kloppenburg and Rodríguez, 1992; Feinsilver, 1996: 118).

The advance payment was designed to eliminate the problem of a time lapse between a product moving from the first stages of bioprospection to being marketed. Furthermore, it would focus attention on the need to arrest the process of deforestation and genetic erosion in Costa Rica. As Eisner observed, the advance payment for the right to commercialize the chemical discoveries of Costa Rican biologists would serve to compensate the costly process of conserving the country's natural resources (Eisner, cited in Segelken, 1991: 2).

The director of INBio was quoted as saying (Lyons, 1991: 28) that the advance payment would help to establish a beachhead against tropical deforestation and generate some employment and public awareness that biodiversity is also a valuable economic resource. Outside assessments were equally upbeat. According to a report by the London Environmental Economics Centre, 'INBio's contract with Merck & Co. provides a pioneering example of how the use of biodiversity in prospecting can generate financial flows in support of biodiversity protection and the development of taxonomic knowledge' (Aylward et al., 1993: 53).

By 1993, however, some senior professionals at INBio were suggesting that the income from royalties would not be forthcoming in the near future and that the advance payment simply reflected, more accurately, the real cost of obtaining high quality samples:

> INBio does not expect major royalty returns in the immediate future from its biodiversity prospecting but its contract with Merck & Co. has demonstrated that commercial partners will pay the real costs of obtaining prospecting samples at the time of collection. (These costs include sample location, sample identification, preserving voucher specimens for future reference, and preservation and management of the target populations, in addition to such visible costs as those for collecting and preparing samples.) With this mindset, royalty possibilities become part of a long-term portfolio. (Sittenfeld and Gámez, 1993: 76)

The hope for the future was that 'with just five successful formulas from agreements with pharmaceutical companies, the Costa Rican forests will generate for the country foreign exchange equal to that of banana exports'[7] (Rodrigo Gámez, director of INBio, in an interview with Fuentes, 1991: 6-B).

Another benefit which bioprospecting would bring to the country would be in the area of tropical forest conservation. As mentioned above, part of the advance payment ($100,000) was immediately invested in this activity. It was also intended that economic benefits would be obtained from bioprospecting without disturbing the tropical forest, through the use of non-invasive methods of extraction associated, in particular, with chemical prospecting. According to Thomas Eisner (1989–90: 33), 'once biological activity is discovered, the usual procedure is not to harvest the source organism, but to identify the responsible chemical so that it can be produced synthetically. Chemical exploration is thus compatible with biological conservation.'

The other major benefit for the host country would be in the field of scientific and technological development.[8] It was hoped that pharmaceutical companies would set up operations in Costa Rica, and that even before that happened the process of bioprospecting and initial analyses carried out locally would be accompanied by technology transfer in the related scientific fields. In fact, approximately half of the advance payment from the INBio–Merck agreement went on training ($120,000) or on equipment, either for the biodiversity inventory ($285,000) or chemical extraction ($135,000) (Laird, 1993: 110, citing Sittenfeld, 1992). Technology transfer was expected to create professional jobs for local specialists who had studied abroad and who, upon returning to Costa Rica, often could not find suitable employment. These professionals would be adding value to raw materials in their native country (Eisner, 1989–90: 33).

Advantages and uncertainties for Merck & Co.

In line with Eisner's conceptualization of the chemical prospecting model, he considered that one of the advantages for the pharmaceutical company would be the fact that, from the outset, the laboratories would be near protected areas and it would be possible for them to test fresh samples *in situ* and in different seasons. Given their proximity, much smaller quantities of sample species and specimens would be required. According to Merck & Co.,

> The collaboration with INBio will expand Merck's inventory of biological samples that are investigated by Merck's ongoing screening program. INBio also offers Merck the opportunity to work with the unique biological diversity located within the Costa Rican biosphere, a high level of government support, an established network of scholars, and the commitment to provide trained peopole to support the effort locally. (Merck & Co., 1991: 4)

Although Merck expressed some scepticism about the possibility of developing successful commercial products, particularly in the short and medium terms, the company recognized other advantages of the agreement. When George Albers-Schonberg of Merck's natural products division was asked about the rationale of the contract with INBio if in the past 25 years Merck has only marketed five drugs discovered by screening natural extracts, he answered:

> One reason is the precarious state of the world's tropical forest. Merck executives have woken up to the fact that a vast reservoir of potential drugs is rapidly disappearing, and that it may be now or never for chemical prospecting. The emergence of faster screening techniques is another key factor. In the past, Merck has only dabbled with natural compounds, but it now realises that for a relatively modest investment it can enter a partnership that could yield thousands of extracts for screening. (Joyce, 1991: 39)

Indeed, for Merck the investment *was* quite modest, amounting to approximately half a million dollars a year, out of a research budget of more than one billion dollars (Feinsilver, 1996: 119). Another advantage for Merck & Co. was the fact that the agreement with INBio would enhance significantly the company's image and reputation for environmental responsibility.

Assessing the Benefits and the Model

Seven years after the INBio–Merck agreement was signed, and following other bioprospecting agreements in different parts of the world, we can begin to assess more realistically the expectations of 1991. On balance there would seem to be a significant gap between the 'win–win' rhetoric surrounding the initial agreement which claimed that INBio, Merck, 'the environment' and 'Costa Rica' would all benefit.

What is clear from the experience to date is that the benefits associated with bioprospecting in general, and the INBio–Merck agreement in particular, have accrued largely to a specific sector of the scientific and technical community. Furthermore, the resources, knowledge and influence gained through various processes of negotiation, consultation and knowledge transfer have served to increase the power of this sector. Certain other stakeholders with intimate knowledge of biodiversity, and whose livelihoods and cultures may be affected by biodiversity loss and conservation efforts, are largely excluded from the benefits of bioprospecting and relevant negotiating or policy processes. We refer, in particular, to community groups, indigenous and peasant populations, and their representatives.

A tool for conservation?

There is considerable debate internationally about whether or not bioprospecting is a useful tool for conservation. Several organizations continue to argue that it is. UNCTAD, for example, has developed a 'Biotrade Initiative', arguing that it is possible for biodiverse countries to generate income by adding value to their genetic resources and trading them under more favourable terms. Conservation International also continues to think that bioprospecting agreements are a valuable tool in promoting the conservation of biodiversity (Bell, 1997: 2). After analysing revenues from the sale of bioprospecting rights, however, some commentators have argued that they may not generate any significant gain for conservation and endangered habitats, and that the international community ought to start to look actively for other alternatives for financing conservation (Simpson *et al.*, 1994).

In Costa Rica it would seem that the expectations associated with the INBio–Merck agreement in relation to conservation were exaggerated. As noted above, the initial agreement allocated $100,000 for conservation. According to its 1996 Annual Report, INBio had transferred since 1992 – that is, over a period of five years – an accumulated amount of approximately $200,000 to SINAC under the Ministry of Environment and Energy (MINAE). This derived from the 10 per cent advance payment of each research project budget in biodiversity prospecting. This gives an annual average of $40,000, which was used by MINAE for conservation purposes in Coco Island National Park. (INBio, 1996: 11 and 25).

The amount appears insignificant when compared to the real conservation needs of the country. According to a citation in Pereira and Vargas (1992: 10), about $1 billion would be needed in the next ten years to underwrite expropriation of land and the inventory of species and their conservation within the public areas which are under government protection. Somewhat more conservative estimates were provided that same year by Mario Boza, Vice-Minister of MIRENEM, who stated in an interview that the country needed $600 million to preserve its forests. He mentioned items such as expropriation of land, reforestation and an operational fund to run the national system of protected areas. He did not mention, however, the time span involved (Sánchez, 1992: 6-A).

Moreover, it is impossible to think that the employment generated by the advance payment could be a determining factor in creating the capacity to arrest deforestation in the country, as had been hoped. In fact, by the mid-1990s deforestation showed signs of once again increasing, while SINAC was finding it extremely difficult to address the problem, especially in some crucial protected areas such as in North Huetar and the Osa Peninsula.

Furthermore, as INBio's 1996 report affirms, the financial resources earned from bioprospecting's advance payment have been invested in the Coco National Park, an uninhabited island far off the coast which has both research and tourism potential.

Unequal investment of this nature could well contribute to the unequal development of the country's protected areas and deny many local communities located in or near protected areas benefits to which they should be entitled.

The claim that the INBio–Merck agreement promoted 'non-invasive' techniques and procedures that were compatible with conservation can also be questioned. Once a biological element shows positive activity, the company needs larger quantities of the raw material to continue its research for the development of new products. According to several authors (Simpson and Sedjo, 1992: 2; Beese, 1996: 7), a pharmaceutical company would need several kilograms in the initial stages of chemical analysis. If these tests are promising, the company will need hundreds and then thousands of kilograms of material for clinical tests.[9] Another possibility would be to learn to domesticate the organisms in farms near the original ecosystem (Beese, 1996: 7; Sittenfeld and Gámez, 1993: 94), which would mean the creation of monocultures near the protected areas which are by nature biodiverse.

Royalties, revenues and corporate philanthropy

With respect to the royalties, we agree that if a few pharmaceutical products were successfully marketed it could mean significant foreign exchange revenues for Costa Rica. However, the expectations surrounding both the possibility that commercial products would be developed and the amount of foreign exchange Costa Rica would earn through royalties appear to have been excessively high.

It is often pointed out that only one in ten thousand substances tested actually provides a potential lead (Lyons, 1991: 28; Sittenfeld and Gámez, 1993: 75). According to Feinsilver, the odds for producing a commercially viable drug from a sample derived from bioprospecting are between 80,000 and 250,000 to one (Feinsilver, 1996: 120). Although the exact number is not known because this information is part of the discretional clauses of the contract, some observers estimate that the INBio–Merck agreement was to provide the company with access to between 1,000 and 3,000 samples over the initial two-year period (Aylward et al., 1993: 49). As Feinsilver points out, the quantity supplied by INBio was relatively small (Feinsilver, 1996: 119).

Once a product is developed and marketed, a pharmaceutical company can make very large sales. For example, in 1990 Merck sold $735 million dollars of Mevacor, a medicine made from a natural product. The development of a few 'blockbuster' drugs could, therefore, generate substantial royalty payments for Costa Rica. But the likelihood of developing such a drug from leads provided by INBio appears very limited. Moreover, much more modest sales and royalty payments would be likely if a product were developed. Indeed, the cost-benefit calculation of the 'present value' of a bioprospecting agreement to the supplier of samples can yield a fairly modest amount. Reid et al. make such a calculation for a product that generates net annual revenues of $10 million. Assuming a supply of 1,000 samples a year, a 10-year research and development period, a 15-year patent protection period, a 5 per cent discount rate and royalties of 3 per cent, they calculate the present value to be in the range of $52,500 to $461,000, depending on whether chemical or natural leads are involved (Reid et al., 1993: 17).

Thus it appears that, while there are possibilities of important findings in the future, it is not tenable to continue to assert that advance payments themselves will cover the divide between the 'here and now' and the time when a product begins to generate royalties for investment in ecological and social initiatives.

Neither is it tenable to assert that the advance payment is somehow related to

corporate philanthropy or evidence of a heightened level of environmental awareness or responsibility on the part of Merck. For example, Merck officials agree that
the contract was good business and a potential boon to conservation, adding that:

> We can't be spending our research money to save Costa Rican rain forests. This is not a
> 'feel-good' thing. It's a real, viable way to demonstrate that there are treasures in these
> areas ... and that you can make the conservation areas economically viable. (Lyons,
> 1991: 27)

The distribution of benefits and the issue of biopiracy

While some obvious benefits have flowed from these agreements, concerns have
arisen regarding how these benefits are distributed and, in particular, the limited
transfer of benefits to local communities. Here we need to underscore that the
riches in the natural protected areas are constituent parts of a national heritage
which are being appropriated privately without consulting the citizens in general
and the local communities or indigenous peoples in particular.

The resources derived from the INBio–Merck agreement have gone primarily
towards supporting a limited number of protected areas (improvements in infrastructure, training, and so on), human resource development and the strengthening
a fairly restrictive 'biological' or 'technocratic' approach to conservation rather than
one which recognizes the importance of integrating local communities in conservation efforts.

Apart from the direct economic transfers, mentioned above, which INBio and
Merck derived from the agreement, it has also served to strengthen the influence of
INBio in the national policy process. Through its bioprospecting activities INBio
developed as an 'intermediary' institution which facilitated access to genetic and
biochemical resources, generated new transfer mechanisms and stimulated a certain
type of conservation. This mission, above and beyond the agreement itself, pre-
supposed a linkage with the national planning and policy process associated with
land use, conservation and information systems. It also called for cooperative relations
and linkages with a range of public and private institutions which have made
contributions to INBio and were not part of the terms of the first contract (Gámez,
1989; Gámez et al., 1993; Gámez and Gauld, 1996; Sittenfeld, Lovejoy and Coen,
1996; Mateo, 1996).

In many countries the search for species and specimens in bioprospecting is often
based on local or indigenous knowledge of the plants. One of the reasons for using
ethnobotany or ethnozoology is the amount of time and money saved by using this
knowledge as leads to improve and make screening more efficient (Beese, 1996: 29;
Chapela, 1996: 43, citing King). The use of this latter knowledge has been promoted
at times by companies and research institutions such as Shaman Pharmaceuticals,
the US National Cancer Institute, and Merck & Co. itself as a part of research
activities not connected with INBio (Joyce, 1991: 40; Caporale and Dermody,
1996: 92–3).

Around the time of the first Conference of the Parties to the Convention on
Biological Diversity, held in the Bahamas in 1994, some NGOs began to replace the
term bioprospecting with biopiracy (RAFI, 1994). They were concerned that
bioprospecting agreements between transnationals and institutions in the South
were, in effect, a new way of plundering resources instead of a means for developing
a more equitable relationship of North–South cooperation. It was argued that the
agreements would not only give the transnationals access to cheap raw materials but

also ownership of the 'indigenous' knowledge associated with these resources – knowledge that would be expropriated through the protection of intellectual property (Chapela, 1996: 43; Feinsilver and Chapela, 1996: 235). Many organizations continue to oppose bioprospecting. They want to stop the patenting of medical products which come from indigenous and local communities; these include, for example, the neem tree, turmeric, cat's claw, aloe and many others. From this perspective, indigenous and local communities are certainly not seen as 'winners' in bioprospecting initiatives.

In the case of bioprospecting carried out by INBio, the biologist Daniel Janzen, a professor at the University of Pennsylvania who worked closely with INBio, and Thomas Eisner, known as the visionary of chemical prospecting, developed the idea that this technique should rest on the knowledge generated by well-trained bioprospectors entirely on the basis of the study of plants and animals, instead of using local or indigenous knowledge as the starting point (Joyce, 1991: 39).

Here we want to stress the following: scientific or technical knowledge is not absolutely free of local or indigenous knowledge. The director and former deputy director of INBio themselves recognize this. Writing about the taxonomists' role in biodiversity prospecting, Sittenfeld and Gámez (1993: 79–80) affirm that 'In fact, the three legs of the biodiversity prospecting "stool" are ecological knowledge (which includes ethnobiological information), phylogenetic knowledge, and the use of modern screening techniques.' In its 1996 report, INBio accepts that it had signed an agreement with the Italian company Indena to 'search for compounds with antimicrobial and antiviral activity in plants used in traditional Costa Rican medicine'. The report makes the point, however, that what is being utilized is not traditional indigenous knowledge but 'popular [knowledge], in the public domain and [associated with products] common in our markets' (INBio, 1996: 30).

While the term 'biopiracy' is generally used in connection with the appropriation of indigenous or 'Southern' knowledge and resources by scientists, transnationals and 'the North', it could also be applied to the privatization of public resources. This latter concern is particularly relevant in the Costa Rican context, where the natural wealth of SINAC, Costa Rica's patrimony, has the tendency of being appropriated by private interests. We hope that this tendency will be tempered as a result of the recently enacted Law of Biodiversity. The fact that bioprospecting and protected area conservation are being increasingly organized and administered by private institutions limits the possibility of upholding the principle of national sovereignty in relation to biodiversity and the maintenance of natural resources in the public domain, if nothing is done to arrest this trend (see also: Commandeur, 1993; Hardon, 1996).

The institutional context favouring the INBio–Merck agreement

As noted earlier, the INBio–Merck agreement has often been held up as a model for North–South cooperation and business–NGO partnerships. The assumption has been that it will be replicated in other countries in the South that are rich in biodiversity. But it is not at all clear to what extent the model is, in fact, replicable, given the specific context in which it developed.

Some of the concerns regarding replicability relate to the fact that Costa Rica enjoys certain 'comparative advantages' which made the agreement possible. Such conditions may not be found in many other developing countries. For such an agreement to happen, it is not enough that there be a transnational corporation with the necessary technical know-how and a developing country with a rich source of biodiversity. The host country must also possess certain institutions and technical capacity. Other bioprospecting agreements may well be implemented elsewhere but we should not expect that they will replicate the INBio–Merck model exactly.

In this regard there are several conditions in Costa Rica that should be noted. First, specific features of Costa Rica's political history and development process, including the country's socio-political culture, democratic tradition and strong civil society, have historically encouraged the state to play an important role in safeguarding the nation's biodiversity and in negotiating different kinds of agreements. In spite of these conditions, there has been a gradual transfer of some public functions to private organizations. Such a trend has been encouraged by certain processes and policies associated with globalization and structural adjustment, and was apparent at the time when INBio negotiated its first bioprospecting agreement.

Second, population dynamics and settlement patterns also favoured the establishment of a National System of Conservation Areas (Gámez and Ugalde, 1988) which forms part of the Ministry of Environment and Energy (MINAE). The scope for carrying out such work was facilitated by the fact that there exists, to some extent, a regulatory framework backed up by certain institutions. It should be pointed out, however, that a considerable amount of taxonomic classification, extraction of samples and synthesis remain unrecorded, some of it taking place on private lands, being subsumed under agreements established with national institutions, or simply carried out illegally.

Third, the country has a relatively large scientific and research community associated with public, private and 'mixed' organizations. The fact that the country has qualified national scientists as well as international research centres has also contributed to the generation of basic information on environmental questions and to stimulating the development of environmental consciousness. The scientific and research community has also played an important role in ensuring that environmental considerations are integrated into national development policies.

Fourth, the Costa Rican government has recently undertaken important institutional changes which adopt biodiversity as an organizing principle for its development strategies, and new laws have been designed to ratify international norms in the environmental realm.[10] The National System of Sustainable Development (SINADES), for example, identifies an explicit role for the major actors of civil society, interacting with government, in biodiversity conservation.

Fifth, Costa Rica has also been a pioneer in negotiating 'joint implementation' agreements. The types of national contexts and circumstances mentioned above enable Costa Rica to be a relatively strong partner in any environmental agreement with foreign institutions or enterprises. The Costa Rican state and other institutions have been pioneers in negotiating joint implementation agreements not only in bioprospecting but also in relation to carbon offset programmes and debt-for-nature swaps.

National policies conducive to joint implementation have been reinforced by trends and institutional changes occurring regionally. Important declarations of principles and political directives for the region as a whole emerged, for example, in 1994 with the signing of the Central American Alliance for Sustainable Development. Internationally there is growing acceptance of basic standards associated with environmental and social responsibility, the need to cost environmental services adequately, and the positive role that joint implementation can play in terms of environmental protection and North–South cooperation. Costa Rica has successfully positioned itself to be at the forefront of new international initiatives related to environmental protection.

The Future of Bioprospecting

Whether or not Costa Rica will benefit from bioprospecting depends not only on the development of commercial products and the way benefits are distributed but also on whether, in fact, it has a future. Bioprospecting is confronting new challenges from combinatorial chemistry, which turns several time-consuming tasks into a very quick process, notably the work of collecting thousands of biological specimens and synthesizing an active ingredient (Amato, 1994: 1399).

Opinions on future trends, however, are divided. While some believe that the future of the pharmaceutical industry lies with combinatorial chemistry,[11] others believe that there is still a long road to be travelled before science is able to synthesize all the pharmacological properties of natural products, and that therefore innovative products will continue to come from nature for quite some time (Feinsilver and Chapela, 1996: 244). According to Beese, today most scientists still consider that new molecules can only be detected in nature and not produced synthetically, but rapid technological advances could overcome this limitation and combinatorial chemistry may soon provide a cheap and ample source of molecules (Beese, 1996: 24).

What is clear is that several transnational pharmaceutical companies have begun to turn their attentions to biotechnology companies which specialize in combinatorial chemistry (Beese, 1996: 24). There is also talk of another trend which is considered important for the future, namely gene therapy, which aims to treat illnesses through the manipulation of genetic material from the patient him or herself (Feinsilver and Chapela, 1996: 244). This would also eliminate the need for medicines to combat some diseases.

Bioprospecting and Responsibility

From the above analysis it is apparent that much remains to be clarified regarding corporate responsibility in this field and whether the type of bioprospecting agreement entered into by INBio and Merck & Co. can contribute in a meaningful way to conservation and development.

The dynamics of bioprospecting and the pharmaceuticals industry, as well as the way resources related to bioprospecting agreements and their results are distributed, present a number of challenges especially to low-income countries like Costa Rica which are rich in biodiversity. We have seen that the prospects for developing commercial products and realizing large foreign exchange revenues from royalty payments appear quite finite, to say the least. If they do materialize it is likely to take many years. But it is not certain whether the pharmaceutical industry will have a long-term interest in bioprospecting in tropical forests, given recent technological developments in other fields. The direct benefits for conservation have also been fairly minimal. Furthermore, the range of stakeholders that has benefited from the INBio–Merck bioprospecting agreement has been somewhat restricted, particularly in view of the fact that local communities have been largely excluded. Another concern we have noted is that the INBio–Merck agreement has not only benefited, first and foremost, a sector of the scientific and technical community, but it has also served to reinforce the power of this sector and its capacity to influence the orientation of government policy on conservation and development. As a result, other – more community-based and participatory – approaches that may be more conducive to environmental protection and sustainable human development have been marginalized.

Some of these concerns would be less relevant if the agreement had been seen as a straightforward commercial transaction. Instead, it was generally packaged and publicized in such a way that bioprospecting in general, and this type of agreement in particular, were portrayed as able to make a unique contribution not only in relation to science and corporate research and development, but also in terms of conservation and development in the South.

Clearly it is necessary to look for better ways to mesh conservation, human development and profits, and to establish and clarify the mechanisms through which social actors associated with bioprospecting can realize this new potential. There are also other concerns which persist and await a response. For example, is Chapela (1996: 41) correct in saying that given the intrinsic or structural interests involved, bioprospectors have no real commitment to conservation in the broad sense? And what about Gereffi's analysis of the pharmaceutical industry and its relationship with less developed countries, which concludes that the promotion of any national interests not compatible with the direct interests of the transnational companies will be parried by the foreign firms, given that they represent costs to the transnationals (Gereffi, 1983, cited in Chapela, 1996: 41). At present, there is clearly some mutual interest in conservation in view of the fact that the transnationals prefer secure sources of biodiversity and high-quality samples and information, and can boost their corporate image as a result of their association with the environment. Beyond the issue of the actual amount which transnationals are prepared to allocate for conservation is the question of whether pharmaceutical companies such as Merck & Co. are even willing to continue to contribute to the conservation of tropical forests if, for example, they reorient their investments towards combinatorial chemistry, which no longer requires biodiversity elements as sources of raw materials.

A basic issue that has to be addressed in any discussion of this nature is whether tropical forests and biodiversity can only be saved by selling them. We are of the opinion that conservation responds to other ethical, aesthetic and broader economic and social values. Bioprospecting takes us into a complex reality, many of whose effects and outcomes are not immediately apparent. It is clear that a more realistic and circumspect assessment of the benefits, potential and risks of bioprospecting is needed. It is also clear that the discourse and declarations associated with environmental and social responsibility that characterize certain international and bilateral agreements on biodiversity conservation and bioprospecting are somewhat inflated.

It is also necessary to establish the rules of the game in order to clarify who has the right to enjoy the benefits of biodiversity resources in protected areas and collective intellectual rights. This is particularly so if we recognize that taxonomic and research processes related to biodiversity take place primarily on public land, but are managed and negotiated on the basis of private sector norms. When issues of rights and responsibilities are considered, these new ways of appropriating collective resources give rise to concern. They have generated tensions and polemics among different actors and stakeholders, especially, for example, when the government has granted considerable rights to private entities to use public resources and undertake public tasks, arguing that the public sector is unable to continue ensuring the responsibility for biodiversity and the national inventory.

Environmental and social responsibility also presupposes the existing linkages between popular or traditional knowledge that provides 'leads' for taxonomic classifications and bioprospecting. What some consider to be the preliminary stages of bioprospecting should be acknowledged and adequately compensated. They should take into account the contributions from local knowledge, culture and the accumulated wisdom in various parts of human civilization which form the basis for perceptions of, and relations with, the environment. Furthermore, for ethical, cultural, economic and ecological reasons, even if this contribution is compensated, bioprospecting agreements ought by no means to be considered a *sine qua non* for patenting of processes and products derived from biodiversity resources.

The Convention on Biological Diversity recognizes that local and indigenous communities are important actors in the bioprospecting process. It also calls on national legislatures to respect, preserve and maintain the knowledge, innovations and local practices related to conservation and sustainable use of biodiversity. This decision has important implications for bioprospecting agreements. It is necessary to take a previous step, in which the local and indigenous communities located in or near the area elected for research or bioprospecting approve the agreement after fully understanding the general terms of the negotiation. These terms would include the definition of the benefits which accrue from the use of the genetic and biochemical resources and the associated knowledge derived, as well as the establishment of intellectual community rights.

One of the basic assumptions underpinning bioprospecting agreements is the idea that it is necessary to sell forest resources in order to preserve the forest. But this is easier said than done. Existing policies in this field, and the means and capacity for control, are very imprecise and often untested, unclear and in flux. In this same vein, the terms of negotiation with regard to risks and the security of new biotechnologies, as well as the ways to guarantee certificates of origin and access to samples or extracts, are in the experimental stages.

Moreover, the marketing terms for genetic materials or extracts and the negotiations regarding regulations, prices and the distribution of benefits among various stakeholders are as uncertain as the time the process will take and the possibilities of adding value to the biologically active molecules identified. The extracted samples of raw materials, and the local knowledge that provides clues or leads regarding their potential use, are severely undervalued in the marketplace. The process of adding technological value to the raw materials requires a sophisticated technological infrastructure and highly skilled human resources. But countries rich in tropical biodiversity generally lack such resources. The large Northern pharmaceutical, seed and agrochemical companies do have them, however, and, as a result, negotiations for joint ventures with developing countries have tended to increase in recent years – but in asymmetrical ways.

Similarly, we should be aware of the contradictions in the concept of patenting medicines for human health and for food security for the vast majority of people. The restrictive nature – monopolistic and discretionary – under which bioprospecting and biotechnology are conducted makes it difficult to agree with the proposition that their products will be the answer to human hunger and disease.

Clearly there is an important role for the state to play in clarifying the rights and responsibilities of the different social actors involved in or affected by bioprospecting and biodiversity use and conservation. It is essential that the formulation of policies and laws in this field, and their implementation, be based on a participatory process that involves not only government planners, scientists, the large environmental NGOs and corporate entities, but also other civil society stakeholders.

Partly in response to the criticisms that have emerged, primarily in the universities and the National Assembly, regarding the way bioprospecting is carried out in Costa Rica, certain changes have recently occurred in policy and legislation related to forests, wildlife and biodiversity. The new Biodiversity Law mandates the establishment of the National Commission of Biodiversity Management. Represented on the Commission will be environmentalists, peasants, indigenous peoples and public universities. Together with a few other stakeholders, they will set the rules and procedures for bioprospectors, including those working with INBio. From now on, INBio's arrangements with any interested enterprise ought to follow those rules and procedures, in contrast to the past, when regulations were very loose or non-existent.

The process of drafting the 1998 law was unique in that the main participants included not only the traditional social actors and institutions which have shaped environmental policy in Costa Rica, but also others, including smaller environmental NGOs, grassroots organizations and the public universities. An important aspect of the law is its formal recognition of 'intellectual community rights' which aim to protect certain forms of local resource management practices and indigenous knowledge associated with biodiversity use and protection. With this law, Costa Rica in fact became the first country to incorporate comprehensively and systematically into national law the principles and guidelines contained in the Convention on Biological Diversity. One such principle was that a broad range of stakeholders should be consulted in any process leading to a bioprospecting agreement, and not just the main parties directly involved, as in the case of the INBio–Merck agreement.

Notes

1 In its modern variant, 'bioprospecting' involves the search for genetic and biochemical sources of lead compounds for products with commercial application, primarily in the pharmaceuticals, agrochemicals, biotechnology and cosmetic industries.

2 The analysis presented in this chapter derives from both secondary sources and an action-research process which has attempted to engage multiple stakeholders at both national and local level in Costa Rica in a dialogue on biodiversity issues and bioprospecting.

3 The elements and components of tropical forests are of interest to bioprospectors since they are rich in materials with chemical defences to repel predators. Among the prescribed medicines in the United States, about 25 per cent are based on substances derived from plants and microbes or synthetically derived from those sources.

4 An initial review indicates that Monsanto was the first to utilize the term 'bioprospection' in 1991 when it signed an agreement for several million dollars and for three years with the botanical gardens of Missouri to collect soil and plant micro-organisms (Joyce, 1991).

5 The first phases of collection and initial screening are carried out in the country of origin and the succeeding phases which are more sophisticated technically, such as characterization, are conducted in the country where company headquarters are located (Eisner, 1989–90: 32).

6 Joyce (1991: 37) believes that Eisner is the visionary in chemical prospecting, Rodrigo Gámez, the director of INBio, its engineer, and Daniel Janzen, a field botanist with 20 years' research experience in Costa Rica, its architect.

7 At the time of writing, bananas were Costa Rica's major export product.

8 It was not until recently that plant biotechnologists met at the First Workshop on Plant Biotechnology in Costa Rica which addressed the 'Present Situation and Perspectives' (August 1997). Their purpose was to assess the field and to organize. The emphasis was on technical aspects and processes of biotechnology as well as questions of economic profitability and intellectual property. The social and cultural costs and effects were not yet part of the agenda for discussion.

9 In the case of taxol (an active ingredient of the tree *Taxus brevifolia* which has properties against ovary and breast cancer), phase one of the clinical tests required more than 120,000 pounds of *Taxus brevifolia* – equivalent to more than 12,000 trees – which caused concern about the negative impact of the collection (Cragg *et al.*, cited by Beese, 1996: 17).

10 The latest is the Biodiversity Law No. 7788, enacted in May 1998.

11 A spokesperson for the US Association of Pharmaceutical Manufacturers argues that we are entering a new cycle 'which is not the search for materials since this is too burdensome and fraught with the possibility of failure.... The companies are adopting a focus on rational design of drugs...' (*New York Times*, 27 June 1995, cited by Feinsilver and Chapella, 1996: 244).

References

Amato, Ivan. (1994), 'Drug Discovery on the Assembly Line', *Science*, 264 (3 June), 1399–402.

Aylward, B. *et al.* (1993), 'The Economic Value of Species Information and its Role in Biodiversity Conservation: Costa Rica's National Biodiversity Institute', discussion paper 93–06, London Environmental Economics Centre, International Institute for Environment and Development, London.

Beese, J. (1996), 'Pharmaceutical Bioprospecting and Synthetic Molecular Diversity. The Convention of Biological Diversity and the Value of Natural Products in the Light of New Technological Developments', draft discussion paper.

Bell, J. (1997), 'Biopiracy's Latest Disguises', *Seedling*, 14 (2) (June), 2–10.

Camacho, M. A. (1997), 'Desarrollo rural y cambio institucional', in *Revista Perspectivas Rurales*, 1 (1997), 85–98, Master's Program in Rural Development, Universidad Nacional de Costa Rica, Heredia.

Caporale, L. and M. Dermody (1996), 'El descubrimiento de medicamentos y la diversidad biológica: colaboraciones y riesgos en el descubrimiento de nuevos productos', in *Biodiversidad, biotecnología y desarrollo sostenible en salud y agricultura: conexiones emergentes*, Organización Panamericana de la Salud, Washington, DC.

Chapela, I. (1996), 'La Bioprospección en la era de la información: un análisis crítico de la iniciativas de conservación asociadas con el descubrimiento de nuevos fármacos', in *Biodiversidad, biotecnología y desarrollo sostenible en salud y agricultura: conexiones emergentes*, Organización Panamericana de la Salud, Washington, DC.

Commandeur, P. (1993), 'Latin America Commences to "Biotechnologize" Its Industry', *Biotechnology and Development Monitor*, 14 (March), 3–5.

Cragg and Snader (1991), 'The Taxol Supply Crisis. New NCI Policies for Handling the Large-Scale Production of Novel Natural Product Anticancer and Anti-HIV Agents', *The Journal of Natural Products*, 56 (10), 1657–68.

Eisner, T. (1989–90), 'Prospecting for Nature's Chemical Riches', *Perspectives* (Winter), 31–4.

El Financiero (1997), 'El INBio tiene siete contratos internacionales', *Semanario* (weekly), San José, Costa Rica, 12.

Feinsilver, J. (1996), 'Biodiversity Prospecting: A New Panacea for Development?', *CEPAL Review*, 60 (December).

Feinsilver, J. and I. Chapela (1996), 'Comentario: Llevará la prospección de la diversidad biológica para obtener fármacos al descubrimiento del "oro verde"?', in *Biodiversidad, biotecnología y desarrollo sostenible en salud y agricultura: conexiones emergentes*, Organización Panamericana de la Salud, Washington, DC, 242–7.

Fuentes, J. L. (1991), 'Bosques producen más que sólo tucas', *La República* (newspaper, San José), 16-B.

—— (1993), 'Wild Biodiversity as a Resource for Intellectual and Economic Development: INBio's Pilot Project in Costa Rica', Proceedings of the Norway/UNEP Conference on Biodiversity, Directorate for Nature Management, Norwegian Institute for Nature Research, Centre for Environment and Development, University of Trondheim, Norway.

—— (1996), 'Inventories: Preparing Biodiversity for Non-damaging Use', in F. Di Castri and T.

Jones, *Biodiversity, Science and Development: Towards a New Partnership*, International Union of Biological Sciences (IUBS), Cambridge University Press, Cambridge.

Gámez, R. (1989), 'Threatened Habitats and Germplasm Preservation: A Central American Perspective', in L. Knutson and A. Stoner (eds.), *Biotic, Biodiversity and Germplasm Preservation: Global Imperatives*, Kluwer Academic Publications, Netherlands.

Gámez, R. and I. Gauld (1996), 'Costa Rica: An Innovative Approach to the Study of Tropical Biodiversity', in F. de Castri and T. Jones, *Biodiversity, Science and Development: Towards a New Partnership*, International Union of Biological Sciences (IUBS), Cambridge University Press, Cambridge.

Gámez, R. and A. Ugalde (1988), 'Costa Rica's National Park System and the Preservation of Biological Diversity: Linking Ecology with Socio-economic Development', in F. Almeda and C.M. Pringle (eds.), *The Diversity of Conservation of Tropical Rainforests*, Academy of Sciences, San Francisco.

Gámez et al. (1993), 'Costa Rica's Conservation Program and National Biodiversity Institute (INBio)', in W. Reid et al. (eds.), *Biodiversity Prospecting*, World Resources Institute, Washington, DC.

Gereffi, G. (1983), *The Pharmaceutical Industry and Development in the Third World*, Princeton University Press, Princeton, New Jersey.

Hardon, J. (1996), 'National Sovereignty and Access to Genetic Resources', *Biotechnology and Development Monitor*, 27.

INBio (1996), *Annual Report*, Instituto Nacional de Biodiversidad, Heredia, Costa Rica.

Janzen, D. (1992), 'A South–North Perspective on Science in the Management, Use and Economic Development of Biodiversity', in K. Hindar Sundlund and A. H. D. Brown (eds.) *Conservation of Biodiversity for Sustainable Development*, Scandinavian University Press, Oslo.

Jonas, H. (1995), *El Principio de responsabilidad: ensayo de un ética para civilización tecnológica* (Spanish translation), Herder Publications, Barcelona.

Joyce, C. (1991), 'Prospectors for Tropical Medicines', *New Scientist*, 152 (189) (October), 36–40.

King, S. (1994), 'Establishing Reciprocity: Biodiversity Conservation and New Models for Cooperation between Forest-dwelling Peoples and the Pharmaceutical Industry' in T. Greaves (ed.), *Intellectual Property Rights for Indigenous People*, a sourcebook, Society for Applied Anthropology, Oklahoma.

Kloppenburg, J. and S. Rodríguez (1992), 'Conservationists or Corsairs?', *Seedling*, 9 (2 and 3), 190–218.

La Nación (1997), 'País podría quedar sin bosques en 50 años' 9 October, p. 16A.

La República (1997), 'Caso de Osa revela debilidad de legislación, Ley Forestal insuficiente para mantener parques', 20 September, p. 6A.

Laird, S. (1993), 'Contracts for Biodiversity Prospecting', in W. Reid et al. (eds.) *Biodiversity Prospecting: Using Genetic Resources for Sustainable Development*, World Resources Institute, Washington, DC.

Lyons, S. (1991), 'Research Pact May Help Rain Forests Pay for Their Keep', *The Boston Globe*, Monday, 4 November.

Mateo, N. (1996), 'Wild Biodiversity: The Last Frontier? The Case of Costa Rica', in C. Bonte-Friedheim and K. Sheridan (eds.), *The Globalization of Science: The Place of Agricultural Research*, ISNAR, The Netherlands.

Mendelsohn, R. and M. Balick (1995), 'The Value of Undiscovered Pharmaceuticals in Tropical Forests', *Economic Botany*, 49 (2), 223–8.

Merck & Co. (1991), 'INBio of Costa Rica and Merck Enter into Innovative Agreement to Collect Biological Samples While Protecting Rainforest', news release, Media Relations, Merck & Co., Rathaway, New Jersey.

—— (1998) www.merck.com

Pereira, A. and W. Vargas (1992), 'Comercio con especies, un negocio lucrativo', *Seminario Universidad*, 1 May.

Pistorius, R. and J. van Wijk (1993), 'Biodiversity Prospecting. Commercializing Genetic Resources for Export', *Biotechnology and Development Monitor*, 15 (June), 12–16.

Poveda, Luis (1997), 'Medicine alternativa, indígenas y nómadas sabios', interview by Eduardo

Mora in *Ambientico*, 50 (May), 8–14.

RAFI (1994), *Pirating Medicinal Plants*, Occasional Papers Series, 1 (4) (November).

Reid, W. *et al.* (eds.) (1993), *Biodiversity Prospecting: Using Genetic Resources for Sustainable Development*, World Resources Institute, Washington DC.

Salazar, Roxana, *et al.* (1996), *Avances y tendencias de la certificación forestal en Costa Rica*, Fundación Ambio, San José.

Sánchez, Aquileo (1992), '$600 millones cuesta conservar los bosques', in *La República* (San José), 24 March, 6-A.

—— (1993), 'Patrimonio nacional cae en manos privadas', in *La República* (San José), 4 June, 5–A.

Segelken, R. (1991) 'Merck Obtains Stake in Cornell–Costa Rica "Chemical Prospecting" Venture', *Cornell University News Service*, 20 September, Ithaca, New York.

Simpson, D. and R. Sedjo (1992) 'Contracts for Transferring Rights to Indigenous Genetic Resources', *Resources*, 109 (Fall), 1–5.

Simpson, D., R. Sedjo and John Reid (1994), 'The Commercialization of Indigenous Genetic Resources: Values, Institutions and Instruments', paper presented at conference: 'Biological Diversity – Exploring the Complexities', Tucson, Arizona, 25–27 March.

Sittenfeld, A. (1992), 'Tropical Medicinal Plant Conservation and Development Projects: The Case of the Costa Rican National Institute of Biodiversity (INBio)', paper presented at the Rainforest Alliance Tropical Forest Medical Resources and the Conservation of Biodiversity symposium, January, New York.

Sittenfeld, A. and R. Gámez (1993), 'Biodiversity Prospecting by INBio', in W. Reid *et al.* (eds.), *Biodiversity Prospecting: Using Genetic Resources for Sustainable Development*, World Resources Institute, Washington, DC.

Sittenfeld, A., A. Lovejoy and J. Coen (1996), 'Managing Biodiversity for Agriculture Research: Building Awareness for the INBio Experience: the Case of Costa Rica', draft paper, based on the document 'A Proposal for Source-country Sustainable Resource Use in the Field of Biodiversity Prospecting: Conservation, Policy Capacities and Business Development', prepared for the United Nations Industrial Development Organization (UNIDO).

The Environmental and Social Effects of Corporate Environmentalism in the Brazilian Pulp Industry

RICARDO CARRERE

Introduction

Responsibility for many of the world's environmental and social problems lies directly or indirectly with large corporations. People – their customers – are becoming increasingly aware of this and are demanding that companies include environmental conservation and social considerations in their productive activities. In the long run, 'business as usual' could result in economic losses and even closure. In general terms, it can thus be said that corporations are being forced to change. Corporations have three alternatives: (1) 'business as usual', disguised under an environmentally and socially concerned discourse; (2) real environmental and social responsibility; and (3) a combination of 1 and 2.

Many corporations, particularly the largest, have in recent years acknowledged the need to incorporate environmental protection in their activities in response to growing public concern over such issues. The question is how much of their environmental policy is genuinely oriented to environmental conservation and how much is simply a public relations exercise. This chapter analyses this question by examining a sector of Brazilian industry which produces market pulp.[1] This sector was chosen for the following reasons.

It is dominated by five large corporations which, to some extent, have recognized the need to include environmental and social concerns in their discourse and/or activities. Their association has produced and distributed a booklet which explains the environmental and social advantages of eucalyptus cultivation by the industry (ABECEL, undated). Each company integrates pulpwood production with pulp production and has modern pulp plants. They are owned by several powerful shareholders, including national economic groups and foreign investors, as well as state-owned enterprises. These corporations carry out large-scale operations, both in the plantation and in the industrial areas. Their raw material supply is produced in extensive plantations of fast-growing tree monocultures, mostly eucalyptus, aimed at feeding their large mills which produce, on average, approximately 500,000 tons of pulp annually. Production is oriented towards three main Northern markets: the European Union, the USA and Japan. The European market has been particularly influential in the inclusion of environmental issues by the five corporations.

By examining the policies and practices of the major companies in this sector this chapter will consider how much this discourse corresponds with reality and examine the underlying reasons for such discourse. To address these questions, I will examine in greater detail the policies and activities of one company, Aracruz Cellulose. The first reason for highlighting Aracruz is that it is not only the world's largest producer of bleached eucalyptus pulp, but also operates the world largest pulp mill of any kind. Second, it is the Brazilian pulp company that appears to be most committed to environmental conservation. An additional reason is that I visited the area where Aracruz operates during July 1997, and was able to dialogue with both the company and local people (indigenous peoples, trade unions, NGOs and some government officials), thus obtaining first-hand information.

The approach used in this inquiry consists of describing and commenting on the stated environmental and social concerns of several corporations and then confronting these claims with both documented evidence and the perceptions of local people affected by the companies' activities. Although the results of this study cannot be extended to other corporations, they are of use in identifying ways to improve the performance of corporations with respect to environmental protection and social responsibility, as well as to further the debate on the currently prevailing development model.

The Brazilian Market Pulp Industry

The Brazilian Association of Cellulose Exporters (ABECEL) is composed of the five main corporations producing market pulp in Brazil: Aracruz Cellulose, Bahia Sul Cellulose, Cellulose Nipo-Brasileira, Jari Cellulose and Riocell. Together they produce 90 per cent of Brazil's bleached eucalyptus pulp for export, averaging more than two million tonnes of exports annually, thus supplying half the world demand. Only one of them (Jari Cellulose) produces some long fibre pulp (from planted pines) in addition to eucalyptus pulp.

Aracruz Cellulose SA: The biggest of them all, Aracruz is currently producing 1.2 million tons of pulp per year from wood fibre harvested on its 132,000 hectares of eucalyptus plantations (its land holdings total 203,000 hectares in the state of Espírito Santo and the southern part of the state of Bahia). Aracruz also has a private port, specializing in pulp shipments. The company's shares are owned by the Lorentzen Group (28 per cent), Mondi Minorco Paper (28 per cent) and the Safra group (28 per cent), while the Brazilian National Economic and Social Development Bank (BNDES) owns a further 12.5 per cent.

Bahia Sul Cellulose SA: This company produces 500,000 tons of bleached eucalyptus pulp, consisting of both market pulp (45 per cent for export and 10 per cent for the domestic market) and pulp for its own paper production (45 per cent), three fifths of which is also exported. The company owns 114,000 hectares of land in the state of Bahia, of which 68,000 hectares are planted with eucalyptus. Its shares are owned by the Suzano group (35 per cent), Companhia Vale do Rio Doce (29 per cent), BNDES (26 per cent) and the International Finance Corporation (3 per cent).

Cellulose Nipo-Brasileira SA (CENIBRA): Located in the state of Minas Gerais, this corporation produces some 400,000 tons of pulp, 80 per cent of which is exported. Its land holdings consist of 155,000 hectares, of which 88,000 are planted with eucalyptus. Companhia Vale do Rio Doce (currently being privatized) owns 51.5 per cent of the shares, while the Japan–Brazil Pulp Resources Development Co. (composed of the Japanese Overseas Economic Development Fund and some 20 private corporations of the pulp and paper industry) holds the rest of the shares.

Jari Cellulose SA: The company's mill produces approximately 300,000 tons of pulp annually, 55 per cent of which is long fibre and 45 per cent eucalyptus. Eighty per cent of the pulp is exported. The firm's extensive land holdings in the states of Pará and Amapá include some 90,000 hectares of eucalyptus and pine plantations. The company is owned by a consortium of 23 Brazilian companies, among which the main ones are the CAEMI group (40 per cent of shares) and Amapá Florestal e Cellulose SA (AMCEL).

Riocell SA: Situated in the state of Rio Grande do Sul, it produces annually some 300,000 tons of bleached eucalyptus pulp, mostly for export. It is also the main pulp producer for the Brazilian rayon industry. The firm owns more than 70,000 hectares of land, 53,000 of which are planted with eucalyptus. Its main shareholders are Klabin (a large producer of pulp and paper), Votorantim (the country's largest private conglomerate) and the Iochpe finance company.

Aracruz

Aracruz is probably the company which has taken most seriously into account the need to respond to the growing international concern about the environment. Its directors participated actively in the preparation of the corporate community's position for the 1992 Earth Summit, which resulted in the publication *Changing Course* (Schmidheiny, 1992), produced in association with what is now the World Business Council for Sustainable Development (WBCSD) and distributed to government delegates prior to UNCED. The company's environmental publicity has been widely disseminated, both by the company itself and through the WBCSD, as well as by journalists and researchers. Aracruz has also supported the London-based non-governmental International Institute for Environment and Development in a two-million dollar study on the 'sustainable paper cycle' (IIED, 1995), which aimed to provide a 'comprehensive, undisputed and independent analysis of the world's pulp and paper industry from a perspective of sustainable development' (Aracruz, 1997a). IIED had previously conducted research for Shell International's troublesome plantation project in Thailand – from which Shell later withdrew in the face of organized local opposition and delays in getting government approval. In 1992, IIED had praised Aracruz's activities in the following words: 'Aracruz Cellulose SA, with government support, took control of much degraded land within the tattered fragments of natural forest, and has established major *Eucalyptus* plantations. In doing so, it has begun to improve the local environment and social conditions' (Bass, 1992b).

The company produces printed and visual materials aimed at different audiences and is carrying out research on the potential environmental impacts of its activities, all aimed at proving that 'all of the Company's activities are carried out under the principles of sustainable development, which involves promoting social and economic growth in harmony with nature' (Aracruz, 1996a).

According to Aracruz, its activities do not appear to have negative impacts either in the plantation or in the industrial areas, because 'the Company has been fully committed to the principles of sustainable development since its inception'

(Kaufmann, 1996). The company states that it preserves biodiversity, protects the soil and protects water resources (Aracruz, 1997b).

In respect to biodiversity, Aracruz stresses that it 'preserves tropical rain forests in the 56,000 hectares of native reserves on its properties that are interspersed with the eucalyptus plantations'. In order to further reassure concerned people (particularly Northern customers), it stresses that its 132,000 hectares of eucalyptus plantations are 'some 3,000 kilometers from the Amazon rainforest region'. It also states that the company 'does not use any wood from tropical rain forests, nor from any other kind of native forests. Aracruz pulp is produced solely from sustainably managed eucalyptus plantations.' Such plantations are publicized as 'a complement to, and not a substitute for, tropical forests. Indeed, fast-growing plantations actually help reduce the world's – and Brazil's – wood deficit by alleviating the main pressures on native forests and consequently helping to preserve them' (Aracruz, 1996a).

The above statements demand comment. Aracruz operates in the area previously dominated by a type of forest – the Mata Atlántica – which is, in fact, under far greater threat of extinction than the Amazonian forest. The Mata Atlántica is also at least as rich in biodiversity as the Amazonian forest. Failure to disclose such facts leaves the company open to the accusation that it is trying to mislead concerned citizens.

Second, the fact that the plantations are 'interspersed' with native forests is not the result of the company's initial concern over environmental conservation, but its simple adherence to government legislation, which established a ban on cutting native forests on a 10-metre strip along the margin of all watercourses. The company only later realized that these remaining forests helped to maintain an ecological balance, which had positive results for its plantations. The company is now planting native species to expand the riparian buffer zones in an extension of some 4,500 hectares. Again, this action aims at complying with new legislation, which establishes that the riparian forest areas must now be widened to a 30-metre strip. As this coincides with Aracruz's experience concerning the importance of the buffer zones to protect its plantations, it is in the company's interests to act in accordance with government legislation (ABECEL, undated). Is this corporate environmentalism or merely expedience?

Last, pulpwood plantations in Brazil do not alleviate pressures on native forests. Forest destruction in Brazil is mostly related to changes in land use (conversion to cattle raising and agriculture), the use of wood as an energy source and the use of timber for the wood industry. That the Brazilian pulp industry does not rely on native species is not because of environmental considerations but because wood from native mixed forests is not suitable for modern pulp production.

Aracruz also asserts that it has planted eucalyptus only in areas where the natural forest was cleared before its arrival. This claim contradicts accusations that Aracruz felled and burned more than 50,000 hectares of forest during its first phase of tree planting (FASE, 1993; Miranda, 1993a). Even when the exact number of hectares deforested by the company remains unclear, local indigenous people still remember forest being felled by chains pulled by two tractors. José Luís Ramos (head of Caieira Velha Tupinikim Indian village) recalls that when he was seven years old 'we went to see the cutting of the forest. We saw this big machine cutting down everything together with another machine, one on this side, the other on that side, and that way they cut the trees'. A Guarani Indian remembers that when they arrived in 1967 (the same year that Aracruz started its activities) 'there was rain forest everywhere. We liked it because it was pure native forest' (ECTG/CIMI,

1996). One of Aracruz's minority shareholders (the Storebrand Scudder Environmental Value Fund) is somewhat more forthright than the company, recognizing that 'Aracruz deforested small amounts of native forests' when the level of environmental consciousness of the business community was extremely low in Brazil and 'Aracruz was not an exception' (EVF, 1997).

Aracruz's plantations are composed of only two species of eucalyptus (*E. grandis* and *E. urophylla*). In order to achieve higher yields with the wood best suited for pulp making and reduce risks associated with low diversity (for example, possible pest attacks), the company carries out important genetic research. Its plantations consist of separate blocks of clones of more than 100 hybrids of the two species mentioned above (Aracruz, 1996a).

In answer to criticisms about low biodiversity, the company's first answer is that 'the biodiversity of eucalyptus should not be compared with that of native rain forests ... but rather with other crops' such as wheat, soya, sugar cane and coffee. This answer is complemented by saying that 'the ecosystem of eucalyptus and native reserves offers shelter, nourishment and even conditions for reproduction for the wildlife' and that in Aracruz areas 'more than 1,700 species of fauna have been found' (Aracruz, 1996a). Such a claim is strongly contested by local indigenous peoples whose hunting and fishing opportunities have declined since the introduction of eucalyptus plantations (ECTG/CIMI,1996). According to them, most of the wildlife has disappeared from the area as a result of the activities of Aracruz (personal communication with local residents).

With respect to soils, Aracruz claims that 'independent research has proved the beneficial effects of Eucalyptus on many soil properties, including structure, water storage capacity, drainage and aereation, among others' and that a number of facts from its own experience contradict 'the theory that euclayptus plantations impoverish the soil'. Among those facts, the firm points to the 'constant increase in forestry productivity, including the regions where the first plantings took place 27 years ago'. The company explains the improvement in soil in terms of 'the intense deposition of organic matter on the soil' and the fact that eucalyptus seeks nutrients in the subsoil layers and brings them to the surface, thus recovering the soil's fertility levels (Aracruz, 1997b).

Three comments should be made on the above. First, the increased productivity after three rotations may in no way be considered proof of sustainability. Many other Green Revolution agricultural crops have been extremely productive during their first harvests, but have resulted ultimately in soil degradation. Increased productivity may simply be the result of increased chemical applications (fertilizers). Furthermore, while productivity measured in terms of wood production may increase, productivity in terms of other biomass and water production may in fact decrease. Second, the balance between deposition of organic matter (estimated by Aracruz at 7 tons per hectare/year) and wood extraction (some 200 tons/hectare every 7 years) is clearly negative. In the case of Aracruz, where trunks are removed together with their bark, the nutrient export is even greater, given that the bark contains many of the nutrients used by the trees. Finally, the surfacing of nutrients from the subsoil implies the use of the subsoil's nutrient 'capital', which will eventually be depleted. Bringing subsoil nutrients (and deeper-lying water) closer to the surface is not necessarily desirable if it means merely the depletion of another layer of soil.

Aracruz has recently implemented a number of measures for soil protection. Based on the results of a study conducted jointly with the Brazilian Agricultural Research Company (EMBRAPA), 'significant changes were implemented in soil preparation operations, the recommendation of genetic materials to be planted, weed control, fertilizer use and insect and disease protection'. As a result, there is now no burning during site preparation, no ploughing and no understorey removal (which were previously carried out as normal management practices). With respect to fertilization, a new technique to avoid the use of 'excessive amounts' of chemical fertilizers 'which otherwise could be leached to the water table or to the rivers', was only implemented in 1994 (Aracruz, 1997b), which means that the company polluted water in the region for more than two decades. While these recent improvements in the company's environmental management are to be welcomed, they also prove that the company has not always adhered to sustainable development. The fact that Aracruz contradicts itself about its past performance raises the question as to whether its claims about the present and the future can be relied upon.

Another contradiction can be found in the 1996 introduction of mechanized tree harvesting equipment. Aracruz's publication 'The Eucalyptus and Sustainable Pulp Production' (1996a) includes a box summarizing methods 'used by Aracruz to lessen potential environmental impacts'. One such method establishes the 'use of forestry equipment with suitable dimensions, tire gauges and working pressures, so as to minimize soil compacting'. Two months later, *Aracruz News* (No. 4) welcomed the introduction of large harvesting machines (fellers, log processors and forwarders), under the argument that they would improve operational efficiency and productivity (Aracruz, 1996b). These caterpillar tractors, however, will undoubtedly compact the soil. Clearly, in this case, economic interest has taken precedence over environmental considerations.

Aracruz also claims to be protecting water resources and has publicized – and even supported – studies proving that eucalyptus plantations have no negative effects on water resources. Like many other plantation advocates, the company stresses that this species 'uses water more efficiently, consuming less water per unit of biomass produced than other species' (Aracruz, 1997b). Such statements hide the fact that the large-scale plantations consume enormous amounts of water and can deplete water resources at a regional level. It is therefore irrelevant to say that they use water 'more efficiently' to produce biomass.

The fact is that only in 1994, when all of its eucalyptus had already been in place for many years, did Aracruz begin to monitor water in its plantation area. This research is being conducted at a 280-hectare watershed and none of its findings have yet been made public. Many of the impacts of plantations on the local water resources, however, had already occurred before this watershed experiment began. Rogério Medeiros, National Coordinator for the Environment of the National Federation of Journalists, who has been monitoring Aracruz's activities since their inception, states that 156 streams have disappeared in the region during that period and that wells are drying up in a number of areas; even a river, the San Domingos, has stopped flowing (FASE, 1993). During our visit to the area, local residents showed us a number of dried-up water courses where they used to fish. It was quite obvious that water used to flow there and that it flowed no longer. The depletion of water resources has impacts not only on local people and their productive activities but also on local fauna, which are highly dependent on water for survival. Even though part of the problem of the depletion of water resources in the state of Espírito Santo can also be attributed to large-scale deforestation processes, the problem, at the local level, seems to have a much more direct link with Aracruz's plantations.

Another fact contradicting the claim that 'the Company has been fully committed to the principles of sustainable development since its inception' is its use of pesticides and herbicides. Leaf-cutting ants constitute the main threat to local plantations. For years, the company used Mirex, a toxic and persistent organochlorine, to combat these ants. It has recently changed to Mirex-S, a pyrethroid, more environmentally friendly than organochlorines. More recently (1997), Aracruz has begun to use biodegradable bait bags that 'exclusively attract the main species of leaf-cutting ants', which makes them 'safer for non-target animals' (Aracruz, 1997c). This means that past ant-killing activities did, in fact, impact on 'non-target animals'.

Herbicides are also widely used by the company. It has changed from Goal to Roundup (Glyphosate) which, it claims, is less harmful than cooking salt. Given the company's forestry management practices, a vast amount of Roundup must be used. Such practices allow the trees to regrow after the first cut, but after the second cut, all the sprouts are sprayed with Roundup, in order to replace them with a new, faster-growing and higher-quality eucalyptus clone. During our visit we frequently came upon landscapes of brown-coloured coppice – killed with Roundup.

The activities of Aracruz have also had other important impacts on local people. First, the enormous area bought by the company since the 1960s was not, contrary to company claims, empty; rather, thousands of indigenous people and subsistence farmers lived there. In order to overcome local resistance to the takeover, mainly from black communities and small agricultural producers who had recently migrated from other states, a strategy which combined physical and symbolic violence was used. Land purchases were made through two people: a military officer and a local black leader, a combination which had an especially clear meaning given the dominance at that time of the military dictatorship (Miranda, 1993b). Approximately 7,000 families are said to have been removed, through violence and coercion, from the areas Aracruz occupied, including several thousand people who received no compensation (FASE, 1993; Valarelli, 1992). Crucial to these expulsions was the negligence or collaboration of local authorities, including the then governor of Espírito Santo state, Artur Gerardt, who later became president of Aracruz (FASE, 1993).

Local indigenous peoples were also subject to expulsion. According to Eugenio Francisco, a Tupinikim Indian, 'When the company came, the people left. They weren't able to defy it. They were forced to leave and even threatened.... The company took everything. They gave us some money, but what they had to pay they didn't' (ECTG/CIMI, 1996). José Luís Ramos, the head of Caieira Velha village, recalls that in 1967 Aracruz, with the support of the state government, 'felled large areas of forest and planted eucalyptus across the region, including on our land. In a little time, this company destroyed around seven Tupinikim villages, expelling us, and today we are surrounded by a sea of eucalyptus' (Miranda, 1993a).

Three principal options were left to the people expelled: emigrate to other rural areas; move to a life of underemployment in the *favelas* or shanty towns of cities; or work for the company, mainly on the plantations. Aracruz plantation work, however, has been described as so dangerous and unhealthy that few workers can remain on the job more than ten years (Inyaku, 1993). According to the same source, over 50 per cent of those who have worked for long periods on the plantations suffer from serious work-related health problems as a result of their tasks. It is also claimed that the company tends to dismiss long-term plantation employees without compensation, replacing them with younger people (Inyaku, 1993). Salaries are kept low by the abundance of unemployed people in the region.

Unemployment has increased owing to the crisis of another export monoculture crop, coffee; other factors are the company's dispossession of local people and migration to the Aracruz 'development pole'.

Yet opportunities for even low-paid, health-endangering jobs have become limited as tree harvesting and other plantation work have become increasingly mechanized (IBASE, 1994). According to Aracruz, the new tree harvesting equipment has meant a 'reduction of the workforce for this phase of operations from over 1,100 to under 350 people' (Aracruz, 1996b). While these machines process 140 trees per hour, chainsaw operators process only 10. The company stresses that 'worker comfort and safety have improved dramatically' with these machines, but says nothing of the 750 workers affected. Plantation work has also increasingly passed to outside contractors, where working and salary conditions are even worse. In a process which began in 1993, Aracruz has reduced its workforce from 7,000 to 2,700 employees. Outside contractors supply another 2,500 workers for Aracruz activities (Aracruz, 1997b).

Aracruz attempts to divert attention from its record by advertising itself as having voluntarily built several recreation centres, schools, vocational training centres and health centres, at a cost of over US$15 million. What the company does not mention, however, is that, as part of the plant expansion project, the BNDES demanded that Aracruz both reinforce social structure in the regions where it operates and provide 80 per cent of the total funding required to do so (Gonçalves et al., 1994).

Aracruz's claim that it does not usurp agricultural land is contradicted by the way the firm has bought land in some areas. In Bahia, for example, Aracruz purchased land previously dedicated to small-scale cultivation of mamão, a local fruit. Although a company director suggested that mamão production was in decline, it had in fact provided a viable livelihood for local farmers (Gonçalves et al., 1994). In general, the company's insistence that its activities are compatible with agriculture makes little sense given its propensity for buying the best agricultural land, on the grounds that it makes mechanization easier. Aracruz owns a full 15 per cent of the plains in Espírito Santo (FASE, 1993).

The Tupinikim Indians, meanwhile, found that soils on land returned to them after having been used for eucalyptus planting did not regain their old levels of agricultural productivity, having become sandy. Furthermore, the indiscriminate use of the herbicides Goal and Roundup and the ant-killer Mirex have been blamed for the wholesale poisoning of animals (FASE, 1993).

The pulp and paper industry is considered to be one of the more polluting industries in the world. Aracruz claims, however, that its industrial processes are clean and that 'strict controls over the pulping process guarantee the safety of the product, and effluent quality levels that meet international regulations' (Aracruz, 1997b). With respect to liquid effluents, the firm states that 'regular analysis shows no traces of dioxin while AOX concentrations – the parameter normally used for measuring organochlorines – are below 0.25 kg per tonne of pulp in the combined final effluent, which is considered very low'. Tests carried out have 'never discovered any significant alterations to the receiving body' (Aracruz, 1996a). The firm goes as far as saying that 'our effluents have caused virtually no impact on the ocean ecosystems' (Aracruz, 1996c). Regarding atmospheric emissions, we were told by Aracruz managers that they consisted mostly of water and sulphur, with no harmful effects apart from the strong odour of the emissions.

The company incorporated new technology for non-chlorine pulp bleaching in late 1993. This was in response to foreign consumer demand for chlorine-free pulp.

A company directive stated that 'without the new technology, we would lose sales of 150,000 tonnes of pulp on the international market' (IBASE, 1993a). It is for this reason that the firm runs three different types of industrial processes among its four production lines. One uses chlorine gas (43 per cent of total output), two others are 'elemental chlorine free' – ECF (47 per cent) – and only the newest one is 'totally chlorine free' – TCF (10 per cent) (ECTG/CIMI, 1996).

Even though Aracruz is now investing in new equipment to eliminate the use of chlorine gas, it is important to look into its past record, to see if 'the Company has been fully committed to the principles of sustainable development since its inception'. The pulp mill was first inaugurated in 1978, but information on final effluent indicators are only available since 1984 (AOX, since 1990), and the evolution of these indicators seem to show that the statement that 'our effluents have caused virtually no impact on the ocean ecosystems' is simply untrue. Official company information is presented in Table 4.1.

Table 4.1
Aracruz Environmental Performance Indicators (Final Effluent)

Year	AOX (kg/adt)	BOD5 (kg/adt)	COD (kg/adt)	TSS (kg/adt)	COLOUR (kgPT/adt)
1984	-	20.10	121.3	13.90	660.0
1990	2.90	21.12	104.0	24.63	428.8
1991	0.91	4.98	42.3	3.56	322.5
1996	0.27	2.10	25.0	1.90	77.5

Kg/adt – Kilos per tonne of air-dried pulp; KgPt/adt – Kilos of platen per tonne of air-dried pulp;
AOX – Absorbable organic halides; BOD5 – Biochemical oxygen demand (5 days);
COD – Chemical oxygen demand; TSS – Total suspended solids; COLOUR – Colour of effluent.
Source: Aracruz, 1997b

According to the above indicators, the company has improved its effluent treatment dramatically since 1984: in most cases a 10-fold improvement. While this can be considered a major achievement, it also shows that the company's past performance has been appalling. The year 1991 seems to be the starting point of a new, more concerned attitude towards the marine environment, which does not appear to have been the case in the period 1978–90. This conclusion coincides with a statement from Aracruz's environmental manager, who says that 'results regarding offshore water quality improved significantly as of 1991, when the six biological lagoons entered into operation, providing intensive secondary treatment of effluents' (Aracruz, 1996c).

According to some local observers, the company's control systems are aimed more at hiding pollution problems than at curbing them. The company has a computerized system for monitoring atmospheric conditions. The system is allegedly used for the discharge of airborne emissions when the wind is blowing away from urban centres. The firm's incinerator, which is used to burn containers of toxic chemicals, is located near its tree nursery and is now hidden behind a eucalyptus plantation. Local people claim that it is used when the wind is blowing in the right direction and when there are no visitors in the area. Although such practices can be considered positive regarding urban people's health, they still hide the fact that the mill continues to pollute the air in the region, and that such pollution will affect rural populations. According to the same sources, liquid effluents are discharged into the ocean mostly at night, particularly when there are few fishermen in the sea. The Pulp Industry

Workers Union (SINTICEL) has accused Aracruz of incorrect management of both waterborne and airborne emissions (FASE,1993). Local activists claim that chemical releases into the Atlantic have killed and poisoned both fish and vegetation.

One of Aracruz's main unsolved problems concerns its attitude towards the indigenous peoples who were already living in the area at the time of its arrival. What the firm conceives as 'sustainable development' clearly differs from the indigenous peoples' view of sustainable development. According to the firm, it was in the mid-1960s, when the state of Espírito Santo was in a situation of economic stagnation, that the federal government 'set into motion a strategy ... to foster development and diversify the state's economic activities' and 'Aracruz participated in this effort' (Aracruz, 1997b).

From the perspective of the indigenous peoples, their area had been used sustainably for centuries and they had no major livelihood problems. In spite of the destructive activities of a 'development' process which had begun in the 1940s – a process which included the granting of lands by the federal government to the Vitória Iron and Steel Company (CONAVI) which deforested some 10,000 hectares of forest – 60 per cent of the area of the municipality of Aracruz was still covered with native forests. These forests ensured food, housing, medicine and other goods and services for the indigenous peoples (ECTG/CIMI, 1996).

The Tupinikim had been living in the area at least since the arrival of the Portuguese and, as owners of the territory, welcomed the arrival in 1967 of a group of Guarani Mbyá from southern Brazil. They did not welcome, however, the simultaneous arrival of Aracruz Cellulose, which purchased 10,000 hectares of land from CONAVI and a further 30,000 hectares from the federal government. Indigenous practices, which had ensured the sustainable use of resources for the present and future generations became unviable after the initiation of the activities of Aracruz. 'The reduction of the territory and the deforestation of the native forest were two determining factors that jeopardized the physical and cultural survival of the Tupinikim and the Guarani' (ECTG/CIMI, 1996).

The indigenous peoples' struggle began that same year, when two Guarani and one Tupinikim went to Brasília to denounce the invasion of their lands by Aracruz to the Indian Protection Service (SPI). The struggle has continued since, with Aracruz using its economic and political strength in order to avoid an equitable demarcation of lands where the Tupinikim and Guarani people can live in accordance with their own cultural norms. In 1993, the indigenous people who had lost their land to Aracruz launched an international campaign to get it back.

As part of this campaign, indigenous representatives went to Norway in early 1997 to seek support for their struggle, given that the company's chairperson, Erling Sven Lorentzen (who is also one of the principal shareholders), was born in that country. SINTICEL, the company's main trade union, wrote a letter of 'support and solidarity for the just struggle of the Tupinikim and Guarani Indians' and made clear that 'the retrocession of the lands to the Tupinikim and Guarani Indians will not disadvantage the company, since it has been proved that Aracruz Cellulose has been exporting wood because of the fact that the eucalyptus production exceeds the capacity of the pulp mill' (SINTICEL, 1997). This was judged as high treason by the company, which not only suspended *sine die* all meetings with SINTICEL, but also banned the union leaders from entering the plant and held individual meetings with the company's employees, trying to divide the trade union.

In summary, it seems relevant to quote the remarks of a team which carried out research in the area:

Aracruz assumes the image of protector of the environment, but its eucalyptus trees have dried streams, destroyed the local fauna, impoverished the soil, impeded the regrowth of native plant species, and drastically reduced the area available for cultivating basic foodstuffs (in a country where many people die of hunger). This is not to mention land concentration and the expulsion of the rural population, which has contributed to increasing the urban population and the degradation of living conditions in the cities. Where is the sustainable development here, we might ask? (Gonçalves *et al.*, 1994)

Bahia Sul

Bahia Sul Cellulose also presents itself as a defender of nature and blames the poor for environmental degradation. The hunting practised by local people to supplement their poor diet, for example, is treated in the company's literature as an 'ecological crime' which the firm is striving to curb. The firm's preservation of the remnants of native forests on its properties is presented as a guarantee for the survival of 'nature' against degradation by the poor (Miranda, 1992).

An industry journalist reported approvingly in 1992 that 'environmental considerations were important both in the location of [Bahia Sul's] plant and in its construction':

> Apart from Bahia Sul's conservation of 30 per cent of its forest land for native species and its planting of 20,000 such trees annually, extensive studies were produced prior to construction to assure the aquatic environment was safe. Features of the mill include oxygen delignification (a cleaner bleaching process), primary and secondary effluent treatment and biomass energy production. (Higgs, 1992a)

Such statements are misleading. They ignore the fact that, before the region was opened up to 'development', local people had been using natural resources in a far more responsible manner than the company is using them today (Miranda, 1992). They are also contradicted by the fact that Bahia Sul used only an exceptionally low 7.2 per cent of its total mill construction costs on contamination control equipment (Gonçalves *et al.*, 1994). This is in sharp contrast to the approximately 20 per cent figure common in industrialized countries (CEPEDES/CDDH, 1992).

Also unmentioned are other socio-economic dangers that Bahia Sul's investments pose for the region as a whole, such as those related to dependence on a single monoculture. In the case of cacao cultivation in Bahia, this dependence led to repeated crises attributable to climatic irregularities, pests, and falling international commodity prices over which local producers had little control. Dependence on monocultures of eucalyptus for the pulp and paper industry may bring similar problems. The reduction in size of the state's agricultural area has already forced it into greater dependence on costlier food imports from other regions, with negative repercussions on the quality of life of poorer groups (CEPEDES/CDDH, 1992; Miranda, 1992).

To make way for Bahia Sul, the families from nearly 8,000 small properties in the region were driven from their land. Evictees who became forestry employees are now by and large worse off than small producers who managed to keep their properties (Gonçalves *et al.*, 1994). Bahia Sul has not proved to be an efficient creator of jobs. Each one of the existing 5,500 jobs at the company has required an investment of between $226,000 and $338,000, with much of the capital deriving ultimately from public funds. According to a study conducted by local NGOs (CEPEDES/CDDH, 1992), an alternative development project (based on diversified agriculture) with a similar level of investment could generate 150,000 jobs at a cost of a mere $8,300 each. In the forestry sector, the company employs only one person per 45 hectares, while agricultural activities provide work to at least 18 per hectare; *mamão* production requires 1.5 workers per hectare (CDDH, 1993). Moreover, contrary to company claims, many of the jobs which have been provided have not gone to local people, who often lack the required qualifications (Miranda, 1992).

In addition, living and working conditions have hardly improved. The large numbers of people attracted to the Bahia Sul site by the company's advertisements for construction workers precipitated a sharp rise in housing rents. For labourers who lodged alone, living conditions were dreadful. Rooms measuring three by four metres lodged six or more workers, with one toilet per 32 men. Family problems were exacerbated by extended separations. Some 5,000 workers lived in such conditions over a three-year period, with the population around the construction site occasionally surging as high as 13,000. The resulting strikes delayed completion of the plant. The infrastructure for health, education, drainage, housing and security could not cope with the large influx of migrants. New shanty towns sprang up, and poverty, violence, crime, disease and prostitution increased (CEPEDES/CDDH, 1992; CDDH, 1993; Gonçalves *et al.*, 1994).

A mega-project of the Bahia Sul variety implies enormous concentrations of capital, land and political power. As it generates little employment in relation to the level of investment, little of this capital and power ever filters down to the deprived in society. As a result, large firms such as Bahia Sul come to wield disproportionate political clout and the states in which they are located run the risk of suffering from a modern 'feudal' syndrome in which large holders of land and capital become 'lords' who attempt to dictate policy. Before Bahia Sul even commenced operations, official complaints were being aired about the use of company funds in election campaigns (CEPEDES/CDDH, 1992). Years later, an advance payment of taxes by Bahia Sul was used by the Bahia government to surface the roads most used by the company's lorries (Miranda, 1992). Public reaction to the growing power of the company eventually forced the state government of Bahia to demand, in 1989, that the firm suspend the acquisition of new lands – a situation which paralleled events in Espírito Santo with Aracruz.

The environmental problems caused by Bahia Sul Cellulose are also significant. In southern Bahia, where the company is located, only approximately 60,000 hectares survive of a forest which, in 1930, covered one and a half million hectares. These remnants are part of the endangered Mata Atlántica forest (CEPEDES/CDDH, 1992). Although the company was not responsible for this deforestation process, Bahia Sul's eucalyptus plantations threaten the survival of this forest mainly because it takes over crucial areas which would otherwise have regenerated into native forest. Unless these areas are allowed to regrow, the strict conservation of a few tiny areas of untouched Mata Atlántica forest, such as those preserved by Bahia Sul, has little meaning.

Bahia Sul's eucalyptus plantations are also affecting both the quantity and the quality of local water. Inhabitants of the town of Veracruz, for example, have declared that, as the result of a nearby eucalyptus plantation, several wells have dried up and they have had to dig down a further three metres in order to find water. Insecticides, fertilizers and herbicides used on the plantations also contaminate watercourses, taking their toll on aquatic fauna. The inhabitants of the fishing community of Caravelas have gone to the courts to demand an investigation into the reduction in crabs and other species – a reduction which has been linked to the use of agrochemicals (CEPEDES/CDDH, 1992). Local residents fear that water contamination from Bahia Sul's industrial plant will only add to their problems.

CENIBRA

CENIBRA's claim to green credentials comes in the form of a five-year strategic plan developed in 1991 to assure 'sustainable development' (Higgs, 1992b). As a result of this plan, 240 hectares of pine and eucalyptus surrounding the plant were to be enriched with local species in order to encourage the return of other indigenous species. In addition, some 1,000 hectares of Mata Atlántica forest on the River Doce were to be preserved, while company land on the banks of the same river was to be reforested with native species. At CENIBRA's mill, meanwhile, the plan called for company-monitored measures to control effluents, as well as the initiation of production of chlorine-free pulp.

Several aspects of this plan call for comment. First, the planting of indigenous species and the preservation of a few areas of native forest (the latter, far from being a voluntary measure, is a legal obligation) are essentially cosmetic measures to pacify local people and environmental groups in the North, although they also limit the risk of pest infestations in the company's plantations. Second, effluent-treatment systems were installed only in 1988 – 11 years after the mill came on-line – and only after heavy pressure from local people (Gonçalves, M.T., 1995). Their installation thus hardly demonstrates trustworthiness regarding environmental matters. Similarly, chlorine-free bleaching techniques began to be used only as a result of demand from the European Community, and are used exclusively with pulp destined for the European market (JATAN, 1993). Furthermore, CENIBRA's 'sustainable development' plan fails to mention a number of destructive realities about the company's operations. One such reality is the way CENIBRA's projects and those of other companies such as CVRD, ACESITA and Belgo Mineira concentrate vast areas of land in a few hands in a process often marked by violence. For instance, according to the Japan Tropical Forest Action Network (JATAN) (1993), FLONIBRA (a subsidiary of CENIBRA) used various methods to acquire land:

> sometimes it purchased land at above market prices; at other times residents were chased away with violence. It also often resorted to deception; for instance it would first move a FLONIBRA insider onto land adjacent to the farmer's land and set up a local conflict; then a third party would be sent in who would act as a 'mediator' between the two and offer to purchase the farmer's land.

FLONIBRA is also reported to have felled secondary forest used by indigenous people, obliging them to emigrate to nearby towns (JATAN, 1992). As elsewhere in Brazil, the concentration of land with good soils in a few hands has undermined subsistence agriculture and led to increased urban migration and the weakening of autonomy and local social ties (Guerra, 1992; Gonçalves, M.T., 1995). Wage labour, meanwhile, has proved an inadequate substitute for small-scale farming in both economic and cultural terms. In the words of one worker, 'the salary that we earn does not go very far ... it is only enough to survive on' (Gonçalves, M.T., 1995). As a result of large plantations taking over agricultural areas, Minas Gerais has had to import food from other regions. As the holdings of plantation firms accumulate (ACESITA, for example, has 250,000 hectares, Belgo Mineira 100,000 and CENIBRA 155,000), the dependence of local towns on a few businesses grows, and the influence of such companies on decision-making processes increases. One result is yet more industrial projects and tree plantations (Guerra, 1992; JATAN, 1993).

CENIBRA's relationship with its workers, meanwhile, has been authoritarian and exploitative. While, according to one interviewed worker, wages were initially good and there was a strong trade union, salaries declined considerably after CENIBRA stepped in to manipulate union elections through pressure and fraud. The company also dismissed unionized workers and started contracting out both industrial and forestry tasks to other firms. This move, aimed at reducing costs, resulted in even lower wage levels and a smaller worker population, making unionization even more difficult (Gonçalves, M.T., 1995). Working conditions are often inadequate, with many plantation chainsaw operators suffering from nervous disorders and other health problems (JATAN, 1993).

CENIBRA is also moving into contract farming through the Fazendeiro Florestal programme, operated in conjunction with a state agency. Through this programme, seedlings, fertilizers and ant poison are provided to individual farmers if they plant eucalyptus on their own land. This allows the company to increase its forestry base in a way other than through simple acquisition of land. The farmers are contractually obliged to sell CENIBRA wood at the 'market price', which is established by the company itself (Gonçalves, M.T., 1995).

The environmental impacts of CENIBRA plantations include destruction of native forests and loss of biodiversity (Guerra, 1992; JATAN, 1993; Gonçalves, M.T., 1995). Fertile agricultural land has also been taken over. Not only does CENIBRA not restrict its plantations to 'degraded' land; contrary to its stated policy, it also plants on pronounced slopes (Guerra, 1992) – a practice which can result in serious erosion. Soil ecology has also been affected. Because the thick layer of plant material associated with plantations cannot be mineralized rapidly by microorganisms, organic acids are formed and calcium, potassium and magnesium ions are replaced by hydrogen ions in the upper layer of the soil. This implies a lower pH, which affects the availability of nutrients to plants. The long-term productive capacity of the soil is endangered and it is not known how much longer the same land can keep on producing eucalyptus wood (Guerra, 1992). Tree bark which, according to the Food and Agriculture Organization (FAO), contains the best part of the nutrients taken from the soil by the tree, is removed from the site and used in the pulp mill for energy generation, further reducing soil fertility (JATAN, 1993).

Local people have observed, moreover, that the rate of replacement of underground water tables has slowed. This is attributable to the increased surface run-off associated with plantations and with the high water consumption of eucalyptus. Finally, the use of pesticides such as Aldrin and Mirex has resulted in the contamination of soils and watercourses, with proven high rates of fish mortality (Guerra, 1992). The company has even begun to spray herbicides from the air, endangering local agriculturalists (Gonçalves, M.T., 1995).

The environmental impacts at CENIBRA's pulp mill have been equally serious. The first complaints of water pollution date from 1977, the year the plant started up, and they have continued ever since. Yet only at the end of 1986 did the company formally commit itself to installing an industrial and sanitary effluent treatment system, giving itself a 30-month deadline. Since 1990, CENIBRA has submitted monthly reports to the appropriate state agency but without making them public (Gonçalves, M.T., 1995). Although scientific data on air pollution around the pulp mill is unavailable, JATAN members visiting the plant in 1992 remarked that 'we couldn't avoid noticing the horrible smell present in all of the plant and we felt sorry for the people who had to work there' (JATAN, 1993).

Jari

According to journalist Richard Higgs, 'Jari is very proud of its almost surgical blending of plantation species in among the predominant and thriving natural forest' – a practice which helps 'to prevent the spread of pests and disease'. The company also maintains reserve areas and carries out research into native species which may be of economic use. Like other pulp firms, Jari has recently displayed much concern about chlorine pollution, although this concern had remained dormant for 14 years before 1992, when European consumers began calling for non-chlorine-bleached pulp (Higgs, 1993). Jari's own public relations efforts have received a boost from Paulo de T. Alvim, a leading Brazilian agricultural planner, who has claimed that the Jari plantations reduce global warming because they grow, whereas the tropical forest that had occupied the site previously had been in equilibrium with the atmosphere, neither absorbing nor emitting carbon (Fearnside, 1993).

Such claims conceal a great deal more than they reveal. For example, although the company is legally obliged to preserve 50 per cent of the native forests it controls, it has already felled around a third of them in order to supplement shortfalls in gmelina (the tree initially adopted for plantations by the firm), with species such as *Jacaranda copaia*, which in 1982 made up around 20 per cent of its wood supply. Some 1,200 hectares of the forests Jari claims to be protecting are being felled each year (Shell/WWF, 1993), mostly for energy generation and for the expansion of its plantations (Fanzeres, 1995). In 1992, the official national environmental conservation organization, the Brazilian Institute for Environmental Renewal (IBAMA), rejected the company's request to cut 5,000 hectares of dense forest which it wanted to replace with plantations (IBASE, 1993b). The felling of such native forests has resulted not only in loss of native trees but also in loss of habitat for a very large number of other species.

Additional environmental problems centre on the project's continuing reliance on monoculture. Forestry experts never tire of pointing out Jari's serious mistake in choosing gmelina as a plantation species (Bass, 1992a; Shell/WWF, 1993). This 'error', however, is merely one instance of a much more general problem which foresters seem far less eager to acknowledge, and which the current Jari project also exemplifies, namely, that in a large-scale monospecific plantation of any fast-growing species, a fungus, virus, insect or other animal which can find food may well be able to decimate the entire plantation in a short time. Pest infestation, moreover, was only one of the environmental problems afflicting the Jari project. When the gmelina felling rotation was shortened to avoid fungus attacks, nutrients began to be extracted from the soil at a higher rate. It is estimated that most of the potassium and phosphorus will have disappeared from the estate by the end of the twenty-first century (Shell/WWF, 1993). Meanwhile, soil compaction and erosion have resulted from the use of heavy forestry machinery (Bass, 1992a).

Nor has the company shown itself to be particularly concerned about water and aquatic life. Effluents from the plant are eliminated by the simple traditional procedure of dumping them directly into the Jari river. This has resulted in fish kills downriver from the plant. The fertilizers and the agrochemicals used by the company also contaminate local watercourses (Shell/WWF, 1993). Jari's 'environmental answer' to its energy needs, a hydroelectric dam on the Jari river (Knight, 1991; Higgs, 1993), would destroy one of the most beautiful and historic sites of Amapá state, Cachoeira Santo Antonio (Fanzeres, 1995).

The claim that Jari's plantations help alleviate global warming (an argument also used by Aracruz), has been convincingly refuted by scientist Philip Fearnside (1993), who points out that 'the much greater standing biomass of the forest [replaced by Jari] as compared to the plantation means that the effect of Jari is emission rather than removal of atmospheric CO_2'. This means that the CO_2 released through the cutting of the forest to make place for the plantation is more than the CO_2 sequestered by the trees growing in the plantation.

In the social area, Jari is accused of widespread abuse. When it was first set up, the company had to invest in a great deal of social infrastructure in order to attract the large forestry and industrial workforce which was needed. Some 3,000 housing units were built, as well as four schools, a 1,100-bed hospital, clinics, supermarkets, a radio station and 11,000 kilometres of roads (Higgs, 1993). Despite these investments, however, 'work-crew contractors were notorious for their treatment of workers brought in from the poor north-eastern states' (Bass, 1992a). This situation was reflected in a constant turnover of staff at all levels, which reached rates of 200–300 per cent per year (*ibid.*).

After the company changed hands in 1992, new social problems emerged. Between 1988 and 1993 the number of workers fell from 8,000 to 4,500. In the forestry sector, many workers were replaced with machines. Many migrants were thus left unemployed in a region with few other potential employers. In the service sector, meanwhile, the company began to pass the responsibility for hospital, school and restaurant management on to local and federal authorities (Higgs, 1993). In other words, having attracted a large number of workers and their families to the project in its initial stages, Jari then shunted the long-term costs of their welfare on to the state. According to a local journalist, 'the legacy of the Jari project has been a shantytown in the middle of the jungle' (Gonçalves, M.A., 1995).

Riocell

In recent years Riocell has responded to both domestic and foreign environmental pressures with various 'green' claims. For example, Klabin, one of the main shareholders, invites visitors to view company operations 'so they can see for themselves that we are not cutting down the rainforest'. Alfredo Lobl, a Klabin director, has stated that of the 330,000 hectares owned by the company, some 100,000 are preserved as native forests. 'We support environmental education programmes for 18,000 school children', Lobl adds (Marcus, 1993). Another Klabin director, Celso Foelkel, has insisted that 'rather than plant huge tracts of monocultural eucalyptus, the company has tried to integrate its growth as far as possible into the countryside ... nobody can say Riocell has a green desert' (Higgs, 1992c). This last remark seems to imply that other companies (such as Aracruz, Bahia Sul, CENIBRA and Jari), do have 'green deserts'. Riocell, like other Brazilian manufacturers, has also begun to produce non-chlorine-bleached pulp.

These 'environmentalist' initiatives, however, simply make a virtue of commercial necessity and hardly reflect a thoroughgoing commitment to change. It is the difficulty of finding large contiguous tracts of land for planting in Rio Grande do Sul, for example, and not a policy to 'fit into the area', that has forced Riocell into a pattern of dispersed holdings across the region. Similarly, it is pressure from the European market, and not a determination to be socially responsible, that is pushing the company into non-chlorine-bleached pulp. As director Alfred Freund explains: 'We decided to go this way [elemental chlorine-free pulp production] because we're market oriented. Europe's our main market and Germany's important to us' (Higgs, 1992c). To discover where Riocell's priorities really lie, it is necessary to examine other aspects of its record.

When the firm began operating in 1975, it claimed to have invested $100 million in an effluent treatment system. According to environmentalists, however, the company installed a sludge treatment unit only in 1987 (AGAPAN, 1992). In 1992, it was still being accused of dumping more than 60 tonnes of organochloride compounds yearly into the Guaiba river, which provides the drinking water for Porto Alegre (Schinke, 1992a).

That same year, facing heavy opposition from environmentalists and others in its attempt to secure official approval to double its production capacity, Riocell apparently tried to bribe a local government official who opposed the expansion (Schinke, 1992 a,b). When this did not work, the company went on to tell the state governor that if he did not approve the project, the company would move to another state. The governor finally passed the project when the state government received a $170 million loan from the Inter-American Development Bank for the decontamination of the Guaiba river basin (Schinke, 1992b). Interestingly, Riocell had financed several studies at the local university which showed that fish bred in water contaminated with effluent from the plant had developed serious genetic abnormalities (AGAPAN, 1992).

Conclusions

Corporations are not philanthropists: their business is making profits. This results in a contradiction with the concept of sustainable development. This is made clear in a statement by Aracruz chief executive Luiz Kaufmann, who states that: 'We share the opinion that the main responsibility of a company is to generate wealth through investment, carrying out its activities in harmony with nature and society.' Unable to solve the implied contradiction between 'creating wealth' and 'harmony with nature and society', he admits that 'before any other consideration a company must generate profits and cash flow to guarantee its own growth and survival, and adequately remunerate its shareholders' (Kaufmann, 1996).

That is exactly what all five companies discussed in this chapter do. During the first phase of their activities, they concentrated on trying to reduce investment costs. This meant externalizing as many costs as possible, using their power for that purpose. Their political and economic strength allowed them not only to obtain subsidies from the state, but also to have the state's coercive power on their side against local people's opposition. Externalization of environmental impacts was also made possible by the state's willingness to turn a blind eye to the companies' activities.

Corporate environmental concerns only surfaced once the companies began to make profits, which allowed them to make 'green' investments to curb some of their more polluting activities (for example, industrial effluents). But even when they went into the black, two other conditions were necessary for corporations to take such steps: strong social pressure, either from customers abroad or from local organized citizens' groups; and approval and enforcement of strict environmental legislation.

Of these conditions, the first seems to have been the more important. Most of the companies' commitments on environmental protection constitute an answer to customer concerns and, to a lesser extent, local pressures. Such is the case with the issue of the use of chlorine gas which pulp companies are being forced to phase out. Legislation, when it exists, has seldom been enforced; when it has, it has usually been with the approval of the corporations (for example, when patches of native forests have been conserved). In cases where pressures have not been sufficiently strong – and even when legislation exists – the companies have continued to externalize impacts, as is reflected in the attempt by the Tupinikim and Guarani to get their lands back from Aracruz.

When environmental or social concerns put the companies' future at stake, they tend to use their strength to misinform the public. For example, they cannot accept that their large-scale tree plantations have equally large impacts on the environment and on society, because that would jeopardize their activity as a whole. They therefore resort to public relations exercises aimed at convincing the uninformed public that plantations are good for the environment. Instead of trying to find an equitable solution to the indigenous land issue, Aracruz hired a well-known US public relations company, Burson-Marsteller, to counteract the international campaign launched by the Tupinikim and Guarani Indians.

Rain forest conservation and environmental protection have become catchwords for many customers and therefore the companies must not only sell a product, but the product must also contain an answer to those concerns. The potential profits lost through the non-exploitation of rain forests, for instance, allow them to make more profits by selling an 'environmentally friendly product'. Yet the analysis presented in this chapter shows that, in spite of their stated policies, the activities of all five corporations have resulted in important negative impacts – both social and environmental – in the regions where they operate. One reason is simply the large scale of their operations, which results in equally large-scale impacts.

The main question, therefore, is not whether these companies are truly committed to work in 'harmony with nature and society' – they are not – but whether this is, in fact, possible. It is extremely difficult for a large-scale, profit-oriented company to adapt without heavy and constant public pressure to the logic of sustainable development, and even less so if the concept also includes 'social equity'. If the negative impacts of corporate activities can be curtailed, it is through a combination of pressure from citizens' groups and government enforcement of environmental legislation. This combination forces corporations to invest money which they would not have invested otherwise. Only then does such investment begin to make sense from a market perspective.

The introduction to this chapter noted three possible alternatives for corporations: (1) 'business as usual', disguised under an environmental and socially concerned discourse; (2) real environmental and social responsibility; and (3) a blend of the first two alternatives. Analysis of the activities of the main companies in the Brazilian market pulp industry leads to the conclusion that none of these firms can be classified under the second alternative. Rather, all of them fall under the third, with some much nearer to the first than to the second. Although it seems *prima facie* almost impossible for these corporations – given the large scale of their operations, the political power they wield and the profit motive that drives them – to carry out their activities while treating environment and society with proper respect, they will respond to pressures from society and governments aimed at mitigating some of their worst practices. The general conclusion, however, is that large-scale investments such as these are incompatible with both environmental protection and social equity.

It is therefore extremely important to go beyond the question of whether corporations are committed or not to environmental protection and to analyse seriously the issue of pulp and paper production and consumption. The current pattern of production in the South (large-scale fast-growth monoculture tree plantations, large pulp mills), aimed at supplying an ever increasing consumption of paper in the North, is proving to be unsustainable. It seems necessary, therefore, to downgrade the size of the pulp mills and to diversify raw materials used in pulp production, adapting the mills to a variety of resources available at the local level. At the same time, Northern countries must acknowledge that paper consumption cannot grow indefinitely and that already unsustainable current consumption patterns are affecting people's livelihoods in Southern countries.

Notes

1 The term 'market pulp' refers to pulp which is produced as a commodity to be traded on the open market. This chapter deals specifically with the Brazilian market pulp industry, which does not include vertically integrated paper companies which produce pulp primarily as an input for their paper production.

References

Aracruz Cellulose (1996a), 'Aracruz Cellulose and Sustainable Eucalyptus Pulp Production. Questions & Answers', Corporate Communications, Rio de Janeiro, March.

—— (1996b),' Harvesting: Mechanized, Safer and More Efficient', *Aracruz News* 4 (2), May.

—— (1996c), 'Monitoring the Marine Surroundings', *Aracruz News* 4 (2), May.

—— (1997a), 'Facts about Aracruz', *Aracruz News* 7 (3), May.

—— (1997b), *Facts & Figures 1997*, Aracruz.

—— (1997c), 'Nature: The Best Ally for Pest Control', *Aracruz News* 8 (3), July.

Associação Brasileira de Exportadores de Celulose (ABECEL) (undated), 'Cultura do eucalipto pela indústria brasileira exportadora de Celulose'.

Associação Gaúcha de Proteção do Ambiente Natural (AGAPAN) (1992), 'Dioxins from Pulpmill: South Brazil' in haz.pulpmills electronic conference, 11 February.

Bass, Stephen (1992a), 'Building From The Past: Forest Plantations in History', in C. Sargent and S. Bass (eds.), *Plantation Politics: Forest Plantations in Development*, Earthscan, London.

—— (1992b), 'Corporate Plantations Aiming for Sustainability: Aracruz Cellulose', in Sargent and Bass (Box 4.2).

Centro de Defesa dos Direitos Humanos (CDDH) (1993), 'Eucalipto-celulose. Desenvolvimento para quem?', CDDH, Texeira de Freitas-BA.

Centro de Estudos e Pesquisas para o Desenvolvimento do Extremo Sul da Bahia/Centro de Defesa dos Direitos Humanos (CEPEDES/CDDH) (1992), 'Eucalipto: uma contradição, impactos ambientais, sociais e económicos do eucalipto e da celulose no Extremo Sul da Bahia', CDDH, Eunápolis-BA.

Environmental Value Fund (EVF) (1997), 'The Storebrand Scudder Environmental Value Fund's Position on Aracruz Cellulose SA', ms.

Executive Commission of the Tupinikim and Guaraní/Conselho Indigenista Misionario Leste (ECTG/CIMI) (1996), 'International Campaign for the Extension and Demarcation of the Indigenous Lands of the Tupinikim and Guaraní', ECTG/CIMI, Aracruz, August.

Fanzeres, Anna (1995), personal communication.

Fearnside, Philip M. (1993), 'Tropical Silvicultural Plantations as a Means of Sequestering Atmospheric Carbon Dioxide', ms, Manaus, 29 June.

Federação de Orgaos para Assistência Social e Educacional (FASE) (1993), 'Inquerito civil sobre fomento florestal', FASE, Vitória.

Gonçalves, Múcio Tostá et al. (1994), 'Exploração florestal no norte do es e sul da Bahia – impactos e alternativas. Estudio de caso: exploração florestal, indústria de celulose e ocupação do espaço regional. Relatório final', FASE/IBASE, Rio de Janeiro, May.

Gonçalves, Múcio Tosta (1995), 'Pau que nasce certo e entorta a vida dos outros: Monocultura de eucalipto e produção de celulose no Vale do Aço', Comissão Pastoral da Terra/Centro Mineiro de Estudos e Pesquisa sobre Ambiente e Florestas/Pacific-Asia Resource Center, Belo Horizonte.

Gonçalves, Marco Antonio (1995), 'Fábrica de papel desencadeia crise no Amapá : Champion adquire fatia da floresta amazônica', *Parabólicas* 2 (12), November.

Guerra, Claudio (1992), 'A Case Study in Brazil: Environmental Impacts on the Piracicaba River Basin', International Institute for Hydraulic and Environmental Engineering, Delft, August.

Higgs, Richard (1992a), 'Bahia Debut', paper, September.

—— (1992b), 'Brazil's Japanese Connection', paper, September.

—— (1992c), 'Riocell: Growing Fast', paper, September.

—— (1993), 'Jarí: The Mill in the Jungle', paper, August.

Instituto Brasileiro de Análises Sociais e Económicas (IBASE) (1993a), 'Cronologia sobre a indústria de celulose no Brasil', in for.plantation electronic conference, 6 November.

—— (1993b), 'Cronologia sobre a indústria de celulose no Brasil' in for.plantation electronic conference, 3 March.

—— (1994), 'Cronologia sobre a indústria de celulose no Brasil', in for.plantation electronic conference, 10 October.

International Institute for Environment and Development (IIED) (1995), 'The Sustainable Paper Cycle: A report for the Business Council on Sustainable Development', draft, IIED, London.

Inyaku, Tomoya (1993), 'Why Brazilian Pulp Is Cheap', in for.paper (APC electronic conference) 22 April.

Japan Tropical Forest Action Network (JATAN) (1992), 'Report on Eucalyptus Plantation Schemes: Investment Activities by Japan's Paper Industry in Brazil and Chile', JATAN, Tokyo.

—— (1993), 'Report on Eucalyptus Plantation Schemes in Brazil and Chile by Japanese Companies', JATAN, Tokyo.

Kaufmann, Luiz (1996), 'Message from the CEO', *Aracruz News* 4 (2), May.

Knight, Patrick (1991), 'Brazil: A Growing Force in World Pulp and Paper', P & PA, August.

Marcus, Amanda (1993), Klabin enjoys lead role among Latins, PPI, November.

Miranda, Moema (1992), 'O extremo sul da Bahia e a avassaladora chegada da modernidade. II relatório de viagem ao extremo sul da Bahia', FASE/IBASE, Rio de Janeiro, October.

—— (1993a), 'Indios reivindicam suas terras', in for.plantation (APC electronic conference) 14 July.

—— (1993b), 'Nas pontas do extremo: outras histórias, outros tempos', FASE/IBASE, Rio de Janeiro, April.

Sargent, Caroline and Stephen Bass (eds.) (1992), *Plantation Politics: Forest Plantations in Development*, Earthscan, London.

Schmidheiny, Stephan, with the Business Council for Sustainable Development (BCSD) (1992), *Changing Course: A Global Business Perspective on Development and the Environment*, MIT Press, Cambridge, Mass.

Shell International Petroleum Company and World Wide Fund for Nature (1993), *Tree Plantation Review*, 11 Vols., Shell/WWF, London.

Sindicato dos Trabalhadores nas Indústrias de Papel, Celulose, Pasta de Madeira para Papel, Papelão e Cortiça de Aracruz (SINTICEL) (1997), letter, 8 May.

Schinke, Gert (1992a), 'Alerto: Riocell escandalo', in haz.pulpmills (APC electronic conference), 12 June.

—— (1992b), 'Brazil Pulp Mill Scandal', in haz.pulpmills (APC electronic conference), 10 June.

Valarelli, Leandro Lamas (1992), 'Complexos Florestais de Celulose: O Mito da Modernidade', *Proposta*, 53 (May).

5 Corporate Environmental Responsibility in Singapore and Malaysia

The Potential and Limits of Voluntary Initiatives

MARTIN PERRY and SANJEEV SINGH

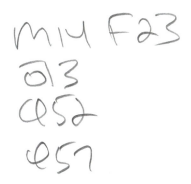

Introduction

The neighbouring South East Asian countries of Singapore and Malaysia have contrasting environmental reputations. The small city state of Singapore, with a population of 4 million and a population density of 6,150 per sq. km, is often seen as a model green city. That reputation rests partly on its efforts to control urban congestion and pollution as well as the retention of green landscapes within the built environment. Malaysia, on the other hand, with a total population of around 20 million distributed between the comparatively urbanized peninsula and the less developed states of Sabah and Sarawak, has a poor environmental image. Deforestation, loss of biodiversity and the marginalization of indigenous populations in resource management decisions account for much of that negative image.

The real comparative environmental performance is a good deal harder to judge than immediate impressions suggest, not the least as Malaysia's GDP per capita is a third of Singapore's. On current income, Singapore ranks amongst the world's top ten richest countries. Its elevation to this group has been rapid but Singapore has yet to accept officially the status of developed country. That mantle would bring economic implications and international obligations, potentially including responsibilities under the climate change convention. Government reticence aside, Singapore's affluence arguably makes Western expectations of environmental responsibility a relevant performance benchmark, particularly as its economy is built on the investment of foreign transnationals. Malaysia, on the other hand, is still managing a transition to industrial society. Around a quarter of the workforce are employed in agriculture and nearly half the population live outside urban areas. Malaysian law makers have demonstrated a willingness to strengthen environmental protection. High-income status may yet be achieved with a greater proportion of its land area designated as protected natural environment than found in many older industrial nations. This may be a reasonable expectation, however, given the ecological significance of tropical forests.

Advocacy of corporate 'voluntary' environmental initiatives – understood as any actions taken to reduce environmental impacts and promote awareness of

97

environmental impacts that have not been required by government regulation – to strengthen environmental management can be justified in Singapore and Malaysia, although for different reasons. Singapore is the regional headquarters for many transnationals with branch establishments across South East Asia (Perry *et al.*, 1997). Demands to demonstrate a strong environmental commitment within Singapore, especially where this extends to the ecological footprint of business organizations, may accelerate the potential environmental leadership role that transnational corporations can play. As a 'developmental state', the priority has been to maximize immediate economic opportunities and to protect business organizations from scrutiny by NGOs or the wider community. Consequently, although *per capita* incomes now exceed those of many older industrial countries, interest in environmental responsibility lags behind that which might be expected on the basis of Western experience.

Malaysia has experienced a greater growth of environmental concern than Singapore, at least judged by the activity of environmental NGOs that are seeking to apply informal pressure on corporate and regulator behaviour (CAP and SAM, 1996; Harding, 1996; Gonzalez *et al.*, 2000; Salleh, 2000). Surveillance by international pressure groups is also significant for resource-based industry and this adds to the pressure for voluntary environmental initiatives. Rising incomes, a significant presence of foreign transnationals and official acceptance of local environmental pressure groups give reasons to believe that voluntary improvement will play an increasing role in Malaysia. That likelihood is further increased by the World Bank's efforts to promote informal regulation, involving various forms of community pressures on business to improve environmental performance, and other new ways of making environmental policy (World Bank, 2000).

The influences that encourage voluntary environmental initiatives, the type of action taken and the extent to which it may substitute for other forms of environmental regulation form the basis for the discussion that follows. It commences with a review of the motivations thought to encourage voluntary behaviour over other ways of promoting environmental improvement. The extent to which such action should be seen as an alternative to governmental regulation is then discussed, noting, amongst other issues, that voluntary action is often closely related to regulatory enforcement. The discussion then turns to a review of corporate voluntary environmental initiatives in Singapore and Malaysia, including original survey results from a sample of foreign-owned TNCs in both countries. The concluding section comments upon the significance of the voluntary action observed in Singapore and Malaysia.

Corporate Greening

TNCs have given environmental issues more coherent and active attention than previously but it remains doubtful that this indicates a permanent and substantial shift in management practice. Corporate environmentalism in older industrial countries is being encouraged by economic, political and industrial organization attributes. Economic conditions support acceptance of increased environmental responsibilities if there are opportunities to obtain market benefits and production cost savings. The existence of a 'win–win' situation has been widely speculated upon but, as discussed further below, the ability to profit from investment in environmental improvement may be less than initial optimism suggested. Political advantage arises where organizations perceive opportunity to accommodate the environmental challenge and use their responsiveness as evidence of their progressive responsibility (Levy, 1997). Industrial organization influences environmental investment partly in the way that individual firms must exert influence on their suppliers and contractors or themselves come under pressure from customers to improve environmental performance. An organization seeking to upgrade performance must ensure that suppliers and contractors support its investment; otherwise the risk of 'contamination by association' can be a major disincentive to action. Globalization and the growth of 'buyer driven commodity chains' (Gereffi, 1994) in many labour-intensive consumer goods industries have accentuated this constraint. Such commodity chains rely on tightly specified contracting relations between independent companies, but the enforcement of contracting conditions among organizations of varying capacities and experiences is often difficult (Utting, 2000).

The form that corporate environmentalism takes can be linked to different motives for taking action. Three broad motives may be differentiated, each associated with characteristic actions (Table 5.1): to gain strategic advantage; to avoid strategic disadvantage; to act responsibly (Eden, 1996; Bansal, 1997). When these motives and strategies are considered, the long-term commitment of TNCs to voluntary environmental initiatives is questioned.

Table 5.1
Motives for and Constraints on Corporate Greening

Motive	Action	Limitation
Strategic	Green marketing Clean technology	Consumer advantage Economic return Industrial modernization
Avoiding disadvantage	Certification Codes of conduct Supply chain relations	Public trust Industry commitment Legislation
Acting responsibly	Triple bottom line	Stakeholder management

Strategic advantage

Many organizations have come to believe that there is profit to be made from 'green business'. At the most immediate level it is often claimed that being environmentally cleaner can bring cost savings. Pollution prevention pays where there are readily available opportunities to save resources and clean-up costs, and to recycle materials at lower cost than using all new materials. Beyond cost savings, there is the possibility of increasing market share by making 'environmentally friendly' products or developing new products on the basis of their environmental advantages. Presenting the organization as environmentally sensitive may offer ways of enhancing reputation through acquiring a positive image, obtaining good publicity and encouraging customer loyalty. The long-term benefits obtained from this may include better recruitment of young staff who are perceived to be particularly attracted to companies with progressive environmental reputations.

The sustainability of green corporatism motivated by strategic advantage will be influenced by the extent to which competitive advantage is realized. Consumer survey evidence frequently indicates that there is an increased willingness to pay for environmental improvements but actual expressions of this tend to be most evident in a limited range of household products, such as detergents, paper and certain food items. Early optimism about the profitability of green marketing is generally not being fulfilled. Even where governments have contributed to the promotion of 'green' products their sales have often been low (Eden, 1996: 9). Although in market research surveys people express preferences for 'clean' products, it is not clear that they will act on those preferences or necessarily believe that a 'green label' is a reliable indicator of a product's qualities (Esty *et al.*, 2000: 83). Similarly, just how far the corporate world can go with 'eco-efficiency' is a matter of increasing contention. Some claim big opportunities exist (Porter and van der Linde, 1995; Flavin and Tunali, 1996) while others are sceptical about the extent of win–win opportunities (Jaffe *et al.*, 1995). In the case of newly industrializing economies, the growth of capital-intensive manufacturing may be at the expense of homegrown producers with methods adapted to local resource conditions. In the case of the pulp industry in South East Asia, for example, industrial modernization results in fewer and more capital-intensive producers that make less use of locally recycled inputs than the producers they displace (Sonnenfeld, 1999).

Avoiding disadvantage

Companies may voluntarily raise their environmental standards because of perceived threats in not doing so. One aspect of this may be to match the behaviour of competitors so as to avoid placing themselves at a strategic disadvantage. This disadvantage may be a loss of market share if the strategies of competitors prove effective or it may be a loss of reputation or standing. The impact of poor publicity can be seen directly in the reaction of individual company share prices to good and bad environmental news (see World Bank 2000: 61). The evidence of this relationship is greatest where there is bad publicity. Indeed environmental transgressions can be more damaging indirectly, through their impact on equity values and reputation, than directly through the financial penalties that may be imposed by regulators (Piesse, 1992). Eden (1996) quotes survey evidence that over two thirds of companies see environmental issues as threats 'requiring defensive or corrective actions' rather than as providing new market opportunities.

When the goal is to avoid disadvantage, the motive for corporate environmentalism is partly to deflect or pre-empt new legislation. To deter demands for legislation, TNC self-regulation needs to attain a high degree of credibility. This is far from straightforward as in many countries businesses sustain lower levels of public trust than many other institutions (Simmons and Wynne, 1993; Eden, 1996). Previous efforts to pre-empt regulation by industry self-regulation have frequently failed because compliance to voluntary codes has been weak (Roht-Arriaza, 1995: 534).

Acting responsibly

The above motivations lead to voluntary environmental actions that are to varying degrees the incidental by-product of profit-driven actions. Other pressures on business that have less immediate linkage to profit or returns on investment are adding to the acceptance of larger environmental responsibilities than in the past (Patten, 1991). This is frequently discussed in terms of the need for business to establish legitimacy in the eyes of consumers, the public at large and government – legitimacy being defined as a 'generalized perception or assumption that the actions of an entity are desirable, proper, or appropriate' (Suchman, 1995: 574).

Beyond the need to keep pace with changes in what society perceives to be acceptable, environmentally sensitive business organizations are facing new demands to demonstrate their legitimacy as their global reach increases (Grolin, 1998; Rodgers, 2000). This argument perceives that the legitimacy conferred by national governments through regulation, law making and representation of public opinion has lessened due to the political emphasis on deregulation and the internationalization of business activity. In this vacuum, corporate business has been under pressure to find new sources of legitimacy. This need affects all aspects of global business but especially environmental performance because of the high profile and scientific uncertainty of environmental issues, as well as public scepticism about the effectiveness of government regulations (Jacobs, 1997: 56). To bolster its reputation, corporate business is being encouraged to seek the acceptance and endorsement of major stakeholder groups, giving rise to so-called 'extended stakeholder management'. To keep this dialogue within manageable proportions, partnerships between business corporations and environmental NGOs have become one method of implementing extended stakeholder management (Lober, 1997).

The extent to which engagement with stakeholders will continue to be viewed as worthwhile is uncertain. Corporate engagement with environmental NGOs is partly predicated on the belief that this will contain adversarial relations with NGOs and that partnerships can be confined to specific issues rather than the overall environmental performance of the business (Murphy and Bendell, 1997). Both outlooks run into conflict with the expectations of environmental NGOs, particularly those with the greatest capacity to confer legitimacy based on their wide networks and accountability to constituencies in society (Rodgers, 2000: 47). More generally, it has been argued that self-regulation has doubtful capacity to increase the legitimization of business environmental practices (Eden, 1996: 122). The chemical industry's code of practice 'Responsible Care' illustrates this in the case of a sector that arguably has particular need to retain public confidence in view of its pollution intensity. Responsible Care requires that adherents seek to match best practice environmental management and to assist other chemical companies to do likewise. Part of this involves increased information transparency. Even so, it has been argued that this has not reduced the legitimacy gap faced by the chemical industry (Simmons and Wynne, 1993). Responsible Care has left unaltered the public perception that chemical companies selectively release information about their environmental impacts and have greater influence over government than does the public at large.

Voluntary Environmental Initiatives and Self-Regulation

Across many areas of social concern there has long been a debate about the desirability of voluntary compliance as an alternative to government regulation (Hawkins, 1990; Petts, 2000). This discussion can exaggerate the independence of separate approaches and overlook the variability of command and control regulation. Enforcement mechanisms, for example, may stress prevention and consultation or they may stress enforcement, including severe penalties for transgressing regulation. Advocates of voluntary environmental management have now joined this debate, adding their criticism of command and control regulation.

In environmental matters, advocates of voluntary approaches suggest that there are efficiency gains in giving industry choice over their investment in environmental improvement, and less need for monitoring and enforcement agencies than where mandatory standards are imposed. In addition, the flexibility to determine its own standards and priorities is said to make business more positive about improvement than where regulation enforces specific actions. To the extent that voluntary regulation does not depend on legislation and political agreement, moreover, it can be enacted quickly and maintain responsiveness to current problems. In practice, voluntary action can be closely dependent on regulatory enforcement for three reasons: (1) participation in so-called voluntary initiatives is frequently determined by the efforts of third parties, including government regulators; (2) government regulation may form a benchmark against which voluntary efforts are designed; (3) conversion of voluntary measures into legislation is possible and not necessarily opposed by 'first movers'.

Third party involvement

Voluntary environmental initiatives have grown partly because government is influencing their design and implementation. In other words, a good deal of the activity classed as voluntary environmental improvement is not purely self-motivated. Public agencies encourage the willingness to participate by establishing frameworks or institutions that variously help to develop, administer or verify voluntary initiatives. Voluntary action has also been a reaction to government efforts to publicize voluntary initiatives and threats to strengthen regulation in the absence of voluntary improvement (Gouldson and Murphy, 1998). A Canadian study, for example, identified four reasons for 'voluntary' action: (1) the threat of regulation; (2) public concern and industry perception that public image affects business; (3) financial advantage, through the direct returns from environmental improvement and improved standing with financial agencies; (4) peer pressure, especially that transmitted through industry associations (Labatt and Maclaren 1998).

A potentially diverse and incoherent range of voluntary environmental initiatives tends in practice to be highly ordered because of the influence of external agencies in encouraging action. A threefold distinction summarizes much voluntary activity: (1) self-regulation; (2) voluntary agreements; and (3) voluntary challenge (Labatt and Maclaren, 1998). Self-regulation comprises action initiated by individual businesses or industry associations, as in the form of voluntary codes of practice (UNCTAD, 1996). Voluntary agreements involve some form of partnership between business, either individually or through their industry association, and government agencies or environmental campaign groups (Murphy and Bendell, 1997). Under the voluntary challenge, most of the initiative for developing, disseminating and monitoring lies with government rather than industry. Government presents the scheme as a challenge to a target community, possibly including a specified time and standard to be complied with. For example, challenges for specified reductions in toxic chemical releases or reductions in packaging may be given to groups of companies. An East Asian example is the PROKASIH (Clean Rivers) programme introduced in Indonesia in 1989 that is credited with eliciting substantial pollution reduction from industrial plants in 11 provinces and 23 river basins (Afsah *et al.*, 1996). PROKASIH covered about 5 per cent of Indonesian manufacturing facilities but was conceived as a prelude to formal comprehensive regulation (Pargal *et al.*, 1997).

Regulation as a benchmark

Mandatory targets and regulatory controls are often an important reference point for voluntary action (Gouldson and Murphy, 1998). For example one of the concerns expressed by business in complying with certified environmental management standards is the uncertainty as to appropriate improvement targets (Netherwood, 1996). Progressive businesses may be prepared to exceed regulatory minimum standards but a framework of regulatory standards and systems may be looked to as a performance benchmark. A statutory benchmark is needed, for example, to capture reputation advantages from behaviour that exceeds the compliance standard. In addition, government agencies may devise and monitor voluntary programmes. As noted above, the threat of regulation is frequently cited as a prime motive for participation in voluntary initiatives. It is important, therefore, that voluntary initiatives are recognized by government regulators if they are to forestall mandatory controls.

Relationship to mandatory regulation

Business participation in voluntary action is frequently to curtail mandatory regulation but it is doubtful that it ultimately persuades government not to act or that business necessarily have this as their intention (Roht-Arriaza, 1995; Eden, 1996). In industrial countries, the pressure to initiate, integrate and strengthen environmental regulation is strong. This pressure diffuses to newly industrializing economies through concern to maintain access to industrial markets and through obligations under international environmental agreements (Deans, 1998; Esty et al., 2000). In this context, voluntary action is more likely to delay new regulation rather than entirely displace it. Nonetheless there is still an incentive to be a 'first mover' as it can provide opportunity to influence the form that regulation takes as well as minimizing the risk of being non-compliant when mandatory controls are introduced. Furthermore, statutory enforcement may not be opposed as it reduces the opportunity for competitors to free-ride on the environmental initiatives of progressive organizations.

Corporate Voluntary Initiatives in Singapore and Malaysia

Singapore and Malaysia responded to deteriorating environmental conditions in the 1970s primarily through command and control regulation. Positive results were obtained from these measures. In Singapore, comprehensive regulatory standards and investment in environmental infrastructure has enabled the city state to maintain economic growth and promote itself as a 'clean, green city' (Ministry of Environment, 1992). Statutory requirements for environmental impact assessment (EIA) in respect of significant development projects are a strength of Malaysian regulation (Markandya and Shibli, 1995). This has increased the prior investigation of potentially serious impacts. Perhaps more importantly, EIAs provide opportunity for third parties to challenge proposals initiated or endorsed by government agencies (see case study of Penang Hill in Harding, 1996). This is important in Malaysia because government is often closely involved in development projects that have serious environmental impacts, such as the Bakun Dam (Rasiah, 1999: 33). As well as impact assessment, a much-cited Malaysian success has been the clean-up of the palm oil industry. Although sometimes presented as evidence of the effectiveness of market-based incentives (Markandya and Shibli, 1995), the reduction in organic pollution was ultimately achieved through strict enforcement of mandatory standards (World Bank, 2000: 44).

In both countries, the tightening of standards and extension of regulatory controls has been a more important response to new concerns and gaps in original environmental controls than investment in alternative environmental management strategies, either in the form of economic instruments or voluntary initiatives. Environmental policy in Malaysia and Singapore is influenced by dependence on international trade and foreign direct investment (Bankoff and Elston, 1994). This has introduced Western environmental expectations to both countries with standards above those demanded by domestic regulation. There is a concern that standards in Western markets will be converted into *de facto* non-tariff barriers. Governments have encouraged voluntary responses, recognizing that higher standards across the board would disadvantage those businesses not exposed to international pressure. This is seen in the help given to obtain ISO 14001 certification of environmental management systems with assistance targeted on exporters and suppliers to TNCs (Zarsky and Tay, 2000: 150). Comparatively high levels of certification have thus been achieved in South East Asia, although not to the levels predicted by the earlier diffusion of ISO 9000 certification for quality management systems (Table 5.2). Before assessing the significance of this and other voluntary actions, we briefly review environmental issues in Singapore and Malaysia.

Table 5.2
ISO 14001 Certifications in South East Asia

Country	Number of certified organizations July 2000	Number expected by the end of 1999 based on ISO 9000 uptakes
Malaysia	175	700
Singapore	87	120
Thailand	283	140
Indonesia	77	125
Philippines	53	100

Source: ISOworld, 2000; Tanner et al., 1997

Environmental Issues in Singapore

The Singapore government's environmental management has been driven by economic considerations (Bankoff and Elston, 1994). This has resulted in the enforcement of comprehensive land use and emissions standards, as well as invest-ment in environmental infrastructure. The primary purpose of this intervention has been to maximize economic activity and population within the small city state. A tendency to equate a clean environment with a green environment is an indicator of this, as in the Ministry of Environment-sponsored annual 'Clean and Green Week', that tends to emphasize activities such as waste removal from beaches and anti-littering campaigns. Substantial gaps can be identified in Singapore's environmental performance, as indicated by five issues.

First, environmental legislation omits a commitment to a formal EIA process, in contrast to other South East Asian countries (Briffett, 1996). Government unwillingness to introduce EIA reflects concerns about its potential to delay or inhibit economic development, increase costs and introduce 'extraneous issues' into the development process. Rather than a transparent and contestable decision-making process, develop-ment decisions are made internally by state development agencies and senior ministers (Bankoff and Elston, 1994). Advocates of EIA suggest that its absence has stifled public debate about the environment and has resulted in inadequate attention being given to environmental considerations (Hesp, 1995; Hilton and Manning, 1995).

Second, the 'green initiatives' fostered by the government's environmental agencies have not incorporated ecological principles. For example, the Nature Society has criticized the areas selected as nature reserves, noting that most are of no ecological significance while locations important to migratory wildlife and endemic species have been taken for development (Hesp, 1995: 139). Similarly parks and roadside planting of trees give a green appearance, but the vegetation is typically exotic and unhelpful to native fauna (Corlett, 1992).

Third, public environmental consciousness over issues such as product recycling, green consumerism and ecological awareness is low. Surveys of environmental behaviour among Singaporean students and women have shown that Singaporeans are generally ignorant of and resistant to incorporating environmental protection in everyday life by minimizing domestic waste, using recycling bins or buying environmentally friendly products (Lau, 1993; Ng, 1994; Savage, 1995).

Fourth, Singapore's public and private agencies have been slow to develop an environmental leadership role in the region, despite the island's economic wealth and trade and investment linkages to neighbouring countries. The widespread destruction of tropical rain forest in Indonesia through illegal land clearance has been one such opportunity, particularly as Singapore investors are involved in many of the illegal operations (Harwell, 2000: 316). Singapore has supported declarations by the Association of South East Asian Nations (ASEAN) and provided remote imaging technology to help monitor the outbreak of fires, but this has done little to stem the unfolding environmental disaster (Shepherd, 1997). Similarly, although Singapore has a major stake in the shipping and petroleum industries, it has done less than Japan to promote marine environment initiatives in the region (Chia, 1995).

Fifth, business in Singapore has tended to view regulatory compliance as the extent of its responsibility. An investigation of business awareness of and investment in clean technology concluded that 'the public and private sectors in Singapore are not aware of cleaner production concepts' (Tay, 1995: 421). It was found that local companies viewed environmental issues as a major deterrent to profit generation and typically lacked the information, resources, technology and labour needed to adopt clean production. Foreign TNCs showed greater awareness and commitment to environmental management than local companies, mainly because of the need to meet the expectations of corporate management. This research suggested that introducing stringent effluent and emission regulations would be the most effective way of advancing cleaner production, as well as offering financial incentives to companies that exceed regulation requirements.

These performance gaps arise partly from the absence of community interest in environmental issues. The island's limited land area and near total loss of natural environment has reduced awareness of development–environment conflicts. Even so, environmental concerns have been one of the few issues on which there has been organized community action to oppose government proposals (Perry *et al.*, 1997). A further and perhaps more important explanation, therefore, is the government's tight control of information.

Since independence (1965), a People's Action Party (PAP) government has retained a monopoly of political control. The PAP has used its dominance to curtail opposition to its policies and to build an 'oligarchic elite' that has 'merged government, state structures and para-political organizations, and has co-opted and sponsored civil society actors' (Gomez, 1999: 1). Citizen participation in issues that pose immediate development threats to the city state, such as waste generation and water consumption, is solicited, but larger environmental activism has not been encouraged. Such activism might challenge government preferences to accelerate population growth (from the present 4 million to near 6 million) and oppose plans to increase investment in pollution-intensive petrochemical industries. It might also bring demands for greater action on regional environmental issues that would compromise the government's reluctance to criticize neighbouring governments. At present, PAP claims about its effective management of environmental issues and the necessity of its development strategies go largely unchallenged. An exception is the Singapore Nature Society, which has instigated a number of successful campaigns to protect areas of importance to wildlife. It remains as one of the few active NGOs, although cooption of senior members has muted its voice in recent years. More generally, the political environment has acted against the development of a vocal middle class concerned about environmental or other public matters in Singapore (Jones and Brown, 1994; Perry et al., 1997). Green label products, for example, have met little consumer interest even amongst the affluent (Wong, 1997).

Stakeholder groups also tend to be reluctant to campaign for greater business accountability. In comparison with the role played by the International Chamber of Commerce in promoting environmental best practice in Europe and North America (Hansen and Gleckman, 1993; Brophy and Starkey, 1996), the Singapore International Chamber of Commerce has not taken up environmental causes on the grounds of lack of interest among its members (Teng, 1997). The Singapore Confederation of Industry did promote a revised version of the International Chamber of Commerce's Business Charter for Sustainable Development. The Singapore version omits eight clauses, including the one which calls for companies to report annually on their environmental performance and progress. The Confederation believed that disclosure would be seen as a threat, especially among Chinese-owned business that operate with a tradition of secrecy and person-to-person communication rather than written declarations and formal agreements (Teng, 1997). The Singapore Environment Council, a government-supported NGO with a remit to promote environmental awareness in the community and among business, has in recent years sought to foster business environmental responsibility. Its principal tool has been an annual Singapore Environmental Achievement Award given to an individual company demonstrating proactive environmental responsibility.

The absence of community interest and influence removes a potentially important source of pressure on companies. Investment in environmental responsibility is deterred where there is little return in terms of status within the community or among consumers. On the other hand, because of the strong presence of foreign TNCs in the Singapore economy, corporate pressure on Singapore subsidiaries and affiliates can be an important stimulant of voluntary action. This dual context can be seen in three sources of evidence about the incidence of voluntary environmental initiatives: (1) corporate environmental reporting; (2) ISO 14001 policy statements; (3) responsible care.

Environmental reporting

The voluntary reporting of environmental impacts and initiatives in company annual reports has become widespread amongst organizations accepting an obligation to extend their environmental responsibilities beyond regulatory compliance (Collier, 1995; Brophy and Starkey, 1996). A review of annual reports produced by 264 publicly listed companies in Singapore (all those with operations in Singapore) for the financial years 1995/6 and 1996/7 found that 6.5 per cent of companies made reference to the environment in both years (Perry and Teng, 1998). The content of disclosure was minimal. Two thirds of the reports with environmental references had no more than two sentences of comment. In terms of the space occupied, the most extensive reporting was by two companies that reported in both years with over ten sentences of information (a property company, DBS Land, and a car distribution company, Cycle and Carriage). Neither case included any data relating to environmental impacts.

A follow-up survey that obtained a 30 per cent response from non-disclosing companies (66 out of 221) and a 45 per cent response from disclosing companies (14 out of 31) found three main reasons for the absence of significant environmental disclosure: (1) a perception that their organization had no environmental impacts; (2) a lack of perceived benefit, either in status with consumers or within the business community; (3) lack of pressure from the government. Government direction to disclose environmental information was identified as the influence most likely to cause a change of practice.

Government has not sought to encourage disclosure, partly from the perspective that ISO 14001 is a greater priority, and calls for disclosure are seen as a deterrent to environmental certification. For the present, the absence of any cases approaching a serious commitment to disclosure is perhaps a more significant indicator of environmental apathy than the overall low disclosure rate. Singapore's public companies are small compared with the organizations that have invested most in environmental reporting. On the other hand, the absence of reporting on pollution-intensive activities can be seen as a shortfall compared with international practice.

Representatives of three foreign TNCs, selected because of their leadership in environmental reporting in their home country, were interviewed as a further part of the study (Perry and Teng, 1998). The interviews revealed that leadership was not being transferred to Singapore. The low level of public and government interest in environmental issues was given as the reason for not disclosing information. One environmental manager commented: 'The level of awareness is very low, who will care if you report environmental initiatives or not? No one will'. An organization accredited to the European Eco-Management and Audit Scheme (EMAS) advised that it would cease to report in Singapore were it not part of the EMAS requirement to distribute an annual environmental report for each operating site. The Singapore environmental manager indicated that the town council covering the factory site, to whom he had sent his report, had asked not to receive it. This caused the manager to comment: 'Why create trouble for yourself when there is no requirement at all in Singapore to report such information to the public?'

ISO 14001 policy statements

As noted above, the promotion of ISO 14001 certification has been the main way in which the government has sought to foster voluntary action in the business community. The promotion has included expenditure of around S\$1million (US\$570,000) up to September 2000 on financial grants to local companies. These grants can provide 70 per cent of the cost of engaging a consultant to a maximum of S\$40,000 (US\$23,000). Public support is also given to two industry–government committees involved in ISO promotion work and to the Singapore Accreditation Council, a body that accredits certifying agencies to gain international acceptability. No regulatory concessions are granted to organizations obtaining certification, but government agencies may be influenced by it in the allocation of their regulatory enforcement effort.

The impact of ISO 14001 on business behaviour can be judged by examining the policy statements of certified companies (Singh and Perry, 2000). Examination of 52 of the first 55 certificates awarded in Singapore found that 12 policy statements made no commitments beyond necessary conditions for certification (such as the need to have top management involvement and to continuously improve the environment management system) and a pledge to comply with legislation (Singh and Perry, 2000). A similar number (14) made two or more commitments beyond those required for certification. The additional commitments most frequently made were: (1) some positive action to be taken, such as the elimination of ozone-depleting chemicals; (2) product modification to reduce environmental impacts; (3) working with suppliers, contractors, and customers to promote environmental responsibility, recognizing the impact of product life cycles. In addition, a few organizations had a commitment to exceed legislative and other regulatory require-ments. IBM (Singapore) Pte Ltd was the sole company to include all four of these types of commitment in its policy. Overall policy statements with two or more beyond-the-minimum commitments were only produced by foreign-owned TNCs. On the other hand, with the exception of European-owned TNCs, all types of business organization included at least some organizations with minimal environ-mental policies. As well as examining the policy statements, the study went on to examine the process through which the policy had been generated and its subsequent implementation. Interviews with 25 organizations found four where the policy was linked to significant management prioritization of environmental improvement. All four were foreign-owned transnationals (the Singapore branches of IBM, Molex, Tetra Pak and Lucent Technologies).

Overall, the investigation of policy statements concluded that certification has generally induced little action amongst Singapore-based organizations. In some instances it would appear to encourage no additional activity above that which is required to comply with government regulations and the minimal requirements of the certification process itself. The performance of foreign-owned companies typically falls short of the types of commitments being made by business in their home countries, but it is among Singapore-owned organizations that least change is taking place.

Responsible Care

The Singapore Chemical Industry Council (SCIC) officially joined Responsible Care in October 1999, having stated its intention of doing so in 1990. The interim was spent in spreading interest in the programme and ensuring a sufficient number of members had the capacity to join. The petrochemical and chemical sectors currently account for around a fifth of value-added in Singapore's manufacturing sector and are dominated by global corporations. Singapore economic promotion agencies have sought to capitalize on the island's long-established role as an oil depot and refining base for the region to expand these activities still further (Perry et al., 1997). Land reclamation has created purpose-designed production space on offshore islands and financial incentives have offset capital investment costs. Despite the sector's extensive land requirements and potential risk to nearby high population densities and vulnerable ecosystems, government agencies continue to prioritize the sector.

Companies that join Responsible Care accept ten guiding principles and a code outlining expected management practices. These commit organizations to match industry best practice with respect to the health, safety and environmental aspects of their operations, to accept product stewardship obligations and to work cooperatively which each other, the community and governments to advance Responsible Care. When launched, 50 of the 180 members of SCIC committed themselves to the programme. One year later the participation had grown to 65, of which 80 per cent were foreign-owned TNCs, the prime drivers of the spread of Responsible Care to Singapore. For foreign TNCs, it provides a structure for attaining common standards among their international branches and of ensuring suppliers and customers attain similar performance. Such concerns among foreign multinationals, rather than local pressure to participate in the programme from government or the community at large, explain the launch of Responsible Care in Singapore. Subsequently, government has given some recognition to the initiative by joining its organizing committee.

Responsible Care is new to Singapore with its focus on assisting organizations improve working practices and reporting systems. Much of the impetus for achieving this comes from TNCs and their willingness to assist local companies. In North America, Responsible Care has been criticized as an attempt to present the industry in a favourable light so as to pre-empt new legislation and regulation (Eden, 1996). In Singapore, the programme may be accredited with some positive outcomes. It provides a framework in which foreign TNCs are taking increased steps to extend environmental responsibilities to overseas branches. This is important in Singapore, where the absence of community and other pressures have resulted in environmental issues being a low priority.

Environmental Issues in Malaysia

Malaysia exhibits most of the environmental problems that are typical of many developing economies (for an overview see CAP, 1998). These include the over-logging of primary forest resulting in the loss of wildlife habitats, soil erosion and the displacement of indigenous communities; air and water pollution from industry and urban transportation, especially in the main centres of economic activity (Kuala Lumpur and the Kelang Valley, Penang and Johor); and the dumping of hazardous waste. The incidence of problems has changed with Malaysia's economic progress but generally increased incomes have yet to be translated into improved environmental conditions (Sham Sani, 1999; Rasiah, 1999). Part of the problem is that urbanization is still increasing and this intensifies the environmental impacts from industry and population. The urban population almost doubled from 1980 to 2000 and is expected to double again by 2020 (World Resources Institute, 1997). Hence pollution problems tended to increase despite the strengthening of environmental governance in the 1990s (Sham Sani, 1999: 13–15).

The overall industrial contribution to pollution shows some changes in the intensity of discharges. Particulate discharges increased in the initial phase of industrial growth but have declined from their high in the mid-1990s (Markandya and Shibli, 1995; Rasiah, 1999). Other air emissions (sulphur dioxide, nitrogen dioxide, carbon monoxide and hydrocarbons) continued to increase through the 1990s, with all emissions except hydrocarbons at least doubling 1987–97 (Rasiah, 1999). Organic pollution of water courses, as measured by biochemical oxygen demand (BOD), dropped in the 1980s but has since increased, with manufacturing a major contributor (Jenkins, cited in Rasiah, 1999). In 1998, three quarters of river monitoring stations recorded some degree of significant pollution, of which the agricultural sector and manufacturing were the major sources for a fifth of the rivers examined (Environmental Quality Report, 1998: 9). In coastal waters, oil and grease contamination is widespread and increasing, with more restricted problems of copper, mercury and lead levels exceeding proposed standards adjacent to some industrial areas (Environmental Quality Report, 1998: 13). A World Bank study in the early 1990s identified hazardous waste as likely to be the principal industrial pollution problem in future years (Markandya and Shibli, 1995). Hazardous waste generation increased by 18 per cent from 1992 to 1998, with the major industrial sources including metal finishing, chemicals, electronics, printing and packaging (Environmental Quality Report, 1998: 9). New controls on hazardous waste were included in the Environmental Quality (Amendment) Act of 1996, the original legislation having provided Malaysia's overall legal umbrella for pollution control since its original enactment in 1974.

Monitoring of individual business behaviour continues to find a high incidence of non-compliance. This may reflect surveillance effort rather than attitudes to environmental responsibility, but it does suggest that business acceptance of regulatory obligations needs to be strengthened before increasing the reliance on voluntary improvement initiatives. With the exception of periods of economic slowdown (1985–90 and 1997–8), the number of environmental offences prosecuted under the Environmental Quality Act has increased. In 1992, for example, 130 cases were prosecuted compared with 253 in 1998 (Environmental Quality Report, 1998: 51). In 1998, a total of 3,889 manufacturing industries were inspected, of which 86 per cent were judged compliant to sewage and industrial effluent regulations and 78 per cent were judged compliant to air emission regulations. Industries in which foreign investment dominates, such as electronics, had a compliance rate of 86 per cent and 89 per cent under the respective regulations; in the chemicals sector, the respective compliance was 88 per cent and 94 per cent. The Environmental Quality Report for 1998 noted that non-compliance by manufacturing was frequently due to failures to maintain abatement equipment or to upgrade capacity with increases in production capacity. Such problems were suggested to be most prevalent amongst small and medium-sized enterprises, many of which were said to be operating without appropriate control equipment. The compliance checks tend to concentrate on large enterprises with potentially the greatest impacts, and so probably do not capture the full extent of non-compliance (Markandya and Shibli, 1995).

A further indicator of business attitudes to environmental impacts can be obtained from those who legally choose to exceed emission standards. Malaysia operates a system that allows emission levels to be exceeded on receipt of a 'contravention licence', for which there is a fee and associated abatement charge. There has been a large reduction in the fees so collected from the rubber and palm oil processing industries (Sham Sani, 1999: 20). This improvement partly reflects the comparative isolation of individual processing facilities in these industries, making environmental impacts easier to monitor than where industry operates from urban locations (World Bank, 2000). Even with the potential added impetus of community surveillance, it appears that environmental commitment remains a low priority. Under the licensing regulations governing 'prescribed premises' (that includes rubber and palm oil processors) an excellent compliance record can lead to the award of licences for more than the normal one-year period. In 1998, 20 of the 143 licensed rubber factories had been granted extended licences (14 for two years, six for three years). Of 328 licensed palm oil mills, 97 had been granted extended licenses (70 for two years, 27 for three years) (Environmental Quality Report, 1998: 22).

A shortage of monitoring and enforcement capacity has been identified as a critical problem with Malaysia's current environmental policy regime (Markandya and Shibli, 1995). It means that apart from large establishments in the palm oil and rubber sector, industry is largely self-monitored. The 1996 amendments to the Environmental Quality Act included substantial increases to the penalties for a range of environmental offences (see Sham Sani, 1999: 33). This change sought to increase the compliance pressure on industry, although in the past courts were generally reluctant to impose maximum penalties. A public complaint system exists and this can trigger enforcement action. An increase in the number of public complaints on environmental issues occurred during the 1990s. This took place alongside an increase in media coverage and growing public awareness of environmental issues, reinforced in the Seventh Malaysia Five-Year Plan, which included an emphasis on environmental awareness.

A significant difference with Singapore is the stronger role that environmental NGOs are playing in encouraging environmental protection. Long-established environmental and consumer protection campaign groups have been joined by groups representing business interests. The Malaysian International Chamber of Commerce and Industry (MICC) established an environmental committee in 1992, the same year that the Business Council for Sustainable Development was formed. The timing coincided with the broader inclusion of environmental issues in the Malaysia Five-Year Plan and the awareness among international companies that they were particularly exposed to any tightening of regulation. As well as providing business with collective representation to government, much of the committee's effort is now devoted to the organization of an environmental award, the Prime Minister's Hibiscus Award. The award recognizes organizations that have demonstrated environmental leadership and is co-organized with the Federation of Malaysian Manufacturers and ENSEARCH, an NGO representing environmental scientists and managers. In 2000, 39 companies (36 subsidiaries of TNCs) received recognition, indicating that they met the criteria for the award.

Community-based environmental campaign groups have attained a high profile, partly through their use of public law suits, a tactic that Singapore-based NGOs have avoided (Tay, forthcoming). An early and well-known example of this was the Asian Rare Earth case in which NGOs supported a group of villagers in legal action against a private company for its improper storage and disposal of hazardous materials, an action that also implicated a government agency for maladministration. The legal standing on which NGOs have sought to challenge government decisions has been unclear, but their right to participate in environmental decisions has gradually attained recognition. Thus, even though NGO action has often not been successful, it is changing the way that issues are dealt with and is bringing greater voluntary willingness to minimize environmental impacts (Harding, 1996). On the other hand, the suggestion that NGOs have become the 'public watchdog' for environmental care (Sham Sani, 1999) may overstate the situation. Few groups have large memberships and much of the environmental activism originates in Penang, the small island that has seen rapid economic transformation because of its success as an electronics manufacturing base (see Gonzalez et al., 2000).

Environmental NGOs remain critical of the lack of enforcement and coordination of regulation (Consumers Association of Penang and Sahabat Alam Malaysia, 1996) but government has shown an increased willingness to accept outside influence on environmental performance. When Austria became the first country to designate a quality mark for tropical timber and raised import tariffs on tropical timber, as part of its efforts to improve timber harvesting practices, it was Malaysia that promptly protested the measure to the GATT (Roht-Arriaza, 1995). The internationalization of Malaysian timber companies has brought a change of attitude. The Malaysia Minister of Primary Industry, who oversees the Malaysian timber industry, has stated that companies should follow basic guidelines of good corporate citizenship, including obeying national laws and not taking advantage of weak governments (Nordin, cited in Sizer and Plouvier, 2000: 97). Increased international criticism of its domestic forestry policies has produced similarly significant changes of attitude. A National Timber Certification Centre has been established and the government, in partnership with industry, has invested substantial resources to create the Malaysian Criteria and Indicators for Sustainable Forest Management as the basis for an independent third-party certification mechanism. Changes in business behaviour nonetheless appear to be slow to emerge. To date, just one Malaysian TNC is said to be making serious efforts to incorporate sustainability principles in its forestry management, and even it continues to be subject to substantial criticism of its activities (Sizer and Plouvier, 2000: 98).

Environmental Performance of Foreign TNCs in Singapore and Malaysia

A study of TNC environmental practices published in 1988 (ESCAP/UNCTC, 1988) included case studies of Singapore and Malaysia. These were based on small samples of TNCs and pre-date contemporary environmental expectations. Consequently, a new survey of foreign-owned TNCs in Singapore and Malaysia was undertaken in 2000 to examine the extent and character of 'voluntary' environmental action as well as the motivations underpinning such action. The focus of the survey was on actions undertaken by TNCs in the host country, either Singapore or Malaysia.

The surveys covered industrial establishments identified in a published business directory for which a present address and named contact could be obtained following a telephone request for this information. Foreign-owned industrial activities were the focus of the survey because it was thought that they would exhibit greater voluntary action than locally owned and service organizations. In Singapore, 400 questionnaires were mailed to environmental officers and other persons identified as responsible for environmental management in each organization contacted. This compares with 640 wholly foreign-owned establishments listed in the latest Census of Industrial Production (Economic Development Board, 1998). In Malaysia, 450 questionnaires were mailed to establishments listed in the KBD Dun Business directory for foreign companies in ASEAN.

There were 89 useable responses in Singapore, a 22.25 per cent response rate, and 91 useable responses in Malaysia, a 20 per cent response rate. The respondent organizations are broadly in line with the ownership distribution of foreign companies in the two countries, although non-Japanese Asian TNCs are underrepresented in the Malaysian responses. The responses from both countries were concentrated in three sectors: electronics, chemicals and chemical products, and fabricated metal products (Table 5.3). The respondents also shared similar characteristics in terms of: (1) pollution intensity (predominantly being either of high or medium intensity); (2) organizational size (predominantly being either small or medium-sized TNCs); (3) nationality (around half are Asian respondents and the United States or Europe account for a similar proportion of the remainder); and (4) average age of capital (predominantly either 5–10 or 11–15 years) (Table 5.3). The capital age, pollution intensity and size characteristics may result in a low representation of organizations

Table 5.3
Summary of Respondent Characteristics

SINGAPORE

Pollution intensity (%)*		Nationality of parent company (%)	
High	40.5	Asia	48.5
Medium	47.0	USA	20.0
Low	12.5	Europe	28.0
*Organization size (%)***		Others	3.5
Large	14.5	*Sector (%)*	
Medium	34.0	Electronics	36.0
Small	51.5	Chemicals and Chemical Products	20.0
Average age of the plant (%)		Food, Beverages, and Tobacco	2.5
Less than 5 years	12.4	Fabricated Metal Products	20.0
5–10 years	31.5	Machinery & Equipment	10.0
11–15 years	28.1	Rubber & Natural Resource Based Products	1.0
16–20 years	14.6	Petroleum and Petroleum Products	2.5
More than 20 years	13.5	Others	8.0

MALAYSIA

Pollution intensity (%)*		Nationality of parent company (%)	
High	39.5	Asia	54.0
Medium	55.0	USA	25.0
Low	5.5	Europe	20.0
*Organization size (%)***		Others	1.0
Large	11.0	*Sector (%)*	
Medium	36.0	Electronics	40.5
Small	53.0	Chemicals and Chemical Products	15.5
Average age of the plant (%)		Food, Beverages, and Tobacco	4.5
Less than 5 years	3.3	Fabricated Metal Products	18.5
5–10 years	45.1	Machinery & Equipment	4.5
11–15 years	25.3	Rubber & Natural Resource Based Products	7.5
16–20 years	15.4	Petroleum and Petroleum Products	3.5
More than 20 years	11.0	Others	5.5

Singapore: N = 89

Malaysia: N = 91

* Pollution intensity was measured according to the effort required to comply with environmental regulations.

** Organization size refers to the size of the parent company distinguished as follows:

One or more of the following applies

Small TNC	1	Less than 500 employees in home country
	2	1–5 affiliates in overseas locations
	3	Operations in no more than 3 countries
Medium-sized TNC	1	Less than 500 employees in home country
	2	6–20 affiliates in overseas locations
	3	Operations in 4–10 countries
Large TNC	1	More than 500 employees in home country
	2	More than 20 affiliates in overseas locations
	3	Operations in more than 20 countries

that are most exposed to environmental pressure, to the extent that large, old, high-pollution plants are not present. More generally, it must be expected that a postal survey of environmental performance is likely to gain fewer responses from those establishments with a poor environmental record. Consequently, without a much greater response rate no claims can be made about its representativeness of all TNCs in Malaysia and Singapore. Differences between respondents and the attributes of those claiming to be most active are the matters that we focus upon.

Respondent organizations were classified according to the extent to which they had implemented the following actions: (1) set environmental performance standards above government regulations; (2) allocated environmental responsibilities to senior managers; (3) completed an environmental review of their establishment within the previous five years; (4) agreed an environmental policy statement; (5) implemented an environmental management system; (6) included environmental performance in the investment criteria for new technology; (7) participated in community-based environmental projects; (8) taken steps to increase environmental awareness and responsibility amongst the workforce. Using these criteria, the environmental commitment of organizations was classified as high, medium or low (Figure 5.1).

Participation in at least six of the eight actions was needed to be classed as high, whereas low performers had not undertaken more than one of the actions. In the case of the last three listed criteria, various responses were possible, some of which indicate additional commitment above the minimum threshold. Such responses were used to identify high performers. These criteria and the range of responses are as follows.

Investment criteria: High performers indicated one of two options relating to the priority given to environmental impacts in the selection of new technology: (1) best available environmental technology; (2) best available environmental technology not entailing excessive cost. Lower options were to select either: (1) environmental technology at a reasonable cost; (2) environmental technology sufficient to meet local regulations.

Community project participation: Participation in any one of four types of community project was required, with multiple participation possible for the most active organizations: (1) sponsoring a community event or environmental initiative; (2) public reporting of their environmental impacts; (3) dialogue with community groups or an NGO or both; (4) green labelling.

Workforce education/training: Participation in at least three of seven types of workforce initiatives was required, again with the possibility that active organizations exceed the threshold: (1) environmental training; (2) environmental awareness orientation for new employees; (3) display of environmental policy around the workplace; (4) copy of policy given to each employee; (5) newsletter on environmental issues; (6) environmental awareness events; (7) environmental suggestion scheme.

The criteria for high performance may be viewed as a comparatively low threshold compared with environmentally advanced corporations in older industrial countries. There is, for example, no reference to product stewardship, public information disclosure or the delegation of environmental responsibilities to all categories of employee. On the other hand, an organization that has implemented six or more of the actions identified suggests a consistent effort to raise their

Figure 5.1
Environmental Action among TNCs in Singapore and Malaysia

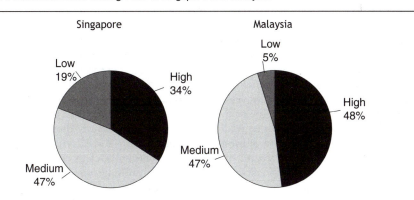

High: 6–8 environmental actions
Medium: 2–5 environmental actions
Low: one or none of the environmental actions

Environmental action	Percentage of respondents					
	Singapore			Malaysia		
	High	Medium	Low	High	Medium	Low
Environmental standards above government regulations	76.7	28.6	5.9	65.1	32.6	0
Allocation of environmental responsibility to senior managers	76.7	63.4	0	93.0	51.4	0
Environmental review completed within 5 years	100	88.1	17.6	100	97.7	40.0
Environmental policy statement agreed	100	78.6	17.6	97.7	76.7	0
Implemented environmental management system	100	66.7	0	93.0	44.2	0
Environmental criteria included in new technology investment	83.3	57.1	58.8	86.0	62.8	60.3
Participation in or sponsoring of community-based environmental projects	73.3	16.7	11.8	62.8	16.3	0
Workforce education and training	96.7	45.2	11.8	93.0	25.6	0

environmental performance. At the other end of the scale, there is little uncertainty that organizations classified as 'low' are not participating in voluntary environmental initiatives. For medium-level organizations, the scale is intended to capture organizations with environmental actions that bring immediate benefits without a strategic commitment to voluntary improvement.

In both countries, medium performance accounted for almost half the respondents, but Malaysia had a larger share of high performers: 48 per cent versus 34 per cent in Singapore (Figure 5.1). The difference in the share of high performers is statistically significant (chi square value = 8.851, df = 2, p<0.05), but additional evidence is required to determine the real extent of difference. Our indicators do not capture the extent of effort invested in individual actions and tell us nothing about the actual environmental impact of an organization. Moreover, as noted above, while generally it may be expected that responses will over-represent active organizations, there may be differences in the willingness of low performers to identify themselves. In Singapore, where companies are under little community pressure to address environmental issues, inactive companies may be more willing to identify themselves than in Malaysia. The greater share of most active organizations in Malaysia keeps open the possibility that informal regulatory pressure from civil society organizations is encouraging more voluntary action in that country than Singapore, but the survey evidence alone does not confirm whether this is actually so.

Amongst high performers in both countries, all eight actions measured in the survey have strong participation. Medium performers exhibited participation in fewer actions, especially those indicative of an overall organizational commitment to environmental responsibility, namely: setting environmental standards above regulatory requirements; participating in community environmental projects; workforce education and (notably in the case of Malaysia) implementing an environmental management system. Low performers have little participation in any actions except some recognition of environmental impacts in technology selection and, in the case of Malaysia, completion of an environmental review (which might be explained by EIA requirements).

A check was made on the classifications by examining the distribution of environmental expenditure that is made to comply with regulation and that which is voluntary. When account is taken of pollution intensity, organizations classified as high performers are associated with a higher proportion of discretionary expenditure than other respondents (Table 5.4). This gives some reliability in the survey responses and classification of respondent organizations.

Explaining environmental commitment

Previous investigations of industry and environment in developing and newly industrializing economies have suggested a number of determinants of environmental performance at the establishment level (see World Bank, 2000 for reviews of recent studies). Drawing on that evidence, firms were cross-classified according to their environmental classification and a number of variables that, it was thought, might explain their classification (Table 5.5). Overall, it was found that few of the explanatory variables were associated with higher performance and that there was no consistent experience between Singapore and Malaysia.

In Singapore, employment size is linked to some extent to environmental effort, with larger firms tending to be more active. When the data are dichotomized into those with more or less than 1,000 employees and those with high or other levels of environmental action, large organizations have a statistically significantly higher share of organizations that implement the widest range of actions (chi square value = 10.804, df = 1, p<0.05). A second, but not statistically significant association (chi square value = 1.164, df = 1, p>0.05) exists with home country nationality. Whereas around a quarter of the total sample are high performers, the share among North American organizations increases to almost 44 per cent.

Table 5.4
Reasons for Environmental Management Expenditure among Pollution-Intensive Organizations
According to their Environmental Commitment

Motivation for environmental expenditure	Percentage of total environmental expenditure					
	Singapore			Malaysia		
	< 25	26–50	51–100	< 25	26–50	51–75
High commitment						
Regulatory compliance	2	8	0	2	4	11
Voluntary environmental action	0	4	6	3	7	6
Medium commitment						
Regulatory compliance	1	5	2	0	3	7
Voluntary environmental action	2	1	5	2	5	4
Low commitment						
Regulatory compliance	0	2	1	0	0	0
Voluntary environmental action	1	1	1	0	0	0

In Malaysia, the data indicate that neither employment nor ownership has an impact on performance. There is a statistically significant increase in environmental action among pollution-intensive respondents (chi square value = 4.590, df = 1, p<0.05). A sectoral bias in which chemicals, petroleum and fabricated metals generate the highest proportion of high performers is consistent with the impact of pollution intensity, but the small number of responses (5) claiming low pollution intensity precludes definitive conclusions from the survey evidence. Location has a small impact on performance, with establishments located near to residential areas having the largest share of high performers, but the participation is not significantly higher than that of establishments isolated from residential communities (chi square value = 6.631, df = 3, p<0.10). Similarly, establishments making finished products (implying a direct interface with consumers) are more likely to be high performers than those supplying industrial customers, especially where it is an internal customer, but again not to a significant degree (chi square value = 1.200, df = 1, p>0.05).

Motivation for voluntary action

Respondents were asked to rank a range of influences encouraging voluntary action. Pressure to conform to environmental criteria set by the corporate head office is most frequently given as the most important driver of voluntary action in both countries (Table 5.6). Increased workforce environmental awareness is the second-ranking main influence. Secondary influences were dispersed across the four possible options so that overall a diverse set of motivations are at work encouraging voluntary action. Although the spread of responses gives some confidence in their reliability, it must be acknowledged that environmental managers are likely to prefer to identify internal drivers as the influences promoting voluntary action. External pressure suggests that matters are somewhat outside their control and that credit for the benefits obtained cannot all be claimed by the organization. Below we offer a partial check on this by comparing the motives for action against the benefits claimed to be obtained. It should be recognized, however, that this is an area that ultimately needs to be addressed through more detailed investigation.

Table 5.5
Percentage Distribution of Firms by Ownership, Pollution Intensity, Location, Size, Type of Product Manufactured and Sector

Singapore

	Percentage of respondents		
	High	Medium	Low
Ownership			
Asia (N = 43)	32.6	39.5	27.9
USA (N = 18)	44.4	38.9	16.7
Europe (N = 25)	28.0	64.0	8.0
Others (N = 3)	33.3	66.7	0
Pollution intensity[1]			
Intensive (N = 36)	41.7	30.6	27.8
Moderate (N = 42)	23.8	64.3	11.9
Low (N = 11)	45.5	38.4	18.2
Location			
Near to residential population (N = 36)	27.8	50.0	22.2
Isolated from residential population (N = 45)	35.6	46.7	17.8
Mixed residential and industrial population (N = 8)	50.0	37.5	12.5
Size (employees)			
Less then 50 (N = 14)	14.3	50.0	35.7
51–100 (N = 22)	22.7	59.1	18.2
101–500 (N = 34)	32.4	44.1	23.5
501–1000 (N = 9)	44.4	55.6	0
More than 1000 (N = 10)	80.0	20.0	0
Type of product manufactured			
Finished product (N = 45)	35.6	42.2	22.2
Partly finished product for plants under same ownership (N = 6)	50.0	50.0	0
Partly finished product for other manufacturers (N = 29)	27.6	55.2	17.2
Mix of above options (N = 9)	33.3	44.4	22.2
Sector or type of activity			
Electronics (N = 32)	43.8	46.9	9.4
Chemicals and Chemical Products (N = 18)	27.8	50.0	22.2
Food, Beverages, and Tobacco (N = 2)	50.0	50.0	0
Fabricated Metal Products (N = 18)	27.8	33.3	38.9
Machinery and Equipment (N = 9)	44.4	22.2	33.3
Others (N = 10)	10.0	90.0	0
Age of Technology			
Less than 5 years (N = 11)	23.3	4.8	11.8
5–10 years (N = 28)	20.0	35.5	41.2
11–15 years (N = 25)	30.0	28.6	23.5
16–20 years (N = 13)	13.3	14.6	17.6
More than 20 years (N = 12)	13.3	16.7	5.9

[1] Pollution intensity: refer to the definition under Table 5.4

(Table 5.5 cont.)

Malaysia

	Percentage of respondents		
	High	Medium	Low
Ownership			
Asia (N = 49)	49.0	46.9	4.1
USA (N = 23)	52.2	39.1	8.7
Europe (N = 18)	38.9	55.6	5.6
Others (N = 1)	0	100	0
Pollution intensity			
Intensive (N = 36)	61.1	36.1	2.8
Moderate (N = 50)	38.0	56.0	6.0
Low (N = 5)	40.0	40.0	20.0
Location			
Near to residential population (N = 52)	55.8	38.4	5.8
Isolated from residential population (N = 21)	42.9	57.1	0.0
Mixed residential and industrial population (N = 17)	23.5	64.7	11.8
Isolated from residential and industrial community (N = 1)	100	0	0
Size (employees)			
Less than 50 (N = 1)	0.0	100	0.0
51–100(N = 6)	50.0	33.3	16.7
101–500 (N = 38)	39.5	55.3	5.3
501–1000 (N = 17)	52.9	47.1	0.0
More than 1000 (N = 29)	55.2	37.9	6.9
Type of product manufactured			
Finished product (N = 47)	57.4	38.3	4.3
Partly finished product for plants under same ownership (N = 9)	22.2	77.8	0
Partly finished product for other manufacturers (N = 26)	46.2	46.2	7.7
Mix of above options (N = 9)	22.2	66.7	11.1
Sector or type of activity			
Electronics (N = 37)	45.9	45.9	8.1
Chemicals and Chemical Products (N = 14)	64.3	35.7	0
Food, Beverages, and Tobacco (N = 4)	25.0	75.0	0
Fabricated Metal Products (N = 17)	64.7	23.5	11.8
Machinery and Equipment (N = 4)	25.0	75.0	0
Others (N = 15)	33.3	66.7	0
Age of Technology			
Less than 5 years (N = 3)	2.3	2.3	20.0
5–10 years (N = 41)	46.5	41.9	60.0
11–15 years (N = 23)	27.9	25.6	0
16–20 years (N = 14)	9.3	20.9	20.0
More than 20 years (N = 10)	14.0	9.3	0

Table 5.6
Influences (Other than Regulation) Motivating Environmental Action

Influences for voluntary action	Most important influence			
	Singapore		Malaysia	
	Frequency	%	Frequency	%
Corporate head office environmental criteria conformance	40	45.5	44	48.4
Community, NGOs, and media	7	8.0	9	9.9
Consumers (located in high-income economies)	18	20.5	21	23.5
Workforce	18	20.5	34	37.4

Respondents
N (Singapore) = 89
N (Malaysia) = 91

Perceived benefits of voluntary action

Respondents were asked to rate the relative importance of the following possible benefits that might be obtained from their voluntary investment in environmental management: (1) market advantages because of enhanced reputation with consumers; (2) cost savings; (3) raised status of the plant within the corporate group; (4) enhanced confidence in the environmental awareness of the workforce; (5) improved relations with regulatory agencies; (6) reduced environmental liabilities; (7) shareholder evaluation of the organization enhanced; (8) improved relations with the community, NGOs and media. The overall response indicates that the first three of these advantages are most frequently claimed in both Malaysia and Singapore (Figure 5.2). Other possible advantages are important for only a comparatively small proportion of organizations.

The establishments surveyed are typically a small part of a transnational organization and this means that they can be a minor influence on shareholder appraisal. Perhaps for this reason, enhanced confidence among shareholders is not identified as a main advantage. Interestingly, in Singapore improved relations with regulators is more frequently cited than reduced environmental liabilities, whereas in Malaysia it is the other way round. An interpretation of this may be that the high visibility of operations in the small city state, combined with the enforcement of regulation, reduces the likelihood of potential environmental liabilities. As noted above, limited resources for enforcement in a larger territory may permit poor practices to survive. In neither country is an improved image in the community cited frequently as the main advantage by more than a few respondents. On the other hand, when the second most important advantage is considered, a greater range of advantages is claimed in Malaysia than Singapore (Figure 5.3). In Malaysia, both improved image in the community and improved relations with regulators are cited by a fifth of the respondents as the second most important advantage. These scores are consistent with the different conditions influencing formal and informal regulation in Malaysia compared with Singapore.

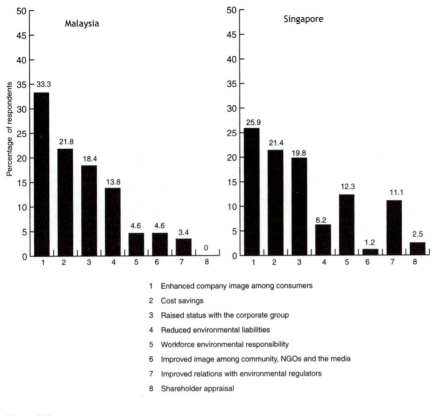

1   Enhanced company image among consumers

2   Cost savings

3   Raised status with the corporate group

4   Reduced environmental liabilities

5   Workforce environmental responsibility

6   Improved image among community, NGOs and the media

7   Improved relations with environmental regulators

8   Shareholder appraisal

Figure 5.2
Main Advantage from Investment in Voluntary Environmental Initiatives in
Singapore and Malaysia

Of course some caution is required in interpreting what respondents indicate has been the main advantage of their environmental management. They may, for example, be reluctant to cite reduced liabilities as an advantage since it is indicative of poor management practices in the past. On the other hand, there is a good correlation between organizations that supply final goods and those citing enhanced reputation with consumers as the key advantage. In Singapore, of 21 TNCs that see enhanced image with consumers as the key advantage, 13 manufactured final products. In Malaysia, 17 of the 29 TNCs were manufacturing final products. Some confidence in the result can be taken from the way that TNCs indicating improved reputation with customers as their main advantage from environmental action are also typically TNCs directly exposed to consumer pressure.

It is interesting to consider whether the advantages reported vary between those with high and low investment in environmental initiatives. The difference in the response of these two groups could suggest that there is an incentive for investing in environmental management as it leads to distinct advantages for high performers. The extent of difference can be examined in the case of Singapore where there is a comparatively large share of low performers (Figure 5.1). Cost saving is seen as the

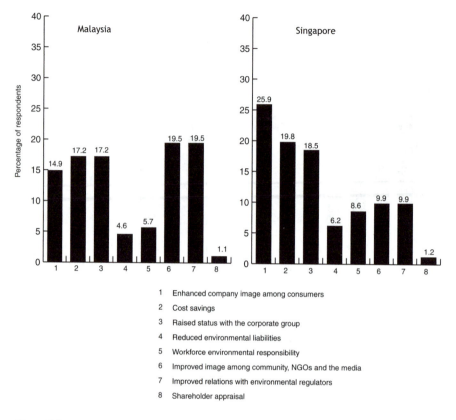

1   Enhanced company image among consumers

2   Cost savings

3   Raised status with the corporate group

4   Reduced environmental liabilities

5   Workforce environmental responsibility

6   Improved image among community, NGOs and the media

7   Improved relations with environmental regulators

8   Shareholder appraisal

Figure 5.3
Second Main Advantage from Investment in Voluntary Environmental Initiatives in
Singapore and Malaysia

key advantage among organizations with both high and low environmental
commitment. The main differences relate to (1) the greater importance of an
enhanced status within the corporate group for those with a high environmental
commitment than those with a low commitment, and (2) improved workforce
awareness, which is seen as a key advantage achieved (after cost savings) among
organizations with low commitment (27 per cent as compared to 7 per cent in the
case of organizations with high commitment) (Figure 5.4). This result reflects how
actions to raise the environmental awareness of the workforce are amongst the most
frequent voluntary actions among organizations with low commitment.

The significance of improved corporate status in motivating organizations to
increase their investment in environmental initiatives is open to alternative inter-
pretations. The absence of this advantage may reflect the lack of priority given to
environmental performance by the group or the branch's low performance (or both
situations). As a partial check on which explanation applies, the motivation for and
advantages obtained from voluntary environmental initiatives were compared
according to the extent of existing activity. Among existing high-activity organizations in Singapore, 80 per cent indicate that conformity to the standards set by

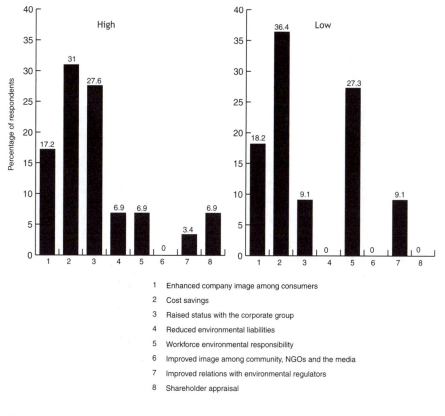

1 Enhanced company image among consumers
2 Cost savings
3 Raised status with the corporate group
4 Reduced environmental liabilities
5 Workforce environmental responsibility
6 Improved image among community, NGOs and the media
7 Improved relations with environmental regulators
8 Shareholder appraisal

Figure 5.4
Main Advantage from Investment in Voluntary Environmental Initiatives by High and Low Performers in Singapore

parent firms is the most important motivation for investment in environmental action compared with 30 per cent for low-activity organizations. In Malaysia, two thirds of high performers were motivated by such standards compared with none of the low performers. Thus it appears that most establishments belonging to organizations that are encouraging higher environmental standards have raised their performance and that they are being recognized for this by their parent company. A small group of establishments with similar corporate environmental interests have yet to take action and gain recognition. This provides a pool of organizations that might be expected to become active. On the other hand, a substantially increased level of participation will depend on corporate interest in environmental responsibility extending to more organizations and for already active organizations to set higher standards for their branches than currently exist.

ISO 14001 and environmental commitment

In Singapore, 37 (41.5 per cent) respondents had a certified environmental management system (two certified to EMAS, the rest certified to ISO 14001) compared with 47 (51.6 per cent) in Malaysia. In Singapore, certified respondents comprised

Table 5.7
Motivation to Implement an Environmental Management System (EMS)

Motivation*	Certified EMS				Non-certified EMS			
	Singapore		Malaysia		Singapore		Malaysia	
	Frequency	%	Frequency	%	Frequency	%	Frequency	%
Required by the corporate head office	32	86.5	38	80.9	17	81.0	7	58.3
Cost savings	28	75.7	37	78.7	10	47.6	6	50.0
Enhanced image among consumers	28	75.7	42	89.4	9	42.9	8	66.7
Improved relations with government regulating agencies	14	37.8	25	53.2	9	42.9	6	50.0
Improved relations with community, NGOs and media	13	35.1	29	61.7	4	19.0	7	58.3
Encouragement by host government	10	27.0	11	23.4	10	47.6	5	41.7
Number of organizations	37		47		21		12	

*Respondents can provide multiple motives

82 per cent (18 of 22) of the organizations with most environmental action and 39.5 per cent (19 of 48) of the medium-level organizations. Corresponding figures for Malaysia were 84 per cent and 26 per cent. As would be expected, no organizations with low levels of action had a certified environmental management system.

By definition, certification implies that several of the other environmental actions examined in the survey are in place. While it may sometimes be associated with additional environmental action, it is important to note that two of the most substantial voluntary actions – adhering to environmental performance targets above regulatory requirements and incorporating environmental criteria in the selection of new investment – are not significantly more frequent amongst certified organizations than others. In addition, it is also worth noting that certification is not more prevalent amongst the most pollution-intensive organizations in Singapore. Of the 36 organizations in Singapore indicating that a high degree of effort was required to comply with environmental regulation, 43 per cent have certification compared with 57 per cent of those with medium or low compliance effort. Similarly in Malaysia, where the respective proportions are 51 per cent and 49 per cent, pollution intensity does not appear to motivate certification.

Perceived market benefits seem to motivate organizations to obtain certification as compared with operating with a non-certified environmental management system (Table 5.7). In both countries, improved image with customers is more frequently cited as a motive amongst those with certification than those without, with cost savings being almost as important a differentiating influence. Parent company instruction is an important reason for certification in both countries, although in Malaysia it is slightly less important than consumer image. In both countries, government agencies have actively encouraged certification but it seems this has had most impact on encouraging the adoption of a non-certified management system.

Codes of conduct

The emphasis on the social responsibility of business and self-regulation is seen in the emergence of environmental codes of conduct. A code of conduct may be specified by a parent company for its affiliate operations, a multilateral organization for certain types of business, a buyer for its suppliers or an industry association for its members (Jenkins, 2000). In Malaysia, 30 of 91 respondents were covered by at least one code of conduct, with one third of the firms having codes being affected by at least two codes. Almost three quarters of the companies covered by a code of conduct were high performers. For all but one organization, at least one of their codes was set by the parent company, with customer or industry association codes the only other notable source. Given that enforcement may be expected to be greatest where the code is associated with an independent party, these results underline the limited importance of codes as an influence on our sample of TNC branches. Respondents in the chemical industry most frequently identified being covered by an industry association code, most probably Responsible Care. Customer codes existed among respondents in the electronic and fabricated metals sectors. Of the 30 organizations that were covered by at least one code of conduct, 25 were from pollution-intensive sectors like chemical and chemical products, fabricated metal products, rubber and natural-resource-based products, and petroleum refining and petroleum products. Two organizations specified the OECD as the source of a code of conduct but none identified other multilateral agencies as a source.

Conclusion

During the 1990s, voluntary 'self-regulation' was promoted as a viable way of increasing business contributions to sustainable development. It was championed for its flexibility in addressing environmental issues and for the incentives it provided for environmental innovations compared with compliance to uniform regulatory standards. Voluntarism became a popular idea among some international and government agencies, which came to see environmental regulations as stifling of industry competitiveness, costly to society and unhelpful in promoting a commitment to improve environmental performance. The review offered in this case study of Singapore and Malaysia casts some doubt on the overall contribution that voluntary action may make. There are reasons to believe that interest in voluntary action will decline as companies fail to obtain the extent of economic or public relations benefits that may have been expected. Much of the case for voluntary action has been based on an exaggerated comparison with traditional forms of regulation which has overlooked, for example, how these can be enforced with differing degrees of coercion and flexibility. The above analysis suggests that there is some scope to benefit from voluntary action in Singapore and Malaysia, but this is partly because there has been little pressure on companies to be proactive in these countries.

When TNCs are asked what motivates their investment in environmental initiatives, the most important driver identified is corporate pressure to standardize the environmental performance of their affiliates in different foreign locations. This can be seen as a commitment to higher standards, although it is also a possible source of cost savings by reducing the variability in management procedures and technology. Nonetheless, the general effect is to increase environmental responsibility in host economies because TNC environmental policies typically encompass more activities than do formal regulations. The survey indicates that organizations coming under corporate pressure are the most active investors in environmental initiatives. Consequently, an important source of any increased participation will be corporate conversion to environmental improvement. This influence would seem to be greater than conditions in the host economy, in the form of either government or informal pressure. Although it is possible that some of the corporate interest comes from trends in affiliate locations, it is more likely that they are influenced by expectations in their home economies, where their customers and investors are located.

The survey has not confirmed the importance of several influences thought to be associated with corporate environmental commitment. Among the explanatory variables examined, size (as measured by employment) emerged as the only significant influence on environmental performance in Singapore. Larger organizations have taken most action to increase their environmental responsibility, but pollution intensity, market characteristics or dependence on brand images were found not to be important. The small size of the sample may explain the lack of association but it also suggests a context in which companies regard regulatory compliance as sufficient in the absence of community questioning of their environmental performance. On the other hand, high pollution intensity had a small impact in encouraging environmental action in Malaysia. This may be linked to less consistent enforcement of regulation in a larger and less well-resourced territory, as well as the greater risk of community action against environmental infringements than in Singapore. Some confirmation of this is given by the greater frequency with which improved community relations are cited as an advantage to be gained from environmental action.

The small sample on which the survey is based makes it difficult to interpret the absence of expected influences on TNC environmental behaviour but it does suggest that management preferences and organizational capacities to absorb higher environmental responsibilities are a significant influence that need consideration in future studies. Other research has found, for example, an association between 'lean' manufacturing and green manufacturing (Florida, 1996). This perspective argues that firms that are innovative in terms of their manufacturing process are likely to be the most imaginative in addressing environmental costs and risks. This possibility arises because essentially the same set of skills and procedures are being utilized. It implies that organizations may not be accepting new responsibilities so much as making full use of their innovative capacity.

Corporate commitment is a prominent driver of environmental initiatives in the absence of other pressures in Singapore, and caution should be exercised in assuming that corporate pressure affects all foreign affiliate locations. In the survey, the relatively limited motivation offered by improved community standing to voluntary action is striking. Presumably this shows how little the Singapore public or media notice corporate environmental behaviour, reflecting confidence that government regulation is managing the issue and ensuring that organizations act responsibly. It also needs to be recognized that the Singapore operations are typically a small part of a transnational organization with limited capacity to influence investor appraisal, which might be a further motivation for voluntary action in the home country. Similarly, the strong enforcement of regulation in Singapore has reduced action motivated by the wish to reduce potential environmental liabilities.

The significance of the action taken by TNCs is difficult to assess without impact data but the overall impression is that substantive activity is limited to a small proportion of organizations. The low participation in environmental initiatives may be criticized but equally it can be seen to highlight the limited advantage that an organization gets from such investment. There has been a tendency in much of the literature to assume that corporate support of voluntary environmental initiatives should and can be adopted across all sectors. This overlooks how the possibility of and incentive for participation is likely to vary considerably between industries. Consumer interest in green products, for example, continues to be highly variable between products. Goods such as washing detergents and certain types of packaging attract significant environmental concern, while clothing and computers, for example, remain less susceptible to green marketing. Both the Singapore and Malaysian samples include a relatively large proportion of final goods manufacturers. Although improved market standing through enhanced image among customers is a fairly important motivation among these firms, it is not the prime motivator of action nor the principle advantage obtained for the most active organizations.

In both Singapore and Malaysia, governments have seen ISO 14001 as an important indicator of voluntary business commitment to environmental improvement. Based on the evaluation of environmental policies of certified organizations in Singapore, it was concluded that for the most part it is encouraging little additional activity. The survey of foreign transnationals tends to confirm this to the extent that it was not encouraging substantive voluntary actions more than could be found amongst non-certified organizations. The assessment of ISO 14001 needs to be different in Malaysia, where there remains a significant problem of pollution from 'backyard' small industries. For such firms adoption of an environmental management system can be a stimulus to important improvements in the absence of resources to ensure regulatory compliance.

For the present, voluntary corporate environmental action cannot be seen as an effective substitute for government regulation. Commitments to prioritize environmental impacts in their investment decisions, or to ensure that all parts of their organizations adhere to home country standards, are limited to a minority of companies. Signs that some TNCs are adhering to performance standards above local regulatory requirements should be viewed as an opportunity to tighten regulation. In the absence of community interest in the environmental performance of business organizations, government-enforced upgrading of performance standards is important to reward those firms that invest ahead of regulatory requirements.

References

Afsah, S., B. Laplante and D. Wheeler (1996), 'Controlling Industrial Pollution: A New Paradigm', policy research working paper No. 1672, World Bank, Washington.

Angel, D. and M. Rock (2000), *Asia's Clean Revolution: Industry, Growth and the Environment*, Greenleaf, Sheffield.

Arora Seema and T. N. Cason (1996), 'Why Do Firms Volunteer to Exceed Environmental Regulations? Understanding Participation in EPA's 33/50 Programme', *Land Economics*, 72 (4) (November), 413–32.

Bankoff, G. and K. Elston (1994), *Environmental Regulation in Malaysia and Singapore*, Asia Paper 2, University of Western Australia Press in association with Asia Research Centre, Nedlands.

Bansal, P. (1997), 'Business Strategy and the Environment', in P. Bansal and E. Howard (eds.), *Business and the Natural Environment*, Butterworth-Heinemann, Oxford, pp. 173–94.

Briffett, C. (1996), 'Monitoring the Effectiveness of Environment Impact Assessment in Southeast Asia', *Asian Journal of Environmental Management*, 4 (1), 53–63.

Brophy, M. and R. Starkey (1996), 'Environmental Reporting', in R. Welford (ed.), *Corporate Environmental Management: Systems and Strategies*, Earthscan, London, pp. 177–200.

CAP (1998), 'Land: Emerging Issues and Challenges', declaration and recommendations at Penang National Conference 1997, Consumer Association of Penang, Penang, Malaysia.

CAP and SAM (1996), *Case of the Malaysian Environment*, Consumer Association of Penang and Sahabat Alam Malaysia, Penang, Malaysia.

Chia, L. S. (1995), *Protecting the Marine Environment of ASEAN from Ship-Generated Oil Pollution and Japan's Contribution to the Region*, VRF Series No. 245, Institute of Developing Economies, Tokyo.

Collier, J. (1995), *The Corporate Environment: The Financial Consequences for Business*, Prentice Hall, London.

Corlett, R. (1992), 'The Changing Urban Vegetation', in A. Gupta and J. Pitts (eds.), *Physical Adjustments in A Changing Landscape: The Singapore Story*, Singapore University Press, Singapore, pp. 190–214.

Deans, J. (1998), 'A Legal Look at Environmental Risks and Liabilities in Asia', *Asian Journal of Environmental Management* 6 (1), 1–12.

Economic Development Board (1998), *Census of Industrial Production*, Economic Development Board, Singapore.

Eden, S. (1996), *Environmental Issues and Business Implications of a Changing Agenda*, John Wiley and Sons, Chicester.

Environmental Quality Report (1998), *Malaysia: Environmental Quality Report 1998*, Department of Environment, Ministry of Science, Technology and the Environment, Kuala Lumpur, Malaysia.

ESCAP/UNCTC (1988), *Transnational Corporations and Environmental Management in Selected Asian and Pacific Developing Countries*, Economic and Social Commission for Asia and Pacific, Bangkok.

Esty, D., M. Pangestu and H. Soesastro, H. (2000), 'Globalisation and the Environment in Asia: Linkages, Impacts and Policy Implications', in D. Angel and M. Rock (eds.), *Asia's Clean Revolution – Industry, Growth and Environment*, Greenleaf, Sheffield, pp. 63–87.

Flavin, C. and Tunali, O. (1996), Climate of Hope: New Strategies for Industry, Island Press, Washington D.C.

Florida. R., (1996), 'Lean and Green: A Move to Environmentally Conscious Manufacturing', *California Management Review*, 39 (1), 80–105.

Gereffi, G. (1994), 'The International Economy and Economic Development', in N. Smelser and R. Swedberg (eds.), *The Handbook of Economic Sociology*, Princeton University Press, Princeton, NJ, pp. 206–33.

Gomez, J. (1999), *Self Censorship: Singapore's Shame*, The Think Centre, Singapore.

Gonzalez III, J. , K. Lander and B. Melles (2000), *Opting for Partnership: Governance Innovation in Southeast Asia*, Institute of Governance, Ottawa and Kuala Lumpur.

Gouldson, A. and J. Murphy (1998), *Regulatory Realities: The Implementation and Impact of Industrial Environmental Regulation*, Earthscan Publications, London.

Grolin, J. (1998), 'Corporate Legitimacy in a Risk Society: The Case of Brent Spar', *Business Strategy and the Environment*, 7, 213–22.

Hansen, M. W. and H. R. Gleckman (1993), 'Environmental Management of Multinational and Transnational Corporations: Policies, Practices and Recommendations', in R. V. Kolluru (ed.), *Environmental Strategies Handbook*, McGraw-Hill, New York, pp. 749–95.

Harding, A. (1996), 'Practical Human Rights, NGOs and the Environment in Malaysia', in A. Boyle and M. Anderson (eds.), *Human Rights Approaches to Environmental Protection*, Clarendon Press, Oxford, pp. 227–44.

Harwell, E. (2000), 'Remote Sensibilities: Discourses of Technology and the Making of Indonesia's Natural Disaster', *Development and Change*, 31, 307–40.

Hawkins, K. (1990), 'Compliance Strategy, Prosecution Policy and Aunt Sally: A Comment on Pearce and Tombs', *British Journal of Criminology* 30, 444–66.

Hesp, P. (1995), 'The Environmental Impact Assessment Process in Singapore with Particular Reference to Coastal Environments and the Role of NGOs', *Journal of Coastal Conservation*, 1 (2), 135–44.

Hilton, M. and S. Manning (1995), 'Conversion of Coastal Habitats in Singapore: Indicators of Unsustainable Development', *Environmental Conservation*, 22 (4), 307–22.

ISOworld (2000), http://www.ecology.or.jp/isoworld/english/analy14k.htm

Jacobs, M. (1997), *The Green Economy: Environment, Sustainable Development and the Politics of the Future*, Pluto Press, London.

Jaffe, A., S. Peterson, P. Portney and R. Stavins (1995), 'Environmental Regulation and the Competitiveness of US Manufacturing: What Does the Evidence Tell Us?', *Journal of Economic Literature*, 33 (1), 132–63.

Jenkins, R. (2000), 'Corporate Codes of Conduct: Self-regulation in a Global Economy', paper prepared for the UNRISD Workshop on Promoting Corporate Responsibility in Developing Countries: The Potential and Limits of Voluntary Initiatives, Geneva, 23–24 October 2000.

Jones, D. M. and D. Brown (1994), 'Singapore and the Myth of the Liberalizing Middle Class', *The Pacific Review*, 7 (1), 79–87.

Labatt, S. and V. Maclaren (1998), 'Voluntary Corporate Environmental Initiatives: A Typology and Preliminary Investigation', *Environment and Planning C*, 16, 191–209.

Lau, T. L. (1993), 'Environmental Issues: Singapore Student Awareness', academic paper, Department of Geography, National University of Singapore, Singapore.

Levy, D. (1997), 'Environment Management as Political Sustainability', *Organization and Environment*, 10 (2), 126–47.

Lober, D. (1997), 'Explaining the Formation of Business–Environmentalist Collaborations: Collaborative Windows and the Paper Task Force', *Policy Sciences*, 30, 1–24.

Markandya, A. and V. Shibli (1995), 'Industrial Pollution Control Policies in Asia: How Successful Are the Strategies?', *Asian Journal of Environmental Management*, 3 (2), 87–117.

MIDA (1997), *1997 Annual Report*, Malaysia Industrial Development Authority, Malaysia.

Ministry of Environment (1992), *Green Plan*, Ministry of Environment, Singapore.

Murphy, D. and J. Bendell (1997), *In the Company of Partners: Business, Environmental Groups and Sustainable Development Post Rio*, Policy Press, Bristol.

Netherwood, A. (1996), 'Environmental Management Systems', in R. Welford (ed.), *Corporate*

Environmental Management System and Strategies, Earthscan, London, pp. 35–58.

Ng, S. K. (1994), 'Environmental Consciousness among Women in Singapore', academic paper, Department of Geography, National University of Singapore, Singapore.

Pargal, S., H. Hettige, Manjula Singh and D. Wheeler (1997), 'Formal and Informal Regulation of Industrial Pollution: Comparative Evidence from Indonesia and US', policy research working paper No. 1797, World Bank, Washington DC.

Patten, D. (1991), 'Exposure, Legitimacy and Social Disclosure', *Journal of Accounting and Public Policy*, 10, 297–308.

Perry, M and T. S. Teng (1998), 'An Overview of Trends Related to Environmental Reporting in Singapore', *Environmental Management and Health*, 10 (5), 310–20.

Perry, M., L. Kong and B. Yeoh (1997), *Singapore: A Development City State*, John Wiley and Sons, Chichester.

Petts, J. (2000), 'The Regulator–Regulated Relationship and Environmental Protection: Perceptions in Small and Medium-sized Enterprises', *Environment and Planning C: Government and Policy*, 18 (2), 191–206.

Piesse, J. (1992), 'Environmental Spending and Share Price Performance: The Petroleum Industry', *Business Strategy and the Environment*, 1 (1), 45–54.

Porter, M. and C. van der Linde (1995), 'Green and Competitive: Ending the Stalemate', *Harvard Business Review* , September–October, 120–34.

Rasiah, R. (1999), 'Transnational Corporations and the Environment: The Case of Malaysia', occasional paper No. 4, Cross-Border Environmental Management in Transnational Corporations, UNCTAD and Copenhagen Business School, Copenhagen.

Rodgers, C. (2000), 'Making It Legit: New Ways of Generating Corporate Legitimacy in a Globalising World', in J. Bendell (ed.), *Terms for Endearment*, Greenleaf, Sheffield, pp. 40–9.

Roht-Arriaza, N. (1995), 'Shifting the Point of Regulation: The International Organisation for Standardisation and Global Law Making on Trade and Environment', *Ecology Law Quarterly*, 22, 479–539.

Salleh Mohamed Nor (2000), 'Access, Power and Governance of the Environment: Global and Local Perspectives', in R. Rahim and K. J. John (eds.), *Access, Empowerment and Governance in the Information Age*, NITC, Kuala Lumpur, Malaysia.

Savage, V. R. (1995), 'Eco-education in Singapore', in G. L. Ooi (ed.), *Environment and the City: Sharing Singapore's Experience and Future Challenges*, Times Academic Press, Singapore, pp. 313–30.

—— (1998), 'North–South Environmental Issues: Eco-education in Southeast Asia', in V. R. Savage, L. Kong and W. Neville (eds.), *The Naga Awakens: Growth and Change in Southeast Asia*, Times Academic Press, Singapore, pp. 261–84.

Sham Sani (1999), *Environmental Management Issues and Challenges in the Next Millennium in Malaysia*, Environmental Management Programme, Universiti Kebangsaan Malaysia, Bangi, Malaysia.

Sheperd, C. (1997), 'Gloom Across the Horizon', *Asiaweek*, 3 October, 37–52.

Simmons, P. and B. Wynne (1993), 'Responsible Care: Trust, Credibility and Environmental Management', in K. Fisher and J. Schot (eds.), *Environmental Strategies for Industry: International Perspectives on Research Needs and Policy Implications*, Island Press, Washington DC, pp. 201–26.

Singh, S. and M. Perry (2000), 'Voluntary Environmental Initiatives: ISO 14001 Certified Organisations in Singapore', *Asia Pacific Veiwpoint*, 41 (3), 269–78.

Sizer, N. and D. Plouvier (2000), *Increased Investment and Trade by Transnational Logging Companies in Africa, the Caribbean and the Pacific*, World Wide Fund for Nature, Brussels.

Sonnenfeld, D. (1999), 'Logging versus Recycling: Problems in the Industrial Ecology of Pulp Manufacturing in Southeast Asia', in W. Wehrmeyer and Y. Mulugetta (eds.), *Growing Pains: Environmental Management in Developing Countries*, Greenleaf, Sheffield, pp. 243–54.

Suchman, M. (1995), 'Managing Legitimacy: Strategic and Institutional Approaches', *Academy of Management Review*, 20 (3), 571–610.

Tanner, D., R. Bellamy and C. Mason (1997), *Environmental Management in Asia: A Guide to ISO 14000*, Regional Institute of Environmental Technology, Singapore.

Tay, J. H. (1995), 'Singapore', in K. Saurai (ed.), *Cleaner Production for Green Productivity: Asian*

Perspectives, Asian Productivity Organisation, Tokyo, pp. 370–421.

Tay, S. (forthcoming), 'Business and Sustainable Development in South East Asia', *UBC Journal of Business Administration*.

Teng, T. S. (1997), 'Business Environmental Disclosure in Singapore', unpublished honours thesis, Department of Geography, National University of Singapore.

UNCTAD (1996), *Self-Regulation of Environmental Management: An Analysis of Guidelines Set by World Industry Associations for their Member Firms*, UNCTAD, Geneva.

Utting, P. (2000), 'Business Responsibility for Sustainable Development', occasional paper No. 2, United Nations Research Institute for Social Development, Geneva.

Wong, C. K. (1997), 'The Geography of Supermarket Retailing and Green Product Availability in Singapore', academic paper, Department of Geography, National University of Singapore, Singapore.

World Bank (2000), *Greening Industry*, World Bank, New York.

World Resource Institute (1997), *World Resources 1997–98*, Oxford University Press, New York.

Zarsky, L. and S. Tay (2000), 'Civil Society and the Future of Environmental Governance in Asia', in D. Angel and M. Rock (eds.), *Asia's Clean Revolution – Industry, Growth and Environment*, Greenleaf, Sheffield, pp. 128–54.

PART II

Promoting Corporate Environmental Responsibility

Mechanisms and Strategies

6

Disturbing Development
Conflicts between Corporate Environmentalism, the International Economic Order and Sustainability

RICHARD WELFORD

M14 Q52 O13
F23 Q57 Q56

Introduction

There can now be little doubt that the environmental damage caused to the planet over the last few decades has reached a point where it is causing untold damage to humans and to other species. Much of that damage is irreversible and the massive use of non-renewable resources has taken little account of the needs of future generations. The situation is getting worse, impacting on human health, biodiversity and the social infrastructure of many societies. There is now clear evidence of climate change and that we are losing the areas of wilderness left on the planet at an alarming rate. Governments have directed little real effort at reversing these trends, preferring to leave the task to the voluntary efforts of businesses, pressure groups, other non-governmental organizations and individuals. Perhaps more than anywhere, the environmental crisis is most acute in the developing world, where it is directly impacting upon the lives and health of local populations and contributing to many of the social problems which we now observe.

The environmental crisis is not a phenomenon which is going to happen sometime in the future unless we do something: we are *now* faced with many serious environmental problems. Business has to accept a very large share of the responsibility for this situation. Businesses are central to a system of production and consumption which is destroying life on Earth; if we continue along this path, not one area of wilderness, indigenous culture, endangered species, or uncontaminated water supply will survive the global market economy. The often uncritical acceptance of trends towards globalization and the emphasis on the need for (naive measures of) economic growth make the situation worse. If trends towards globalization mean that production shifts to low-wage economies where labour is continuously under pressure to produce more and at lower costs, we can hardly view this as consistent with development. In parallel, if growth in the first world simply results in underdevelopment in the Third World, then this simply widens the inequities, which are inconsistent with a move towards sustainable development.

Given the current international economic order, it is likely that future environmental crises, which are inevitable, will occur not in countries at the root of the

135

industrialization process, but in those which are currently growing at the fastest rates, where business activity is expanding rapidly and where institutional structures are least able to deal with the consequences of accelerating production and consumption. These are the developing countries, which have long been neglected in the debates over the appropriateness of corporate environmental management strategies and tools.

This chapter examines the conflicts between sustainable development, the current international economic order and contemporary corporate environmentalism. It does so in three main parts. We begin by considering trends and contradictions associated with free international trade and globalization. The next section moves on to describe current corporate environmentalism in the context of modernism. We then identify changes at the level of the firm which would be more consistent with a move towards sustainable development, and consider policy reforms and frameworks that would encourage corporate environmental and social responsibility.

The International Economic Order

In line with the move towards the globalized, free market economy, governments have created an international environment of deregulation because free markets, unrestrained by governments, are supposed to result in higher economic growth as measured by gross national output. The primary responsibility of industrial policy seems to be to provide an infrastructure which will help corporations expand their commercial activities. In this respect, governments seek to enforce the rule of law with respect to property rights and contracts – without which the capitalist system comes to a halt. Privatization has been espoused over the last fifteen years and we have seen valuable national assets shifted from the control of governments to the private sector in the name of efficiency. Thus the very role of governments has been to transfer more and more power to the corporate private sector.

Around the world, governments and inter-governmental agencies have shifted towards a more conservative view of economics and industry. Embracing social democratic principles and democratic capitalism, the left talks increasingly of 'the stakeholder society' and less of vested interests and the living standards of the working classes. But, in general, mainstream political parties have not embraced green ideas. They have operated on the edges of the environmental debate, waiting to see if the green vote will be significant enough for them to respond. They have, therefore, consistently lacked any real leadership on environmental issues and their policies have been devoid of any radical green ideas or vision. The green political agenda (weak as it is) represents a tension between pressure groups, indigenous protesters and human rights activists, on one hand and, on the other, the vested interests of the large corporations seeking cheap labour and plentiful resources. This is a battleground where politicians have consistently feared to tread. The resulting outcome is that the more powerful business world is allowed to continue its march oblivious to burning rain forests, rare habitats, dangerous waste sites, unsustainable consumption patterns and the legitimization of greed.

More fundamentally, however, we must now recognize that politicians and governments no longer have sole control over the management of nations. They may still be able to wage war with their massive stocks of destructive arms when opinion polls desert them, but the management of the economic process has to be done in cooperation with business. Of the hundred biggest economic institutions in the world today, about half are countries and half are companies. Businesses have become expert at shaping societies and cultures. Indeed, it is business which has created the consumer culture, the fast food culture, and insatiable materialism. It is business which would like to set out its vision of the world's monoculture with its global products, global messages and mass markets. It is even business which supports and sponsors the politicians and political parties which will give it what it wants. Money can buy a lot of votes – one way or another. Thus to look to governments for radical change would be tantamount to expecting the big cats to become vegetarian – it isn't in their nature.

Moreover, large corporations have a significant advantage over governments. They are able to cross national boundaries much more easily. The transnational corporations with their massive stock of private capital are much more influential on the global stage than any government or even inter-governmental agency can be. The capital which they use to broker agreements replacing vital natural resources with industrial plant is essentially nomadic. This means that the large corporation is able to change the direction of development of the many countries dependent on its patronage, to suit whatever short-term objective seems paramount at any point in time. What development there is in the Third World, for example, is often directed, dependent development, and the aspirations of indigenous populations and local environmental concerns are rarely given any real priority. The institutions of government and the inter-governmental agencies which are supposed to protect the greater interest are therefore failing.

There is, therefore, what we might call a 'governance gap'. Whilst we have seen the growth and globalization of business we have not seen an equivalent globalization of government and democracy. There have been virtually no successful initiatives to introduce international regulations governing the behaviour of companies and there is no requirement for companies to be accountable to a global audience, but only to be financially accountable in those countries where they decide to declare their profits. This represents a fundamental problem: the power of corporate elites far exceeds the power of any democratically elected institution. In many ways corporations really do now rule the world (Korten, 1995).

Moreover, companies are very happy to work with many governments in developing countries and support them, even when they are not democratically elected and their record on human rights is poor. There is a mutual understanding between such governments and business that the bottom line is to support each other's aspirations. This often translates into collusion between governments and businesses to maintain low wages and poor working conditions, as well as financial support for government elites. And very often it results in the corruption of government institutions. Fees are paid to politicians and senior government officials, siphoned out of countries and into secret bank accounts. Undemocratic governments are able to control dissident voices, often with the tacit cooperation of corporations.

Thus, without the necessary governmental controls, we have seen some hitherto beneficial corporations turned into finance-driven institutions which thrive on market tyranny. They move smoothly across national boundaries, colonizing ever more of the planet's valuable living spaces. They plunder wilderness in the name of progress, destroying ecosystems and people's livelihoods. People are displaced, their values ignored and the dominant corporate culture invades traditions, beliefs and long-established ritual. The large corporation, the transnational business, is detached from place. It wanders around the world picking off smaller enterprises and influencing sovereign democratic processes. But even productive business is threatened by the globalized financial system which it itself helped to create. This system is less interested in the production of real wealth through productive innovation and more interested in the extraction of money. Thus, as Korten (1995) points out:

> The big winners are the corporate raiders who strip sound companies of their assets for short-term gain and the speculators who capitalize on market volatility to extract a private tax from those who are engaged in productive work and investment.

Although depressing, the message here is not one of despair. It is within our means to reclaim the power that we have yielded to the institutions of money and recreate societies that nurture cultural and biological diversity. There are huge opportunities for developing social, intellectual, spiritual, and ecological advancement beyond our present imagination. But first we must challenge the existing order.

Business so often begins with the premise that globalization is a reality and there is nothing that can be done to stop the trend. End of story. In taking this line it cleverly sidesteps any debate over the inherent contradictions between globalization and sustainable development. And by ignoring that debate, business fails to acknowledge its role as a major barrier to sustainable development. Three sets of contradictions seem particularly pertinent. Let us deal with each one in turn.

Responsible business and the international economic order

Business responsibility in relation to social and environmental aspects is constrained by the pressures which globalization exerts upon companies. The need to make profits in a highly competitive international marketplace means that costs have to be continually driven down. There is little room in corporate budgets for anything which is not perceived as strictly necessary or for anything which does not have a short payback period in a traditional business sense. Such intense competition drives out any scope for creativity, reflection and responsibility. For many Northern companies, simply surviving and maintaining employment in such a hostile environment is difficult enough.

As if to make the situation worse, competitors in low-wage economies with access to Northern markets are able to undercut domestic firms. Low wages become a major source of competitive advantage and therefore high wages (as paid to workers in the North) become a source of inefficiency. Job cuts are made or the company itself relocates to low-wage economies. Human beings become little more than factors of production and when the globalized system makes them inefficient they are simply substituted out of production.

The emphasis on cost reduction as a source of competitiveness often, therefore, turns out to be destructive. Moreover, even when companies switch to producing in low-wage economies, that is not the end of the potential for cost reduction. The exploitation of the natural environment follows, with firms clearing forests, mining in unsustainable ways and convincing governments to let them have access to more and more resources in order to aid development. Social and environmental responsibility comes pretty low down on any such business agenda. And when breaches of any such responsibility are easy to hide (as they commonly are in the Third World), then it is unlikely even to figure at all.

The international economic order and sustainable development

It has to be recognized that growth and development are different things. In some cases a degree of growth has benefited development. However, the type of growth we are now witnessing is often not consistent with development. Since the latter implies a qualitative improvement in the lives of human beings, it is difficult to see how low-wage economies, the destruction of natural resources and the undemocratic political power of corporations are consistent with such development. Moreover, economic growth in one part of the world actually requires a degree of underdevelopment in other parts of the world in order to provide the cheap labour and resources to fuel competitiveness. Thus the international economic order becomes divisive and stimulates as much underdevelopment as it creates growth.

Moreover, what development does occur is often not sustainable either economically or environmentally. It is too often based on treating the environment as a free good and tends to result in high levels of pollution. It relies on easy access to resources. But such factors cannot last for ever and there is an inevitability about economic collapse following environmental collapse. The future could as easily be about resource wars as it is about some harmonious free-enterprise global economy.

The whole process of globalization means that goods, services, capital and, to a lesser extent, labour are free to move around the world. This greatly reduces the ability of individual firms to develop policy instruments and other measures consistent with sustainable development. The introduction of environmental regulations or taxation could lead to a degree of (perceived) uncompetitiveness and result in less favoured treatment by powerful transnationals. Thus there is a power vacuum and national governments are unable to respond in a way that promotes sustainable development.

Indeed, the international economic order, with the support of multilateral financial agencies and the World Bank, takes Third World countries in completely the wrong direction. As Herman Daly points out, 'free trade, specialization, and global integration mean that nations are no longer free *not* to trade. Yet freedom not to trade is surely necessary if trade is to be mutually beneficial.' The upshot, he argues, is likely to be not only serious conflict between nations but also between classes within nations (Daly, 1996: 157). The international economic order imposes economic austerity measures on the South in order to promote the free market economy, reduce wages and cut government spending. These sorts of policies are inducing not development but planned underdevelopment. The rights of individuals in developing countries become secondary to the whims of IMF economists and the power of commerce in such a system. It is, of course, true that commerce has enriched countries and increased material standards of living, but in so doing it has also created powerful individuals, ruling families and a corporate elite. The benefits of trade and globalization which do accrue to developing countries are not well distributed.

Business and sustainable development

Clearly the constraints discussed above mean that business actually has a very hard task if it wants to internalize policies and strategies which are consistent with the move towards more sustainable development. But the way companies behave makes the situation even worse. Since firms seek to maximize profits (even though much of those profits is consumed inside the firm rather than distributed to shareholders), there will always be an incentive for them to externalize costs. In the first world there are many social and environmental costs which are imposed on companies: minimum wages, national insurance contributions, welfare programmes, health and safety measures, pollution control, liability for accidents, and so on. Many of these costs can be externalized simply by a shift of location. Indeed, what globalization creates is a process of lowering standards which companies are often happy to accept. In such a context, it becomes extremely difficult to adopt policies which could move us towards sustainable development but which would result in costs being imposed on business.

Instead, the business community espouses the voluntary approach which requires us to to sit back and trust companies to adopt methods more consistent with sustainable development. But most people do not actually trust big business any more. There is little evidence that corporations are taking the sorts of measures required or that they are even interested in sustainable development. Unfortunately, there is rather a lot of evidence of corporate involvement in human rights violations, illegal payments to governments and negligence over pollution controls.

Business has yet to realize that if the international economic order continues in its present form, and the demands of sustainable development are ignored, they are bringing about their own demise. There is an environmental crisis in the world but perhaps it is not yet of the magnitude which will force business (and governments) to face up to their real responsibilities. The problem is that when business eventually gets around to acknowledging its true role, it may be too late. Until then, it will continue to push the type of modernist agenda which we now consider.

Corporate Philosophy and Practice

Modernism

The free market, the global economic system and its consequential unsustainable path are founded on the vestiges of modernism. Modernism originally referred to the civilization that developed in Europe and North America over the last several centuries and became fully evident by the early twentieth century. But the modernist tradition, characterized by capitalism, a largely secular culture, liberal democracy, individualism, rationalism and humanism (Cahoone, 1996), is now rapidly spreading to the developing world. It is being upheld not only by northern corporations but also by transnationals and other companies from developing countries whose business strategies are based on the same principles. There is now, therefore, a global corporate culture which believes that natural resources are there for the taking and that environmental and social problems will be resolved through growth, scientific advancement, technology transfer via private capital flows, free trade and the odd charitable hand-out.

Modernism has seen new machine technologies and modes of industrial production that have led to an unprecedented rise in material living standards in the North but have often resulted in exploitation in the South. The continuation of this process, with its emphasis on output growth and free trade, is what has become so unsustainable. The results are easy to see: environmental destruction, anthropocentrism, the dissolution of community, the loss of individuality and diversity, the rise of alienation and the demise of tradition. Even notions of development are now often equated only with economic growth. As Shiva and Bandyopadhyay (1989) point out:

> The ideology of the dominant pattern of development derives its driving force from a linear theory of progress, from a vision of historical evolution created in eighteenth- and nineteenth-century Western Europe and universalized throughout the world, especially in the post-war development decades. The linearity of history, presupposed in this theory of progress, created an ideology of development that equated development with economic growth, economic growth with expansion of the market economy, modernism with consumerism, and non-market economies with backwardness.

It is undeniable that capitalism has been a great wealth creator because it has unlocked the potential to use basic natural resources and process them into valuable material objects. However, it is also undeniable that, because growth has been so rapid, current wealth is being generated by stealing it from future generations. How will future generations continue the process when there are no resources left? Can this be left to the ubiquitous free market system to sort out?

Given its power in the modern world, business must be seen as both central to the problem and central to the solution. If we are to avoid further environmental and social crises, there is no alternative but to change the way in which businesses and markets allocate resources. At present, however, that very system rewards those businesses which can produce goods at the lowest possible capital and labour costs whilst largely ignoring the value of nature and environmental degradation. Many businesses would agree that there must be change. The conflict is over the degree of change. To date businesses in the North that have begun to respond to environ-mental issues have done so in quite piecemeal and marginal ways. In the developing world most businesses have done even less. Thus as globalization produces a shift of the manufacturing sector towards low-wage economies, the process actually makes the environmental situation worse.

Business leaders are not stupid; many are aware of what is happening in the world around them and recognize the need for some action. But they are often unsure of what to do and feel constrained by the international economic order which requires them to continually drive down their costs. As environmental awareness has increased, there have been calls for businesses to respond in a more environmentally responsible way. Some have begun to do so but in ways that generally ensure that their environmental strategies do not conflict with their need to make profits. Business has wanted to make sure that the definition of environ-mental protection and social responsibility is consistent with its other objectives. The more radical goals and policies associated with 'deep' green politics are not consistent with the other aspirations of business which will always be put before the environment. The interests of people in developing countries are less important than the needs of shareholders and customers. Moreover, in the globalized marketplace the exploitation of workers in the Third World is fully consistent with the need to maintain competitiveness.

Since there is very little analysis of what a business really is and of its place in society (in terms of social responsibility and politics), there is very little under-standing of what business could become. Furthermore, change is often resisted by shareholders, managers and others who are generally satisfied with the performance of their corporations in the context of the current economic system. Free-market capitalism does little to solve these problems. It is not the great dynamic entity which its proponents espouse; rather, it actually creates a good degree of inertia. The single-minded emphasis on profit, efficiency, cost reduction and growth dwarfs issues such as employment, protection of the environment, social responsibility and sustainable development.

Business, therefore, stands at the edge of a massive potential transformation. With their huge power, large corporations can begin to challenge the economic order if they really wished to do so. But large corporations must be persuaded, cajoled or even forced to realize that it is in the interests of all human beings for them to change. However, it seems that only a minority are currently committed to change or have any coherent vision about how to behave more responsibly. The reality is that most corporations duck and dive, invest in smoke screens, hide behind science and technology, and espouse gradualist, marginal solutions in response to societal pressures.

Business can and will have to be different if we fully integrate the principles of sustainable development into the international economic order. Hawken (1994) reflects the view of many who believe that there is now the potential for a transformation in the role and responsibilities of business. The marginalism of modernism will not be enough and change will have to be radical and thorough. It may be that business, in the future, will be unrecognizable when compared to the commercial institutions of today. That scenario is entirely possible but it is currently blocked by business itself and the globalized system in which it operates. Increasing the importance which we attach to development issues in the Third World must be a starting point, along with challenging those who try to interpret sustainable development in narrow terms which often ignore the social aspects of that concept. Indeed, even the term 'sustainable development' is often shortened to 'sustainability'. The concept of development becomes an afterthought or, worse, simply ignored. And the term sustainability itself is often interpreted even more narrowly in terms of only environmental sustainability. There is a need to consider the development side of the issue in greater detail than has so far been the case.

We should not be surprised to see so much inertia in businesses. Industry cannot imagine that it can survive in a world of adjustment which may require cutbacks, decentralization, less rather than more, and free trade being replaced by fair trade. The driving force is more and more profit and the accumulation of ever greater stocks of capital. There is an emphasis on maximizing shareholder value with much less regard to the impact of consequent strategies on other stakeholders. The basic premise turns out to be that the action which yields the greatest financial return to the individual or firm is the one that is most beneficial to society. We rarely bother to examine, however, just how profits are made, or ask if they are justifiable or in the interests of the wider international community which has worked to produce them. There is insufficient debate over the sources of those profits and just how they are attained. Perhaps when profits are declared there should be some sort of transparent statement relating to just how they were derived and what were the associated social and environmental impacts. Paul Hawken (1994) makes a very perceptive point about corporate profits:

> The language of commerce sounds specific, but in fact it is not specific enough. If Hawaiians had 138 different ways to describe falling rain, we can assume that rain had a profound importance in their lives. Business, on the other hand, only has two words for profit – gross and net. The extraordinarily complex manner in which a company recovers profit is reduced to a single numerically neat and precise concept. It makes no distinctions as to how the profit was made. It does not factor in whether people or places were exploited, resources depleted, communities enhanced, lives lost, or whether the entire executive suite was in such turmoil as to require stress consultants and outplacement services for the victims. In other words, business does not discern whether the profit is one of quality or mere quantity.

It is not unlikely that social crisis, rather than environmental degradation, will be the force that will eventually bring about fundamental change. Since using labour more than absolutely necessary becomes a source of inefficiency, there is always an incentive for business to employ fewer people, to pay them less, to shed labour whenever possible and to replace human with technological capital. We are therefore moving into a world where fewer and fewer people will be involved in the productive process and therefore the number of people benefiting from the activities of industry will decline. It is difficult to see how social systems can continue to support growing numbers of unemployed people who in many countries become homeless beggars, criminals, drug addicts and residents of refugee camps.

Eco-efficiency or 'business as usual'

Slowly, the pressures on companies to change are building. As a result a number of large corporations (mainly from the North) have actively engaged in the environmental debate during the past ten years. Some industrialists have considered the arguments of traditional environmentalists but have generally found them too threatening or too difficult to operationalize (Welford, 1997). It is not surprising, therefore, that they have sought out a discourse on the environment which fits within their other aims and objectives.

The discourse is that of 'ecomodernism'. It is typified by the following paragraphs taken from the original Declaration of the Business Council for Sustainable Development (Schmidheiny, 1992):

> Economic growth in all parts of the world is essential to improve the livelihoods of the poor, to sustain growing populations, and eventually to stabilize population levels. New technologies will be needed to permit growth while using energy and other resources more efficiently and producing less pollution. Open and competitive markets, both within and between nations, foster innovation and efficiency and provide opportunities for all to improve their living conditions.

Thus ecomodernism's frame of reference is the here and now, working within the present institutional framework. It sees private capital as a main instrument for change and emphasizes the role of the free market. Moreover, ecomodernism is actually defined to satisfy the wider interests of business. Schmidheiny (1992: 99) reflects this when he argues:

> Companies now have to work with governments to spread environmentally efficient production processes throughout the global business community.... This will require significant technological, managerial, and organizational changes, new investments, and new product lines ... it will be increasingly in a company's own interests to develop cleaner products and processes.

At the centre of ecomodernism we find the search for 'eco-efficiency'. I have never found a very clear definition of what this really means but the minimalist definition provided by Schmidheiny (1992: 98) suggests that it is simply 'the ratio of resource inputs and waste outputs to final product'. Thus using traditional business tools of systems and audits, eco-efficiency essentially works on the trade-off between industrial activity and the environment, continuing to do 'business as usual' and adding in concern for the environment. This definition is technologically oriented and implies that solutions can be found which will allow the rich North to consume more and more whilst using fewer and fewer natural resources. The tool of eco-efficiency sees no alternative to businesses setting the environmental agenda and controlling the greening of growth through the vehicle of technology transfer via private capital.

Ecomodernism, therefore, with eco-efficiency as its flagship tool, represents 'business as usual'; not a break with what went before but a continuation of it. It adds an environmental dimension to the traditional growth path but does not allow that dimension to change the path radically. Perhaps more importantly, the ecomodernist trend has been subtly designed to reinforce the growth trend, justify the power of private capital, promote globalization and ignore most of the social dimensions of sustainable development.

Ecomodernism as a philosophy is a response to concern about the environment held by people and institutions who are persuaded of the need for marginal change rather than something more fundamental or radical. As such, it represents the hijacking of traditional notions of environmentalism (however disparate) which exist within various ecosocialist, ecoliberal and ecoradical groups. Indeed, rather than impart any new green values, ecomodernism actually destroys the debate amongst ecologists. The ecomodernist approach takes us away from, not closer to, a greener future (Welford, 1997).

The sterility of ecomodernism is also one of its key characteristics. Its emphasis on positivism and rationality and its conservative nature mean that it denies the existence of spiritual dimensions to the debate which are at the heart of deeper green politics. It calls for technological change in a way which assumes that all technology is good and leaves out any mention of the importance of engaging human beings in a move towards sustainable development. Moreover, and very importantly, ecomodernism is wedded to the ideals of maintaining the wealth of the rich (in terms of both individuals and countries). There is a hidden recognition that growth in one area often creates underdevelopment in another but this seems to be of little consequence to the ecomodernists. The clear implication is that there is always something which will have priority over ecological action. Essentially, ecological action becomes an add-on feature of 'business as usual', given emphasis when time and resources allow, or when crisis or public pressure requires a response.

There is clearly a great deal of overlap between models of eco-efficiency and the technological-fix school of thought. This is essentially a defensive position which sees science and technology as bulwarks of traditional notions of capitalism. Industry in the North continues to defend its domination of the world order by increasing productive capacity through the displacement of labour in favour of capital. This leaves the majority of citizens fighting over an ever-shrinking share of the pie whilst a small, powerful, industrial elite seeks to maintain its vested interests through marginal adaptations to the demands of the rest of us. There is simply no systematic consideration of the full social consequences of allowing this sort of technological determinism. There is no debate over the rights of people and the right to work within whatever economic system exists. This is the world of industrial imperialism.

It is not surprising that alternatives to ecomodernism frighten the corporate establishment and that their response has been to make sure that the type of environmentalism adopted is consistent with their own aspirations. Any model of environmentalism outside of ecomodernism would involve a break with 'business as usual'. It would challenge the pillars of free trade, scientific and technological domination and the orthodoxy of economic growth.

Those who advocate eco-efficiency talk about 'ecology' when they really mean 'environmental protection' because they do not perceive there to be any difference. Ecologists know that the scale on which we do things is too massive, complex, unwieldy, exploitative and alienating. This is never considered by business because the economic system demands greater scale. Mass demand, mass markets, mass consumption and globalization come to dominate any notion of the greening of industry. Even the population explosion is rarely considered because it does, after all, present new market opportunities. Eco-efficiency does not only fit within the growth paradigm, it is subtly designed to reinforce it.

The ecomodernist approach sees the future as being a product of what went before. Environmentalism, it asserts, must therefore be embedded in what is here and now. The postmodern perspective, which associates the environmental debate more clearly with a break from the past, is largely ignored. The usual approach taken to environmental management strategies is therefore largely integrationalist. In other words, corporate environmental management is integrated into (or, worse, bolted on to) 'business as usual'. The most significant question, therefore, revolves around the importance attached to environmentalism. If integration is equivalent to the watering down of environmentalism, then it must be seen as a step backwards.

It is increasingly clear that when we discuss environmentalism many of us are essentially speaking very different languages. The rhetoric surrounding ecomodernism lacks any real vision and ignores the complex social and cultural issues which many of us see as central to sustainable development. It lacks any real dialogue and is largely applicable only to the developed world. Those who want to discuss more radical forms of environmentalism are often ignored and sidelined by business. It is asserted by those with power that there is no alternative to the model they have chosen. But they rarely seek the opinions of those who propose alternatives. Corporations rarely consult, for example, powerless indigenous populations in developing countries. Those who demand a greater degree of self-determination and locally oriented development models are told that the world is not like that. It treats globalization as a 'given', not something to be challenged.

When industry is under pressure, a common strategy is to create business fora or clubs to further increase their power and to provide evidence that they are taking action. One such club is the influential World Business Council for Sustainable Development. Established by wealthy businessmen, it has pushed a line wholly consistent with ecomodernism. Such clubs are created when public restlessness makes industry feel lonely. They are essentially fortresses built to fend off the attacking environmentalists. They may engage in consultation and consensus building, but that 'consensus' is usually well-defined a long time before any consultation takes place.

A common characteristic amongst businesses is to do only as much as is perceived to be absolutely necessary. At the same time, what little is done is often given an extraordinarily high profile. For example, it is increasingly common for businesses to draw up an environmental policy. That may be a good starting point, but all too often one hears 'that's our policy, we've got one – it shows we are doing something'. The reality is that too often nothing much happens subsequently. Even those companies which produce environmental reports (and they are sometimes produced for very dubious reasons) still operate as if the environment were an add-on to give them a competitive advantage. Too often any environmental strategy exists outside of the day-to-day running of the firm. This add-on rhetoric is dangerous. Those advocating the addition of environmental protection to 'business as usual' fail to recognize the fundamental faults in the system itself and fail to deal with the real challenge facing industry: to do business differently.

Many environmentalists recognize the need for action on the demand side when considering the levels of consumption taking place in the West. But the debate in industry always returns to supply-side measures because tackling the demand side means challenging issues such as growth and market share, which are sacred tenets to large corporations. Businesses find it almost impossible to conceive of a situation in which they are selling less and the emphasis is on ecology and quality rather than growth and quantity. Increasing populations in developing countries are therefore not viewed as posing severe environmental problems but perceived as a new market in which to sell goods. The cigarette manufacturers in the North, whilst worried about litigation, are less worried about falling sales in the developed world when they know that there are millions of people in developing countries who can be targeted in their marketing campaigns.

Managers in the ecomodern firm like simple solutions (and one-page documents) and this is what eco-efficiency offers. They claim that they are busy and need fast, practical and cost-effective solutions to environmental problems. They therefore fail to respond to the scale of the environmental problem and to recognize that there is no single, simple solution to a very complex debate. I find it interesting that seemingly rational managers who claim to care about both the financial and environmental performance of their companies become almost unstable (and often aggressive) when one asks about their social performance as well as environmental performance. They either choose deliberately to ignore their social liabilities or, more often, are clearly unaware of the social dimension of sustainability and are reluctant to engage in any debate. The eco-efficiency fix rules, therefore, and actually becomes equated with sustainable development. Social issues are consistently marginalized.

Environmental managers too often seek out only the technical and scientific solutions to their environmental problems. Eco-efficiency actually encourages this and is therefore welcomed. Again, managers are either unaware of the social and cultural dimensions of their activities or are so scared by such ideas that they dare not even consider them. They simply do not know where to start, because they are unaware of the alternatives or are so constrained by a limited corporate culture that they dare not even contemplate anything new.

Since the alternative environmental agenda is diverse and complex and offers no simple solutions, ecomodernists are provided with a stick to beat more radical thinkers. Obstruction through detail is one of the most powerful weapons of the ecomodernists. If one cannot provide them with clear agendas for change, with a detailed (and costed) strategy for implementation, then they feel unable to act. What they do not realize is that the move towards sustainable development is an uncertain path which involves a good degree of groping in the dark. Uncertainty over other green alternatives only adds weight to the more certain strategy of ecomodernism. It supports the culture of continuity of the past rather than change. They are willing to take on marginal changes to 'business as usual', and therefore tolerate or even embrace ecomodernism – but radical, creative thinking is not on the agenda.

If our ultimate aim is to move towards a sustainable development path, we must consider not only the piecemeal nature of the eco-efficiency approach but also a fundamental methodological question. We must ask whether the basic concept of efficiency is in fact an appropriate measure of sustainable development at all. Efficiency is essentially a neoclassical concept based on optimization. But in the case of the environment we know that to optimize involves an almost impossible trade-off between the many different effects of industrial production. Eco-efficiency turns out to be a complex, messy and inaccurate process, often related to assumptions about these different environmental effects. When one adds the important social dimension of sustainable development into the eco-efficiency function, we reach an impossible calculation, because it is so complex and uncertain. Such complexity results in businesses leaving the social dimension aside because it would be impossible ever to conceive of a concept associated with social efficiency. Perhaps the concept of efficiency needs to be replaced with consideration of issues such as ethics, equity, equality, empowerment, education and ecology. But we must recognize that there are no simple models to deal with these issues.

This chapter is not trying to suggest that all the attempts made by industry to improve its environmental performance are bad. It does suggest, however, that to date most attempts are inadequate and that ecomodernism has a life outside of other discourses on environmentalism. Moreover, it has been suggested that there are huge barriers in the achievement of even marginal environmental improvements because of the nature of the international economic order and its emphasis on growth and globalization. Neither the ecomodernist model nor the present structure of the international economic order are consistent with a move towards sustainable development.

Thus, I want to paint a picture of considerable concern but not necessarily one of despair. The concern is associated with a view that ecomodernism, although powerful and growing in popularity, might lead to marginal environmental improvements but lacks the real radicalism needed to bring about sustainable development. We live in a period of rapid change and this is likely to accelerate in the new millennium. Environmental awareness amongst individuals is exploding. Increasing numbers of people are looking towards new solutions to the problems in their lives and there is a growing distrust of business activity. Industry will have to respond to that change and although it is now advocating a powerful environmental agenda inconsistent with that change, it will have to come to accept the limitations in ecomodernism and embrace the many radical alternatives to that limited discourse. Industry must recognize such change and grasp the opportunities which it presents. This is the focus of the next section of this chapter.

Achieving Change

There are many radical environmental agendas which we could consider here as an alternative to ecomodernism. The work of 'bioregionalists' tells us that it is the scale of industrial production and exchange which is at the root of the problem. Others challenge trends towards globalization and call for a new protectionism. There are those who call for zero growth strategies in the North to allow environmental space for the South to develop. Some continue to hint at the need to replace capitalism with something else but are usually very vague about what that something else might be. The trouble with all such policy prescriptions is that it is almost impossible to see such radical change being implemented in the short run. We do live in a global economy and many developing countries and their large corporations are benefiting enormously from their abilities to sell their goods worldwide. Although we know that economic growth is, at times, extremely environmentally damaging, it is nevertheless the cornerstone of every country's economic policies and seen, in the developing world, as the way to improve standards of living for many millions of people. When one visits countries in South East Asia there is no doubting that this is the case. Thus, although we have argued that there is massive conflict between business, the international economic order and sustainable development, the process of change must start with what is achievable here and now and then build into the more radical dimensions of social and environmental responsibility consistent with sustainable development.

It is pointless laying out an alternative strategy which has no hope of being adopted by large corporations which are driven by a desire to gain competitive advantage and growing market shares globally. Whilst many people within such organizations (including senior executives) may be personally committed to environmental improvement, the corporate culture of many large companies in developing countries is such that there is little room for environmental policy unless it can be seen to enhance existing business performance. Thus everything suggested below is capable of being operationalized in the short run.

We must recognize an important paradox here. This chapter has described ecomodernism as inadequate, partly because it is about supporting marginal change to a 'business as usual' philosophy. But it is also being argued that strategies for moving towards sustainable development must be consistent with the aims of the corporation (at least in the short run). This is a paradox but not necessarily a contradiction. Unlike ecomodernism which represents marginal change, something much more far-reaching is being advocated here: a new philosophy towards production, consumption and accountability; a recognition of all the facets of sustainable development and how these can be built into a transparent framework; and the recognition that enhanced competitiveness is achievable through differentiation strategies based on social and environmental excellence. This goes far beyond the rhetoric of ecomodernism. Whilst only a start on a long road towards the achievement of sustainable development, it is argued that this agenda is both achievable and superior to the ecomodernist rhetoric.

The challenge, therefore, is to go beyond the narrow and marginal approaches associated with ecomodernism and to create a degree of change within the constructs of the modern global industrial economy. Whilst it must be accepted that businesses will find this harder to achieve than adopting tools associated with eco-efficiency, nevertheless, the benefits of going beyond marginalism may be significant. That is not to suggest that the policies advocated here are cure-alls. They are not; rather, they are policies and tools for businesses in the short term. In the longer term there will have to be debate about the nature of the international economic order which is at the root of so much unsustainable behaviour.

Here we point towards three areas which ought to be addressed:

- sustainable production, consumption and accountability;
- sustainable development at the corporate level;
- competitive advantage through social and environmental differentiation.

Let us deal with each issue in turn.

Sustainable production, consumption and accountability

One area where corporate environmental management literature is almost silent relates to the definition of sustainable production: a concept which would seem to be important. Here, sustainable production is seen as production which is economically, environmentally and socially responsible. Moreover, 'economically responsible' might be defined as both economic for the producer (that is, profitable) and for those involved in the production process (that is, in relation to fair wages, employment, and so on). Thus a useful definition of sustainable production is as follows: to produce less, of higher quality and durability, with much lower environmental and social impacts at higher levels of employment, whilst making an acceptable profit or surplus.

The implication is simple. We should make fewer throw-away goods and more products of quality which will last longer and create less waste. Re-use, recycling and all such associated practices need to be increased. But a fundamental part of sustainable production is to increase levels of employment. Here the argument is simple. If, in the search for ever-increasing efficiency and lower and lower costs, companies continue to use less labour and more capital, social upheaval led by those unemployed who become disenfranchised from society is likely to occur. We have already noted that labour is becoming more uncompetitive as capital productivity increases. But such capital productivity is essentially being subsidized by the environment through, for example, cheap energy costs which do not internalize the true environmental costs of resource loss and pollution. If energy (and therefore capital) costs accurately reflected their true costs, then a switch back to labour usage would occur, increasing both employment and reducing environmental damage.

The word 'production' is, of course, quite misleading. When we talk of production we take it to mean the creation of something new. In actual fact, production is really about changes in the state of things: one substance or form is converted into another. Thus production is really about conversion and any creation which takes place must be associated with destruction. Now, if we begin to see production as inevitably destructive, it takes on a much more negative connotation. This is not to advocate that all production should be ceased, just that production is only truly justified when the value of what is being produced outweighs the value of that which is destroyed. This can be linked to the concept of product justifiability (Welford, 1996) where companies might be expected to consult with a wide range of stakeholders about the needs and costs of a product. This is likely to be linked to full life-cycle assessments of products.

Sustainable production needs to be matched with sustainable consumption if the outcome is to be truly effective. More sustainable consumption, of course, requires individuals as well as businesses to accept a good degree of responsibility themselves. Not everything can be left to businesses. More and more people have to recognize that increasing levels of consumption do not make for happiness. Moreover, higher levels of consumption in the North simply contribute to the unhappiness of people in the South impacted by the globalization trend. There is, nevertheless, a huge role which businesses can play through education. Perhaps more than any other institution in the world, business has a direct communications line with millions of people: its consumers. Linking marketing with education and campaigning could influence people in a more direct way than any educator or individual campaigner. Consider, for example, the impact that a corporation like Coca-Cola might have if it printed environmental messages on every can and bottle of Coke which it sold. We return to the important issue of education below.

As a start, however, sustainable production and consumption require there to be a wider involvement of all company stakeholders in a move towards sustainable development. A transparent pluralist approach facilitates this and allows for a degree of accountability through an assessment of progress, using techniques such as social auditing. Thus social auditing takes account of not only the internal pluralism within an organization but external pluralism as well. It also supports a greater degree of organizational transparency (Welford 1996). Social auditing is, therefore, a process to induce and promote new forms of democracy and accountability in the workplace and beyond.

The rationale behind using a social auditing approach for a business wishing to move towards sustainability is to acknowledge the rights of information to a wide constituency – that is, to attend to societal pluralism. Firms using the audit process would be conceived of as lying at the centre of a network of social relationships which are articulated in a manner akin to a stakeholder model. Stakeholders are commonly understood to be those groups or individuals who can affect or are affected by the organization's social performance and objectives (Freeman, 1984). Put another way, social auditing recognizes the concepts of stewardship and accountability, and this in turn acknowledges that the whole of society has rights to information about actions taken on its behalf (by businesses, for example). Thus the social auditing process allows business to engage with its stakeholders (representing, in part, societal interests), responding to their views and, where necessary, explaining and justifying its actions. But it is not a one-way flow. Businesses are also able to influence their stakeholders so that the ultimate outcome derives from consensus.

Respect for pluralism is developed as organizations become more transparent. That is, information is used to reduce the distance between the organization and the external (and internal) participants so that stakeholders can 'see into' the organization, assess what it is doing with the resources that determine future options and react (or not) accordingly. As Gray (1994) argues, the impact of such information on this constituency and its associated response can be assumed to encourage the new practices necessary for sustainable development. If accountability and transparency are embraced, then the corporation will find itself more closely in tune with its wider constituents and the company will develop its culture from a recognition of different stakeholder expectations and needs. But this is by no means an easy process. There will be trade-offs that have to be made if sustainability is to be pursued.

The social audit process means that employees' (internal stakeholders') values and expectations are accounted for alongside those of other external stakeholders. The social audit provides a medium in which the employee's values and expectations can be measured against other employees from different departments, levels or backgrounds, as well as against various other stakeholders. The resulting deeper appreciation of the diverse stakeholder pressures upon a company breeds greater respect and trust between stakeholders. A relationship characterized by trust and mutual respect is a fruitful basis for employee participation. An open dialogue between management and employees on problems raised is necessary to deal with conflicts and resistance.

The social audit gives the employee a chance to compare and contrast core company values not only with their own but also with those of other employees and external stakeholders. The important point to stress is the importance to a social audit of an overarching and explicit framework of values written in terms of corporate values, visions, aims and objectives. This is important because it provides the basic parameters for the ongoing dialogue between the various stakeholders and management. An explicit values framework avoids the anarchic flaws of this type of 'accounting receptivity'. In other words, it avoids a business degenerating into an unmanageable scramble of values, multiple aims and multiple measures of performance. In this way a firm can provide a sustainable direction to its activities.

Sustainable development at the corporate level

There exists a strange and fruitless search for a single definition of sustainable development amongst people who do not fully understand that we are really talking here of a process rather than a tangible outcome. This search is most apparent amongst positivist researchers who grope for a hard core of definitions and data which they can manipulate to produce simple solutions and singular answers to very complex concepts. Such simplifications cannot exist in the postmodern world and they simply hide a scientific research bias which is not appropriate to a highly political issue such as sustainable development. The search for a single definition of this concept is futile, even if it maintains the employment of a few academics.

Many argue that the concept of sustainable development is not appropriate to analysis at the corporate level. It is commonly argued that it can only be analysed and measured within a spatial dimension. Whilst that may be true, it is nevertheless important to recognize that business is central to the sustainable development process and that, therefore, we ought to be able to conceive of a framework whereby the firm would, at least, be operating in a way which is consistent with moves to sustainable development. That is we turn our attention to next.

Strategies are needed to translate conceptual ideas into practical reality. This requires a more radical assessment of environmental strategy. The challenge that faces the economic system is how to continue to fulfill its vital role within modern society whilst ensuring sustainability. The emphasis to date has been on piecemeal moves towards environmental improvement and these moves have often been in the wrong direction. I advocate a model which is a combination of many different people's work and has developed over the last couple of years. It is based on six Es: environment, empowerment, economics, ethics, equity and education. We can view these as six areas where companies should have a clear policy and agenda for change. Table 6.1 outlines these policy areas along with suggested tools for

Table 6.1
Policy Areas and Tools for Sustainable Development

Policy area	Indicative tools
Environment	Life cycle assessment
	Environmental management system and audits
	Functionality assessment
	Resource management
Empowerment	Team building
	Participation
	Equal opportunities
	Declaration of rights
Economics	Profits/surplus
	Employment
	Quality
	Long-term financial stability and investment
Ethics	Transparency of objectives
	Openness to concerns
	Honesty
	Values statement
Equity	Fair trade policy and activity
	End-price auditing
	Development aid
	Sponsorship
Education	Training
	Customer information
	Community involvement
	Campaigning

operationalizing a change process. The sustainable firm will not only use these tools to achieve its sustainable development objectives in these six areas, but will also report on progress. This model is essentially a 'policy in, reporting out' framework where the activities of the firm are transparent. In other words, the company is expected to have a policy in each of these six areas, to operationalize that policy using the indicative tools suggested in Table 6.1, and then to report on progress. No firm will be able to produce a perfect profile in all six areas (even if that could be defined). Reports should detail progress in each element and demonstrate a degree of continuous improvement. They should also point to areas which still require attention and produce objectives and targets for the next reporting period.

It is worth briefly reviewing the sorts of idealized outcomes which an individual business should move towards in each of these six areas.

Environment

The environment is to be protected with minimum use of non-renewable resources. Environmental performance will be monitored and measured and it is likely that there will be an environmental management system in place with regular audit activity. Products will be assessed according to a life cycle assessment and redesigned where practicable to reduce environmental impact. Products will also undergo a functionality assessment to determine whether there is a better way of providing the benefits of the product. There will be strong connections along the supply chain to integrate all stages of the product's life. After production, firms will, as far as possible, manage the use and disposal of the product through product stewardship procedures. Much emphasis will be placed on local action, including close connections with local community initiatives and protection of the health and safety of all employees and neighbours.

Empowerment

All employees must feel part of the process of improvement and must be empowered to recognize and act on their own obligations as well as to work together closely with colleagues. There will be strong participation of the workforce with respect to decision making, profit sharing and ownership structures. The organization will be open to new suggestions made by anyone in the workforce and workers will be rewarded on the basis of contribution to this overall ethos as well as work done. Human capital will be valued and workers will not be treated as simple factors of production. There will be enshrined rights within the organization relating to equal opportunities and individual freedoms.

Economy

The economic performance of the firm will be sustainable in that it will be sufficient to provide for ongoing survival, the continued provision of employment, the payment of dividends to shareholders and the payment of fair wages to all concerned in the organization. Financial audits will be extended to a justification of profits made and a demonstration that they have been made though good business practices rather than cost-cutting exploitation. There will be periodic new investment in both physical capital as well as human capital (through education and retraining). Business relationships should be mutually advantageous to all parties concerned, so that supply chain stability will exist. Jobs are a central part of sustainability and the provision and growth of employment will be encouraged. Products made will be of good quality, durable and suitable for the purposes for which they were intended.

Ethics
The organization will have a clear set of values which it will publish and which will be reassessed periodically through the social audit process. The firm will at all times be honest and open to questions about its ethical stance, providing evidence relating to any activities which are being challenged. It will be a transparent organization and relations with subsidiaries, contractors and agents will be clearly identified. Ethics are not something which the organization simply declares, it must translate them into practice via codes of conduct, education, communication and information. Businesses serve a variety of purposes for different stakeholders. Therefore we might argue that, as a necessary condition, business activities are justifiable only in so far as they can be shown to meet the legitimate requirements of stakeholders.

Equity
Issues associated with equity exist both inside and outside the organization. Closely linked with empowerment issues there must be a clear statement of rights and equal opportunities within the firm. Trade along the supply chain must be equitable and, particularly with regard to international trade, there must be assurances for workers in developing countries, for indigenous populations and for human rights. End price audits of goods whereby a product's final price is broken down into an analysis of who gets what share of that price is immensely valuable and can be used to demonstrate that subsistence wages being paid to the poor in Third World countries is not the whole basis of the product's provision. The distribution of the benefits of product (or service) provision must be demonstrated as being just. Where appropriate, the firm will be involved in wider development initiatives though technology and know-how transfer, sponsorship, charitable donations and the provision of development aid to partners in developing countries.

Education
Education is at the root of the sustainable development process. We will make little progress if we are not able to communicate the challenge and educate people to live in a more sustainable manner. Every business can be an educator because of its close links with both employees and customers: it should provide suitable information and education to anyone working for it or purchasing its products and services. The firm can also be involved in community initiatives. It can be involved in public campaigns and the process to raise awareness more generally. It can work closely with campaign groups and non-governmental organizations through general co-operation, more specific sponsorship, the secondment of staff and similar initiatives. It is capable of bringing about much more sustainable consumption.

The 6Es approach therefore provides a set of ideals which the company can work towards. It contains a number of values and issues too commonly ignored in business; in many respects it challenges the business to accept a much wider responsibility for all its actions. The starting point is simply for management to think about these issues and through interaction with the workforce and other stakeholders to produce policy statements in each of the six areas. However, that must be followed by concerted action as the company seeks out the road towards sustainability.

Competitive advantage through social and environmental differentiation
The nature of globalization and the fact that companies in developing countries have developed rapidly by gaining international competitiveness cannot be ignored. Thus any form of corporate environmental management adopted by companies in

developing countries must be fully consistent with, or even enhance, competitive advantage. There needs to be a shift in the social and environmental emphasis. Rather than seeing corporate environmental management within the 'business as usual' context, the environment and the concept of sustainable development can actually be at the forefront of competitiveness strategies, driving environmental, social and economic performance in positive directions. Rather than putting the emphasis of competitiveness on cost reduction strategies, which we have already seen are often inconsistent with sustainable development, there is a need to see competitiveness enhanced through a degree of differentiation – that is, by improving the perception which consumers have of a company and its products. This emphasis can be fully consistent with sustainable development.

Many companies in developing countries have been very successful at increasing their competitiveness, making them, in many cases, world leaders in the industries in which they operate. The maintenance of that competitiveness is vital for the continued success of such firms. It is sometimes assumed that strategies and tools associated with environmental protection and sustainable development will be costly and may reduce such competitiveness. But here it is argued that operational-izing the types of changes advocated in the previous two sections can actually add to, rather than detract from, competitive advantage.

The trend towards globalization and the removal of barriers provides a new framework for competition. This is imposing a need for strategic reorientation by companies. It is my contention that environmental management and sustainable development at the corporate level, along with their associated strategies and tools, provide one effective method to increase the competitiveness of companies which see care of the environment as a new and integral part of business operations. More-over, as technology matures and as quality issues become a standard for doing business, environmental management and social responsibility provide a new impetus for the firm to gain advantage over its competitors. Whilst some of those strategies might reduce costs (the ubiquitous win–win situation), that is not the emphasis here. Rather, more attention is placed on the area of differentiation, where social and environmental aspects of sustainable development will have most impact as con-sumers become more and more sophisticated and as responsibility is increasingly expected of businesses.

Differentiation consistent with sustainable development requires a company to:

- develop sound environmental and social performance;
- engage in effective and educational marketing and distribution strategies;
- communicate its performance in a transparent and honest way to stakeholders.

Thus, differentiation strategies can improve both the competitiveness of firms and their social and environmental performance. What is more, if firms are able to further differentiate their products and corporate image through sustainable production and accountability strategies, and by reporting on their performance in relation to sustainable development (via the 6Es or some other model), then we can see how, working within modern global economies, sustainable development and environmental protection might actually be facilitated by companies. This goes much further than corporate environmental management strategies associated with ecomodernist approaches. Whilst competitive strategies to enhance sustainable development may seem inevitable, given increased consumer sophistication and pressures from competitors and along supply chains, there are nevertheless ways in which the process can be accelerated. In this respect, environmental policy has an important role to play. We now return, therefore, to macro-level considerations and examine the sorts of policy changes which can both reduce the conflict within the international economic order and, at the same time, encourage businesses to think and act in a way which is more consistent with sustainable development.

Policy frameworks capable of enhancing competitive advantage

Companies are dynamic and capable of responding to change in productive and innovative ways. Indeed, Porter and van der Linde (1995) effectively show that changes in environmental policy can bring about significant environmental improvements as firms adjust their activities and innovate to avoid the costs and penalties of regulation and market measures. There is a need to develop a policy framework capable of stimulating the sorts of changes advocated in the previous three sections of this chapter. In particular, we would want to find ways of pushing businesses towards activities more consistent with sustainable production and consumption, rewarding moves towards sustainable development and encouraging competitive strategies which can deliver such change. Whilst there is insufficient room here for a full analysis of all possible policy changes, we would highlight three areas for consideration: environmental taxes, social accounting procedures and consumer information, and targeted protectionism.

Environmental taxes

Few would disagree with the proposition that the environment is undervalued because in many instances it represents a free good. Moreover, because the capitalist system is unable to fully account for long time scales, many non-renewable resources are also massively undervalued and used in a completely unsustainable way. These relatively simply arguments make taxes on environmental damage very attractive.

However, there are even more compelling arguments for the introduction of environmental taxes when one recognizes that the consequence of the environment actually subsidizing production activities (through raw materials and particularly energy) is to make labour increasingly expensive and uncompetitive in relation to capital. This situation is compounded when one considers that virtually all governments receive very large amounts of their taxation revenue from income taxes on workers and taxes levied on employers for employing labour. Thus a shift away from taxes on employment (which must be seen as a good) and towards taxes on environmental damage (a bad) must be regarded as a Pareto improvement. Moreover, taxes on inputs into production processes which are environmentally damaging would make them much more expensive relative to alternatives such as reuse and recycling.

Such fiscal readjustments will inevitably lead to more sustainable production activities. But they will also stimulate firms to find more environmentally responsible ways of producing goods if they are to maintain their competitiveness. The total tax take from the company need not increase (and may decrease) since increases in materials and energy costs will be associated with decreases in labour costs (direct employment taxes will fall and wages will also fall as decreased income taxes make it increasingly likely that workers will be prepared to take jobs at lower gross wages).

Social accounting procedures and consumer information

Few companies currently engage in social accounting or social auditing. Those that have, however, report considerable benefits. If more standardized procedures existed for social accounting and reporting, a benchmark would be created for all firms to follow. Moreover, this would provide for standardized information which could be provided for consumers. An extension of the International Standards Organization's work on environmental performance evaluation (ISO 14001) would be a good starting point.

With the cooperation of industry, such reporting could become a standard. Procedures for verification would ensure useful consumer information with which to make more informed choices. As noted above, this could increase the competitiveness of companies as to which are able to publish the most impressive reports and are thus able (in an objective way) to differentiate their corporate image from that of others. Social and environmental accountability and policies in line with sustainable development then become an integral part of the profile of a firm. Moreover, those unable to provide adequate information are more likely to be targeted by consumer groups which could organize more effective boycott activities, with verified information (or the absence of it).

Targeted protectionism
We saw earlier that many companies are able to provide goods at cheap prices by ignoring social and environmental responsibilities. Free trade can encourage the activities of unscrupulous companies (or associate firms whose activities are easier to hide) which attempt to drive down costs through human and ecological exploitation. In such circumstances, targeted protectionism is not only justified – it is to be encouraged. It is widely accepted that the activities of many large transnational corporations are too difficult to control and that the nomadic nature of much of their capital means that they often have more power than the governments which are supposed to regulate them. However, whilst it may be difficult to control their production activities, it is relatively easy to control their markets. And without their markets they cannot exist. Thus, consumer activities and boycotts, as suggested above, need greater support. Where appropriate, action at a national or international level can be taken against companies until they put misconduct right. Companies whose markets are potentially threatened will soon adopt policies which prevent this from happening.

Conclusions

This chapter has suggested that many large companies (including some in developing countries) are adopting corporate environmental management strategies and tools. Whilst this is to be encouraged, we should question the real effectiveness of many of the tools being used. Although companies may perceive that their actions are right, we must ask whether what they are doing is, in fact, the right thing. The trend associated with ecomodernism is not sufficient if our aim is to bring about a situation consistent with sustainable development.

Nevertheless, we have demonstrated that the fault cannot be attributed entirely to business alone. Companies often struggle with a globalized economic order which is inconsistent with sustainable development and which forces them to continually drive costs down in order to survive. In such a system it is little wonder that business views environmental protection and social responsibility as a relatively low priority. But in a world where businesses are increasingly powerful and where they are often more effective than governments in bringing about change, we should expect them to take a lead.

Thus we are left with the question of what companies ought to try to achieve. We must recognize that we live in an increasingly globalized economy where companies will survive only if they can maintain a degree of competitive advantage. Rather than seeing this as a barrier to social and environmental improvement, we ought to regard it as an opportunity. In this respect, companies can build upon the competitive advantage which already exists, stressing real differentiation strategies associated with environmental protection and social responsibility. Through a greater degree of accountability and transparency, and effective communications, they can create a new norm which requires every business to perform in a way more consistent with sustainable development.

This chapter, therefore, advocates a clear definition of sustainable development as applied to the corporate setting and sets out a model consistent with this aim. It calls on companies to pursue policies of sustainable production: producing less, of higher quality, reducing environmental and social impacts and increasing levels of employment. Social accounting and social auditing are seen as ways of tracking and reporting on achievements in this area, and this, in turn, will help to differentiate the corporate image of the company, leading to a degree of competitive advantage. While this may seem a tall order, there are some signs that businesses are responding to the challenge. With the increasing availability of information about firms (provided both by themselves and by their detractors) on media such as the Internet, it is going to be much easier for consumers to make informed choices about the products they buy. Moreover, as crises associated with environmental degradation and social conflict increase, so too will the demands from individuals for change. Changes in civil society, with NGOs and coalitions of individuals being more willing to assert their power, will intensify the pressures on business.

Policies consistent with such aspirations are, nevertheless, still required to accelerate the move towards sustainable development. They include the widespread introduction of environmental taxes, a framework for social auditing and consumer information, and targeted protectionism against companies which can be identified as consistently underperforming or unnecessarily exploiting humans or the ecological base. The proposals advocated in this chapter go far beyond the aspirations and tools associated with ecomodernism and eco-efficiency. They nevertheless work within the existing globalized economy where companies in developing countries will be able to develop effective and efficient strategies to enhance their competitive positioning. We must challenge the ecomodernists to do more, to throw away their own highly restrictive assumptions and models and to take the next big leap forward in engaging with sustainable development. This is both achievable and necessary.

At present, however, this chapter argues that we see a very 'disturbing development'. Interestingly, the word 'disturbing' has two different meanings and both are appropriate to the situation described here. Firstly, the dominant trends of corporate environmentalism, globalization and free trade are disturbing in that they are worrying. They conflict with the process of sustainable development and act as a serious impediment to any change consistent with that concept. Secondly, the conflicts inherent between sustainable development, the international economic order and corporate environmentalism are disturbing in as much as they may be disrupting what otherwise might be progressive development in the South. This is because the emphasis on cost reduction in the globalized marketplace requires a degree of underdevelopment in low-wage economies in order to satisfy the needs of the North and wealthy elites in the South. Unless we can tackle the conflicts at the root of the international economic order, therefore, 'disturbing development' will continue.

References

Brown, L. (1995), *State of the World*, Worldwatch Institute/Earthscan Publications, London.

Cahoone, L. E. (1996), *From Modernism to Postmodernism: An Anthology*, Blackwell, Oxford.

Daly, H. E. (1996), *Beyond Growth: The Economics of Sustainable Development*, Beacon Press, Boston, MA.

Freeman, E. (1984), *Strategic Management: A Stakeholder Approach*, Pitman Publishing, Boston, MA.

Gray, R. H. (1994), 'Corporate Reporting for Sustainable Development: Accounting for Sustainability in 2000 AD', *Environmental Values*, 3 (1).

Hawken, P. (1994), *The Ecology of Commerce: How Business Can Save the Planet*, Weidenfeld and Nicholson, New York.

Korten, D. C. (1995), *When Corporations Rule the World*, Earthscan Publications, London.

Porter, M. and C. van der Linde (1995), 'Green and Competitive: Ending the Stalemate', *Harvard Business Review*, 73 (5).

Schmidheiny, S. (1992), *Changing Course: A Global Business Perspective on Development and the Environment*, The MIT Press, Cambridge, MA.

Shiva, V. and J. Bandyopadhyay (1989), 'Development, Poverty and the Growth of the Green Movement in India', *The Ecologist*, 19 (3) (May/June), 111–17.

Welford, R. J. (1996), *Corporate Environmental Management: Systems and Strategies*, Earthscan, London.

—— (1997), *Hijacking Environmentalism: Corporate Responses to Sustainable Development*, Earthscan, London.

7

Environmental Regulation of Transnational Corporations

Needs and Prospects

MICHAEL HANSEN

Introduction

Holding foreign stock worth US$4 trillion in 1998, investing more than US$600 billion abroad annually and controlling two thirds of international trade, the world's 60,000 transnational corporations (TNCs) and their 500,000 foreign affiliates are the central organizers of the emerging global economy (UNCTAD, 1999). The role of TNCs in the global economy has increased dramatically in recent years, as indicated by the surge in foreign direct investment (FDI) by TNCs. FDI has displayed growth rates significantly above those in both GNP and exports. The accelerating internationalization of economic activity in general, coupled with the growing role of TNCs in particular, has raised concerns over the environmental consequences of this process. At the macro level, it is feared that variations in environmental control costs between North and South could prompt TNCs to relocate polluting productions to less developed countries (LDCs) (Leonard, 1988). At the micro level, it is feared that TNCs may apply 'double standards' in their international operations; in other words, a set of high standards in OECD countries and a set of much lower standards in LDCs, thus exposing populations, the environment and workers in LDCs to undue risks (Castleman, 1985).

From the late 1960s onwards, there have been extensive political as well as academic debates as to whether and how to mitigate these perceived environmental maladies of TNC activity. These debates have not resulted in international regulation addressing environmental concerns related to TNC activity and, in recent years, have largely subsided. It is, however, probable that debates on environmental regulation of TNCs will resurface in the years to come as the role of TNCs in the global economy grows and as environmental concerns over economic globalization intensify. Given this background, it is useful to recapitulate the debates that have taken place regarding the environmental regulation of TNCs and to re-evaluate the arguments presented. Part 1 of this chapter provides an historical overview of the policy debates on TNCs and the environment. Part 2 presents the various arguments advanced in connection with these debates and assess their merits. Part 3 outlines a future scenario of environmental regulation of TNCs.

159

The Debate on Environmental Regulation of TNCs

The following overview of the historical evolution of the debates on environmental regulation of TNCs will focus mainly on the activities at the United Nations, as this organization in many respects has been the locus for these debates. It is argued that in spite of intense efforts throughout the 1970s and 1980s to develop a framework for international environmental regulation of TNCs, a regulatory vacuum had in fact emerged by the mid-1990s.

The 1970s: the advent of regulatory activism

Essentially the history of regulatory activism in relation to TNCs and the environment is the history of an international debate on the role of TNCs in the global economy merging with the international environmental debate. This section will first describe the advent of the debate on economic regulation of TNCs, and then examine how this debate became linked to the emerging environment debate.

Economic regulation of TNCs

The contemporary debate on international economic regulation of TNCs dates back to the late 1960s and early 1970s. At that time, it was mainly concerned with the question of how to promote economic development in LDCs. Although the developing world experienced rapid growth in the late 1950s and 1960s, many LDCs felt that this transformation was too slow. In particular, there was widespread frustration among LDCs that the multilateral institutions were responding too slowly to the development challenge. In order to strengthen the LDC position in international economic debates, 77 LDCs created the Group of 77 (G77) at the 1964 United Nations Conference on Trade and Development (UNCTAD). This group was able to shape the international debate on economic and social development for the next two decades. One of the main intellectual inspirations contributing to the formation of this group came from the Latin American economist Raul Prebisch. Essentially he argued that the Third World was placed in a dependency position in relation to the OECD countries, due to structural deficiencies in the international economy. Prebisch became the first head of the newly formed UNCTAD secretariat which was to become a significant Third World voice in the international economic debate in the years to come. By the early 1970s, the G77 initiatives had developed into a broad-based call for a New International Economic Order (NIEO) aimed at radically restructuring the international economic system. The NIEO called for increased national control over natural resources, freedom from outside intervention, a reaffirmation of the right to nationalize foreign holdings, and international control and regulation of the activities of TNCs.

The G77 effort in relation to TNCs rested largely on the perception that TNCs often work against the interests of the host country. TNCs may create enclave economies within the host country and extract resources without transferring to the host country any of the benefits normally associated with industrial operations. This highly critical perception was supported intellectually by books such as Vernon's *Sovereignty at Bay* (1971), Servan-Schreiber's *The American Challenge* (1968), or Barnet and Müeller's *Global Reach* (1974): all portrayed investment by TNCs in LDCs as largely hostile and damaging, and stressed the monopoly power of TNCs *vis-à-vis* host countries. A major implication was that tough regulatory action was needed in order to reduce the rents captured by TNCs and to mitigate their adverse effects on economic, social, political and cultural conditions in LDCs.

At the national level, this critical perception led many LDCs to establish regulatory frameworks which directly targeted foreign direct investment by TNCs. Restrictions were placed on TNC market shares, imports and profit repatriation. Moreover, TNCs were subject to regulations related to technology transfer, exports, domestic participation in investment projects, the siting of production facilities, and the local content of products. At the international level, the critical perception of TNCs prompted the economic and social branch of the United Nations (ECOSOC) to launch a new programme aimed at monitoring and controlling the activities of TNCs. The institutional foundation of this programme became the United Nations Centre on Transnational Corporations (UNCTC). The UNCTC was a small secretariat for the Commission on Transnational Corporations, a subcommittee of ECOSOC. The UNCTC was mandated by the Commission to solve three tasks in relation to TNCs: to monitor the activities of TNCs and provide reports on developments in international investment; to provide LDCs with expertise and advice in their dealings with TNCs; and, finally, to draft proposals for normative frameworks governing the activities of TNCs.

The normative activity of UNCTC soon focused on the establishment of an international code of conduct for TNCs. In 1977 a working group began to prepare the code and presented the first draft in 1978. The latest draft of the code, which appeared in 1990, called for TNCs, *inter alia*, to respect national sovereignty, adhere to social and cultural norms of host countries, promote environmental and consumer protection, disclose information at the request of governments, and abstain from corrupt practices. In return, TNCs would be guaranteed equal and fair treatment, adequate compensation in the case of nationalization and expropriation, and the right to transfer payments between headquarters and affiliates (UNCTC, 1990).

While the UNCTC worked on developing a code of conduct, normative activities on TNCs were undertaken by other international organizations. In 1976 the OECD members agreed to a set of voluntary Guidelines for Multinational Enterprises, partly as an alternative to the UN code of conduct. The OECD guidelines established norms with respect to disclosure, confirmed the basic principles of non–discrimination and national treatment[1] and, in general, codified the policies and practices that most OECD countries were already following. Like the UNCTC code, the OECD code was voluntary, but the stipulated responsibilities of TNCs, as well as the rights of states, were much more limited than those of the UN code. Moreover, whereas the UN code was intended to be all–encompassing, the group of signatories to the OECD code was confined to OECD countries. The ILO also undertook normative activities in this field, issuing in 1977 the so-called Tripartite Declaration of Principles Concerning Multinational Enterprises and Social Policy. The ILO code focused mainly on labour practices and, like the OECD guidelines, was much less inclusive than the UNCTC code. It stipulated recommendations to governments, TNCs and employers concerning employment and industrial relations matters, while also addressing workplace health and safety issues. Finally, UNCTAD drafted a code on Restrictive Business Practices and a code of conduct on Technology Transfer, both of which had implications for TNCs. These codes were adopted by the General Assembly of the UN in 1980.

Environmental regulation of TNCs

By the late 1970s and early 1980s, the international community increasingly began to focus on the environmental aspects of TNC investment. During this period a series of catastrophes, accidents and incidents involving OECD-based TNCs received enormous media attention. Concerns over the environmental aspects of TNC practices culminated in 1984, when an accident at an Indian subsidiary of the US chemical giant Union Carbide killed several thousand people in Bhopal.

In 1985, the UNCTC began work on the environmental aspects of TNC activity. This work included both substantial research (see, for example, UNCTC, 1985, 1988, 1991; ESCAP/UNCTC, 1988) as well as normative activities. With regard to the latter activity, the Centre included a chapter on the environmental responsibilities of TNCs in the draft code of conduct. This chapter calls for TNCs to 'work seriously towards the making of a positive contribution' to the environment in the LDC host country and that their contribution to consumer and environmental protection should be made 'with due regard to relevant international standards'. Moreover, the chapter requests corporations to furnish host countries with all relevant information concerning aspects of their products or processes which may harm the environment.[2]

In the late 1980s and early 1990s, UNCTC expanded its normative activities on the environment. In 1989, a series of 14 'criteria for sustainable development management' was issued by UNCTC and endorsed by ECOSOC. In preparation for the 1992 Rio Conference, UNCTC drafted an elaborate catalogue of 'recommendations' for TNCs, to be included as a separate chapter in the international community's elaborate Action Plan for the Twenty-first Century, Agenda 21. The chapter contained recommendations on the environmental responsibilities of TNCs in five areas: global corporate environmental management; the minimization of risk and hazard; consumption patterns; environmental accounting; and environmental conventions, standards and guidelines (Hansen and Gleckman, 1993). These recommendations provided both minimum and maximum criteria for the conduct of TNCs and were based on existing codes of conduct as well as state-of-the-art practices in the business community. During the same period, the OECD included an environmental chapter in its Guidelines for Multinational Enterprises; the World Health Organization (WHO) adopted an International Code for Marketing of Breast Milk Substitutes and a code on the distribution of pesticides; and the UNEP Industry Office in Paris drafted – in conjunction with industry associations – various sectoral guidelines for industry, including the guidelines of the European Chemical Industry Council (CEFIC) on the safe transport and storage of chemicals.

The 1980s: the conservative backlash

Because the debate on environmental regulation of TNCs was closely tied to the drive to create the New International Economic Order (NEIO), environmental regulation also became one of the main targets when conservative OECD governments reacted against the NIEO in the early 1980s. This 'conservative backlash' and how it affected the environment debate on TNCs will be the topic of this section.

The reaction against NIEO

The NIEO drive lasted roughly from the oil crisis of 1974 until the debt crisis of the early 1980s. By then conservative governments, highly sceptical of the NIEO, had come to power in the major OECD countries. In the United States, the Reagan Administration launched a deregulation and anti-bureaucracy crusade. Similar efforts were undertaken by the conservative British government headed by Margaret Thatcher. At the international level, the NIEO proponents became one of the pet targets of conservative ideologists, and since it was the main locus for the NIEO debate, the United Nations also came under growing attack.[3]

Given their relevance to the debates on the NIEO, attention focused on TNCs as the conservative backlash gained momentum. As the world's largest source of FDI, the United States became the leading opponent of efforts to control TNCs. In accordance with textbook neoclassical economic reasoning, the US position contended that outcomes of international trade and investment generally should be market-driven in order to maximize global welfare, which would be reduced by interventionism in trade and investment; the very merit of a TNC code of conduct was questioned.

As a result of mounting opposition from powerful OECD countries, economic recession and debt crises, the NIEO drive – and with that the drive for an international code of conduct for TNCs – faded during the 1980s. For all practical purposes, attempts to establish a UN code of conduct were abandoned by the mid-1980s. In 1990 there was an attempt by the G77 and the UNCTC to revive the (by then) moribund code, but this effort failed owing to resistance from OECD countries. In 1992, the UNCTC – long at the top of the US conservatives' hitlist[4] – was closed down and some of its activities integrated into UNCTAD. Consequently, the UN programme on TNCs lost the organizational independence that had enabled it to play a central role in the discussion of TNCs and development throughout the 1970s and 1980s. In 1994, the political superstructure of the UNCTC, the Commission on Transnational Corporations, decided to dissolve itself and become a subcommittee of UNCTAD's Trade Council.

Environmental regulation of TNCs
In the light of US opposition to the international economic regulation of TNCs and in view of the Reagan Administration's zealous efforts to roll back environmental regulation in the US,[5] it is not surprising that the US opposed proposals for international environmental codes aimed at TNCs. After the UN code of conduct had finally been put to rest in 1990, the UNCTC attempted to introduce the issue of environmental regulation of TNCs in the Earth Summit agenda by drafting a chapter on the environmental responsibilities of TNCs which, it was hoped, would be included in the Summit's global plan of action, Agenda 21. But in response to pressure from the business community and conservative Western governments, the draft chapter – nicknamed the 'Recommendations' – was removed from the agenda during the preparations for the Rio conference (Gleckman, 1992). The draft was considered too controversial because of its regulatory tone, and because it did not deal sufficiently with issues of property rights and patent protection. Apart from several ambiguous and non-binding recommendations referring to TNCs, dispersed among the 500 pages and 40 chapters of Agenda 21,[6] the issue was to all intents and purposes removed from the agenda. This elimination of the TNC chapter from the UNCED agenda prompted an outcry from some NGOs and LDC delegates. This outcry was amplified when almost simultaneously the UNCTC was closed down by the UN Secretary-General. For many observers, this was a prime example of the business community capturing the international environmental agenda.

The 1990s: corporate self-regulation and NGO activism
By the conclusion of the Rio Conference, it seemed that the debate on environmental regulation of TNCs was in the process of disappearing entirely from the international political agenda. The United Nations had ceased to be a locus for this debate. Nevertheless, the debate was kept alive in various fora which were partly intergovernmental and partly in the NGO and business communities.

The current debate on economic regulation of TNCs

By the late 1980s the rhetoric of NIEO had largely been left behind and the debate on international economic matters become more reconciliatory. As part of this new atmosphere, many LDCs softened their position on TNCs. In particular, the debt crises of the early 1980s led to a re-evaluation of the benefits of FDI. Mexico and China were prime examples of economies opening the gates to FDI; India was another case in point. Consequently, by the early 1990s it had become clear that international regulation of TNCs, in line with the UN code of conduct, was highly unlikely.

This does not mean, however, that TNC-related normative initiatives have been abandoned entirely at the international level; international financial institutions such as the Multilateral Investment Guarantee Agreement (MIGA) or the International Finance Corporation (IFC) have adopted guidelines for FDI. The Uruguay Round Agreement also has significant implications for investment and TNCs.[7] At the time of writing, an international framework for investment is being considered by both the WTO and the OECD. In the WTO, there is discussion about whether an investment treaty should be included in GATT. Although the 1996 WTO ministerial meeting in Singapore failed to reach an agreement on such a treaty, a working group was established to continue deliberations on this issue. In the OECD, too, deliberations on an international investment framework are taking place. In May 1995, trade ministers from the 27 OECD countries decided to initiate the drafting of an investment agreement that should 'provide a broad multilateral framework for international investment with high standards for the liberalization of investment regimes and investment protection and with effective dispute settlement procedures'. Both the WTO and OECD initiatives essentially focus on various distortions to investment and measures to facilitate investment rather than, as was the case with the UN code of conduct, controlling and limiting the activities of TNCs.[8] These various initiatives toward international economic regulation of TNCs remain uncoordinated and unfocused and no 'GATT for investment' has yet materialized. Consequently, bilateral investment treaties remain the preferred way for the international community to prevent disputes related to investment.[9]

New forms of environmental regulation of TNCs

As mentioned above, the issue of the environmental responsibilities of TNCs spurred intense debate at the 1992 Rio Conference. The concluding documents of the Rio Conference, however, failed to address effectively the role of TNCs in sustainable development. In the wake of the Rio conference it seemed that no serious effort was taking place to regulate environmental aspects of TNC activity at the international level. Perhaps as a reflection of the failure of the international community to establish environmental regulation of TNCs, the environmental debates on TNCs of the 1990s seem to have moved outside the intergovernmental arena and into the non-governmental arena. For instance, the business community, through various associations, has organized around this issue and has increasingly become involved in what has been labelled 'self-regulation'. Simultaneously, many non-business NGOs have become involved in this issue since the Earth Summit.

By the early 1990s, the business community was relatively well organized in relation to international environment and development debates. A 1993 survey by the UN estimated that more than 1,000 companies participated in the preparatory process of the Rio Conference, either by being members of the environmental business networks set up to lobby the conference or by participating in events related to the conference. The same survey found that 40–50 companies were extremely active and participated in several Rio-related events or activities (ECOSOC, 1993). Probably the best-known business initiative in connection with the Rio conference was the formation of the Business Council for Sustainable Development (BCSD). The BCSD, a group of 48 companies headed by the Swiss industrialist Stephan Schmidheiny, played a pivotal role in the Rio preparatory process. This group was encouraged by the UNCED Secretary-General, Maurice Strong, to provide business input to the conference. It was influential in shaping the chapter on business and industry in Agenda 21 – an exceptional role for an NGO in the work of the United Nations. The group also issued a report – *Changing Course* – which outlines the role that the business community can play in sustainable development (Schmidheiny, 1992).

Since the Rio conference, green business networks (GBN) similar to the BCSD have grown in number and scope. In 1994, the Green Keiretsu Survey profiled 40 organizations, of which more than 20 'fall fully into the GBN category' (*Tomorrow*, 1994). These were mainly the high profile networks – 'the very tip of a rapidly growing iceberg of industry associations, coalitions, federations and networks that have set themselves new environmental objectives' (*ibid.*: v).

In recent years there has been a notable consolidation of these networks, as symbolized in the 1995 merger between former rival business associations, the World Industrial Council for the Environment (WICE) and the BCSD, to form the the World Business Council for Sustainable Development (WBCSD). Numerous business associations have drafted and disseminated guidelines and standards for environmental conduct among their members. In the early 1990s, the International Chamber of Commerce (ICC) issued the Business Charter for Sustainable Development, which by 1996 had more than 2,000 companies subscribing worldwide. Several industry associations have created industry-specific guidelines and standards for their members – the chemical industry's Responsible Care programme, for example, or the pharmaceutical industry's Guidelines for Good Manufacturing Practice. More importantly, a number of private standards organizations have developed standards for environmental management. This work has resulted in international environmental management standards such as the ISO 14000 series or the European Union's EMAS standard. These management standards outline procedures and practices relating to how companies should organize environmental management. Such standards are currently subscribed to by thousands of companies, mainly in the OECD countries but increasingly in the LDCs as well. Although they are private business initiatives, they are in the process of becoming *de facto* standards for corporate environmental management and are widely endorsed by governments around the world and by international institutions such as the WTO.

The transnational organization of the business community on environmental issues has been paralleled by a transnationalization of NGO work on TNCs and the environment (Risse-Kappen, 1995). This work involves a broad-based alliance of environmentalists, consumer groups and trade unions, as well as development, human rights and religious organizations, all sharing a critical perception of the corporate vision of sustainable development. Most NGOs are highly sceptical of business 'self-regulation' and challenge the emphasis on economic growth, technology cooperation, market reform and enhanced trade and investment links as integral parts of sustainable development. In their critique of business, these NGOs are much closer to the notion of 'limits to growth' espoused by the Club of Rome in the early 1970s, than to the Brundtland Commission's notion of sustainable growth of the late 1980s.

The 1992 Rio Conference became in many respects the heyday of NGO activism with a TNC focus. At a major NGO alternative conference held in Rio de Janeiro during the weeks of the intergovernmental UNCED conference, NGOs organized debates and seminars on international environment and development issues. The NGO community broadly felt that most of the important issues related to the global economy had been removed from Agenda 21, and that the plan of action paid only lip service to the role of trade and foreign direct investment in sustainable development. In the eyes of many NGOs, the Rio conference had essentially been 'captured' by business interests. Skilful lobbying by the business community had succeeded in deflecting the real issues concerning the role of TNCs, making the conference embrace watered-down language of corporate self-regulation: 'Given the abdication of government and the erosion of the environmental movement, the Rio conference became a platform from which business and industry ... were offered an additional opportunity to shape the way the public should think about environment and development' (Chatterjee and Finger, 1994: 111). Greenpeace described business involvement in the Rio Conference as 'a green washing farce'.[10] Others argued that the real agenda in Rio was for the business community to 'deflect' binding international regulation of TNCs by claiming to be clean and by arguing that business self-regulation would do the job (Gleckman, 1992).

In the institutional vacuum created by the perceived impotence of governments to deal with 'the real issues', the reign of TNCs was seen by many NGOs as virtually unchallenged: 'the only currently functioning global agents are ... TNCs' (Chatterjee and Finger, 1994: 111). In order to provide checks on business, the NGO community represented at the Rio conference established the foundation for future NGO cooperation on TNCs by adopting an alternative 'treatise' on the responsibilities of TNCs in sustainable development. This treatise stated that TNCs 'should be held to the highest (environment, health and safety) and labour standards in all countries of operation' and that 'the precautionary principle which places the burden of proof of no harm on the potential polluter rather than on the environment or potential victims should govern TNC practices'.[11] During and after the Rio conference, a host of NGOs including Greenpeace, CERES, Friends of the Earth, Third World Network, the Inter Faith Center on Corporate Responsibility, Multinational Monitor and European Work Hazards Network have launched campaigns targeting TNCs, monitored their activities, published newsletters, issued guidelines for business conduct, and shared information on the Internet. In this way they have kept alive the debate on the international environmental control of TNCs.

Is There a Case for Environmental Regulation of TNCs?

Like any industrial enterprise, TNCs are subject to a host of environmental regulations and other normative frameworks. First and foremost, they have to observe national environmental regulation in the various countries in which they operate. Moreover, they are subject to international environmental conventions (such as the Basel Convention on the export of hazardous waste or the Montreal Protocol on the use of CFCs and other ozone-depleting substances) if these conventions have been ratified by the countries in which they operate.[12] Other 'softer' environmental rules and guidelines also exist; for instance, at the intergovernmental level, codes of conduct and various recommendations contained in Agenda 21, and, at the industry level, various guidelines and business codes such as the ICC Business Charter for Sustainable Development.[13]

While all these rules and regulations are relevant to TNCs, they generally do not target them specifically, given their transnational status, but pertain to all business enterprises. It is possible, however, to envision rules and regulations that *do* target TNCs specifically because of their transnational nature. There could, for instance, be environmental rules similar to those envisaged by the failed United Nations code of conduct for TNCs, or to those contained in the UNCTC 'Recommendations' debated at the Rio Conference. Environmental rules could also be part of a future multilateral agreement on investment. The question to be examined in this section, from a more principled perspective, is whether such rules are warranted at all. This will be done through a presentation of various arguments for and against environmental rules for TNCs and a discussion of the merits of these arguments.

Arguments in favour of environmental regulation of TNCs

Since the late 1970s it has been argued that international environmental rules for TNCs should be established. Essentially two main rationales have been advanced: one takes its point of departure in environmental considerations, the other in economic considerations. Let us examine these rationales in more detail.

The environmental rationale behind regulation
The first environmental argument in favour of regulation of TNCs is essentially moral. This argument holds that certain standards for TNC conduct exist that should never be infringed, even if the erring TNC explicitly or tacitly operates within the requirements of host country laws and regulations. It will be morally unacceptable to most people if OECD-based TNCs relocate polluting and dangerous production to LDCs in order to escape tougher regulations at home; if such TNCs play a central role in the exploitation of scarce natural resources such as rain forests in LDCs; or if they apply significantly lower environment, health and safety standards at LDC production facilities than at home. In cases where such commonly held standards for TNC conduct exist, environmental regulation which specifically targets TNCs should, according to this line of reasoning, be established.

A second argument in favour of environmental regulation of TNCs is related to the transboundary nature of environmental problems. Frequently the environmental problems created by a TNC operating in one country may affect the environment in another country or even the global environment. It is often not realistic to expect a single country to take into due account, when designing regulation, the extraterritorial environmental effects of activities taking place in its territory. An international environmental framework for TNCs would address this transboundary aspect of TNC activity.

A third argument in favour of environmental regulation of TNCs is related to the fact that technology developments and policy liberalization render TNCs more and more 'footloose' and consequently more difficult to regulate by individual states. This mobility of TNCs may encourage countries to apply less stringent environmental standards than neighbouring or competing countries in order to attract investment by TNCs, or just to retain productive capacity. The consequence could be 'a race to the bottom' with regard to international environmental standards (Daly, 1993). To mitigate this effect, many observers feel that international rules pertaining specifically to TNCs should be established.

A fourth argument in favour of environmental regulation of TNCs is that such regulation could compensate for regulatory failure in LDCs. Recent advances notwithstanding, LDC environmental regulation is still characterized by serious shortcomings.[14] These are accentuated by a series of characteristics of the TNC: first, TNCs have considerable bargaining leverage *vis-à-vis* host governments because of their mobility and flexibility. Second, TNCs will often be extremely reluctant to give host country regulators insight into their operations in order to protect financial information or proprietary technology. Finally, as many TNCs hold only minority shares in a joint venture arrangement and/or as the LDC subsidiary is a local entity in a legal sense, it will often be difficult for LDC authorities to hold a TNC responsible for, say, an accident at an LDC affiliate. It could be argued that international environmental regulation of TNCs might compensate for deficiencies in LDC environmental regulation and strengthen the LDC bargaining position *vis-à-vis* TNCs.

The economic rationale behind environmental regulation of TNCs
Originally the arguments in favour of environmental regulation of TNCs were related to concerns over the competitiveness of OECD industries. This concern emerged in the United States in the late 1960s; during this period the economy experienced rapidly growing outward FDI simultaneously with the expansion of environmental laws and regulations. This led some trade economists to suggest that these two trends were related: investment flight was seen to be partly caused by the rapidly growing pollution abatement costs incurred by industry, leading to a subsequent loss of competitiveness.[15] It was even suspected that some countries actively promoted themselves as 'pollution havens' in order to boost competitiveness and attract foreign investors. In this context it was proposed that TNCs should observe certain environmental standards regardless of location. It was hoped that such rules would prevent the environmental dimension from becoming a factor in the international competition for investment capital.

Arguments against environmental regulation of TNCs
The case in favour of environmental rules governing the activities of TNCs is not unchallenged. Thus, two arguments against the pro-regulation position are typically advanced. The first is that such rules will lead to an economically sub-optimal allocation of productive resources internationally. The second is that such rules are not required from an environmental perspective.

The economic rationale against regulation
In the trade community, environmental regulation pertaining to TNCs is generally viewed with great suspicion. Trade economists typically emphasize that internationally harmonized rules for TNCs are economically inefficient. Environmental conditions vary enormously among countries and regions. Densely populated, highly industrialized regions obviously require more stringent environmental measures than do sparsely populated under-industrialized areas. Harmonization of environmental standards, including those pertaining to TNCs, would ignore the fact that countries have different absorptive capacities for pollution and will thereby prevent an optimal allocation of productive resources globally. A stronger version of this argument is that poor countries with large environmental assimilative capacities ought to be allowed to specialize in the production of pollution-intensive products and actively attract FDI from highly polluting TNCs. Such pollution-based development strategies are sometimes referred to as 'pollution haven' development strategies.[16]

Today, trade economists tend to downplay the argument that countries may have different absorptive capacities and that international harmonization of environmental regulation should, therefore, be avoided. Instead they emphasize that such regulations may become disguises for protectionism. For an increasing number of trade economists, 'the issues related to environmental policy and competitiveness are really about avoidance of the protectionist capture of ecological arguments' (Low, 1992: 6). By imposing environmental standards on TNCs, OECD countries *de facto* force LDCs to adopt OECD country standards in industries where TNCs play a large role (Bhagwati and Dali, 1993: 21). Environmental regulation of TNCs will thereby eliminate one source of comparative advantage of LDCs and divert investment away from this region. Moreover, TNCs with the greenest technology (typically located in OECD countries) will have a competitive interest in international regulation requiring high environmental performance. By influencing global decision makers to adopt equivalent environmental standards, these companies will gain competitive advantage *vis-à-vis* less environmentally advanced TNCs, such as those based in LDCs. In other words, environmental regulation of TNCs will be a perfect way for certain OECD-based TNCs to extend market control and weed out competitors not yet capable of meeting high environmental standards and organizing environmental management on an international scale.

A final economic argument against regulation of TNCs is that such regulation would be highly unfair to TNCs. There is no *a priori* environmental reason why TNCs should be singled out while non-TNCs with equal or even worse environmental problems should be allowed to pollute. A framework governing the environmental conduct of TNCs would result in a distortion of foreign direct investment in favour of local investment. This would imply a sub-optimal allocation of investment capital globally. A related argument is that, in many cases, it would not be feasible or it would be disproportionately expensive to require TNCs in their LDC operations to adhere to rules and standards developed for OECD contexts. LDCs often do not have the environmental infrastructure – such as landfills, waste treatment facilities, laboratories and trained personnel – required to support high environmental performance.

The environmental rationale against regulation
In addition to the economic arguments against environmental regulation of TNCs, it is sometimes argued that such rules would be unwarranted environmentally. First, such rules would duplicate already existing environmental regulations at the national and international level. At the national level, most countries have already established environmental regimes pertaining to industry, be it local or transnational. LDC regulations may be inferior to those prevalent in OECD countries, but this only reflects, opponents of regulation would argue, that LDCs give preference to developmental objectives at the expense of the environment and/or that the assimilative capacity of LDC environments are larger than those of OECD countries. The establishment of an international environmental framework pertaining to TNCs would, according to this line of reasoning, infringe on LDC environmental and development priorities. At the international level, many aspects of TNC activity are already covered by various environmental laws, conventions and guidelines issued by international organizations and aimed at solving transboundary environmental problems. In addition, there are numerous regional and bilateral agreements and conventions regulating the environmental aspects of local firms, as well as transnational corporations. To develop new environmental frameworks specifically targeting TNCs would, according to this line of thinking, duplicate already ongoing efforts.

A second environment-related argument against environmental regulation of TNCs is that there is little need to establish environmental safeguards against TNCs. Opponents of regulation argue that the fear that TNCs will relocate polluting production to LDCs to escape pollution abatement costs in OECD countries is largely unfounded. There is virtually no incentive for TNCs to move polluting production to LDCs. Typically, variations in pollution abatement costs between the North and the South are too small to make relocation for environmental reasons profitable. Furthermore, the marginal benefits of investing in the pollution haven have to be measured against the environmental liabilities of moving to the pollution haven in terms of consumer reaction, NGO boycott, strained relations with the host country government and so forth. It has been argued recently, moreover, that leading countries with regard to environmental regulation are also leading exporters of the products subject to tough regulation (Porter, 1991; Porter and van der Linde, 1995). Because national environmental priorities of the most environmentally conscious countries can apparently be reflected in environmental regulations without seriously impeding their competitiveness, environmental regulation to protect competitiveness and prevent investment flight seems less pertinent (Lundan, 1995: 14). With regard to the fear that TNCs will apply lower environmental standards in LDC operations, opponents of TNC regulation may argue that market forces, rather than prompting TNCs to operate with environmental double standards, will encourage TNCs to operate within 'sustainable development configurations' (Baumol *et al.*, 1988) and make them harmonize environmental management systems and standards worldwide (Hadlock, 1994). According to Lundan, it is likely that large TNCs operating in multiple locations will harmonize their standards internally according to the highest standards across all locations, and that those standards 'by virtue of their pronounced presence in the world market, will form the *de facto* standard in global competition' (Lundan, 1996: 38). Further, Lundan argues that 'rather than seeking havens, MNCs adopt the Best Available Technology globally, and possibly transfer it to other production locations around the world, often exceeding local compliance levels and upgrading *de facto* world standards' (Lundan, 1995: 20).

The case for international environmental regulation of TNCs

As demonstrated in the previous sections, there are strong arguments for and against environmental regulation of TNCs. From an economic perspective, advocates of regulation argue that, without such regulation, environmentally responsible countries and companies will lose competitiveness. Opponents of regulation argue that such rules are economically sub-optimal as they prevent countries from exploiting comparative advantages associated with an abundant assimilative capacity, and as they are biased in favour of non-TNCs. Moreover, opponents of regulation argue that there is a real danger that such rules will become disguises for protectionism. From an environmental perspective, advocates of environmental regulation argue that such rules will mitigate a series of adverse environmental effects of FDI and TNC activity and prevent countries from engaging in a regulatory race to the bottom. Opponents of regulation argue that such rules are unwarranted, as many aspects of TNC activity are already covered by national and international environmental law and as the adverse environmental consequences of TNCs which relate to their transnational status are, in any case, limited.

Having presented various arguments for and against environmental regulation of TNCs, this section will assess their merits. On balance, regulation of TNCs would seem to be desirable for four reasons: to guarantee salient environmental values and minimum standards; to compensate for regulatory failure at the national and international level; to encourage high environmental performance and innovation in TNCs; and to facilitate FDI in LDCs.

Guaranteeing environmental minimum standards
Opponents of regulation are probably right that the adverse environmental effects of TNC investment are less serious than often believed. Empirical studies reveal that industrial flight to pollution havens is exceptionally rare (Jaffe *et al.*, 1995; Dean, 1992; UNCTC, 1992; Leonard, 1988; Hansen, 1997) and while environmental double standards may be common, TNCs also tend to be cleaner than comparable local companies (Royston, 1979). Moreover, there is empirical evidence to support the contention that TNCs frequently integrate and harmonize environmental standards at a global scale and operate with high environmental standards regardless of location (Hadlock, 1994; Gladwin, 1987; Clark, 1993; Lundan, 1996; Hansen, 1997).

However, evidence that the adverse environmental impacts of FDI in general may be limited does not imply that environmental regulation of TNCs is unwarranted. Specific TNC activities or investment projects that ignore environmental dimensions may have devastating environmental implications. This was amply demonstrated by the Bhopal catastrophe. Futhermore, while TNCs often operate with high environmental standards regardless of location, there is also evidence to suggest that high environmental performance eludes many TNCs. A 1993 United Nations study of cross-border environmental management in 169 of the world's largest TNCs suggested that around one quarter of these companies had yet to establish cross-border environmental management procedures (UNCTAD, 1993a). And a 1995 survey of cross-border environmental management in 153 Danish TNCs suggested that most smaller TNCs have no procedures to monitor and upgrade environmental performance of affiliates located in LDCs and Eastern Europe (Hansen, 1997). Thus, environmental regulation of TNCs should be established to avoid new Bhopals, and to encourage all TNCs to be environmentally responsible in international operations.

Environmental regulation is also necessary to ensure the continuity of good practice. While the adverse environmental consequences of FDI may be negligible at any one time, this situation may change in the future. Changing conditions in the global economy related, for example, to deregulation, technological developments or improved macro-economic conditions in many LDCs could render at least some industries more footloose, thereby increasing the probability of industrial flight to pollution havens. The future is also likely to see a partial shift in the geographical location of markets where TNCs sell their products. One of the reasons why the dynamics of international production currently seem to bring about favourable environmental responses by TNCs is that their major markets are in the economies of OECD countries, where stricter environmental regulations and standards exist. As countries with less elaborate environmental regulations, such as LDCs or the emerging markets of Eastern Europe, become increasingly integrated into the global economy, market forces might induce TNCs towards double standards and industrial flight. In view of the probability that TNC investment may increasingly have adverse environmental consequences, international environmental minimum standards safeguarding against such consequences seem appropriate.

Compensating deficiencies in current environmental regulation

On balance, the argument that TNCs are already covered by national as well as international environmental law, and that no specific environmental frameworks for TNCs are therefore needed, seems too optimistic. Regarding national environmental regulation, trade economists have argued that specific environmental rules governing FDI will be economically sub-optimal because existing national environmental regulation already reflects the assimilative capacities and environmental priorities of countries. While theoretically valid, this argument is flawed at the empirical level. In reality, it is highly questionable whether the level of environmental regulation in a given country in general, and LDCs in particular, reflects the 'true' assimilative capacity of the environment. Regulation in most LDCs remains highly rudimentary, especially with regard to long-term and diffuse environmental problems, and it seldom reflects environmental costs of production and resource exploitation (Pearce *et al.*, 1993).[17] Moreover, the assimilative capacity of a country's environment is partly determined by the pollution tolerance of its population. But in a situation where the institutions through which public opinion can influence government action are weak, as is the case in much of the developing world (OECD, 1992), there can be no *a priori* expectation that environmental regulations will reflect the preferences of the people. If environmental regulations in LDCs typically do not reflect either environmental costs or the preferences of the people, it seems that the case of the trade economists against environmental regulation of TNCs is seriously impaired.

With regard to international environmental law, opponents of regulation argued that as international law already addresses environmental problems of a transboundary nature, no separate framework for TNCs is needed. However, international environmental law is characterized by a host of problems that weaken this argument: international environmental law is a relatively new policy area; it is highly fragmented among many regional and international organizations; and it has tended to develop 'reactively' and on an *ad hoc* basis (UNCTAD, 1993a: xi). Although there have been significant improvements – especially at the regional level in Europe and North America – environmental cooperation remains weak at the global level. Relatively few LDCs have ratified global instruments such as the 1994 Basel Convention and the 1987 Montreal Protocol. Moreover, in many important areas there are still no internationally applicable frameworks coordinating the activities of national governments. According to a 1993 UNCTAD survey of international environmental law with implications for TNCs, the regulation of international atmospheric regulation is 'relatively underdeveloped'; international regulation of waste problems is confined to trade and subject to at least three different international regimes; the international regulation of hazardous substances is generally limited to non-binding guidelines; and the regulation of flora and fauna is only now beginning to relate to mainstream economic issues (UNCTAD, 1993a: xii). In this situation it would be highly premature to argue that the possible adverse consequences of TNC activity are covered satisfactorily by international environmental law.

The conclusion is that free-flowing investment would be environmentally neutral only if all countries involved in international investment had fully internalized environmental costs and if international environmental law had addressed environmental problems of a transboundary nature. As this is obviously not the case, there is a strong case for regulatory frameworks specifically targeting environmental aspects of TNC activity.

Encouraging high environmental performance and innovation in TNCs

The previous arguments in favour of environmental regulation of TNCs concerned the possible adverse impacts of FDI. However, an equally compelling argument in favour of rules for TNCs is that they may encourage high worldwide environmental performance by TNCs and trigger innovation. For example, by setting standards for cross-border environmental performance, environmental regulation would act as a disincentive to those TNCs ignoring environmental dimensions and operating with blatant double standards, and favour those TNCs applying comparable environmental criteria worldwide. Consequently, regulation of TNCs could facilitate cross-border environmental responsiveness and the implementation of high standards regardless of location, and become an important source of competitive advantage. Furthermore, the adoption of environmental rules for TNCs would strengthen those forces within a TNC working for the standardization of environmental management throughout the corporation at the expense of forces advocating local adaptation and ignoring the environmental dimensions in international operations (Hadlock, 1994).

Facilitating FDI

Rather than diminishing global investment, as feared by many trade economists, environmental regulation of TNCs may in fact facilitate FDI. Of course environmental rules for TNCs would, in the short term, favour domestic over foreign investors, as the opponents of regulation point out. But, in the longer term, environmental rules specifically targeting TNCs might facilitate foreign investment. Such rules could be a way to appease public concerns – justified or unjustified – regarding the environmental impacts of TNC investment and may thereby be a precondition for getting political acceptance for global investment liberalization. Moreover, international environmental rules for TNCs may remove some of the environmental uncertainties often associated with an investment project in LDCs; for instance, the uncertainty associated with the fact that TNCs are often held to higher standards than locally based companies, or that TNCs will often be the first that governments clamp down on if environmental issues become politically salient. By having environmental regulation governing TNCs in place at the international level, host governments, as well as TNCs, will be provided with benchmarks for what they can expect from each other. This would create more transparency in investment projects and minimize conflicts around environmental issues, thereby facilitating FDI. Finally, international environmental regulation of TNCs might ease business for the internationally oriented company by levelling the playing field among the myriad of regional and national standards that are now significant barriers to trade and investment.

The preceding arguments for and against environmental regulation of TNCs are condensed in Table 7.1. The conclusion is that some degree of international environmental regulation of TNCs is desirable. The question to which we now turn is what kind of regulatory action should be taken.

Future Environmental Rules for TNCs: An Outline

What sort of rules should stipulate the rights and responsibilities of TNCs in the environmental field? This section will consider the possible content of such rules – which aspects of TNC activity could be targeted – and discuss a series of generic questions concerning the organization and design of environmental rules for TNCs.

Table 7.1
Arguments for and against Environmental Regulation of TNCs

	Arguments in favour of environmental regulation of TNCs	Arguments against environmental regulation of TNCs
Economic rationales	Mitigate competitiveness effects of variations in environmental control costs	Would cause a sub-optimal allocation of productive resources worldwide
	Ease cross-border business transactions	Unfair to single out TNCs
	Facilitate FDI in LDCs	May become a disguise for protectionism
Environmental rationales	Compensate for regulatory failure at the national and international level	TNC environmental problems are already addressed by national and international environmental regulation
	Prevent flight of polluting industries to LDC pollution havens	Industrial flight to pollution havens empirically insignificant and regulation therefore less pertinent
	Prevent environmental double standards	TNCs should not be singled out for regulation as TNCs generally perform better than non-TNCs and as many TNCs standardize environmental management across borders
	Many TNCs have yet to establish cross-border environmental controls and standards	
	Mitigate a regulatory race to the bottom	International market forces may encourage a *de facto* upgrading of environmental standards worldwide and attempts to regulate TNCs may hamper this process
	Encourage high environmental performance and innovation	

The content of environmental rules for TNCs

A distinguishing characteristic of environmental regulation of TNCs *vis-à-vis* the existing body of national and international environmental regulation is that it specifically targets firms that are involved in international production; consequently it sets environmental standards for TNC conduct in foreign locations that are different from (and presumably above) those imposed by the typical LDC host country. Very few such rules currently exist, but it is possible to select various aspects of TNC activity that could be targeted.

First, environmental rules for TNCs could set standards for the kind of products produced in foreign locations. Such standards could, for instance, prohibit TNCs from producing in foreign locations products that have been banned or severely restricted in the home country. Examples might include OECD-based TNCs producing in LDCs pesticides that have been banned in their home markets, or CFC gases in developing coutries where CFCs have not yet been phased out.

Second, environmental rules pertaining to TNCs could set standards for the production technologies transferred to foreign production facilities. Such requirements could, for example, prohibit or restrict the use of production technologies that are banned or restricted in OECD home countries. Currently, the Basel Convention restricts the export of scrapped production technology to LDCs. Such provisions could be broadened to include the transfer of old production technology within the same company. Technology requirements could also facilitate the transfer of clean technology, for example, by requiring TNCs to use Best Available Technology (BAT) regardless of location.

Third, environmental rules specifically targeting TNCs could set standards for environmental performance in TNCs. TNCs could be required to observe the same environmental standards regardless of location and/or to operate with home country standards regardless of local regulatory standards. Such provisions already exist in various 'soft' regulations, for example Agenda 21 and various international guidelines issued by business associations.

Fourth, TNCs could be required to establish certain cross–border environmental management procedures. For instance, they could be required to conduct regular international environmental auditing or to establish environmental reporting procedures between affiliates and headquarters.[18] It would also be possible to include provisions for cross–border environmental management in certain existing international management standards such as ISO 14000, EMAS or BS 7750.

Finally, environmental rules for TNCs could target their relationship to authorities and populations of the host countries where they operate by requiring them, for example, to provide governments with information on environmental hazards or by including community right-to-know clauses in investment agreements.[19]

The organization and design of environmental regulation of TNCs

Regardless of which function of TNC activity is targeted by environmental regulation, a series of generic questions will have to be clarified when designing such rules for TNCs. There are three key questions: should they be business–led or government–led, should they be unilateral or multilateral, and should they be binding or voluntary?

Business self-regulation or (inter)governmental regulation

Typically, the normative literature on TNCs and the environment distinguishes between intergovernmental measures such as international law or codes of conduct on the one hand, and self-regulation within the international business community on the other. In recent years, business self-regulation has been promoted as an alternative to governmental regulation in various fora. It is the business community's response to the growing environmental concerns worldwide and is believed to be superior to regulation. One of the most prominent proponents of self-regulation, Stephan Schmidheiny, founder of the BCSD, bluntly states that 'it is time for business to take the lead because the control of change by business is less painful, more efficient and cheaper for consumers, for governments and for businesses themselves. By living up to its capabilities to the full, business will be able to shape a reasonable and appropriate path towards sustainable development' (Schmidheiny, 1992: 83). For Schmidheiny, business leaders are better positioned to deal with the highly complex problems related to the environment than are politicians: 'Multinational companies often take a longer-term and more international view than governments themselves. Business people are often more experienced than politicians in the practice of weighing risks and making decisions based on uncertainty. We do it daily.'[20]

In the post-Cold War era, self-regulation has thus become a catchword in international political debates on business and the environment. Self-regulation seems all the more attractive as the failure of the international community to adopt international environmental rules becomes increasingly evident. More and more, governments refer to business self-regulation as the solution to environmental problems. At the Rio conference, the international community explicitly endorsed business self-regulation by encouraging TNCs to adopt international environmental industry guidelines.[21] The chemical industry's Responsible Care programme and the ICC's Business Charter for Sustainable Development are the best-known examples of such activities. By 1996, more than 2,000 companies had adopted the Business Charter for Sustainable Development. Even more companies are currently certified or are planning to become certified according to one of the increasingly popular international management standards. While voluntary, these standards effectively set the stage for corporate environmental management worldwide and are increasingly becoming the passport for companies that want to operate in countries with high environmental awareness.

The self-regulatory efforts of the business community have been motivated by various factors. First, by setting international standards, business has sought to remove differences in environmental regulatory regimes that distort competition. Furthermore, certain industries, in particular the chemical industry, have come under pressure to rebuild a damaged public reputation. Finally, it is possible that the business community through its promotion of self-regulation seeks to deflect binding national and international environmental regulation.[22]

Some of the self-regulation initiatives contain provisions for the cross-border conduct of TNCs. As previously mentioned, the ICC Business Charter for Sustainable Development requires signatories to 'apply the same set of criteria regardless of location'. The Japanese industry association Keidanren, in its Global Environment Charter, requires members to 'make environmental protection a priority at overseas sites' and to 'apply Japanese standards concerning the management of harmful substances'. Similarly, the OECD's series of Guiding Principles for Accident Prevention states that 'hazardous installations in non-OECD countries should meet a level of safety equivalent to that of similar installations in OECD countries'. The ISO 14000 environmental management standard refers specifically to Agenda 21[23] and the ICC Charter as a reference point for companies adopting the standard. If references to environmental responsibilities become more explicit in such initiatives, business self-regulation may become an important means of facilitating cross-border environmental responsiveness in TNCs.

In spite of some noteworthy – and impressive – self-regulatory efforts by the business community, it would be naive to believe that business self-regulation is an alternative to government action. There are at least five ways in which an endorsement of self-regulation as a measure of addressing environmental problems associated with TNC activity should be qualified. First, self-regulation does not come about out of the blue or because corporations suddenly feel a sense of environmental responsibility. In most cases, corporate self-regulation is undertaken in response to pressures by governments or international organizations. Thus, self-regulation takes place in a context where regulators keep an eye on industry, where there is a real probability that regulation in due course will be upgraded, and where regulation is waiting if self-regulation fails. Without the possibility of regulatory action, business self-regulation would quickly lose momentum.

Second, the danger of collusive arrangements in connection with self-regulation cannot be ignored. It could be argued that much of the international green networking taking place within the business community may be collusive activity by leading TNCs undertaken to hold off less environmentally advanced competitors, in particular LDC competitors. International management standards such as EMAS and ISO 14000 could illustrate this. LDC companies may in the longer run have to adapt to such standards if they want access to OECD markets or to become suppliers and sub-contractors to TNCs based in these markets. Thus, those standards may effectively become *de facto* standards in LDC export industries, and what could be seen, from an OECD perspective, as an environmentally beneficial activity could easily be perceived by LDCs as a collusive arrangement set up to keep their producers and products out of OECD markets.

This brings us to a third limitation of self-regulation, namely its lack of legitimacy. Self-regulation is initiated by more or less self-appointed business groups, typically large Northern TNCs. Standards and guidelines such as the ICC Business Charter for Sustainable Development or the environmental management standards issued by the ISO are, for all practical purposes, initiated, drafted and adopted by OECD-based companies for OECD-based companies. LDCs, consumer groups and environmental NGOs have little influence on these activities. As a result many observers view them with great suspicion. The negative reaction of NGOs to the initiatives of the international business community at the Rio conference underscores this point (see Bruno and Greer, 1996; Chatterjee and Finger, 1994). International inter-governmental rules may be the only way to get acceptance from all parties in the global economy, thereby providing the conditions for stability and legitimacy in the implementation of such measures.

Fourth, while self-regulation may be a flexible and effective means of promoting innovation and the competitive pursuit of environmental excellence, self-regulation cannot be employed to secure basic environmental minimum standards. To achieve environmental minimum standards defies the logic of self-regulation; the companies which already have their environmental house in order will gladly adhere to standards set by industry associations, whereas the very companies targeted by such measures will boycott them. Thus, self-regulation is merited in cases where state-of-the-art practices and benchmarks for future regulation are looked for but it is inherently ineffective with regard to environmental safeguards.

Finally, there is a danger of self-regulation becoming a way for TNCs to deflect regulation by governments (Gleckman, 1992); while impressive promotional material may be presented to the public and governments, there is no guarantee that practical action will be taken. Therefore, if self-regulation is to obtain any credibility, it will be necessary for industry associations to develop standardized ways of verifying the implementation of self-regulatory initiatives. As stated by UNCTAD (1996: 33),

> in the absence of a system of international regulations or a binding set of international conventions, managerial leadership in this area is a key to promoting a global standard.... Industry leaders will have to make the case that their principles are being borne out in practice if the case for self-regulation is to carry any credibility.

It is difficult to see how such credibility can be achieved without the participation of governments and international organizations.

In sum, business self-regulation is an exciting mechanism by which the cross-border environmental aspects of TNC activity can be addressed. It is flexible and may encourage innovation and the pursuit of cross-border environmental responsiveness. Given its serious limitations, however, it is important to stress that business self-regulation is a supplement to government-led regulation and not an alternative.

Unilateral versus multilateral regulation
How might government-led regulation be designed to address the environmental aspects of TNC activity? Should it be unilateral or multilateral? It has been suggested that in view of the failure of the international community to agree on international environmental regulation of TNCs, TNC home countries should take unilateral action to ensure that TNCs adhere to certain minimum standards abroad. For instance, home countries could adopt laws requiring domestic firms to observe domestic environmental standards in foreign operations. If the largest OECD countries adopted such rules they would create a *de facto* standard worldwide. Such unilateral measures would not be unprecedented; in the 1970s the United States adopted the so-called Foreign Corrupt Practices Act, which was aimed at bringing the extra-territorial activities of US firms under domestic control in cases of corruption. In line with this legislation, it has been proposed that US environmental standards should apply to US production facilities abroad,[24] most recently in connection with the NAFTA negotiations. While little legislative action in this regard has succeeded, it has now been established that US companies can be held liable in US courts for accidents at non-US production facilities (Buckley 1993: 139, Gleckman, 1992:6).[25]

In spite of its possible merits, unilateral action is a highly controversial way of addressing the environmental problems related to TNCs. Unilateral investment measures are (like the 'countervailing environmental duties' associated with international trade) dangerous because they connote protectionism. Unilateralism may open the spigot for all sorts of restrictions on investment at a time when GATT and other free trade agreements are attempting to minimize such measures. A related problem of unilateralism is associated with monitoring and enforcement; how can a home government monitor and correct TNC conduct in a foreign country and, more importantly, which host government would allow a foreign government to control such measures on its territory? Thus, for reasons of competitiveness and national sovereignty, international measures are clearly the preferred option. As Low suggests (1992: 323), only 'harmony in environmental standards allows the imposition of external preferences without the disharmony of gunboat diplomacy'.

Nevertheless, there are instances where unilateralism may be acceptable. There are softer, incentive-based versions of unilateralism that may infringe less on host government affairs and prove less protectionist. For instance, governments could encourage investors to meet certain environmental standards in investment projects. The Danish state-sponsored investment promotion agency, the Industrialization Fund for Developing Countries (IFU) requests its partners to observe a set of environmental guidelines when starting up production in LDCs. In these guidelines, potential partners are requested to meet Danish standards in investment projects in LDCs; in cases of deviation from Danish standards, partners must observe World Bank standards. Approximately 40 per cent of all Danish investment projects in LDCs are associated with the IFU (Hansen, 1996). Such rules can significantly affect the environmental conduct of Danish TNCs (Hansen, 1997). IFU also assists, in particular, smaller TNCs with environmental improvements in foreign affiliates through guidance and financial support.

Another type of 'soft' unilateralism could be to insist that aid programmes pay greater attention to the environmental performance of investment projects, for instance by funding the environmental measures of small and medium-sized enterprises (SMEs) in foreign locations or by co-funding environmentally benign foreign direct investment in LDCs. This linkage between aid and FDI has received little attention.[26]

Binding versus voluntary regulation

Another issue of contention concerning the design of TNC regulation is whether it should be binding or voluntary. This debate is, of course, influenced by the fact that it is extremely difficult to establish internationally binding rules, whereas voluntary frameworks are more likely to be accepted. Historically, therefore, the efforts of the international community to create rules for TNCs have focused on voluntary codes of conduct, such as the United Nations code of conduct, the ILO Tripartite Declaration of Principles Concerning Multinational Enterprises or the OECD Guidelines for Multinational Enterprises. All these codes have environmental provisions. In addition, certain guidelines and recommendations related to cross-border environmental management have been issued by the international community through fora such as the Earth Summit (see Box 7.1).

It is often argued that such codes and guidelines are ineffective because they are non-binding, whereas international conventions are intended to be legally binding. While there is some merit to this argument, it is also true that guidelines adopted by overwhelming majorities or unanimously in international fora such as the General Assembly of the United Nations are, at least to some extent, adhered to by most nations (UNITAR, 1990: 72–8).[27] Moreover, in time, codes of conduct may well evolve into international customary law. As Gleckman (1992) argues in his assessment of the evolution of TNC codes, 'what we are watching is the evolution of international environmental standards roughly equivalent with the now recognized human rights standard'. While this latter argument is disputed, it is clear that the differences between voluntary/soft and binding regulations should not be exaggerated; there is a wide grey zone between the two types of measure. Consequently, attempts to establish international normative frameworks governing the environmental aspects of TNCs could appropriately start out with voluntary international codes, with a view to reaching more binding frameworks in the future.

However, while international codes of conduct may promote a greater degree of commitment than is often assumed, it is also evident that free riders may undercut

---

Box 7.1

Agenda 21 References to Cross-border Environmental Management Responsibilities of TNCs

- 'Be encouraged to establish worldwide corporate policies on sustainable development' (Ch. 30.22).

- 'Introduce policies and commitments to adopt equivalent or not less stringent standards of operation as in the country of origin' (Chs 19.52 and 20.30).

- 'Arrange for environmentally sound technologies to be available to affiliates owned substantially by their parent company without extra external charges' (Ch. 30.22).

- 'Encourage affiliates to modify procedures in order to reflect local ecological conditions' (Ch. 30.22).

---

the efficiency of such voluntary frameworks in the longer run. Ideally the objective, therefore, must be to establish rules, where sanctions can be imposed in the case of non-compliance. One place where such enforceable rules might evolve is in the context of a Multilateral Agreement on Investment (MAI) which would be binding for signatories and establish arbitration procedures in the case of disputes. Although the MAI negotiations among the 28 OECD countries displayed little receptiveness to consumer and environmental concerns,[28] the draft MAI proposal included references – albeit very general – to the environmental rights and responsibilities of governments and TNCs (OECD, 1997). The WTO is also considering an international investment agreement as part of the GATT framework, and a working group is looking into the issue. In contrast to the OECD negotiations, developing countries will be represented in the WTO negotiations. It is important for negotiators to include substantial environmental provisions in such an agreement. Linking environment and investment in a WTO investment agreement would promote greater environmental discipline and permit the imposition of sanctions in the case of non-compliance, *inter alia* cross-sanctions spanning trade and investment. A typology of possible rules targeting the environmental aspects of TNC activity is outlined in Table 7.2.

Conclusion and Prospects

This chapter began with an overview of the historical evolution of the debate on international environmental regulation of TNCs. Where the 1970s were characterized by regulatory activism, partly spurred by the Third World's drive for a New International Economic Order, the 1980s became dominated by what was labelled a 'conservative backlash'. By the mid-1990s, it seemed that calls for international environmental regulation of TNCs had largely vanished from the intergovernmental agenda, paradoxically at a time when the power of TNCs in the global economy was increasing tremendously. Instead, the debate on the environmental responsibilities of TNCs shifted to the NGO and business communities.

Part 2 examined whether the international community had done the right thing in abandoning efforts to regulate the environmental aspects of TNC activity. On balance it was concluded that there is a need for an international framework governing the environmental aspects of TNC activity. One reason for this is that

Table 7.2
A Typology of Environmental Rules Targeting TNCs

| | Government-led interventions | | Business self-regulation |
	Binding	Voluntary/ incentive-based	
Unilateral measures	Extraterritorial application of national environmental regulation Courts acknowledging cross-border environmental liability	Environmental guidelines issued by national investment promotion agencies (e.g. IFU). Aid programmes subsidizing environmentally benign investment in LDCs	Keidanren's Global Environment Charter BS 7750 Canadian Chemical Manufacturers' Responsible Care programme
Multilateral measures	Provisions for TNCs in international environmental law Inclusion of environmental measures in an international investment treaty International customary law	Agenda 21 recommendations Environmental provisions in codes of conduct for TNCs, e.g. the United Nations code of conduct for TNCs or the OECD Guidelines for Multinational Enterprises IFC and MIGA environmental guidelines	Business Charter for Sustainable Development International environmental management standards such as ISO 14000 or EMAS

although there is evidence that TNCs are increasingly doing the right thing in international operations in terms of environmental performance, there are certainly exceptions to this rule. One need remember only the Bhopal catastrophe to realize that these exceptions could have immense consequences. Moreover, there is no guarantee that the adverse environmental effects of TNC activity will not become more common in the future. Technological developments and policy liberalization will make TNCs increasingly footloose and this may increase the probability that FDI by TNCs will have adverse environmental effects on LDC host countries. A second reason why regulation of TNCs is warranted is that both national and international environmental law is currently insufficiently developed to address cross-border economic activities. International regulation of TNCs could compensate for some of the deficiencies of environmental law. Third, rules for TNCs are needed in order to support state-of-the-art environmental practices of leading TNCs and to facilitate the dissemination of environmentally sound technologies worldwide. Finally, the existence of harmonized rules for TNCs may ease cross-border business trans-actions and appease TNC critics, thereby facilitating FDI to LDCs.

When considering how such regulation should be designed, Part 3 identified various measures. First, various voluntary and incentive-based measures were assessed, including self-regulatory efforts of the business community and guidelines by international organizations. There is considerable scope for pursuing TNC excellence in international operations and the development of new benchmarks for cross-border environmental conduct through business self-regulation. While such efforts are important they will need to be supplemented by regulatory action of a more binding nature. This needs to be undertaken by the international community in order to uphold basic environmental values and prevent free riding. In this regard, the option of unilateral measures by countries dominating international investment was considered. Such measures could stipulate standards for the environmental conduct of TNCs abroad. However, it was argued that they should be adopted only as a last resort as, all too easily, they may become disguises for protectionism. Instead, international environmental provisions are preferable. Such provisions could, it was suggested, be included in the broader multilateral agree-ment for investment currently being considered by the WTO. The inclusion of environmental provisions in such an agreement would mirror the trend of recent years to include environmental provisions in international trade agreements such as GATT, NAFTA and the EU.

What are the prospects for the adoption of international rules stipulating environmental standards for TNCs? The politics of TNCs, environment and development in the 1990s do not suggest that the international community is in the process of coming to grips with this issue. Failure to address the environmental aspects of FDI may radicalize the NGO community and make NGOs further question the legitimacy of TNCs. Without environmental regulation of TNCs, it will be increasingly difficult to build frameworks of confidence between business and communities; consequently, investment projects may be impaired. Moreover, the unpredictability provided by lack of ground rules for environmental conduct may expose TNCs to arbitrary decisions by governments reacting to domestic opinion hostile towards TNCs. The issue is not simply whether TNCs harm the environment or not; the very perception of negative effects of TNCs, as in the negotiations over NAFTA, may provide a significant political drag on investment liberalization. Eventually, the inclusion of environmental minimum provisions in a future 'GATT for investment' could be the argument that makes such a treaty more feasible and acceptable outside narrow trade and investment circles. Therefore we strongly urge that minimum standards for appropriate environmental conduct be included in a forthcoming international investment agreement. Such provisions would give TNCs a clear indication of the normative expectations they will have to adhere to in international operations and would go some way to appeasing TNC critics. As such, the inclusion of environmental provisions in an international investment agreement could be seen as part of a larger deal liberalizing investment regimes around the world and removing the obstacles to FDI in developing countries.

Notes

1 These two principles are central to international trade and investment law and are the basis of the GATT: the National Treatment Principle (Art. III) states that all imported goods should be treated like domestic goods. The Most Favoured Nation principle (Art. I) states that advantages given to one nation must automatically be extended to other nations.

2 Commission on Transnational Corporations, *Transnational Corporations: Code of Conduct; Formulations by the Chairman*, United Nations, I/C.10.AC2/8, 13 December 1978, pp. 9–10.

3 It should be stressed that the growing critique of the United Nations was based on more than a distaste for its advocacy of the NIEO. Already in the Carter years, the United States withdrew its support for some UN activities, in particular those of UNESCO, partly on ideological grounds but mainly because of mounting evidence of inefficiency and incompetence in this organization.

4 One of the conservative think tanks which ferociously attacked the United Nations was the Heritage Foundation.

5 See Vig and Kraft (1990) for an excellent description of the deregulation agenda's consequences for environmental protection in the United States.

6 Agenda 21's 40 chapters contain 32 provisions referring directly to TNCs (UNCTAD, 1996), although the implications for TNC activity of these provisions seem highly limited: there is no logic as to which of the 40 themes addressed in Agenda 21 include provisions for TNCs and which do not. Many of the provisions deal with trade-related issues such as the export of hazardous waste that have little direct relevance for TNCs (White, 1989). Finally, the recommendations pertaining to TNCs are, as is the case with most of the recommendations of Agenda 21, general and non-binding, with no specific targets or deadlines.

7 For instance, the chapter on Trade Related Intellectual Property Rights (TRIPs) has broad implications for TNCs as they possess the bulk of patents worldwide. Also, the separate agreement on Trade Related Investment Measures (TRIMs) obliges GATT signatories to scrap rules requiring TNCs to use local inputs or to export a certain proportion of production. However, it should be stressed that the Uruguay Round failed not only to address the problems related to 'national treatment' of TNCs but also to include investment in services. Moreover, it failed to open the discussion of the highly contentious issue of investment incentives.

8 For instance, both the OECD and WTO initiatives include the following investment-facilitating elements: (1) the right of establishment for foreign investors; (2) the principle of 'most favoured nation' treatment; (3) the principle of 'national treatment'; (4) agreed rules on taxation, repatriation of profit and management; (5) limitations on host country performance requirements; (6) rules for dispute settlement.

9 By 1997, more than 1,300 bilateral investment treaties had been signed (UNCTAD, 1997).

10 In a report issued just in advance of the Rio Conference, Greenpeace claimed that at least nine out of 48 members of the BCSD were engaged in highly dubious environmental practices, despite their claims to be leading companies in terms of environmental responsibility (Chatterjee and Finger, 1994: 130).

11 Mimeo, NGO Global Forum, Rio de Janeiro, June 1992.

12 The United Nations estimates that at least 35 international laws and conventions limit the activities of TNCs, mostly in relation to their trading and marketing practices (UNCTAD, 1993a).

13 See UNCTAD, (1993a, 1996) for a comprehensive description of the various environmental guidelines with relevance for TNC activity.

14 See, for example, Gladwin, 1987. See also Pearce *et al.* 1993:173 ff. for a list of shortcomings associated with LDC regulation.

15 See Leonard, 1988: 67 ff. for a detailed account of the trade economists' debate on the environment. See also Jaffe *et al.*, 1995

16 In 1991, Lawrence Summers, then chief economist at the World Bank, argued that the movement of polluting production should not be restricted by international rules for the following reasons: (1) as the life of a person in an LDCs is worth less than the life of a person

in an affluent country, polluting production with possible health consequences is more optimal in poor countries; (2) the marginal cost of pollution prevention in a developing nation is lower than in a rich nation and therefore polluting production should take place there and not in OECD countries; (3) polluting production is more accepted in poor countries because rich people value the environment more than poor people. The argument was advanced in an internal World Bank memorandum and was, according to Summers, intended as a purely academic argument. However, this memorandum was printed in the *Economist*, 8 February 1992, and led to an international outcry.

17 In the ideal neoclassical world, governmental regulatory intervention could, in accordance with the prescription of Pigouvian welfare economics, ensure that the market 'is getting prices right'. In line with this thinking, a branch within neoclassical welfare economics – 'environmental economics' – seeks to devise ways in which markets, encouraged by government action, could internalize environmental externalities, through measures such as green accounting, taxation and tradable pollution permits (see, for example, Turner *et al.*, 1994 or Pearce *et al.*, 1993).

18 In this regard, the Danish Environment Minister recently proposed that the mandatory green accounting for polluting Danish companies should be extended to include foreign affiliates. *Berlingske Tidende*, 12 (6) (1997).

19 Community right-to-know clauses are requirements stipulating that firms are obliged to provide surrounding communities with information about environmental hazards associated with a given production facility.

20 Statement by BCSD Chairman Stephan Schmidheiny.

21 See Chapter 30 of Agenda 21 (UNCED, 1992).

22 See, for example, Gleckman (1992) for this line of reasoning.

23 This standard's affiliation with the international environment and development debate is quite explicit: for instance, the draft ISO 14000 environmental management standard directly refers to the UNCED process and states in the opening paragraph that it has been designed in response to 'the expressed need ... for further development of international environmental management programs'. The draft standard includes, in Appendix A, a full copy of the Rio Declaration and, in Appendix B, a copy of the ICC Business Charter for Sustainable Development (ISO, 1994).

24 See, for example, Neff *et al.*, 1990 for such proposals.

25 See, for example, UNCTAD 1993c for an account of various measures that can be taken to impose cross-border liability.

26 A possible exception is Wallace, 1996.

27 See also Sauvant and Aranda (1994) for arguments on why soft international law may prove effective.

28 See, for example, http://csf.colorado.edu/sustainable-economics/mai/ or http://www.islandnet.com/~ncfs/maisite/ for NGO concerns related to the MAI negotiations.

References

Barnet, R. J. and R. E. Müeller (1974), *Global Reach: The Power of the Multinational Corporations*, Simon and Schuster, New York.

Baumol, W., J. Panzar and R. Willig (1988), *Contestable Markets and the Theory of Market Structure*, Harcourt Brace Jovanovich, New York.

Bhagwati, J. and H. Dali (1993) 'Debate: Does Free Trade Harm the Environment?', *Scientific American* (November), 17–29.

Bruno, Kenny and J. Greer (1996), *Greenwash: The Reality behind Corporate Environmentalism*, Apex Press, New York.

Buckley, Ralf (1993), 'International Trade, Investments and Environmental Regulation: An Environmental Management Perspective', *Journal of World Trade*, 27 (4) (August).

Castleman, B. I. (1985), 'The Double Standard in Industrial Hazards', in Jane Ives (ed.), *The*

Export of Hazard: Transnanational Corporations and Environmental Control Issues, Routledge and Kegan Paul, Boston.

Chatterjee, P. and M. Finger (1994), *The Earth Brokers*, Routledge, London.

Clark, G. (1993), 'Global Competition and the Environmental Performance of Australian Mineral Companies. Is the 'Race to the Bottom' Inevitable?' *International Environmental Affairs*, 3, 147–72.

Daly, H. (1993), 'Debate: Does Free Trade Harm the Environment?', *Scientific American* (November), 17–29.

Dean, J. M. (1992), 'Trade and the Environment: A Survey of the Literature', in P. Low (ed.), *International Trade and the Environment*, World Bank Discussion Papers, Washington DC.

ECOSOC (1993), *Activities of the Transnational Corporations and Management Division and Its Joint Units: Follow-up to the United Nations Conference on Environment and Development as Related to Transnational Corporations*, E/C.10/1993/7, United Nations, New York.

ESCAP and UNCTC (1988), *Transnational Corporations and Environmental Management in Selected Asian and Pacific Developing Countries*, United Nations, Bangkok.

Gladwin, T. (1987), 'Environment and Development and Multinational Enterprises', in C. Pearson (ed.), *Multinational Corporations, Environment, and the Third World: Business Matters*, Duke University Press, Durham, NC.

—— (1992), *Building the Sustainable Corporation: Creating Environmental Sustainability and Corporate Advantage*, National Wildlife Foundation.

Gleckman, H. (1992), *Transnational Corporations and Sustainable Development: Reflections from Inside the Debate*, internal memo from Department of Economic and Social Development (DESD), United Nations, New York.

Hadlock, C. R. (1994), 'Multinational Corporations and the Transfer of Environmental Technology to Developing Countries', *International Environmental Affairs*, 6 (2).

Hansen, M. W. (1996), 'Danish Foreign Direct Investment in Less Developed Countries and Eastern Europe: A Survey of the International Operations of Danish Companies', working paper, Copenhagen Business School (CBS), Copenhagen.

—— (1997), 'Cross-border Environmental Management in Danish Transnational Corporations', working paper, Copenhagen Business School (CBS), Copenhagen.

—— and H. Gleckman (1993), 'Environmental Management in Transnational Corporations', in K. Kolluru (ed.), *Environmental Strategies Handbook*, McGraw Hill, New York.

ISO (International Standards Organization) (1994), 'Guide to Environmental Management Principles, Systems and Reporting Techniques', Committee Draft, ISO/TC207/SC1/WG2/ 23 September, Geneva.

Jaffe, A.B. *et al.* (1995), 'Environmental Regulation and the Competitiveness of US Manufacturing: What does the Evidence Tell Us?', *Journal of Economic Literature*, 33, 132–63.

Leonard, H. J. (1988), *Pollution and the Struggle for World Product: Multinational Corporations, Environment and International Comparative Advantage*, Cambridge University Press, Cambridge.

Low, P. (ed.) (1992), *International Trade and the Environment*, World Bank Discussion Papers, Washington DC.

—— (1992), 'International Trade and the Environment: An Overview', in P. Low (ed.), *International Trade and the Environment*, World Bank Discussion Papers, Washington DC.

Lundan, S. M. (1995), 'Tighter Environmental Standards as a Learning Opportunity: Revisiting the Pollution Haven Hypothesis', paper presented to the 7th International Conference of the Society for the Advancement of Socioeconomics, Washington DC, 7–9 April.

—— (1996), *Internationalization and environmental strategy in the pulp and paper industry*, PhD. Thesis, Rutgers University, New Jersey.

Neff , A. *et al.* (1990), 'Not in Their Backyards, Either: A Proposal for a Foreign Environmental Practices Act', in *Ecology Law Quarterly*, 17.

OECD (1992), *Environmental Effects of Trade*, Report Com/env/TD(92)4, OECD, Paris.

—— (1997), *The Multilateral Agreement on Investment*, OECD, (HTTP://www.oecd.org/daf/ cmis/mai/), Paris.

Pearce, D. *et al.* (1993), *Worlds without End*, The World Bank, Washington DC.

Pearson, Charles S. (1985), *Down to Business: Multinational Corporations, the Environment and*

Development, World Resources Institute, Washington DC.

Porter, Michael (1991), 'America's Green Strategy', *Scientific American* (April), 168.

Porter, M. E. and Claas van der Linde (1995), 'Green and Competitive', *Harvard Business Review* (September–October).

Risse-Kappen, T. (ed.) (1995), *Bringing Transnational Relations Back: Non-state Actors, Domestic Structures and International Institutions,* Cambridge University Press, Cambridge.

Royston, Michael G. (1979), 'Control by Multinational Corporations: The Environmental Case for Scenario 4', *Ambio,* 8 (2/3).

Sauvant, K. and V. Aranda (1994), 'The International Legal Framework for Transnational Corporations', in *The United Nations Library on Transnational Corporations,* Vol. 20, Routledge, London.

Schmidheiny, S. (1992), *Changing Course: A Global Business Perspective on Development and the Environment,* MIT Press, Cambridge, Mass.

Servan-Schreiber, J. J. (1968), *The American Challenge,* Hamish Hamilton, London.

Summers, L. (1992), 'Foreword', in P. Low (ed.), *International Trade and the Environment,* World Bank Discussion Papers, Washington DC.

Thomas, C. (ed.) (1994), *Rio: Unravelling the Consequences,* Frank Cass, Portland.

Tomorrow (1994), 'In Search of Environmental Excellence', *Tomorrow,* 4 (4).

Turner, R. K. *et al.* (1994), *Environmental Economics,* Harvester Wheatsheaf, New York.

UNCED (United Nations Conference on Environment and Development) (1992), *Agenda for the 21st Century,* A/CONF.151/26 (Vol I-III), United Nations, New York.

UNCTAD (United Nations Conference on Trade and Development) (1993a), *International Environmental Law: Emerging Trends and Implications for Transnational Corporations,* United Nations, New York.

—— (1993b), *Environmental Management in Transnational Corporations,* United Nations, New York.

—— (1993c), *Improving Liability Measures for Addressing Transfrontier Pollution,* Environment Series No. 4, prepublication copy, United Nations, New York.

—— (1996), *Self-regulation of Environmental Management: An Analysis of Guidelines Set by World Industry Associations for Their Member Firms,* UNCTAD, Geneva.

—— (1997), *World Investment Report 1997. Transnational Corporations, Market Structure and Competition Policy,* United Nations, Geneva.

—— (1999), *World Investment Report 1999. Foreign Direct Investment and the Challenge of Development,* United Nations, Geneva.

UNCTC (United Nations Centre on Transnational Corporations) (1985), *Environmental Aspects of the Activities of Transnational Corporations: A Survey,* United Nations, New York.

—— (1988), 'Transnational Corporations and the Environment', in *Transnational Corporations in World Development,* United Nations, New York.

—— (1990), *The New Code Environment,* UNCTC Current Studies, Series A, No. 16, United Nations, New York.

—— (1991), *TNCs and Issues Related to the Environment,* E/C.10/1991/3, United Nations, New York.

—— (1992), 'Transnational Corporations and the Environment', in UNCTC, *World Investment Report 1992: TNCs as Engines of Growth,* United Nations, New York.

UNITAR (United Nations Institute for Training and Research) (1990), *The United Nations and International Business,* UNITAR, New York.

Vernon, R. (1971), *Sovereignty at Bay: The Multinational Spread of US Enterprises,* Basic Books, New York.

Vig, N. J. and M. E. Kraft (1990), *Environmental Policy in the 1990s: Toward a New Agenda,* CQ Press, Washington DC.

Wallace, David (1996), *Sustainable Industrialization,* Earthscan, London.

White, A. (1989), 'The Transboundary Movement of Hazardous Products, Processes and Wastes from the US to the Third World Nations: A Prognosis', paper presented at annual meeting of the Association of American Geographers, Baltimore.

Promoting Corporate Environmental Responsibility

What Role for 'Self-regulatory' and 'Co-regulatory' Policy Instruments in South Africa?

JONATHON HANKS

M14
F23
013   457
052 058

Introduction

Notwithstanding the environmental improvements that have been achieved by the policies and regulations introduced since the late 1960s, there is a growing appreciation amongst environmental policy makers and commentators of the diminishing returns associated with the traditional regulatory approach. This appreciation, coupled with the trend in most OECD countries towards deregulation, and reinforced by the increasing adoption of proactive environmental strategies within industry, has resulted in the widespread use of alternative policy instruments that favour a more cooperative approach to environmental policy making. The logic of using such instruments is convincing: they seek to overcome some of the limits associated with 'command-and-control' regulation by making use of the entrepreneurial dynamism and informational advantages of the business sector; furthermore, they promote the active involvement of the business community in the policy-making process, thereby facilitating the more effective integration of national economic and environmental activities.

A principal aim of this chapter is to consider the relevance of these new policy initiatives for developing countries. This is a controversial issue, at the heart of which rest differing perceptions as to the motivations and intent of business and industry, as well as different visions as to the nature of the environmental crisis and the meaning of sustainable development. Although the chapter adopts a position in favour of a co-regulatory approach to environmental policy making, its principal objective is to serve as a basis for discussion.

The analysis proceeds in two main parts. Part 1 presents an overview of environmental policy instruments, and outlines some of the traditional arguments regarding the merits and shortcomings of different approaches to environmental policy before examining the issue of negotiated agreements in more detail. Part 2 assesses the potential for introducing negotiated agreements in South Africa. Such agreements form a vital component of arguably one of the most comprehensive attempts yet at developing a sustainable economy, the Netherlands' National Environmental Policy

Plan (NEPP). A key question addressed in this chapter is to what extent there exists in South Africa the type of institutional context that would facilitate the implementation of such an approach.

South Africa constitutes a challenging test case for examining the relevance of innovative policy approaches for developing countries. While the country has a relatively sophisticated infrastructure and industrial base, it faces challenges that are common to many developing economies: it has a high unemployment rate, a significant level of poverty and social inequality, and a growing population – all factors that complicate the process of policy-making for sustainable development. The issue is further complicated by the existence of significant government resource constraints, coupled with a general tendency to place economic and social equity issues before environmental concerns.

Policy-making for Industrial Sustainable Development

The process of environmental policy making is typically seen to comprise two distinct steps: the identification of a socially optimal level of environmental protection and the implementation of instruments to achieve that level. Although the focus of this chapter is predominantly on the second stage in the policy-making process, it is important to consider briefly some of the debates associated with setting an 'optimal level of pollution' – or with defining a state of 'sustainable development' – as any underlying assumptions regarding the preferred method of *identifying* the socially optimum level of pollution will influence the choice of policy instruments for *attaining* that outcome.

Sustainable development as a process

Despite the plethora of definitions that have emerged since the 1987 Brundtland Report (WCED, 1987) it is evident that the concept of sustainable development still eludes a single operational definition. That this is the case should not be surprising: at the core of the concept is the notion of 'development', itself an inherently vague concept that reflects a plurality of political demands and expectations. As political decisions are at the heart of the choices to be made, sustainable development cannot be seen as a mere technical problem. Policy makers seeking to achieve sustainability should endeavour first to reach broad agreement on the general purpose and direction of development, making explicit provision for ecological sustainability and social equity as considerations over and above purely economic concerns. This is best achieved through a culture of improved communication and consensus building, as well as through a greater emphasis on the provision of pertinent information, rather than simply through a process of ecological standard setting or pricing the environment (de Graff *et al.*, 1996).

It follows that the focus of any discussion on sustainable development should be on the *process* rather than on defining a single 'tangible outcome'. It is technically not feasible to define the specific ecological limits to growth, nor to ensure that these are respected, particularly where they conflict with immediate demands such as job creation. An integral element of this approach to sustainability is the emphasis placed on the issue of *uncertainty* regarding the nature of the ecological risk. This issue has important implications for a policy approach founded solely on directive-based regulations, and especially on those that mandate specific technology standards in the blind faith that this will guarantee a specified ecological outcome.

Whilst acknowledging the complexities and inherent uncertainties in striving to

Box 8.1
Ecological Modernization: A Theoretical Basis for Co-regulation and Negotiated Agreements?

First introduced as a theory of social change by a group of German political scientists in the early 1980s, ecological modernization challenges the perceived fundamental opposition between economy and ecology and advocates the adaptation — as opposed to rejection and wholesale reorganization — of existing 'techno-industrial' institutions as a means of addressing environmental concerns. While this approach may have shifted the environmental debate to the middle ground, it has nevertheless underpinned a significant process of political change. Key features that distinguish ecological modernization from previous mainstream environmental policy approaches include:

- a shift in emphasis from reactive pollution control to proactive integrated pollution prevention practices, emphasizing the role of technology as a central institution for ecological reform;

- the view that the natural environment should be treated in economic terms as a resource to be paid for, rather than as a free good for the disposal of waste;

- recognizing that uncertainty is inherent in the environmental debate, and thus no longer insisting on unambiguous scientific proof as a precondition for policy intervention (the precautionary principle);

- an appreciation of the important role of the social perception of risk, notwithstanding that this may at times conflict with 'science-based' risk assessments;

- a belief that in many instances the burden of proof should rest with the suspected polluter, rather than with the injured party, thus heralding a general shift from causal to collective liability regimes.

An important feature of ecological modernization theory is its view on the role of the state. Although critical of undue bureaucratic state intervention in managing the processes of production and consumption, it does not dispute the essential function of the state in ensuring environmental protection; instead it argues that the state's role should 'change from curative and reactive to preventive, from "closed" policy making to participative policy making, from centralised to decentralised, and from dirigistic to contextually steering' (Mol, 1998). Concomitant with the increasing institutionalization of environmental issues within the state and the market is a changing role for social movements. Having served as prime initiators whose actions placed the environmental issue within the political agenda, it is suggested that their role should now develop from that of *external* social critic to that of a *participant* (albeit still critical and independent), mobilizing from within for an ongoing ecological restructuring of modern society (*ibid.*).

operationalize sustainable development or to define specific ecological limits, and appreciating the fact that sustainability requires provision for social equity and economic factors, the main focus of this discussion is nevertheless on environmental issues. This is largely in the belief that there is now ample evidence to suggest that natural capital – rather than human-made or social capital – constitutes the primary limiting factor to unbridled economic growth (Goodland *et al.*, 1991). Furthermore, and perhaps more importantly, there is a tendency for many Third World governments to prioritize economic and social equity issues, to the comparative exclusion of environmental issues.[1]

In seeking to raise the profile of environmentalist concerns in the context of poverty and social inequality, it is essential to minimize the potential for any mistrust regarding environmental initiatives that may result from the perceived (and in some instances real) conflict between environmental priorities and competing social needs such as job creation. For this reason it is argued that there is great merit in focusing initial environmental policy endeavours on issues such as 'cleaner production' or 'eco-efficiency', and on the promotion of 'no regrets' options[2] and 'win–win' opportunities.[3]

Such measures would constitute a useful transition as the wider implications of sustainable development become appreciated by both government and the business community, and as more substantial longer-term reforms are considered. Focusing initial efforts on 'win–win' options would not only help to minimize the potential for the divisive jobs-versus-environment debate that might otherwise result; it would also address the profits-versus-costs trade-off by demonstrating that in many instances protection of the environment offers useful financial benefits. In implementing such measures, however, it is important to promote the use of instruments that require information exchange and that enhance the opportunity for consensus building, while as far as possible facilitating the simultaneous achievement of socio-economic benefits.

In adopting this incrementalist approach to sustainable development policy making – as characterized by the social theory of 'ecological modernization' (see Box 8.1) – this chapter strives to develop a pragmatic approach to policy reform.[4] Such an approach, it is hoped, avoids the tendency of many of the more radical environmentalist commentators who criticize the *status quo* and call for substantial institutional reform while frequently failing to come up with any concrete suggestions for feasible action. This author professes to believe in reforming corporations through a combination of regulation and voluntary approaches, rather than either advocating radical transformation or placing undue faith in the ability of free markets alone to resolve the issue (Shrivastava, 1995).

Environmental policy options

To gain a clearer understanding of the policy context for co-regulatory approaches, as well as the distinction between 'self-regulation' and 'co-regulation',[5] it is useful to consider a typology for classifying the various environmental policy instruments. Some of the predominantly used policy typologies include:

- Directive-based regulation/Incentive-based strategies/Information based strategies[6]
- Command and control/Market-based instruments/Industry self-regulation[7]
- Direct measures/Indirect measures/Supportive measures (RSA, 1997)
- Regulated/Negotiated/Induced/Unconstrained[8]
- Public regulation/Co-regulation/Self-regulation.[9]

Although these frameworks are fairly similar in that they differentiate policy instruments according to the degree to which the state – as opposed to the regulated party – is involved in the development and implementation of that instrument, there are nevertheless some important distinctions between them, a key one being the definitions adopted in describing the 'non-traditional' regulatory options. The following groups of policy approaches are particularly relevant:

Directive-based regulation ('Command and control'): This refers to the traditional use of government regulations whereby a public authority sets standards, monitors and enforces compliance to these standards, and punishes transgressions. There are various types of environmental standards, such as ambient environmental quality standards, effluent and emission standards, technology-based standards, performance standards, and product and process standards.

Economic instruments: These are efforts to encourage beneficial behaviour by altering the prices of resources and of goods and services in the marketplace so that they more accurately reflect the environmental costs of production and/or consumption. Examples include pollution taxes, tradeable pollution permits and deposit-refund schemes.

Liability reform: There is a trend in a number of legal regimes towards the imposition of strict liability for environmental damage, in terms of which a corporate entity that may be shown to be the source of the damage is required to remedy the damage irrespective of any due diligence efforts that the entity may have taken.[10]

Co-regulatory instruments: This covers a variety of initiatives where the interactive relationship between the regulator and the regulated is particularly close. Typically, the environmental objectives are set by the public authorities while the methods for achieving that objective are determined by the regulated industry. Although as a broad definition this may be seen to cover several of the policy approaches listed above, it refers in particular to instruments such as negotiated agreements.

Information-based instruments: These include measures taken to enhance awareness on environmental issues, such as technical assistance programmes, advertising, eco-labelling, performance reporting, group empowerment programmes and small business incentive schemes.

Self-regulatory instruments: This refers to a system of self-discipline that is adopted by business in order for it to maintain its acceptance in the market place and to develop a competitive advantage. This discipline is self-imposed, without direct government intervention, and involves industry voluntarily choosing both the environmental target and the measures to achieve this target. Examples include the chemical industry's Responsible Care initiative and the ISO 14000 series of standards.

Directive-based regulation

Since the inception of environmental policy in most developed countries, the predominant strategy for pollution control has generally been one of directive-based regulations (often known as 'command and control'). This normally involves a public authority setting standards and then inspecting, monitoring and enforcing compliance to these standards, and punishing transgressions with formal legal sanction.

Box 8.2
South African Environmental Law:
Demonstrating the Weaknesses of Directive-Based Regulation

Although South Africa has a number of appropriately structured environmental statutes, the good intent and potential of the law in achieving environmental objectives has largely not been realized. There are a number of widely appreciated reasons for this, many of which are common throughout developing countries:

- There is excessive *fragmentation* of the laws, both with regard to their subject matter and their administration, with a number of different agencies being responsible for pollution control without sufficiently effective coordination.

- Environmental law is not sufficiently *enforced*, largely as a result of a shortage of suitably qualified and committed inspectors, government lawyers and administrators. The lack of capacity within government is evident at both national and provincial levels, although it is particularly pertinent in the provinces where the general administrative capacity is described as being at a 'crisis level'.

- The problem of inadequate enforcement has been compounded by the lack of *sanctions* which act as a deterrent, with fines and sentencing provisions being very lenient by international standards.

- Historically there has been a tradition of *insufficient disclosure* of corporate environmental information; this situation, however, has improved in terms of the Right of Access to Information Clause of the new constitution;

- An additional problem that has compounded the application of environmental law in South Africa has been that of strict *locus standi* requirements, although again this issue has to some extent been addressed in terms of provisions within the new constitution.

- The focus of many environmental permits in South Africa has been on setting *individual site-based discharge standards* without sufficient reference to long-term ambient environmental standards. It is suggested that if sustainability is to be achieved, then it is essential that standards are set on a prioritized basis with due consideration to long-term objectives.

- Environmental regulations in South Africa have generally formed part of a series of *end-of-pipe* laws which are media-specific.

- Traditionally the principle of '*best practicable means*' has been applied, demonstrating a general primacy of technical and economic considerations over the environment.

- The current system of setting and enforcing standards is subject to the usual inefficiencies associated with 'command and control' approaches: standards are generally *inflexible*, tend to discourage technological *innovation*, and they require the regulator to use scarce public resources to obtain *information* that is already available to the polluter.

- The development and implementation of an integrated approach to environmental issues in South Africa has been compounded by a *lack of political power* and sufficiently strong leadership in the Department of Environmental Affairs and

Tourism; arguably this is reflective of the generally low priority given to environmental issues within the South Africa government (past or present).

Although initiatives are being taken to address many of these constraints as part of the current environmental policy reform process, insufficient institutional capacity at both national and provincial levels is likely to remain a problem for some time, notwithstanding the efforts being devoted to environmental 'capacity building' in a number of the provinces.[11]

Such an approach undoubtedly has some significant strengths as a means of changing behaviour. Not only does it give the regulator maximum authority to control where and how resources will be allocated to achieve environmental objectives, but it also provides the regulator with a reasonable degree of predictability as to how much the pollution levels will be reduced. Furthermore, there are certain specific situations where directive-based regulations may be seen as the most appropriate and effective means of achieving a desired environmental outcome, a pertinent example being the control of ultra-hazardous materials through specified restrictions or banning.

While it is evident that directive-based regulation has resulted in some significant progress towards meeting public health and environmental objectives, and not disputing the fact that such regulation should remain an essential underlying feature of most environmental policy options, it has nevertheless become apparent that there are several important limitations associated with directive-based regulation, many of which are particularly evident in developing countries. A principal criticism relates to the fact that regulations are inherently inflexible, often resulting in responses that require greater costs for smaller returns; this is particularly the case in those instances where the regulations mandate specific types of solutions (such as end-of-pipe technologies[12]) rather than facilitating the adoption of innovative alternative approaches (such as cleaner production practices) which otherwise may have resulted in environmental benefits being achieved beyond compliance, and almost certainly at less cost.[13]

A feature of directive-based regulation that is of particular significance in the context of developing countries relates to the expectations and demands that it places on government resources, both in terms of setting and enforcing standards. In *setting* appropriate site-specific standards, government is required to develop sufficient knowledge and experience of technical and process issues. Yet much of this expertise rests with industry. The importance of government capacity – in terms of technical, personnel and financial resources, as well as the requisite political will – is also apparent in ensuring the effective *enforcement* of any regulated standards. As is outlined above in the case of South Africa (Box 8.2), the question of institutional capacity is often a key determinant that negatively impacts on the application of otherwise well-considered environmental regulations. Related to this is the danger that the implementation of environmental law becomes largely a procedural exercise, with enforcement becoming a mechanistic application of permit requirements, in some instances relying on non-compliance with legal technicalities rather than on promoting the achievement of long-term environmental objectives.

An area where the regulations themselves tend to be at fault – rather than their application – is the fact that they generally focus on supply-side controls (such as industrial production issues) without paying sufficient attention to important demand-side issues which seek to change consumption patterns. If this imbalance were effectively redressed, there would then be a useful incentive for businesses to invest in environmentally more acceptable products, processes and services with the aim of securing a competitive advantage. Related to this concern is the growing appreciation that conventional regulatory mechanisms are often not effective in addressing some of the more diffuse sources of pollution or in tackling the more complex global environmental problems.

An additional criticism of traditional command-and-control legislation is that it is often media-specific, focusing too narrowly on the management of one of the environmental media (land, air or water). In doing so, it fails adequately to address the impact that action in one medium might have on another, and often may require the introduction of treatment technologies to manage pollutants in each of the various environmental media. Associated with this is the tendency for many regulations to require the installation of end-of-pipe controls, rather than promoting the adoption of proactive pollution prevention alternatives. As is historically evident in South Africa, the administration of media-specific regulations is frequently costly and is subject to bureaucratic inefficiencies, particularly in those instances where there has been a widespread division of responsibilities amongst differing governmental departments. The demands that this has placed on business and industry, regarding for example multiple permit applications, has often resulted in long delays and unnecessary expenditure.

In the light of the various shortcomings associated with the directive-based approach to pollution control, there is growing acceptance by governments of the need for more innovative environmental strategies for industry, moving away from a focus on regulation and control towards greater cooperation and incentives. Broadly, this policy shift may be characterized by the increasing adoption of market-based policy tools and by the development of a more hybrid approach which includes the use of information-based instruments as well as self-regulatory and co-regulatory policy approaches.

Market-based instruments

There is a large body of literature and empirical evidence in support of the view that market-based instruments (MBIs) are, in most cases, inherently more efficient than emission standards in achieving a desired reduction in pollution. This view is straightforward to demonstrate in theory.[14] MBIs act as *incentives* for the development of more cost-effective pollution control technologies and they provide greater *flexibility* in the choice of technology or prevention strategy, thus being more cost-effective in achieving agreed levels of pollution. Furthermore, they may provide government with a source of *revenue* which may be used to support environmental or social initiatives that may contribute to enhanced sustainable development.[15] Although it is not in the scope of this chapter to analyse in any depth the theory and experiences regarding the increased efficiency of market-based instruments,[16] it is nevertheless important to appreciate that despite these possible benefits, the potential of MBIs for promoting improved environmental performance has not been realized. To some extent this is due to a continuing political resistance to their adoption, typified for example by the reluctance in the European Union to implement more widespread environmental charges. This is a significant, though understandable limitation. As Cairncross argues, 'setting proper prices for environmental resources will be one of the hardest political tasks in the coming century; a whole civilization has grown up with bad 'genes' – wrong signals from the market about the proper way to value the environment' (*The Economist*, 1990).

In addition to noting this political constraint, it is important not to underestimate some of the other disadvantages associated with MBIs: they are often less predictable in achieving environmental standards; they are not very effective in monopoly situations; and there may be practical administrative complications in their implementation (Bernstein, 1993; Spence and Weitzman, 1993). This last point is evident in South Africa where one of the apparent reasons for the current reluctance of the Department of Finance to introduce environmental charges is their lack of capacity to administer new taxes,[17] an admission that provides further reason to examine policy instruments that seek to shift responsibility for policy implementation on to the regulated party.

Self-regulation and co-regulatory policy instruments

Various policy instruments exist that seek to change corporate behaviour through information and incentive-based mechanisms (Box 8.3). A common feature of these approaches is their tendency to induce improved environmental management through systems of self-discipline, thereby making use of the entrepreneurial spirit to drive environmental innovation while at the same time reducing a dependency on limited government resources.

If effectively implemented, such instruments are theoretically more cost-effective to society than either directive-based or market-based instruments used on their own. By giving business greater flexibility, within a clear framework of societal expectations and requirements, they help to encourage continuous and innovative self-improvement rather than stopping at compliance with a set performance or technology standard. Instead of adopting the adversarial approach of 'command and control', self-regulation seeks to make use of industry's knowledge and resources, thus reducing the cost to government of having to collect the information, and avoiding situations where governments develop regulations and monitoring systems without an appropriate level of industrial and process experience. Being less dependent upon scarce government resources (such as manpower, technical skills and financial assets), such instruments are particularly pertinent in the context of developing countries where there are numerous pressing social concerns coupled with significant government resource constraints.

Self-regulatory policy instruments – as distinguished from co-regulatory approaches – refer to those instruments that are developed and implemented by enterprises without direct governmental intervention. They reflect a system of self-discipline that is adopted by business in order for it to maintain its acceptance in the market place and to develop a competitive advantage. In an environmental context, self-regulation is a strategy by which companies or sectors of industry, responding to various pressures, choose to regulate themselves by setting standards and codes of practice, introducing monitoring programmes, achieving pollution reduction targets, and so on.

For self-regulation to be a viable option, it is essential that various driving forces be in place to ensure that it is in industry's self-interest to adopt environmental strategies.

The threat (ultimately) of strict government sanction: While the emphasis of self-regulation is principally on self-monitoring and the use of internal incentives for enforcement, the statutory and enforcement powers of government are necessary as the ultimate sanction; the threat of legislation being passed – as opposed to existing regulations

Box 8.3
Examples of Co-regulatory and Self-regulatory Policy Instruments

Negotiated agreements. These are agreements that are entered into between regulatory agencies and private sector enterprises or sectoral organizations, in terms of which the latter undertakes to meet certain environmental commitments.

Reporting and disclosure requirements. These emphasize the positive potential role of information in promoting preventative actions, building on the experiences of Pollution Release and Transfer Registers (PRTRs) in, for example, the USA, Canada, Australia and the UK, as well as the requirements for mandatory environmental reporting in Denmark.

Environmental management systems (EMS) standards such as the ISO 14000 series. These standards, which have been drawn up and are being implemented voluntarily by many in the business community, provide a framework for improving environmental management and performance.

Self-auditing and voluntary disclosure, through the application by government of flexible penalty options. This approach — applied, for example, in the USA — seeks to pursue further the adoption of EMS standards by encouraging more open reporting by industry, and thus shifting some of the resource implications of environmental enforcement away from government towards the private sector.

Voluntary programmes such as those promoted by the US Environmental Protection Agency (33/50, WasteWise, and Green Lights). These initiatives seek to achieve significant environmental benefits beyond what the law requires. By participating in these environmental programmes companies benefit through improved public recognition, access to technical assistance from the EPA, cost savings, and the longer-term rewards associated with innovation. Examples of voluntary programmes in South Africa are the Clean Commute and Green Buildings for Africa programmes, launched in May 1997 with the aim of simultaneously curbing greenhouse gases and promoting economic development.

Eco-labelling and consumer education schemes as a means of facilitating more sustainable consumption patterns. Although eco-labelling schemes are increasingly implemented in OECD countries, they do not appear to be particularly evident in developing regions, a possible reason being that the power of consumer choice remains largely a luxury, being dependent upon the presence of a well-informed and comparatively affluent consumer body.

Life-cycle analysis (LCA), used as a means of facilitating prioritized policy making. The use of LCA is of particular potential value in improving decision making and prioritizing environmental actions by government, business and the consumer. It remains, however, a somewhat imperfect tool.

Codes of environmental practice adopted by industry groups such as:
• the ICC's *Business Charter for Sustainable Development*;
• the chemical industry's *Responsible Care* Programme;
• the Japanese business sector's *Keidanren Global Environmental Charter.*

being enforced – is itself an incentive, with companies that are able to pre-empt legislation often gaining a competitive advantage.

Peer pressure: This typically requires that there are effective sectoral organizations that have the ability to exert meaningful and credible sanctions on their members.

Technical and/or marketing benefits associated with participation in voluntary initiatives: Examples include the marketing benefits associated with having ISO 14001 certi-fication, and the technical assistance offered for example by the EPA to participants in voluntary programmes such as 33/50 and Green Lights; for such initiatives to be of value there needs to be sufficient technical capacity within government and/or a willingness to dedicate resources to access such capacity.

An appreciation of the direct cost savings associated with environmental management: Business is increasingly coming to appreciate that there are useful cost savings to be achieved by implementing cleaner production programmes, and there is a growing acknowledgement that the sustainable use of resources is an essential element of successful long-term business.

The requirement to disclose environmental impacts: By publicizing emission levels, business leaders come to appreciate the true level of their business's environmental impact, as a result of which they may be prompted to improve their performance, not only to reduce newly recognized costs, but also in response to both public and peer pressure; the important role of information may be seen in the USA, for example, where the annual publication of the top 10 TRI polluters – an 'environ-mental Fortune 500' – has proved a powerful incentive towards self-regulatory initiatives.

General public pressure: Environmental issues are receiving an increasingly higher public profile, to which industries have to respond so as to avoid public loss of confidence; in this regard an important role is played by public interest groups. To be effective they should be suitably vocal, relatively well-informed, and with access to sufficient financial resources, all of which are often important limiting factors in developing countries; similarly, consumers need to be able to exercise the power of choice in their consumption patterns, often a luxury when faced with poverty.

 This list of institutional, structural and political conditions that facilitate and en-hance the adoption of self-regulatory initiatives raises the important question of the ability to transfer such initiatives to developing countries where such conditions may be absent or weak – an issue to which we return in the second part of this chapter.

 The list also serves to highlight some of the limitations associated with self-regulation and to confirm that there are various instances in which such instruments may not be the most appropriate policy option. Two of the most significant obstacles with environmental self-regulation are the problem of 'free riding' and the general lack of credibility associated with such initiatives. These two criticisms are often levied against the chemical industry's Responsible Care programme, a prime example of a self-regulatory approach. To overcome such criticisms requires that sectoral efforts be in place to exercise meaningful sanctions on free-rider companies, that there are effective market incentives to comply, and that there is a system of external verification of compliance. The issue of free riding also emphasizes the continuing important role of public intervention as a means of increasing the incentive of firms to comply with any voluntary commitments, and arguably thus confirms the role of co-regulation as an option that may be of wider and more significant application.

While some of the initiatives listed in Box 8.3 require detailed reporting of progress in implementing agreed codes of practices, with the threat of some form of sanction for failure to do so, many are still entirely voluntary and rely principally on peer pressure to induce improved performance. For these industry codes to be effective, mechanisms need to be in place to promote their implementation by members, to monitor and publicly report on adherence, and to have meaningful sanctions in addition to peer pressure alone. It must be acknowledged that this is not always the case, a criticism that has been levied against the ICC Charter in particular.[18]

The case for co-regulatory policy instruments

Appreciating some of the weaknesses with regard to self-regulatory initiatives, and acknowledging the important role of government in defining the preferred environmental objectives, the use of co-regulatory instruments may be seen as a constructive attempt at combining the best of both approaches to policy making. Unlike pure self-regulation, where there is no public intervention, industry may be seen to benefit in that government intervention is more likely to secure the collective action of the sectoral organizations. In contrast to directive-based regulation, on the other hand, firms have greater ability to identify the most cost-effective means of attaining the publicly determined environmental objectives.

As has perhaps become evident from the discussion thus far, it is possible to distinguish two broad arguments in favour of a co-regulatory approach to policy making. The first is that co-regulation may in principle be seen as more conducive to sustainable development in that it ensures active collaboration and co-operation between government and industry, thus facilitating the effective integration of long-term economic, social and ecological priorities. If the business community is to achieve the necessary substantial improvements in resource efficiency, while at the same time meeting increasing demands for employment and redistribution, then it is essential that there be a common understanding between government and industry as to the preferred long-term development path. This requires that there be agreement on the environmental priorities that need to be addressed, as well as a clear appreciation as to how these priorities balance with the requirements of industrial competitiveness and job creation. The development of a shared vision for industrial sustainability and the creation of an environment that is conducive to long-term innovation both benefit substantially from the adoption of co-regulatory policy options.

A second related argument in favour of co-regulatory instruments is that directive-based regulation on its own is not sufficient to address the longer-term issues associated with sustainable development. This is particularly relevant in developing countries, many of which face significant government resource constraints and thus lack the capacity – and in many instances the political will – to ensure the effective development and implementation of environmental law. As indicated earlier, however, this acknowledgement of the importance of the co-regulatory approach is not to deny a continuing role for directive-based regulation. Such regulation is important in that it can act as an incentive for the adoption of self-regulatory initiatives, regulates free riders, serves as the basis for setting any desired social goals, and ensures the maintenance of government independence.

Building on these arguments relating to co-regulatory policy, it is useful to

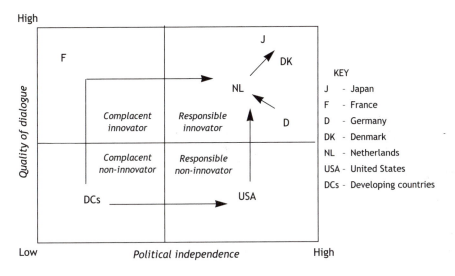

Figure 8.1
Actual and Potential Environmental Strategy Transitions
Source: D. Wallace, *Environmental Policy and Industrial Innovation Strategies in Europe, the US and Japan*

consider the analysis of Wallace (1995) regarding the implications for environmental policy making of the relationship between industry and the regulator. In seeking to identify the circumstances which result in an effective policy – defined as one which promotes industrial innovation – Wallace undertook a comprehensive study of the process of environmental policy making in six OECD countries: the USA, the Netherlands, Denmark, France, Germany and Japan.[19] The possible relationships are summarized in a matrix comprising two factors: the political independence of the regulator, and the quality of dialogue between the regulator and industry (see Figure 8.1). Together, these two factors may be seen to determine the long-term effectiveness of environmental policy making, and in particular its impact on industrial innovation. *Political independence* is seen to be important in avoiding the trap of power-based negotiations, thereby ensuring that industry does not use its superior information to its own advantage. By ruling out the possibility of 'influence peddling' and by maintaining a stable, trusting political climate, it is argued, industry will be more inclined to devote its resources to environmental innovation, including cleaner production practices. Similarly, with regard to the *process of dialogue*, it is suggested that a high-quality flow of information between industry and the regulator is conducive to the development of more innovative solutions by industry.[20]

Applying this model to developing countries, it is apparent that many have adopted 'complacent non-innovator' strategies. As pressures for environmental improvement grow, governments in developing countries may be tempted to sever their close relationship with industry and make a rapid transition to the 'responsible non-innovator' strategy. It is suggested, however, that the preferred route for policy makers in developing countries would be to adopt 'responsible innovator' strategies by promoting more effective industry–regulator dialogue, while maintaining sufficient independence from industry.

While there may be some debate as to where a country such as South Africa is currently situated on this matrix, the focus of policy reform should be on facilitating

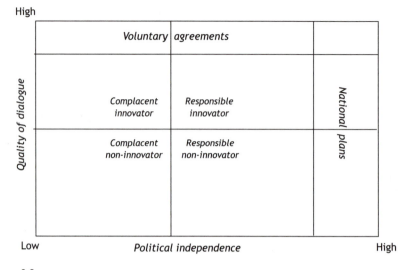

Figure 8.2
The Strategic Effects of National Plans and Voluntary Agreements
Source: D. Wallace, *Environmental Policy and Industrial Innovation Strategies in Europe, the US and Japan*

a transfer towards a 'responsible innovator' strategy rather than succumbing to the possible temptation of introducing aggressive adversarial regulation. In seeking to achieve this transition, it is useful to draw on the experience of the Netherlands in trying to achieve a sustainable economy. The Netherlands is characterized by two features in particular that are relevant to this analysis: the creation of a long-term plan for sustainability and the use of negotiated agreements.

An initial first step in policy making for sustainable development is to reach agreement on long-term developmental objectives. This requires the participation of all stakeholders. By setting long-term objectives, a government is more likely to create a stable and consistent policy framework, which not only has general public acceptance but also formalizes the political independence of government from industry. The function of negotiated agreements is to formalize a high level of dialogue and trust between industry and regulator, thereby promoting the adoption of the 'innovator' strategy. In combination, the use of negotiated agreements and a sustainable national plan facilitate a 'responsible innovator strategy' (see Figure 8.2).

Using these assumptions, it can be seen that there is merit in examining the potential role of negotiated agreements for promoting environmental innovation within industry in developing countries, in the belief that environmental innovation is a necessary (albeit perhaps insufficient) requirement for achieving sustainable development more generally.

Institutional conditions for introducing negotiated agreements

In seeking to make environmental policy making more efficient, most states in the European Union, as well as in other countries such as Canada, Australia and New Zealand, have introduced some form of negotiated environmental agreement. Although the first formal environmental agreement in Europe was concluded as early as 1971, such agreements generally date from the late-1980s and early 1990s. The majority of these agreements relate to waste management and the phasing out of specific substances, although the range of issues covered in the Netherlands is much broader, with industry covenants forming an integral part of the country's ambitious National Environmental Policy Plan.

International experience has shown that while environmental agreements can provide an effective means of achieving desired environmental outcomes, they are not the most appropriate policy instrument in all circumstances. Before agreements can be successfully introduced it is necessary that a number of specific *institutional* and *procedural* conditions be met.[21] As the procedural conditions may be dealt with in the structure of the agreement itself[22] and thus are largely independent of the political–institutional context, it is particularly important (in assessing the potential for introducing environmental agreements in developing countries) to focus on the nature of the *institutional* conditions.

A basic precondition for the development of agreements is that both parties must not only believe there are clear benefits to be achieved in adopting this route, but also be convinced that there is sufficient capacity to fulfil any good intent. For this motivation to be suitably strong, institutional aspects associated with values, social relations and organizational structures are particularly important. In this regard, it is submitted that there needs to be:

- A high level of *environmental awareness* amongst both government and industry, coupled with a good appreciation of the benefits of working together.
- Sufficient *mutual trust* between the various parties. While to some extent this may be dictated by historical political circumstances, it is also possible to improve the level of trust by implementing mechanisms that promote visibility, and by setting long-term mutually agreed objectives and procedures that are consistently applied.
- Some *threat of punitive measures*, as an incentive for the initial development and the continuing implementation of agreements, or alternative incentives. While this is generally taken to imply the need for strictly enforced legal standards, it is important also to appreciate the role of peer, public or consumer pressure. Pressures such as these require a certain type of institutional setting which is likely to include proactive and well-structured business and industry organizations, the existence of active and sufficiently resourced public interest groups, the ability of consumers to exert pressure through the power of choice in their consumption patterns, and public sector capacity to impose sanctions.

The existence of these conditions raises the question as to whether the political-institutional framework in developing countries is appropriate for the development and implementation of negotiated environmental agreements. This issue is now examined in the context of South Africa.

Promoting Co-Regulation in South Africa

Negotiated agreements and the political–institutional context

As part of its project to investigate the role of voluntary approaches to environmental management, the South Africa Department of Environmental Affairs and Tourism (DEAT) apparently made the conscious decision to exclude 'voluntary agreements or covenants', in the belief that these would not work in South Africa until there was greater capacity for more effective enforcement of existing directive-based regulations.[23] Officials in the Department have also expressed the fear that industry might use its greater knowledge to deliberately mislead the government during any negotiation process, thereby ensuring that any targets or commitments would be set at a less stringent level.[24] This not only demonstrates a lack of trust in the environmental motives of industry, but is also a tacit admission of insufficient technical capacity within government. These are significant concerns that provide a visible demonstration of a possible lack of some of the basic conditions required for the successful introduction of negotiated agreements.

Legal sanction versus informal communication

The suggestion that negotiated agreements are dependent upon the threatened enforcement of legal standards is based on the assumption that unless there is a tradition of effective governmental enforcement there will be no incentive for industry either to enter into, or to comply with, environmental agreements. Such a belief is often reinforced in the context of scepticism about the motives of industry. Addressing this concern is crucial to any strategy that seeks to promote the intro-duction of negotiated agreements and other 'voluntary approaches'.

There are several ways to approach this issue. To start with, it may be argued that the historical failure to enforce environmental law in South Africa (and arguably in a number of other developing countries) was dependent upon previous circum-stances — a lack of political will, or a failure to appreciate the importance of the environmental issue — and that this has since changed. Evidence of such a change in South Africa may be seen, for example, in the commitment by the Minister for Water Affairs and Forestry to act severely against industries causing water pollution, an undertaking that has been paralleled by the pledges of various provincial environ-mental administrators to bring high-profile test cases against certain polluting industries.

While one must query the capacity of government to enforce regulations effect-ively across *all* relevant enterprises and business sectors, it may nevertheless be argued that these visibly made commitments will be seen as sufficiently credible to serve as motivating factors for improved corporate action, particularly amongst the larger enterprises that are the most likely targets of any politically motivated activity. It is important to appreciate, however, that any renewed enthusiasm and potential for environmental prosecution is likely to remain limited to the more visible companies and that the structural constraints inhibiting the more widespread adoption of directive-based regulation will probably remain for the foreseeable future.

Arguably, this contention is upheld by the findings of a survey of 200 South African companies (including the top 150 companies as ranked by asset value). The survey found that the main drivers of corporate environmental responsibility were 'government policy/legislation' (83 per cent), 'public opinion' (64 per cent), 'customer demands' (62 per cent) and 'international trade' (51 per cent) (KPMG–IEF, 1997). Although it may be suggested that this response indicates business perception as to what constitutes the most significant *potential* pressure (suggesting that in the absence of such pressure there remains little incentive to improve performance), it is worth noting that, of the companies surveyed, 76 per cent believe that the environment is already a strategic issue, with 36 per cent indicating that environmental issues are considered 'very strategic'. In addition, an overwhelm-ing majority of the companies (84 per cent) maintain that environmental issues are likely to have an increasingly significant impact on their activities over the next five years.

The growing importance attached to the environment as a strategic issue would appear to be confirmed by several initiatives undertaken by industry groups and the level of participation of various individual companies and sectoral organizations in many time-consuming environmental policy processes over the last four years. Industry groups that have been particularly active and that have allocated substantial resources towards the policy processes include the Industry Environmental Forum of South Africa (IEF), the Chemical and Allied Industries Association (CAIA), the Chamber of Mines, the Packaging Council of South Africa (PACSA) and the South African Chamber of Commerce (SACOB). The more active industry associations tend to be those representing sectors that have a high environmental profile, with the most active individual participation coming from the larger and more visible enterprises within each sector. These traditionally more active companies and industry groups constitute the most useful basis on which to focus any efforts at developing negotiated agreements in South Africa.

The fact that there has been a poor tradition of law enforcement is not an appropriate argument against the introduction of negotiated agreements. As we have seen, various types of pressure are exerted on some of the higher-profile companies to motivate them to participate in the process of environmental legal reform, even to the extent where this may involve immediate costs. Furthermore, it can be argued that even if the existing system, founded on directive-based regulation, is not producing the desired result, this in itself is a strong incentive to explore the use of alternative mechanisms. This is particularly so when the existing structural impediments to legal efficacy – such as a profound shortage of government resources – are unlikely to be overcome in the immediate future. In the belief that it would be foolhardy to wait expectantly for sufficient resources to be allocated to environmental enforcement in South Africa, it is suggested that there is thus a need to seek innovative mechanisms that may be less affected by the vagaries of government, and more effective in promoting compliance amongst the low-profile companies.

The argument put forward by DEAT, that an alternative approach should not be attempted in the belief that it would fail until the structures are in place for more effective enforcement, is not only unduly defeatist; it also overplays the role of regulation as the sole motivating factor for improved environmental performance in enterprise. In this regard it is important to acknowledge the significance of other pressures such as public opinion, trade and investment requirements, and the possible market opportunities associated with improved environmental performance. It has been argued, for example, that the adoption of proactive environmental strategies in South African business 'has had little to do with legislation. Trade pressures, investment and more frequent exposure to international norms resulting from the end of South Africa's isolation have stimulated change' (Hobbs and Ireton, 1996).

While these pressures are largely independent of public intervention, they may nevertheless prompt participation in the legislative process in those instances when the regulatory pay-offs relative to the cost of lobbying are in themselves insufficient. As an example of this, one may refer to the chemical industry's Responsible Care programme which was implemented largely with the view of improving the industry's battered public image. Programmes such as this have tended to raise the general level of environmental activity within the particular sector, often exposing that sector to useful initiatives developed elsewhere that have demonstrated the potential value of more proactive involvement with the regulatory authorities.

Although it is apparent that there are additional non-regulatory pressures on companies to introduce environmental management practices, these in themselves may be dependent on important institutional considerations, a number of which may be lacking in developing countries. In response to these observations it is pertinent to consider the arguments of commentators who emphasize the role of information as an important motivating factor for regulatory involvement and legal compliance. These arguments are relevant not only in suggesting that negotiated agreements may be *developed* in the absence of threatened legal sanction, but also in contending that these agreements might be *implemented* in the absence of such sanction. Indeed, it may be argued that informal bargaining, typified by negotiated agreements, may at times be the only effective policy tool when formal legal procedures do not produce the desired result.[25] Arguably this has been the approach in some instances in South Africa where, as in the case of air pollution, instead of enforcing compliance through implementation of legal sanction, a government agency has negotiated a solution with the polluting company. Instead of focusing solely on the possible problems associated with the legal informality of agreements, coupled with the limited coercive power of the existing legal instruments, attention should instead be directed towards the positive impact of the communication-enhancing effects of agreements.[26]

Herein lies potentially the most powerful argument in support of the use of negotiated agreements, even in those instances where there is insufficient regulatory enforcement. The process generates an added value which is its capacity to facilitate creative problem solving and to enlarge the support for the proposed measures through 'informal communication', rather than relying simply on the presumed coercive power of legal instruments (Koppen, 1994). Seen in this light, one of the main problems that may need to be solved relates not to the juridical component but to non-juridical factors such as the provision of information.[27]

Any initial agreements that are to be developed in South Africa (or for that matter in other regimes characterized by weak legal enforcement) should seek specifically to build on the positive motivating influences associated with improved information flows; after all, 'no management tool is more powerful than information' (Cairncross, 1991). There are a number of mechanisms by which information may be seen to act as a strong incentive for improving environmental performance. Demonstrating to senior management how much money and toxicity is leaving their premises in the form of unmonitored waste is likely to serve as a strong motivation to reduce these losses. Furthermore, by ensuring that this information is made available to key stakeholders, the possibility is raised that market pressures – in the form of consumers and agitating community groups – will begin to compete with government as an incentive for improved environmental performance. Raising the profile and the stakes associated with information gathering and dissemination serves as an important mechanism for overcoming some of the 'bounded rationality' that often inhibits companies from implementing the 'no regrets' options associated, for example, with cleaner production.

DEAT may well be concerned that they currently lack the capacity to enforce existing regulations. If anything, however, this should serve as an incentive to explore alternative non-regulatory means of promoting environmental responsibility in the business community, and in particular should signal the importance of using the potential power of information as a means of promoting enhanced behaviour, rather than waiting for the government's institutional capacity to be built up. That may be a long wait!

A culture of consensus and a mature policy framework — can these be developed?

A second area in which the nature of the political–institutional relationship is seen to impact upon the efficacy of negotiated agreements is the belief that the successful implementation of agreements is dependent upon the existence of a culture of consensual policy making, involving 'experienced and credible parties, within both government and industry, that are represented by respected negotiators'.[28] This raises two related issues that need to be examined in the context of South African circumstances: is there an appropriate culture of negotiation and trust between the parties, and is there sufficient experience amongst the regulators to ensure that industry does not abuse its position as a possible monopoly holder of technical expertise? These concerns are evidently shared by the DEAT.

In addressing these concerns it is important to ensure that there are sufficient procedures in place to guarantee both the appropriate disclosure of information by industry and the effective participation of interested and affected parties. This would serve to reduce the chances of industry overwhelming the technical capacity of government or creating the perception that it might do so. As was argued in Part 1, there is also a need to ensure sufficient independence of the regulator from industry. The suggestion was made that this should be achieved by establishing environmental (or broader 'sustainability') objectives and targets, with all key stakeholders being involved in determining these targets. Accordingly, the focus of negotiated agreements should be on the means of action rather than on setting the environmental objective, while also ensuring that there is regular and sufficiently transparent reporting of progress in implementing the agreement. Adopting such measures, it is believed, may to some extent allay the fears of the DEAT expressed earlier.

Although these procedural mechanisms may go some way to addressing stakeholder concerns relating to the informational advantages enjoyed by industry, they do not in themselves result in a culture of consensus building and trust. It may of course be debated whether such a culture is necessary for the success of negotiated agreements; on this issue Mol, for example, observes that 'notwithstanding the fact that these new communicative models of environmental policy making are found in countries with a predominantly consensual policy style, research on and initiatives in joint environmental policy making can also be found in countries with the opposite policy style' (Mol *et al.*, forthcoming).

In examining whether it may be possible to develop a consensual approach to policy making, it is perhaps encouraging to note the experience of the Netherlands, which arguably has managed to overcome the initial 'familiar battle lines between industry and environment ministries' through a programme consciously aimed at creating a more collaborative relationship (Wallace, 1995). While it may be questioned whether the institutional and cultural context in South Africa is sufficiently similar to permit the same change in approach to policy making within the DEAT, there may be some useful lessons that could be applied within the Department, particularly as it seeks now to implement National Environment Strategies and Action Plans, having spent most of its effort in the recent past on policy formulation.

Introducing negotiated agreements in South Africa

Following the first democratic elections in South Africa in April 1994, the country has been engaged in a myriad of legal and policy reform processes within each of the various government departments and ministries. Of particular relevance to this chapter are two environmentally related policy initiatives: the DEAT's Consultative

National Environmental Policy Process (CONNEP), which, after three years, culminated in the publication of a *White Paper on Environmental Management Policy for South Africa*, and the Integrated Pollution Control and Waste Management initiative undertaken jointly by the DEAT and the Department of Water Affairs and Forestry (DWAF), which has also resulted in a White Paper.[29]

It is important to ensure that any proposals for introducing agreements in South Africa are compatible with the aims and objectives of both of these initiatives, and in particular with the basic philosophies and anticipated future actions provided for in the CONNEP White Paper. In this regard it is pertinent to note the DEAT's undertaking to formulate National Environmental Strategy and Action Plans as a means of implementing the policy proposals in this White Paper. This may be seen as a most appropriate opportunity for the introduction of innovative environmental policy instruments, with a view to ensuring that these form part of a process of consultation aimed at setting environmental objectives and targets in an integrated and prioritized manner.

Building on the experience of countries such as the Netherlands, a first step in developing a pragmatic long-term strategy for sustainable development must consist of developing a common understanding on environmental priorities, based on constructive negotiation between all key stakeholders. Due consideration should be given to the demands for increasing industrial growth, while at the same time balancing the concerns of the environmental community with the requirements of competitiveness and employment creation.[30] In implementing this 'shared vision', it is recommended that there be a mutual commitment to meeting specific objectives and targets, with some agreement on the allocation of public and private resources and responsibilities.

To ensure the acceptance of any agreements in South Africa – and arguably in other developing countries – measures will need to be taken to overcome the concerns and scepticism aroused by many industry-based initiatives. This will require a particular emphasis on providing for active stakeholder involvement in the development and implementation of agreements. Furthermore, it is suggested that provision should also be made in the agreements for relevant developmental priorities. These include, for example, concerns pertaining to employment generation, worker health and safety, and the promotion of enhanced environmental performance within small and medium-sized enterprises. Ideally, the introduction of agreements should form part of a strategy that aims at building consensus in defining the principal priorities for attaining sustainability, and that promotes the dissemination of information in a manner that reflects an awareness of the capacity constraints of government. As a means of securing greater commitment to the importance of ecological sustainability, it is suggested that attention should focus initially on promoting the 'win–win' and 'no regrets' options typically associated, for example, with the concepts of cleaner production and eco-efficiency. This is a point that was argued earlier in the context of the perceived environmental priorities as stated by the Minister for Environmental Affairs and Tourism.[31]

Initial negotiated agreements should be developed in those sectors where there are strong industry associations, and where there is some degree of uniformity within that sector, as well as evidence of an ability to exert peer pressure on individual member organizations. In this regard, the South African Chemical and Allied Industries Association may be seen as a useful sectoral organization in the light of its current experience in implementing the Responsible Care programme. Ensuring that contracting parties are well organized, and initially focusing on a limited number of contracting parties, will provide fewer opportunities for free riding, as well as a greater capacity for administering the agreement. As outlined below, in addition to CAIA, there are a number of other sectoral organizations that could contribute to such an initiative.

In the light of experiences in Europe, it may be appropriate to focus initial efforts on single-product/substance combinations and waste generation issues, as agreements in these areas appear to have had the highest degree of success. Given the general shortage of information in South Africa regarding the current levels of pollution and waste generation, a necessary first step prior to setting any detailed targets is the need to improve the quality of baseline data. Improvements in the quality and availability of environmental information as well as securing commitments to the implementation of waste minimization programmes within a well-structured sector, such as the chemical industry, arguably constitutes a valuable test case for the introduction of negotiated agreements in South Africa.

Information as a basis for a pilot negotiated agreement in South Africa

A key theme throughout this chapter has been the emphasis on information disclosure, not only as a means of identifying the desired goals of sustainable development and for monitoring progress in the attainment of those goals, but also in the belief that a central component of any initiative based on 'shared responsibility' – if it is to be credible and successful – must be the existence of a high level of visibility. The need to improve the generation of, and access to, credible environmental information is particularly relevant in South Africa. Arguably the current lack of adequate environmental data will become more apparent following publication of the imminent provincial and national State of the Environment Reports, when it is likely that a number of significant shortcomings in the quality of information will become evident.

Acknowledging the importance of information as a means of ensuring effective and prioritized decision making, and recognizing that the current lack of adequate baseline data militates against the more widespread adoption of co-regulatory policy instruments, it is necessary to focus on improved monitoring and reporting commitments as a basis for the initial introduction of negotiated agreements in South Africa. The possibility of linking these initial reporting commitments to the implementation of cleaner production programmes is also recommended, an issue that is briefly discussed below.

In ascertaining which information to focus on for initial disclosure purposes, it is suggested that this be decided in consultation with key interested stakeholders, though with an emphasis on a more limited number of priority substances. These might include, for example:

- *air emissions:* carbon dioxide, nitrogen oxides, sulphur dioxide, methane and specific hazardous particulates;
- *waste generation:* amounts generated, nature of any specified hazardous wastes (including persistent organic pollutants), and disposal method;
- *water quality:* priority issues include chemical oxygen demand (COD), ammonia, total dissolved solids (TDS), suspended solids, and acidity/alkalinity (pH).

One of the earlier identified constraints regarding the introduction of co-regulatory agreements, which is especially pertinent in the context of poor legal enforcement, is the existence of sufficient pressures to motivate industry to adopt and implement such instruments. There are a number of possible motivations that may be identified as prompting the larger industry sectors in South Africa to invest time and effort in the implementation of agreements.

A principal motivation is that of increasing external pressures from international competitors and trading partners, many of whom may seek to use the lax enforcement of environmental legal standards in South Africa as the basis for discriminatory trading practices. By implementing an agreement which includes a commitment to environmental performance that is comparable to international best practice, the basis for such discrimination is greatly reduced. A second motivation arises from the fact that there is a general appreciation amongst a number of key industry sectors that legislation introducing a pollution release and transfer register (PRTR) system in South Africa is inevitable, and that if this is not effectively structured it will have significant cost implications. The most affected sectors, such as the chemical industry, thus have a strong interest in proposing a reporting methodology that as far as possible builds on existing reporting initiatives. And proposing a system that focuses on practical priority issues – rather than a more exhaustive list of chemical substances – is not only likely to demonstrate the benefits of a prioritized approach, but may also highlight the government's capacity constraints that would otherwise limit the efficacy of more ambitious reporting demands.

A third longer-term motivation is that the development of such an agreement may result in the identification of some significant industry cost savings, particularly if the agreement is linked with a commitment to implement cleaner production programmes. In this regard there is significant potential for pollution inventories in South Africa to act as a powerful stimulus for improved environmental performance by raising management awareness as to the true extent of the quantities of hazardous waste discharged, both in terms of environmental impact and financial cost. By seeking a similar commitment from non-industry sectors to undertake reporting, including a commitment from government to institute ambient-level monitoring and reporting, this would facilitate the adoption of more focused regulatory efforts, and, in a number of instances, may even serve to redirect attention to more polluting, though perhaps less visible, sectors such as transport. Evidently this is in industry's interest, as large manufacturing companies are often the target of costly legislative standards simply because of their higher visibility, rather than as a result of any systematic prioritization based on objective monitoring.

An approach such as this may of course prompt concern by industry that those companies that pre-empt any legal standards through voluntary disclosure of information are likely to find themselves the target of legal enforcement and greater attention, thus reducing any incentive to participate. More balanced or flexible measures may need to be implemented to deal with concerns such as these, which may impact on competitiveness, in an effort to enhance the perceived benefits within industry of implementing agreements.[32]

It is important to appreciate that the use of negotiated agreements should be seen as one of several possible policy options to be considered in conjunction with traditional and more innovative policy approaches. Examples of complementary co-regulatory options include:[33]

- developing 'fully negotiated agreements' between government and industry, along the lines of the various EPA negotiated programmes;[34]
- promoting the widespread adoption of auditable environmental management systems, as a means of reducing the need for government inspections;[35]

- encouraging voluntary self-reporting and policing by reducing penalties for violations that are promptly disclosed and corrected, and that were discovered through voluntary internal audits or compliance management systems.[36]

A concern often voiced by industry is that of commercial confidentiality. While there are many instances when this is no doubt a valid concern, it is arguably an issue that has been overplayed by many in the South African corporate sector and that reflects a mindset that has developed in the culture of protective legislation during the apartheid era.[37] Notwithstanding this arguably unduly defensive perspective, there are nevertheless circumstances when commercial confidentiality needs to be protected. Means need to be found that balance the economic interests of competitive business with the protection, in particular, of worker and community environmental health and safety. One of the suggested methods for protecting commercial confidentiality is the establishment of an independent agency that can act as a clearing house for performance-related information, without necessarily disclosing the direct relationship with a specific industrial process.

The establishment of an independent agency should be considered, drawing for example on the experience of the Netherlands. Not only would such an agency act as a central clearing house for results-oriented data, but more importantly it could serve as an independent body for the verification of reporting data, as well as a centre of expertise for the provision of technical assistance. If appropriately structured and resourced, such a body could be particularly useful as a means of promoting cleaner production initiatives more broadly, as well as addressing the issue of environmental management amongst small and medium-sized enterprises. The potential of linking these activities within an existing agency – such as the CSIR[38] or with a university-based research institution – is an issue that may merit further examination, particularly in the context of those organizations that are proposing to participate as 'recognized service bodies' in some of the current donor-sponsored cleaner production activities.[39]

Regarding the issue of the preferred industry sectors and associated representative bodies, the initial leadership for coordinating any further investigations could be managed by organizations such as the Industrial Environmental Forum of Southern Africa and the CAIA. Both these entities have been particularly active in the policy reform initiatives in South Africa, with the directors of each association sitting on the numerous stakeholder forums and steering committees established to contribute to the environmental policy reform processes. While these two organizations may provide some of the initial leadership and impetus in driving the process forward, they would be well advised to liaise with other significant sectoral organizations such as Business South Africa, the Chamber of Mines and the South African Chamber of Business, all of which have taken an active and high-profile role in the development of environmentally related policy in South Africa.

In addition to these broad sectoral organizations, there are numerous other industry bodies in South Africa that meet most of the institutional requirements described earlier and that could thus contribute to the development of sectoral-specific negotiated agreements (or other co-regulatory initiatives). These include, for example, the SA Petroleum Industries Association, the SA Sugar Association, and the Packaging Council of South Africa. Important potential sectoral organizations at a smaller scale include the American Electroplaters and Surface Finishers (AESF) Society and the SA Deep Sea Trawling Industry Association, two organizations that have expressed interest in becoming actively involved in cleaner production initiatives.[40] In addition to building on the capacity and institutional structures of the various industry sectoral organizations, such a strategy should seek also to make use of the strong tripartite traditions (involving government, business and labour) in developing industry plans. This is apparent, for example, in the activities of the Department of Trade and Industry, which is increasingly adopting a sector-based approach to the development and implementation of policy.

An initial commitment to reporting against certain defined parameters should be linked with commitments to introducing waste minimization and cleaner production programmes. Initially this could be envisaged as being at a fairly generic level involving, for instance, the elaboration of broad guidelines contained in corporate environmental plans (possibly along the lines of the Dutch corporate environmental plans), with more specific targets being set once suitable baseline data have been established, and once there is greater clarity as to the extent and feasibility of possible improvements. As argued earlier, the aim of such targets should be to ensure that they will result in business investing in cost-effective pollution reduction and resource efficiency measures. There is a need, therefore, to consider the value of developing generic guidelines – that focus specifically on cleaner production issues, for example – as well as the benefits (and costs) associated with the establishment of an independent agency for monitoring and technical assistance purposes.

Conclusion

It has been argued in this chapter that co-regulatory policy options, in particular negotiated agreements, have a potentially vital role to play in the achievement of industrial sustainable development in South Africa. The success of such instruments, however, will depend on a number of conditions being fulfilled. Crucial in this respect is whether or not certain institutional conditions exist or might be developed, although certain procedural conditions relating to the content and structure of the agreements themselves are, of course, also important. It is also important to acknowledge that this argument in favour of negotiated agreements does not deny the continuing need for directive-based regulation.

In recommending the introduction of negotiated agreements, it is suggested that this will help to address some of the structural problems that currently impede the achievement of environmental sustainability in South Africa, a number of which are characteristic of the structural constraints in many developing countries. These include, for example, the lack of a long-term vision, which thus militates against the adoption of environmental innovation by industry; the associated problem of legal uncertainty, coupled with the current fragmentation of environmental law, both of which result in general inefficiency; and the paucity of appropriate environmental information, which impedes the development of prioritized decision making.

Through the use of negotiated agreements – by shifting greater responsibility to the business community which has a number of significant resource advantages over government – it is more likely that an effective balance between the needs of economic development and the requirements of environmental protection will be achieved, and that the innovation necessary for realizing ecological sustainability will ensue.

The adoption of negotiated agreements as a policy instrument should be seen as reflective of a broader shift in the role of state intervention in societal processes as a whole, characterized by a move away from the state's traditional unilateral imposition of norms, to a model in which the state 'functions as an horizontally juxtaposed entity, a partner, although *primus inter pares*' (Koppen, 1994). Acknowledging the increasingly apparent limits of using direct outside intervention as a means of achieving a desired result within individual enterprises, there is a growing appreciation that the role of the state should change from that of being a 'hierarchical imposer to a consensus-seeking negotiator' (*ibid.*). This view emphasizes the benefits of active involvement and of shared responsibility. It also expresses faith in the role of information and communicative informality as a means of stimulating the required changes in corporate behaviour. It is in this context that negotiated agreements are seen as a most valuable instrument for achieving sustainable development in South Africa.

Notes

1 This is clearly evident in South Africa where the government's Growth, Employment and Redistribution (GEAR) strategy lacks any reference to environmental issues, placing the emphasis solely on addressing the social and economic elements of sustainable development.

2 'No regrets' options are those options which a company could implement and which would have positive economic and environmental benefits, regardless of the subsequent severity of the initial environmental threat that prompted implementation of that option. As a policy approach, 'no regrets' may be seen to fall between the more demanding 'precautionary principle' and the more limited approach of 'business as usual'.

3 In a speech at the United Nations, reviewing progress made in implementing the Earth Summit commitments, the South African Minister for Environmental Affairs and Tourism stated: 'The new environmental policies being propagated by my Ministry aim at creating "win–win" opportunities by simultaneously promoting both economic and environmental gains. These policies are informed by the recognition that growth and development must be more equitable, less polluting and more efficient in the use of energy and natural resources' (Jordan, 1997).

4 In adopting this approach, the author wittingly (though humbly) becomes one of those who may contribute to the continual surprise of Welford, who states: 'To my surprise I constantly find people who would, in a traditional sense, be regarded as intelligent, who really believe that eco-modernism represents the best way forward. I am astounded by such false consciousness' (Welford, 1997a: 29).

5 There is often considerable confusion regarding this distinction. It has been particularly apparent during the policy reform process in South Africa and has arguably resulted in an unnecessary division amongst those who otherwise share a common belief in the need for substantial policy reform.

6 See, for example, European Environment Agency (1997).

7 This is a frequently used distinction, and is used by the South African Department of Environmental Affairs and Tourism (see DEAT, 1996); see also McKinsey and Co. (1992).

8 As, for example, in Arthur D. Little (1996).

9 See Leveque (1996).

10 For an interesting debate on the role of different environmental liability regimes on corporate environmental behaviour, see Teubner *et al.* (1994).

11 The acute problem of government capacity has been emphasized in South Africa following an investigation into administrative capacity in the provinces (Paseka, 1997; quoted in Greybe, 1997). On the basis of this study it was concluded that it would take at least ten years to build the necessary management skills throughout the provincial public sector. This is likely to remain a particular problem with respect to environmental issues which continue to receive a low priority in terms of central government funding.

12 This refers to technology that attempts to control pollution after it has been created.

13 The suggestion that regulations generally discourage technical innovation is an area of some

dispute, most famously evidenced in the pages of the *Harvard Business Review* following an article by Porter and van der Linde (1995).

14 For useful references see Perman *et al.* (1996).

15 MBIs should not, however, be used principally for revenue-generating purposes. The idea of 'charges' is that they have a steering effect, thus distinguishing them from 'taxes'. If charges are relied upon to raise revenue then there is the danger that governments will not then have the incentive to ensure an effective steering of behaviour.

16 See Perman *et al.* (1996) for useful references on the benefits of market-based instruments.

17 P. Claasen, Department of Environmental Affairs and Tourism, personal communication, 8 August 1997

18 See, for example, Mayhew (1997).

19 An interesting alternative perspective on the relationship between political institutional settings and environmental policy is provided by Mol *et al.* (forthcoming) who contrast, for example, the 'consensual, flexible and closed policy making' of the UK and Sweden with the 'open, adversarial policy making with formal rules and legal enforcement' of the USA.

20 The quality of the dialogue is determined by such factors as the technical competence of officials, the prevalence of personal relationships, and industry's willingness to be open in its communications with regulators (Wallace, 1995).

21 The importance of such conditions is well demonstrated, for example, by the failure of the attempted UK Packaging Agreement, as compared with the more successful Dutch Agreement on Packaging. A more detailed analysis of the conditions and criteria for evaluating negotiated agreements is provided in Ingram (1996) and Hanks (1997).

22 Procedural guidelines for negotiated agreements established by the European Commission include the following:

(1) Interested parties should have the opportunity to comment before the agreement is concluded;

(2) The agreement should take the form of a contract, enforceable under civil or public law;

(3) It should include 'unequivocal' quantified objectives, as well as intermediate milestone objectives that describe the stages to achieve the overall objectives within the schedule

(4) It should provide for monitoring of the results achieved;

(5) The agreement should be accessible to the public with periodic reporting to the authorities regarding the progress made in achieving the agreed milestones;

(6) Dissuasive sanctions should be established such as fines, penalties and the withdrawal of permits.

These are described in more detail in Commission of the European Communities (1996). A useful list of procedural criteria for effective agreements is also provided in New Directions Group (1997).

23 H. Benkenstein, Deputy Director, Sub-Directorate of Environmental Impact Management, personal communication.

24 *Ibid.*

25 See, for example, Koppen (1994), who cites Hucke and others.

26 In this regard, note the arguments of Koppen (1994).

27 See Van Driel, quoted and translated in Koppen (1994: 187).

28 Wallace (1995); analysis of the role of political culture in environmental policy making is also given in Mol *et al.* (forthcoming).

29 Although these two initiatives are directly relevant, the intention is not to deny the potential relevance of the many other environmentally related policy reform processes, including those relating to energy, climate change and water resource issues, which are being carried out within the DEAT, DWAF and the Department of Minerals and Energy (DME).

30 The Dutch experience in developing sectoral targets for attaining national sustainability targets is constructive.

31 See endnote 3.

32 A useful initiative that has the potential to address this concern is the system of flexible penalties introduced in the USA as an incentive for the disclosure of voluntary audit findings.

33 See Hanks and Ireton (1996).

34 In terms of these programmes, government provides technical assistance and facilitates marketing benefits in exchange for commitments to meet and report against objectives; typical examples include the 33/50 and Green Lights initiatives developed by the EPA in the USA.

35 Consideration could be given to the development of auditing and reporting requirements similar to current financial audits, and to finalizing an internationally recognized accreditation system in South Africa.

36 Such an approach has been introduced by the United States EPA.

37 Note, for instance, the blanket secrecy provision in the Atmospheric Pollution Prevention Act. An interesting example of the difficulties that may be encountered in collecting industry information (in this case for research purposes) is provided by Goldblatt who notes: 'The fears encountered during the survey were so serious that one major industrial generator only allowed an interviewer onto the premises after ensuring that he had no pens or paper on him. The company took the notes during the meeting and forwarded them to the interviewing team many months later. So onerous were the confidentiality agreements for the study overall, that all the raw data – the largest collection of hazardous waste data ever gathered in the country – was destroyed after the final report was published to ensure long term confidentiality' (Goldblatt, 1997: 127).

38 The CSIR – formerly known as the Council for Scientific and Industrial Research – is Africa's largest scientific, technological research, development and implementation organization.

39 DANCED (1997). Some of the possible service bodies that were suggested include the CSIR and specific departments and institutes at the Universities of Natal, Cape Town and Rhodes.

40 As indicated by their detailed responses to a recent offer of technical and financial support by DANCED. This interest, at both a sectoral and individual company level, could be seen to constitute useful grounds for seeking to promote the initial adoption of more innovative policy approaches, particularly if, as suggested, they are linked to pollution prevention commitments. The nature of their responses is briefly described in DANCED (1997).

References

Arthur D. Little (1996), 'Sustainable Industrial Development: Sharing Responsibilities in a Competitive World', conference paper prepared on behalf of the Dutch Ministry of Housing, Spatial Planning and the Environment, and the Ministry of Economic Affairs, Brussels.

Bernstein, J. (1993), *Alternative Approaches to Pollution Control & Waste Management: Regulatory and Economic Instruments*, World Bank, Washington DC.

Cairncross, F. (1991), *Costing the Earth*, Economist Books, London.

Commission of the European Communities (1996), *Communication from the Commission to the Council and the European Parliament on Environmental Agreements* (COM(96) 561, 1996), Brussels.

Danish Cooperation for Environment and Development (DANCED) (1997), *Informal Comments on the Possible Way Forward with Regard to DANCED Support to Cleaner Production Activities in South Africa*, 104.SAR.1.DANCED.4.a/5–8 September, Copenhagen.

DEAT (Department of Environmental Affairs and Tourism) (1996), *Environmental Impact Management: Information Document*, DEAT, Pretoria.

The Economist (1990), 'Industry and the Environment – An *Economist* survey', 8 September .

European Environmental Agency (EEA) (1997), 'Environmental Agreements: Environmental Effectiveness', *Environmental Issues Series*, 1 (3), EEA, Copenhagen.

Goldblatt, M. (1997), 'Registering Pollution: The Prospects for a Pollution Information System', in L. Bethlehem and M. Goldblatt (eds.), *The Bottom Line: Industry and the Environment in South Africa*, UCT Press, Cape Town and International Development Research Centre, Ottawa.

Goodland, R., H. Daly, S. El Serafy and B. van Droste (eds.) (1991), *Environmentally Sustainable Economic Development: Building on Brundtland*, UNESCO, Paris.

de Graaf, H. J., C. J. M. Musters and W. J. ter Keurs (1996), 'Sustainable Development: Looking for New Strategies', *Ecological Economics*, 16, 205–16.

Greybe, D. (1997), 'Administration of Provinces "Chaotic"', *Business Day,* 14 August, p. 1.

Hanks, J. P. (1997), 'Towards Industrial Sustainable Development in South Africa: A Role for Negotiated Agreements as Part of a Strategy of "Co-Regulatory" Policy Options', unpublished MSc thesis, International Institute for Industrial Environmental Economics, University of Lund.

Hanks, J. P. and K. Ireton (1996), 'Negotiated Self-Regulation: A Cost-Effective Policy Option for Business Environmental Management', industry position paper written for the Industrial Environmental Forum of Southern Africa and submitted to the Consultative National Environmental Policy Process (CONNEP), IEF, Johannesburg, January.

Hobbs, J. and K. Ireton (1996), 'South Africa: A State of Change', *UNEP Industry and Environment,* 19 (1), 34–6.

Ingram, V. (1996), 'An Environment for Consensus? Building Consensual Commitment through Communication; Negotiated Agreements in Environmental Policy', MSc thesis, Centre for Environmental Technology, University of London.

Jordan, Z. P. (1997), 'Government Policy on Sustainable Development in South Africa' (address to the fifth session of the UNCSD), published as a technical supplement to *Chemical Processing South Africa,* Primedia Publishing, Sandton, June.

Koppen, I. (1994), 'Ecological Covenants: Regulatory Informality in Dutch Waste Reduction Policy', in G. Teubner, L. Farmer and D. Murphy (eds.), *Environmental Law and Ecological Responsibility: The Concept and Practice of Ecological Self-Organisation,* Wiley, London.

KPMG–IEF (1997), *Top South Africa Companies: Environmental Survey 1997,* KPMG, Johannesburg.

Leveque, F. (1996), *Environmental Policy in Europe: Industry, Competition and the Policy Process,* Edward Elgar, London.

Loughran (1997), 'Still Activist after All These Years: Tomorrow's 1997 Environmental Leadership Award', *Tomorrow,* 7 (5), 18–20.

Mayhew, N. (1997), 'Fading to Grey: The Use and Abuse of Corporate Executives', in R. Welford (ed.), *Hijacking Environmentalism: Corporate Responses to Sustainable Development,* Earthscan, London.

McKinsey and Co. (Management Consultants) (1992), *Building Successful Environmental Partnerships,* Washington DC.

Mol, A. P. J. (1998), 'Ecological modernisation: Industrial transformations and environmental reform', in M. Redclift and G. Woodgate (eds.), *The International Handbook of Environmental Sociology,* Edward Elgar, London.

Mol, A. P. J., V. Lauber, V. Enevoldsen and J. Landman (forthcoming), 'Joint Environmental Policy-making in Comparative Perspective', in D. Liefferink (ed.), *New Instruments for Environmental Protection in the EU,* Routledge, London.

New Directions Group (1997), *Criteria and Principles for the Use of Voluntary or Non-regulatory Initiatives to Achieve Environmental Policy Objectives,* New Directions Group, Canmore.

Paseka, N. (1997), *Audit Report of the Provinces of South Africa,* Government Printer, Pretoria.

Perman, R., Y. Ma and J. McGliveray (1996), *Natural Resource and Environmental Economics,* Longman, London.

Porter, M. and C. van der Linde (1995), 'Green and Competitive: Ending the Stalemate', *Harvard Business Review,* 73 (5), 120–33.

RSA (Republic of South Africa) (1997), 'White Paper on Environmental Management Policy for South Africa', *Government Gazette,* 385 (18164), 28 July.

Shrivastava, P. (1995), 'Industrial and Environmental Crises: Rethinking Corporate Social Responsibility', in F. Fischer and M. Black (eds.), *op cit.*

Spence, M. A. and M. L. Weitzman (1993), 'Regulatory Strategies for Pollution Control', in R. Dorfman and N. Dorfman, *Economics of the Environment: Selected Readings,* W. W. Norton, London.

Teubner, G. (1994), 'The Invisible Cupola: From Causal to Collective Attribution in Ecological Liability', in G. Teubner, L. Farmer and D. Murphy (eds.), *Environmental Law and Ecological Responsibility: The Concept and Practice of Ecological Self-Organisation,* John Wiley and Sons, London.

Wallace, D. (1995), *Environmental Policy and Industrial Innovation: Strategies in Europe, the US and*

Japan, Royal Institute of International Affairs, London.

Welford, R. (1997a), 'From Green to Golden: The Construction of Corporate Environmental Management', in R. Welford (ed.), *Hijacking Environmentalism: Corporate Responses to Sustainable Development*, Earthscan, London.

— (1997b), 'Towards a more critical dimension for environmental research', in R. Welford (ed.), *op. cit.*

WCED (World Commission on Environment and Development) (1987), *Our Common Future*, Oxford University Press, Oxford.

New Partnerships
for Sustainable Development

(selected country)

The Changing Nature of Business—NGO Relations

DAVID F. MURPHY AND JEM BENDELL

Introduction

Partnership is not the first word that comes to mind when one thinks about business–NGO relations. Over the past three decades, most relationships between the private sector and civil society have been founded upon conflict.[1] In different sectors and geographical contexts, this pattern of business–NGO relations started to change in the early 1990s with the emergence of formal sustainable development partnerships between these long-standing adversaries. Although most of these business–NGO partnerships to date have appeared in the North, many have significant implications for the South, particularly those that promote international business and trading standards. Furthermore there is some indication that Southern-based companies and NGOs are beginning to collaborate, albeit to a much lesser extent than their Northern counterparts.

Academic inquiry into how NGOs influence corporate policies related to sustainable development is a relatively new venture. Scholarly debates about the potential for partnerships between business and NGOs in the South are even less common. Indeed, there is little empirical research on the nature of conflicts and alliances between NGOs and private sector companies that have led to environmentally and/or socially advantageous outcomes in both the North and the South. Instead, most research in this area focuses on the role of government in mediating conflicts between business and local communities, or on government–NGO relations. Information on direct relations between NGOs and business is largely anecdotal. In order to help fill this gap, this chapter presents three case studies of business–NGO relations on sustainable development with examples from both the North and the South.

First, to illustrate the myriad relations between civil society and business, we provide a broad review of protest and partnership between various NGOs and companies involved in the tropical timber trade since the mid-1980s. Second, to reveal how coordinated global protest affects TNC activities in both the North and South, we focus on relations between Shell and various NGOs in the 1990s. Third, to outline the politics and processes of complex multi-stakeholder North–South partnerships, we describe the Project to Eliminate Child Labour in the Pakistan

Soccer Ball Industry. This case demonstrates the growing importance of environment, health and safety (EHS) standards for the many global companies that have shifted the manufacturing of finished products to factories in the South. Given that this is an emerging area of study, the chapter concludes with preliminary thoughts on the preconditions, processes and outcomes of more collaborative relations between business and NGOs. The case studies presented here also provide a basis for the elaboration of a new theoretical understanding of corporate environmentalism based on 'civil regulation' which is presented in the following chapter.

Planting Seeds of Change: Protesting and Partnering to Save the Tropical Rain Forests[2]

Deforestation emerged as a significant international policy issue and major Northern media story in the mid-1980s (Humphreys, 1997). Since that time the rates of forest degradation have shown little evidence of slowing. Despite lengthy consultations among governments, and rising concern from the public (reaching a peak at the 1992 Rio Summit), rapid deforestation continues unabated. According to some estimates, tropical forests are disappearing at the rate of nearly 1 per cent per year, with the annual deforestation rate in the Brazilian Amazon increasing 34 per cent between 1991 and 1994 (United Nations, 1997; Serrill, 1997).

The main causes of deforestation are logging, mining, iron smelting, cattle ranching, cash cropping, dam construction, road building, housing and hotel development, shifting agriculture and fuelwood collection. This case focuses on the causes and responses to the crisis that directly involve Northern countries and their companies, and specifically the international timber trade. Robert Repetto and Malcolm Gillis argued in 1988 that commercial logging was the top agent of deforestation and around this time it was also popularly considered to be the case.

Government and industry initiatives for rain forest protection

For much of the 1980s and 1990s, governments and various international bodies have attempted to respond to the worldwide concern about tropical deforestation. The first international instrument for tropical forests came with the 1983 International Tropical Timber Agreement (ITTA), which provides a framework for co-operation and consultation between tropical timber producers and consumers on a range of issues. Later, in May 1991, members of the International Tropical Timber Organization (ITTO) approved a 'Year 2000 Target' for sustainable forest management. The general NGO feeling is that the ITTO has been too complacent about tropical deforestation in that it has avoided challenging 'the destructive activities of the timber industry' (FoE—UK, 1992: 5).

At the regional and national levels in the South, some governments have introduced new policy instruments to monitor logging company activities. The South Pacific Forum Code of Conduct for Logging of Indigenous Forests sets minimum standards for the preparation and implementation of work programmes by concession holders. Similarly, the Forestry Commission of Guyana has introduced a code of practice for the operation of natural forest concessions (Murphy, 1997b).

At the international level, the World Business Council for Sustainable Development (WBCSD) commissioned an independent study of the pulp and paper industry. The study recommended that the industry consider developing a code of conduct similar to the chemical industry's Responsible Care, with the added feature of sector-wide monitoring of company performance (WBCSD, 1996).

The first global certification system for well-managed forests, however, was set up in 1993 by civil society working in partnership with business. This scheme, the Forest Stewardship Council, was supported by a variety of NGO and industry members from the North and South; it will be discussed in a later section of this chapter. The reasons why companies in the timber trade have collaborated with NGOs can only be understood by examining the role played by civil society in shaping the deforestation issue since the mid-1980s.

Civil society protest in the South

One of the major stages for deforestation and conflict in the 1980s was Amazonia. The problem was particularly acute in Brazil, where the military junta was trying to 'civilize' the region by facilitating billions of dollars of subsidies and tax breaks for entrepreneurs to buy up land and 'develop' the forest (Revkin, 1990). Unions of rubber tappers led the fight against cattle ranchers and loggers. Meagre rubber-tapper livelihoods were being threatened because rubber barons realized they could make more money by cutting down the trees and grazing cattle. Accordingly, the tappers decided to stage *empates* whereby chainsaw gangs were confronted and asked to leave the land they were clearing. These protests raised the attention of the international media so that 'by the mid-1980s ... indigenous groups and tappers were considered legitimate participants in the debate' (Dore, 1996: 15). One protester who rose to international fame was Chico Mendes, the leader of the Xapuri Rural Workers Union. He soon became a symbol of the human dimension of the deforestation issue. Furthermore, with his involvement 'the authorities could no longer dismiss efforts to save the rain forests as foreigners interfering with Brazilian affairs' (Rowell, 1996a: 214).

The *empates* protests worked as a tactic: by December 1988, some 3 million acres of the Amazon had been saved (Hecht and Cockburn, 1990). After one particular incident, the authorities bought out the prospective rancher so that his plans could not proceed. In revenge, the rancher ordered the killing of Mendes in December 1988. Mendes became the ninetieth rural activist to be murdered in Brazil that year (Hall, 1996). After his death the world's news media reverberated with headlines and leading stories on the rubber tappers and deforestation. Following the international condemnation that followed Mendes' murder, the new civilian administration of President Sarney proceeded to establish a new environmental control agency (IBAMA) to promote a new environmental policy (Nossa Natureza) and set up several protected extractive reserves (*ibid.*). Thus grassroots action by Southern unions backed up by international concern did bring some specific successes. Indeed the combined protests of civil society groups in tropical forest countries in the 1980s began to shape a new international policy debate. In the 1970s and 1980s cattle ranching and logging were almost universally promoted as the best way to develop tropical forest regions. By 1990 they had become a symbol of destruction.

Civil society protest in the North

With increased NGO campaigning and media coverage, the profile of environmental issues rose in most Northern countries in the late 1980s. As the struggles of indigenous peoples against tropical deforestation became known, the role of the timber trade became a key consumer concern. For example, a wooden product such as mahogany came to be associated with the murder of forest dwellers. At this time, local, largely autonomous Rainforest Action Groups (RAGs) in North America, Europe and Australia were formed.

In Great Britain, beginning in the spring of 1991, various RAGs started to take direct action against wood-product retailers. These groups organized mock chainsaw massacres outside Do-It-Yourself (DIY) home improvement and furniture stores with protesters dressed as loggers graphically depicting the destruction of the world's rain forests. Protesters leafleted customers and delivered anti-tropical timber pledges to store managers. The intention was to discourage customers from buying tropical timber products.

Later in 1991, local Friends of the Earth—UK (FoE—UK) groups built upon the initial RAG protests. On one November weekend there were over 100 demonstrations, including 25 to 30 demonstrations outside the outlets of DIY market leader B & Q plc. Subsequently, on 11 December, FoE—UK claimed in a press release that its protests had prompted dramatic policy developments in the DIY retailers B & Q, Texas Homecare and Homebase, who were now committed to 'stop selling environmentally damaging tropical rainforest timber' (FoE—UK, 1991). The anti-DIY demonstrations proved to be highly successful and garnered considerable media and public attention. Customers began to write letters to the retailers and to confront store managers and employees with tough questions about timber sourcing. For the most part, the companies took both the protests and customer letters very seriously.

Meanwhile, the World Wide Fund for Nature International (WWF) was itself beginning to turn to industry, having become disillusioned with protracted international negotiations on a global forest convention and other international policy initiatives. In 1989 WWF had already announced its own 1995 target for the world's timber trade to be sustainable. At the 1992 Rio Summit, governments could only produce the 'toothless' *Non-legally Binding Authoritative Statement of Principles for a Global Consensus on the Management, Conservation and Sustainable Development of all Types of Forests*. Francis Sullivan, then WWF—UK forest officer, believed 'you can't just sit back and wait for governments to agree, because this could take forever'.[3] He felt certain it was right to try and work with people and companies who might be able to get things done.

The emergence of timber industry—NGO partnerships

For the DIY trade, WWF—UK appeared to be a solution to a mounting business problem. Following WWF—UK's 'Forests Are Your Business' seminar in December 1991, ten companies committed themselves to reaching the WWF—UK 1995 target and launched the so-called 1995 Group. The cumulative effects of different forms of environmental campaigning seemed to have taken firm root in the private sector. The 'chainstore massacre' demonstrations and resulting consumer awareness were instrumental, as was the catalytic role of WWF—UK via its forest seminars. Internally, directors of the targeted companies were worried about the public relations and commercial implications of the protests, customer letters and media coverage. Other pressures from investors, insurers and lenders were on the horizon.

To join the 1995 Group, the companies had to agree to phase out, by 1995, the purchase and sale of all wood and wood products not sourced from well-managed forests. In pursuit of this target they had to provide WWF—UK with a written action programme detailing how the company would reach the target and then submit regular six-monthly reports on their progress. It soon became apparent, however, that the participating companies needed a credible system for defining good forest management and for ensuring that products were from such forests.

What was needed was a standard-setting body with a system for verifying product claims. Following 18 months of preparatory work, the Forest Stewardship

Council (FSC) was launched in 1993. The Founding Group consisted of environmental NGOs, forest industry representatives, community forestry groups and forest product certification organizations. Both WWF–International and B & Q, among other organizations, provided financial and logistical support.

The FSC mission statement commits members to 'promote management of the world's forests that is environmentally appropriate, socially beneficial and economically viable' – language consistent with the principles of sustainable development. The FSC accredits certification bodies to ensure that they adhere to FSC principles and criteria when certifying forests as well-managed, and allows them to issue the FSC logo once a chain of custody has been recorded from the forest to the company selling the end product.

By the end of 1995, commercial support for the FSC had spiralled in the UK. The WWF–UK 1995 Group had reached 47 members, accounting for about a quarter of the British consumption of wood products. Although many of the companies did not reach the 1995 target, a significant number had purchased certified timber and had specified where most if not all their timber was coming from. The Group was consequently extended with the revised target that companies would purchase wood only from certified forests by the year 2000. As of late 1997, there were over 80 members in the new Group.

Partnerships between the timber industry and NGOs are growing in other countries. There are similar timber buyers' groups or business–NGO partnerships committed to the FSC in the Netherlands, Belgium, Australia, Austria, France, USA and Sweden. The Dutch 'Hart Voor Hout' initiative dates back to early 1992 and many of its developments paralleled the British experience, namely the catalytic role of protest in leading DIY retailers to seek NGO partners (Murphy, 1996).

The impetus for Northern buyer groups, of course, comes from Northern consumers, campaigners, corporations and NGOs. However, members of Southern civil society also have a voice in the process, through the FSC. Representatives of NGOs such as Foundation of the Peoples of the South Pacific (Papua New Guinea), FUDENA (Venezuela) and SKEPHI (Indonesia) participate in the FSC as either Board representatives or members of specialist working groups. At the national level in the South, FSC working groups have been established to ensure that the global principles and criteria are adapted to the local context (in Brazil and Cameroon, for example). Although only 25 per cent of current FSC members are from the South, the organization is supporting efforts to increase this number. Furthermore, a special working group on social aspects of certification is attempting to find ways in which the social performance of the FSC could be improved (Colchester, 1997).

Before partnerships between timber companies and NGOs, there was no functioning mechanism whereby consumer power in industrialized countries could be captured to promote sustainable forest management around the world. As of December 1997, 5.5 million hectares of forest had been certified worldwide. The absence of a significant number of partnership initiatives in the South suggests that many of the driving forces behind greater responsibility in the timber industry are peculiar to Northern countries. From the above, it is apparent that NGO and consumer pressure in a Northern context often have a profound effect on corporate public image and a perceived need on the company's part to respond positively. Collaborating with a well-known environmental NGO also promises additional benefits to those normally gained from internal environmental management initiatives (Bendell and Warner, 1996). In addition to help with getting the job done, significant public relations benefits may be gained from collaborating with NGOs.

For example, the participation of WWF in the FSC scheme has helped to reassure customers that participating company claims are credible.

Criticism of timber industry—NGO partnerships

Notwithstanding the progress to date, there is considerable criticism about the role and contribution of the FSC scheme. Some have challenged the use of market mechanisms for rain forest conservation by arguing that such schemes fail to address the underlying causes of deforestation and the infringement of indigenous peoples' land rights (Corry, 1993). Others are concerned about how commercial interests might undermine social and environmental matters in the certification process.

Criticism has also come from timber traders and producers that do not support the FSC form of certification. On a practical level, some companies argue that producer certification would be too expensive and bureaucratic to implement across the whole of the industry. Others have difficulty with the FSC in principle, suggesting that non-governmental bodies do not have the authority to 'regulate' a company's forest management practices. This, they argue, is the role of sovereign governments or intergovernmental organizations (Harris, 1996).

Some critics in government, business and civil society argue that the championing of the FSC by Northern NGOs and companies is another example of the industrialized North imposing its perception of environmental problems and remedies upon the rest of the world. Whereas the social, political and cultural contexts in many Northern countries have produced a concerned retail trade and an impetus for certification, the situation in the East and South is different. Japan, the largest importer of tropical timber and timber products in the world, has not yet become an advocate of a sustainable timber trade. Despite the presence of a well-organized environmental movement, there has been limited Japanese NGO pressure and consumer demand for certified wood products (Wadsworth, 1996). The rise of consumer concern and business response in most other Northern countries, therefore, may just serve to shift international trade patterns, with certified timber going to Europe and North America and non-certified timber going to Japan and, increasingly, South East Asia.

The recent moves of companies from countries such as Malaysia, Thailand and Indonesia into the tropical rain forests of Latin America, the South Pacific and the Congo basin is worrying. To illustrate, in Papua New Guinea, Malaysia's largest logging company, Rimbunan Hijau, now controls at least 60 per cent of the government's 21.5 million-acre forestry concession area through more than 20 subsidiaries (Ito and Loftus, 1997). Despite recent attempts to introduce codes of conduct, the prospects for influencing these concessions through legal or market mechanisms appear bleak. Faced with a national debt and a need to attract foreign direct investment (FDI), most governments of tropical forest countries appear to be locked into a 'race to the bottom' of environmental regulation.

New tools and tactics for forest protesters

In response to the apparent inability of governments to curb the ongoing destruction of tropical forests, civil society organizations, both North and South, are developing new tactics and using new tools to influence corporate behaviour (Collinson, 1996; Johnston, 1997). Many protests are aimed at the international timber, oil and mining industries. These protests differ from those in the 1980s in two significant ways. The first relates to the use of information technology and the second to a new focus on Northern markets. Together, these developments are leading to a new level of North—South cooperation in civil society.

The role of electronic information technology in Southern forest struggles first gained major significance during the Zapatista uprising in the forested Chiapas region of Mexico in 1994. Protesters could send their complaints, including those about the environmental degradation of the Lacandon Biosphere Reserve, around the world by electronic mail (e-mail). Journalists and activists on the appropriate e-mail lists accordingly received immediate accounts of the events unfolding: it was the first 'on-line revolution' (Stea, Elguea and Bustillo, 1997: 218). Communication technology is also helping to forge new alliances between local, national and international groups.

The second dimension to Southern group campaigning is an increasing focus on Northern markets. The struggle of the Guarani and Tupinikim Indians in Brazil against the paper and pulp company Aracruz Cellulose is an example of such a strategy. The Guarani and Tupinikim Indians have been contesting the Aracruz operations on their traditional lands for many years. When the government announced that Indians could lay claim to their traditional lands there was hope that the Guarani and Tupinikim would benefit. In 1993 the executive commission of the two tribes submitted an application to annex 13,274 hectares. However, an adjustment to the law in 1996 allowed prospective logging companies to appeal against the claims of forest dwellers. Aracruz launched such an appeal and the Guarani and Tupinikim became concerned that their claim would be rejected. In response they began an international campaign to raise awareness of their cause.

In early 1997, representatives of the tribes, together with Dutch campaigner Winfred Overbeek, visited Norway and Great Britain to put their case to the customers of, and investors in, Aracruz Cellulose. In Norway, the group tried to talk with Aracruz shareholders Den norske Bank and the Lorentzen Group. 'Den norske Bank did not want to talk with the indigenous representatives,' explains Overbeek. Consequently, the representatives took their case to the government – the Bank's major shareholder – and the media. Questions in Parliament and reports on television and radio followed. In response, the Minister of Trade and Commerce stated that there was no way for the Norwegian government to define how Den norske Bank applies its money. The international campaign also included meetings with members of the WWF–UK 1995 Plus Group, the FSC-accredited Soil Association and the Paper Federation of Great Britain. The companies and organizations agreed to examine closely the decision on the demarcation of the disputed lands.

Meanwhile, in the South there appears to be little mileage in establishing communication with the Aracruz management. Against a history of violence – an activist for the tribes, Paulo Cesar Vinha, was murdered in 1993 – prospects for dialogue with Aracruz appear bleak. Indeed, the international campaign of the Guarani and Tupinikim appears to have generated a retaliatory public relations campaign. Aracruz has contracted Burson-Marsteller, the world's largest PR company, to curb growing support for the Indians' international campaign. The Aracruz response, examined further by Ricardo Carrere in Chapter 4, appears to be the antithesis of many other companies who are engaging constructively and openly with civil society in order to help reduce deforestation.

The seeds of change?

This case study has described varying degrees of corporate responsibility for tropical deforestation and a range of tactics employed by NGOs. It appears that some companies are either unable or unwilling to embrace environmental concerns.

Further research is needed to reveal the variety of financial, political and cultural factors that enable some companies to engage NGOs and indigenous peoples on the deforestation issue while others avoid, undermine or kill their critics. For those companies that have moved forward with NGO partnerships, progress appears to have been the result of both personal and organizational commitment. The motivation of key individuals seems to be particularly significant. WWF–International's Francis Sullivan explains:

> Success has boiled down to the commitment of individuals and the support that senior management has given to those individuals.... You have some companies that are not particularly committed themselves, but you have got an individual in there who is unbelievably committed to actually getting the thing sorted out.[4]

The support that these individuals have received in different companies, organizations and countries illustrates how the boundaries of corporate social and environmental responsibility have been shifting dramatically, alongside rapid developments in the tools and tactics of NGOs. We have observed the role of protest, North and South, in raising public and consumer awareness about adverse effects of tropical deforestation. At the same time, market leaders have responded to this pressure as an opportunity to maintain leadership in a changing marketplace. This in turn has cleared the way for some of the more cautious competitors to follow, thereby planting the seeds for a transformation of the timber trade.

After the Shell Shock: Protest, Partnership and the Global Oil Industry [5]

The oil industry is one of biggest sectors in the global economy, with an average daily oil production of 61.9 million barrels valued at over a billion US dollars (Tippee, 1997).[6] The 1997 *Business Week Global 1000* survey of the world's leading companies ranked Shell and Exxon first and second in profits at US\$9.3 and \$7.5 billion respectively. In terms of market value, six oil companies were ranked in the top 50 companies.

The Royal Dutch Shell Group is one of the top three corporations in the world in terms of size, comprising more than 300 individual companies based in over 100 countries. Shell's annual global turnover is in the vicinity of \$100 billion. Until recently Shell had a reputation as an environmental leader dating back many decades. Even before the birth of the contemporary environmental movement in the late 1960s, Shell had begun to respond to public concerns about the environment. Early examples of company initiatives in the UK include environmental education in the 1940s and a Shell Film Unit documentary on air pollution in the 1950s, following the introduction of the British Clean Air Acts. Shell also helped launch the Keep Britain Tidy campaign in 1954.

Suddenly, in the mid-1990s, Shell became the focus of two high-profile campaigns by environmental and human rights NGOs that raised serious questions about the corporation's commitment to sustainable development. As noted earlier, the first of these confrontations came in mid-1995 when Greenpeace opposed Shell's efforts to dump the Brent Spar oil platform in the North Atlantic. This was quickly followed by complaints about Shell Nigeria's use of lower environmental standards in the West African country's Delta region. The company was also accused of implicitly supporting human rights abuses, given its perceived close association with the Nigerian military regime.

The fallout from both of these episodes has had a negative impact upon the image and reputation of both Shell and other companies in the global oil industry. Although the industry has long been a target of NGO and consumer campaigns, Shell's recent experience has brought increased pressure and attention. As a result, Shell and other oil companies are scrambling to find new ways of relating to NGOs, particularly in the South. This case reviews business–NGO relations in the oil industry, with a particular focus on Shell's Nigeria experience.

Strong and aggressive criticism

Historically the oil and gas industry has been among the world's biggest polluters. For many years public opinion polls in the USA have identified the industry as a major polluter (Erskine, 1971). Not surprisingly, the industry was also an early target of environmental campaigners in many northern industrialized countries. In 1963, six oil companies formed one of the first industry environmental think tanks, Conservation of Clean Air and Water Western Europe (CONCAWE), largely in response to 'strong and aggressive' criticism by environmentalists and the general public about the industry's 'gross ecological negligence'. CONCAWE was designed 'to establish "hard facts" [through] professional analysis of the underlying nature of the chemistry and physics involved'. CONCAWE member companies then planned to use this data 'to define the steps needed to redress adverse ecological trends, mishaps and disasters' (Han Hoog, 1993: 4–5).

Despite industry efforts to prevent environmental disasters, the oil and gas industry was implicated in at least 14 major industrial accidents (causing more than 50 deaths each) between 1970 and 1984. Of a total of more than 2,000 deaths, almost 1,500 resulted from accidents in developing countries, including oil, gas, petrol and tanker explosions, offshore-rig collapses and gas pipeline fractures (Shrivastava, 1987). In recent years, the industry has continued to face considerable public scrutiny. Both before and after the Rio Conference, the oil industry faced heavy international pressure about the impact of fossil fuel emissions on global warming. Implementation problems with the Rio climate change agreement have been linked to the political influence of oil lobby groups such as the Global Climate Coalition and the American Petroleum Institute. Lobbying strategies include exaggerating costs of climate action, emphasizing scientific uncertainties and collaborating with governments hostile to action, such as the OPEC states (Newell, 1997a and 1997b). In the lead-up to the December 1997 Kyoto climate change conference, oil industry groups continued to argue against the adoption of tougher targets and regulations to reduce carbon emissions.

The idea of environmental injustice – a linkage between ecological degradation and human rights abuses – has gained worldwide attention, largely as a result of the activities of oil companies such as Shell in Nigeria, BP in Colombia and Texaco in Burma. Various environmental and development NGOs, from both North and South, are working together to challenge oil companies to promote environmental justice on a variety of fronts, often via the Internet.

Shell, the Ogoni and Nigeria

Over the years Shell has faced NGO and consumer pressure over a range of social responsibility issues, most notably concerning its role in South Africa during the apartheid era. Despite considerable international protest in the 1970s and 1980s, Shell refused to pull out of its mining, chemicals and petroleum-related activities in South Africa, insisting that its employees did not suffer any racial discrimination. As noted earlier, on environmental matters the company did not face sustained and organized international protest until the Greenpeace Brent Spar campaign in 1995, which culminated in Shell's decision to abort the deep-sea disposal of the oil platform in the face of growing political and consumer pressure in Europe. Riding the Brent Spar wave, the media then discovered a much more complex and wider environmental and human rights campaign that had been raising serious questions about Shell's role in Nigeria since the early 1990s.

The Shell Petroleum Development Company is a joint venture between Shell (30 per cent), the majority shareholder Nigerian National Petroleum Company (NNPC, 55 per cent) and two other oil companies, Elf (10 per cent) and Agip (5 per cent). Shell Petroleum is the largest Nigerian oil and gas exploration and production company, with 92 oil fields generating one million barrels daily. The company has a 6,200-kilometre network of pipelines and flowlines spread over more than 31,000 square kilometres of the Niger River Delta. Shell employs 5,000 staff directly, including 300 non-Nigerians. According to Shell, more than half of its Nigerian staff comes from the Delta region (Shell International, 1995). Shell Nigeria's annual oil revenue is $11 billion. Nigeria's total oil revenues account for 90 per cent of its export earnings and 80 per cent of total government revenue.

Protest begins

The origins of Shell's recent problems in Nigeria lie in a history of considerable environmental pollution in the Niger Delta region. From 1982 to 1992, 1.6 million gallons of oil were spilled from Shell's Nigerian fields in 27 separate incidents. Forty per cent of spills attributed to Shell worldwide happened in Nigeria. Various Niger Delta communities have experienced Shell's gas flaring 24 hours a day for 30 years (Rowell, 1995). Shell's main antagonist in Nigeria has been the Movement for the Survival of the Ogoni People (MOSOP), an activist NGO with the linked goals of social justice and environmental protection. The Ogoni are an ethnic group of 500,000 people living in 82 communities covering 1,000 square kilometres in the Delta region in the south-east of the country. Most Ogoni are engaged in farming and fishing, with a minority working in the oil industry either for Shell or contractor firms. Shell estimates that from 1987 to 1992 it spent about $2 million on the Ogoni area, about 16 per cent of the community budget for its Eastern Division's operation. By 1993 the company was extracting up to 28,000 barrels of oil per day from Ogoniland (Rowell, 1995).

The first demonstration against Shell was staged in 1987 by the Iko community in the Andoni ethnic area of the Delta. When Shell sought protection from the Nigerian Mobile Police Force, two people were killed, some 40 homes were destroyed and more than 350 people were made homeless (Rowell, 1996b). By 1990, growing numbers of local Delta communities from various ethnic groups started to demonstrate against Shell's activities in the area. Other companies were also targeted, but Shell was singled out as the largest and most visible player in the local oil industry. Shell officials acknowledged that there were 63 protests against the company in 1990 alone. At one demonstration in Ogoniland, 80 villagers were killed by the Nigerian Mobile Police Force. The judicial inquiry which followed criticized Shell on two major counts: first for the company's unfair acquisitions of Ogoni lands for its oil operations; and second for the environmental degradation caused and meagre compensation paid by the company to affected Ogoni communities (Goodall, 1994).

Ogoni leaders signed the 'Ogoni Bill of Rights' in 1990, citing the environmental degradation and limited employment opportunities resulting from Shell's presence in Ogoniland. The Nigerian military regime was also strongly criticized in the Ogoni manifesto. Both Shell and the Nigerian government consequently perceived both MOSOP and its leading figure as direct threats. In 1991, novelist Ken Saro-Wiwa became MOSOP's international spokesperson. Later that year, Ogoni leaders updated the Bill of Rights and authorized MOSOP to internationalize its campaign against the Nigerian government and oil companies operating in Nigeria (MOSOP, 1992). Meanwhile local protests against Shell and other oil companies continued.

The following year MOSOP presented its case to the United Nations Commission on Human Rights. MOSOP also officially submitted its demands to all oil companies operating in Ogoniland, including Shell, Chevron and NNPC. The companies were asked to pay back-royalties and compensation within 30 days or cease their operations in Ogoniland. Throughout 1992 local protests against Shell continued.

Ogoni campaign goes global

By 1993, the Ogoni campaign against Shell and the Nigerian government began to attract international attention. On 4 January MOSOP organized a major rally of 300,000 people against the oil industry to celebrate the Year of Indigenous Peoples. Later that month, MOSOP was accepted as a member of the Unrepresented Nations and Peoples Organisation (UNPO). As a result, the Ogoni case received its first major media exposure, with coverage by CNN, *Time* magazine and the British Channel 4. The latter's *Drilling Fields* launched a series of documentaries on the tensions between Shell and the Ogoni.

Around this time, The Body Shop International took the issue up as one of the company's campaign issues, working in a loose alliance with MOSOP, Greenpeace International, and other NGOs. Various independent journalists and filmmakers also began to lend support to the Ogoni cause. The Shell–Ogoni story had gone global. That story is long and complex. In the interest of brevity, the key events from 1993 to 1997 are highlighted below:

- 1993: As the MOSOP campaign against Shell intensifies, the company decides to withdraw its staff from the Ogoni area in late January, citing intimidation, attacks and the destruction of equipment. Under the protection of Nigerian soldiers, personnel from Shell and an American subcontractor return to the area in April to begin work on a new pipeline. After Ogoni crops are destroyed, local protesters block the path of the bulldozers. Following many days of confrontation between the Ogoni and the soldiers, one person is shot dead and more than 20 are wounded. Shell finally ceases production work in Ogoniland in June. In July 1993, Ken Saro-Wiwa is elected President of MOSOP.

- 1994: In January, three major oil companies announce losses in excess of $300 million during 1993 because of 'unfavourable conditions in their areas of operation' (UNPO, 1995: 51). They call for urgent action to resolve the situation. In April the Nigerian military intervenes in a local conflict between the Ogoni and another ethnic group. Fifteen Ogoni people are arrested without being charged. Nigerian soldiers attack, raid and burn Ogoni villages. More than 20 people are reportedly killed. On 1 May UNPO calls on Shell to use whatever influence it has to persuade the Nigerian government to release Ogoni prisoners. On 21 May four traditional Ogoni elders are murdered by a mob at a local rally.

Saro-Wiwa does not attend the rally. On 22 May Saro-Wiwa and more than 50 other Ogoni men are arrested. Saro-Wiwa is accused of inciting a crowd of his supporters to kill the traditional elders. In July Greenpeace International condemns Shell's 'misguided priorities' and public relations approach to the problems in Nigeria (1994: 22).

- 1995: In January a military tribunal begins to hear the Saro-Wiwa/Ogoni case. From his jail cell, in August, Saro-Wiwa calls on the international community to boycott Nigerian oil. Throughout the year the pressure grows on Shell to use its perceived political influence to seek the prisoners' freedom. On 1 November the *Financial Times* publishes a letter from Anita Roddick of The Body Shop calling on Shell to publicly condemn the military tribunal 'for the sham that it is'. On 10 November Saro-Wiwa and eight other Ogoni are hanged. The World Bank withdraws its loan for Shell Nigeria's planned $4.2 billion natural gas project. On 13 November Shell announces it will proceed with the project. On 17 November Shell organizes an informal Nigeria briefing for 35 British NGOs. Greenpeace is not invited. Global media coverage of the Saro-Wiwa execution focuses on Shell's role and responsibilities. Shell's response to the criticism is that 'politics is the business of government and politicians' and the company 'does not and should not have [political] influence' in Nigeria (NGO Task Force on Business and Industry, 1997: 18).

- 1996: Shell announces new initiatives in Nigeria, including a $850 million upgrade of two crude oil terminals and flow-line renovations to current standards. At Shell's Annual General Meeting in May the company announces that it will conduct a major international review of its Statement of General Business Principles. International protest against Shell continues, particularly via networks of linked activist Web sites on the Internet. Shell's Internet critics range from large organizations such as Amnesty International, Sierra Club and The Body Shop International to lesser-known groups such as Oilwatch, Earthlife Africa, One World Online and the Public Media Centre.

- 1997: In January, the World Council of Churches (WCC) publishes a report which argues that Shell has been justifiably criticized for its operations in Ogoniland. In March, Shell releases its revised business principles, which include for the first time explicit support for human rights. Amnesty International welcomes Shell's move but argues that it is now up to Shell to prove its commitment through practical action. In May Shell publishes its first public report on community and environmental issues in Nigeria. The report establishes new targets, including an end to gas flaring within ten years. Shell also launches a youth training scheme in Ogoniland. In September, the Canadian government introduces a voluntary policy initiative, the International Code of Ethics for Canadian Business, largely in response to Shell's controversial role in Nigeria (Ross, 1997). Meanwhile, various Internet sites continue to call on Web surfers to 'Boycott Shell Now' until the company stops its practice of 'double standards', and supports an independent environmental assessment of the Niger Delta.

Shell continues to face considerable pressure from its critics even as it introduces new environmental and social policies and programmes. Shell has indicated that it will be placing a new emphasis upon implementation procedures. One of the key lessons that Shell appears to have learned from the past few years is the need to enhance its transparency and communication with a wider range of stakeholders. Greater sensitivity to social and environmental concerns has failed, nevertheless, to stop the international protest against Shell. A remarkably diverse coalition of unions, environmental groups, human rights organizations, churches and businesses continues to single out Shell for its tacit approval of the oppressive military regime in Nigeria (Rowell, 1996b). Shell's critics continue to demand that the company should stop practising 'double standards'. They typically argue that Shell's behaviour in Nigeria would not have been tolerated in countries with higher standards (NGO Task Force on Business and Industry, 1997).

Such criticism has not deterred Shell's efforts to develop new relationships with other NGOs. In 1997 Shell attempted to apply the lessons learned from its Nigeria experience to a new gas project in the Camisea region of Peru. The proposed site is located in a pristine rain forest inhabited by indigenous peoples. Shell announced in May 1997 that it had signed an agreement with Red Ambiental Peruana (RAP), a social and environmental network, which empowered RAP members to monitor the social and environmental performance of the proposed project. Shell also supported an elaborate consultation exercise in the Camisea area, which aimed to increase the company's knowledge about local environmental, social and economic issues. These moves did not, however, stop protest against the project by other NGOs and indigenous peoples' groups both locally and globally.

Conflicting messages

The oil industry's overall response to its critics has been mixed in recent years. Industry groups such as CONCAWE continue to believe that a rational approach is essential to the proper resolution of complex issues (CONCAWE, 1996). Under-lying this argument is a belief that the industry can solve complex environmental problems if it merely gets the scientific facts right. At the same time, the industry has indicated that technically sound solutions need to be worked out in partnership with its stakeholders. However, CONCAWE fails to include NGOs among its list of the industry's stakeholders.

Cracks are nevertheless beginning to appear in the previously unified industry front. On the issue of global warming, the world's third-largest oil company, British Petroleum (BP), recently broke ranks. John Browne, BP's chairman, announced in May 1997 that his company has accepted that there is now sufficient evidence to indicate that the burning of fossil fuels is a significant factor in climate change. BP subsequently agreed to work with the Environmental Defence Fund (EDF) to develop a voluntary emissions trading system for greenhouse gases.

BP's new commitment to the precautionary principle[7] and partnership may reveal an oil industry trying to come to terms with the new politics of sustainable development. BP's lead on climate change came at a time when the industry and Shell were still coming to terms with the fall-out over Brent Spar and Nigeria. For its part, BP spent much of 1997 fending off accusations about its complicity in human rights abuses and environmental degradation in Colombia. This has prompted BP to initiate dialogue with a group of British development NGOs to explore issues of mutual concern regarding BP's current activities and future projects in Colombia. As market leaders, Shell and BP have found themselves at the forefront of both organized protest and the industry response to the growing complexity of the corporate role in sustainable development.

As Shell's experience in Nigeria and Peru illustrates, enhanced dialogue and partnership may not be enough to improve the global image of the oil industry. Companies like Shell face a dilemma. They are in the business of extracting natural resources to meet a growing worldwide demand for energy. The opening statement on Shell's Internet Web site makes this clear: 'Everyone must have energy to live. Shell's main business is drawing stored energy from the earth – as oil, gas and coal – and getting it in a useful form to where people want it' (Shell International, 1997: 1). As a business argument, this seems to make good economic sense. However, it does not allow for any fundamental questioning of resource extraction, processing and transportation. There is also no recognition of the need for energy alternatives. Extracting resources and getting them to where people want them may mean that other people and their environments are harmed in the process.

Many argue that without ongoing civil society protest, business will have little motivation or need to change. At the same time, many questions remain about how oil companies should best manage the diverse, complex and sometimes contradictory expectations of their stakeholders. Shell's Group Chief Executive C. A. J. Herkströter (1996) offers a useful starting point: 'We must remain sensitive to the evolving needs and concerns of all our stakeholders. I fully accept that, in this process, we must be prepared to engage in wider debates – including on human rights issues' (1996: 14). His counterpart at BP, John Browne, offers some additional clues as to the future social and environmental agenda of the oil industry: 'We need to go beyond analysis to seek solutions and to take action. It is a moment for change and for a rethinking of corporate responsibility' (1997: 3).

If market leaders like Shell and BP are serious about engaging in wider debates and rethinking corporate responsibility, then perhaps a time will come when the voices of those opposed to a potential project are more clearly heard. In such cases, the most appropriate corporate response might be not to intervene at all. Whether oil companies are prepared to accept 'non-intervention' as a possible solution in some cases remains to be seen.

Postscript

In July 1998, Shell announced that it would not go ahead with the Peru gas project despite having spent $250 million in exploration costs. *The Economist* reported that the Peruvian government and the oil companies could not resolve questions about distribution, pricing and exports. New drilling appraisals had also challenged original output forecasts. No mention was made of the possible role of civil society protest in Shell's decision (*The Economist*, 1998a, 1998b).

Meanwhile, the situation in Nigeria's Delta region remains tense. In October 1998, local protesters seized two Shell helicopters and occupied an oil rig and more than 10 oil relay stations. Local communities in Ogoni and other parts of the region continue to demand compensation from the Nigerian government, Shell and various other oil companies. MOSOP's financial demands remain fixed at $30 billion, the estimated value of Ogoni oil extracted since 1958. MOSOP also wants Shell to clean up degraded Ogoni lands. Although Shell has made overtures to individual community leaders in Ogoni, the company and MOSOP have been unable to resolve their differences. As of early 1999, Shell's exile from Ogoni continues. Although some Shell pipelines continue to cross Ogoni territory, the company has not undertaken any drilling or gas flaring activities there since its withdrawal in 1993.

Shell's new development strategy for Nigeria includes a planned five-year investment of $8.5 billion to develop a number of large off-shore oil fields. BBC reports suggest that part of the project's attraction is that off-shore development will be 'much less prone to the disruption which has severely affected output in the Niger Delta' (BBC Online, 1999).

Just Do It — Justly! The Sporting Goods Industry, NGOs, Child Labour and Global Standards[8]

The business response to sustainable development requires much more than policies and programmes for environmental protection. Social sustainability concerns such as poverty, health and child welfare are also affected by commercial activities, both positively and negatively. At the international policy level, sustainable development encompasses EHS issues in the workplace. In recent years, various United Nations agencies have lent impetus to calls for enhanced corporate environmental and social policy responses in both the North and the South.

In the 1990s, the EHS practices of sporting goods companies such as Nike and Reebok, particularly in Asia, have been under attack by labour and human rights NGOs in both the North and South. For example, the 'NIKE – Fair Play?' Campaign has resulted in meetings between Dutch activists and NIKE officials, at which the company's representatives admitted that the monitoring of its code of conduct was unsatisfactory. Nike's main competitor Reebok has also faced scrutiny, with NGO accusations and media exposés about unfair wages, health and safety violations and the use of child and forced labour in some of its supplier factories in China.

This case describes efforts by industry associations, member firms, manufacturers, United Nations agencies, NGOs and various local partners to develop strategies to prevent and eliminate the use of child labour in the production of hand-stitched soccer balls in Pakistan. The global soccer ball market is worth almost $1 billion in total retail sales. Pakistan produces about 80 per cent of the world's match-grade soccer balls.

The child labour issue

In 1992, the ILO established its International Programme for the Elimination of Child Labour (IPEC) with the aim of working towards the progressive elimination of child labour. By working in collaboration with a wide range of actors, IPEC is seeking to prevent child labour, to withdraw children from hazardous work, to offer alternatives and, in the interim, to improve existing working conditions for children.

Despite 'unprecedented public awareness of the problem ... and broad consensus on the need to do something about it', the ILO notes:

> At the intergovernmental level, the problem of child labour has been caught up in a politically charged debate on human rights, labour standards, ethics and international trade. This partly accounts for the relatively slow progress being made towards concerted international action to tackle the problem, even in its most extreme forms. (1997b: 233)

As of December 1997, less than 60 countries had ratified ILO Convention 138, an international agreement that sets minimum age standards for different kinds of work.[9]

UNICEF's *The State of the World's Children 1997* report focuses on child labour and makes links to global corporate irresponsibility. UNICEF cites the growing impact of a liberalized global economy driven by TNCs as a major contributor to the problem of exploitative child labour. Global competitive pressure brings children into the workforce in many southern countries. Terry Collingsworth insists that government regulation on child labour needs to be safeguarded:

> The child labor issue should drive the larger struggle to regulate fundamental rights in the global economy. As nations lose their sovereign right to prohibit child labor (through stealth provisions in complex trade agreements), there must be a plan to ensure that the global economy does not force countries with reasonable child labor prohibitions to scrap those protections and offer up their children as a source of extra cheap labor in the global marketplace. (1997: 2)

Implementing social protection programmes on the ground, however, remains highly problematic. Despite the existence of national regulatory frameworks on child labour in many Southern countries, 'the weakness of enforcement mechanisms' remains a major obstacle to effective legal protection largely due to 'the nature and scale of the problem' (ILO, 1997b: 241). Monitoring the use of child labour in the large informal sector is particularly difficult.

The general United Nations message to governments and industry groups is that all extreme forms of child labour must end now. Rather than trying to stop child labour outright, consumers, companies and campaign groups are asked to 'target the intolerable' and seek to eliminate all work which is detrimental to the health, safety and future development of children (ILO, 1996, 1997a; UNICEF, 1997). The ILO estimates that some 250 million children are currently working worldwide.

A partnership response

Officially launched in February 1997, the 'Project to Eliminate Child Labour in the Pakistan Soccer Ball Industry' is a multi-stakeholder collaboration that primarily involves the following organizations, some as direct partners and others as project supporters:

- *Bunyad Literacy Community Council (BLCC):* a Pakistani NGO that provides non-formal primary education mainly for girls and women.
- *International Labour Organization (ILO):* a specialist United Nations agency with a tripartite structure, which allows for representation from governments, employer organizations and worker organizations.
- *Pakistan Bait-ul-Mal (PBM):* an organization created by government statute which assists needy widows, orphans, people with disabilities, and the chronically ill, by providing them with assistance for education, housing and rehabilitation.
- *Save the Children–UK (SCF):* the UK's largest international NGO concerned with children's rights and welfare. SCF works in partnership with children, parents, governments, local authorities and NGOs in over 50 countries.
- *Sporting Goods Manufacturers Association (SGMA):* the trade association of North American manufacturers, producers and distributors of sports apparel, athletic footwear and sporting goods.
- *Sialkot Chamber of Commerce and Industry (SCCI):* one of Pakistan's largest and oldest association of business enterprises, based in the Sialkot District of Punjab Province. SCCI represents local soccer ball manufacturers.
- *United Nations Children's Fund (UNICEF):* a specialist United Nations agency dedicated exclusively to meeting the needs of children. It works with other United Nations agencies, governments and NGOs to provide a range of health and education-related community-based services.
- *World Federation of the Sporting Goods Industry (WFSGI):* the Switzerland-based

association of national sporting goods manufacturers that together represent over 12,000 companies worldwide, including leading brands such as Nike, Reebok, Mitre, Adidas and Umbro.

The partnership project has four main aims:

- Prevent and progressively eliminate child labour in the manufacture or assembly of soccer balls in Sialkot District and its environs;
- Identify and remove children under the age of 14 involved in the manufacture or assembly of soccer balls and provide them with educational and other opportunities;
- Facilitate changes in community and family attitudes to child labour, including abuses in the soccer industry;
- 'encourage the Government of Pakistan, the business community in Sialkot and other institutions to explore effective ways to eliminate child labour' (quoted in SCF 1997b: 73).

Two programmes are being developed to enable the project participants to achieve these goals. First, the Prevention and Monitoring Programme is a voluntary scheme open to all soccer ball manufacturers. Participating firms are expected to meet formal registration requirements concerning use of contractors, stitching locations and proof-of-age documentation for workers. Second, the Social Protection Programme is designed to provide affected children and families with educational and financial support, and to raise local awareness about child labour and the need for alternatives.

Project origins

The roots of the Pakistan project lie in the emergence of child labour as a significant political and consumer issue in Northern countries in the late 1980s and early 1990s. In 1992 American Senator Tom Harkin introduced a bill that would have placed import restrictions on products manufactured by child workers. Media coverage initially focused on large numbers of young girls employed in the Bangladesh garment industry and horrific cases of bonded child workers in the South Asian hand-woven carpet industry. One case proved to be particularly significant. Pakistani Iqbal Masih was sold into slavery in 1986 for less than $16 when he was only four years old. After Masih escaped from a carpet factory in 1992 he became a champion of child workers, spoke at international labour conferences and helped close dozens of Pakistani carpet factories. Over the course of his campaign Masih received numerous death threats and in early 1995 was shot dead in his home village. Although most independent evidence suggests that Masih was not killed by carpet industry assassins, his death and the outrage that followed drew worldwide attention to child labour and in particular to the situation in Pakistan (Associated Press, 1995; CEP, 1995; Marcus, 1997).

The specific focus on the soccer ball industry originated in the USA in the aftermath of the locally hosted 1994 World Cup. The American Federation of Labour (AFL–CIO) had already been campaigning on the general issue of child labour since at least 1993. By focusing on child labour in the soccer ball industry, labour and consumer groups helped raise awareness about the issue with politicians, athletes, sports associations, parents, children and, perhaps most importantly, within the business community.

In early 1995 WFSGI approached SCF with a proposal to develop a labelling scheme for soccer balls similar to the Rugmark Foundation's labelling scheme. Established in 1994 with the support of the ILO and a group of South Asian and European NGOs, Rugmark primarily targets European and North American importers and South Asian producers of hand-made carpets. The scheme certifies participating producers according to a set of labour standards and related criteria. Rugmark inspectors monitor factories on a regular basis. Child welfare NGOs are provided access to certified factories to ensure that children are not being employed.

SCF declined the WFSGI offer because of concerns that labelling would shift the focus away from the root causes of child labour in the industry. SCF worried that such schemes were more concerned with meeting the needs of Northern consumers than with a direct response to the problems facing child workers. SCF feared that a labelling scheme might lead to an 'ethical' labelled segment of the market, aimed at niche consumers, while the same companies continue to market unlabelled, 'unethically' produced products to other consumers. This would enable a participating company to be lauded for the ethical label without implementing ethical policies for all products and activities. Furthermore, SCF expressed doubts about potential monitoring problems. Rugmark was experiencing some difficulties in this regard (Hilowitz, 1997).

Throughout 1995 the child labour story increasingly attracted the attention of foreign journalists. Some of these reporters were attacked and beaten up by local people in Sialkot who feared the potential loss of income as a result of adverse publicity in the international media. Local manufacturers also complained that campaigns against child labour had an underlying agenda of promoting adult labour unions internationally.[10] The news reports from Pakistan nonetheless continued to reach their intended audience, particularly in the United States.

Near the end of 1995, in response to growing consumer and political pressure on the soccer ball industry and individual companies, WFSGI in cooperation with the International Olympic Committee (IOC) established the Committee on Ethics and Fair Trade as a new working committee within WFSGI. The new committee was launched in early November at the first WFSGI conference on human rights, which was attended by representatives of the industry, United Nations agencies and NGOs. In the conference report, the new President of WFSGI, Stephen Rubin, admitted that WFSGI had been 'a passive organization frightened to upset its member associations and individual member companies, lest they cease to be members'. It was time, Rubin argued, for the organization 'to become proactive, to stand up and be counted'. He added that 'it is equally important that NGOs and other public sector organizations should back us up' (WFSGI, 1996: 1, 76).

In early 1996 the FoulBall Campaign was launched in the USA by the International Labor Rights Fund (ILRF). The campaign targeted soccer balls originating from Pakistan, China and Indonesia and claimed that these nations extensively use child labourers. The campaign attracted support from average citizens and policy makers alike: 'youth soccer leagues in the US were quick to pick up on it and join. The US Secretary of Labor, Robert Reich, was much interested in it and threw his influence into publicizing the effort, as did a number of members of the US Congress' (Harvey, 1997). By mid-1996, coinciding with football's UK-hosted European Cup, the British Trade Union Congress, the International Textile, Garment and Leather Workers Federation and International Confederation of Free Trade Unions launched an initiative with the Federation of International Football

Associations (FIFA) to target the soccer ball industry. The trade unionists were attempting to raise spectator awareness and to get FIFA to phase out the use of balls produced by child labour.

Meanwhile, the FoulBall Campaign in North America was succeeding in getting its message across to the so-called soccer moms who were accompanying their children to the growing numbers of community soccer programmes. At Nike's 1996 Annual General Meeting, Chairman Phil Knight acknowledged that the company had recently purchased a shipment of Pakistani soccer balls which were 'found to have been manufactured ... using child labour in horrible conditions' (Nando.net and Associated Press, 1996). In many respects, however, working conditions for most child stitchers in Sialkot were not as bad as those faced by child workers in other industries in Pakistan and elsewhere. Nonetheless, the soccer ball story continued to capture public attention, largely because of its media-friendly nature (Marcus, 1997). Consequently, the sporting goods industry continued to face growing consumer and activist pressure, particularly in North America and Western Europe.

Seeking solutions

In July 1996 representatives of Mitre, one of the largest soccer ball brands, organized a visit to Pakistan and invited SCF to accompany them. This visit enabled both Mitre and SCF to develop important contacts on the ground in the Sialkot District where the Pakistan soccer ball industry is based. In particular, SCF initiated discussions with the local industry body SCCI about the need for complementary efforts to ensure that children removed from work do not find themselves in more dangerous and exploitative work environments.

Mitre asked SCF to become involved in a monitoring and labelling scheme, but again SCF declined for reasons similar to those outlined above. However, SCF agreed to undertake a detailed study of the child labour issue in Sialkot. Although three other quantitative studies had already been done, few had gathered qualitative data and all lacked significant attention to the perspectives of children and their families.

By the autumn of 1996 the soccer ball industry was continuing to feel the pressure of the various NGO campaigns. In September the FIFA–labour group coalition mentioned above produced a broad and ambitious code of conduct that left the industry scrambling to respond. Trade associations such as WFSGI and the Soccer Industry Council of America (SICA) were increasingly concerned about the impact of NGO pressure upon the industry's image and the potential loss of markets. In an effort to help it find solutions to the growing storm of controversy, the WFSGI organized a conference in London in November 1996, bringing together industry representatives, many of its critics and other interested parties.

At the conference, WFSGI announced that it was committed to develop a code of conduct for the production of all sporting goods; however, it was one that failed to address 'the full range of labour rights enumerated in the FIFA code' (Harvey 1997). WFSGI also indicated that it had reached agreement with the Pakistan-based Steering Committee on Child Labour (a joint initiative of SCCI and the All Pakistan Sporting Goods Association) to develop a programme to help eliminate the use of child labour in the soccer ball industry. Another outcome of the conference was that SCF agreed to undertake a detailed situational analysis in Sialkot, re-affirming its original commitment made during the Mitre visit.

Partnership agreement signed

Following the London conference, formal negotiations continued between WFSGI, ILO, UNICEF and SCCI in order to finalize a joint project response to the child labour issue. This culminated in the formal announcement in Atlanta on 14 February 1997 of the Project to Eliminate Child Labour in the Pakistan Soccer Ball Industry. Although the official 'Partners' Agreement to Eliminate Child Labour in the Soccer Ball Industry' was signed only by ILO, UNICEF and SCCI, SCF was invited to become a full partner on the Project Coordinating Committee. At the Atlanta launch, the WFSGI, SICA and Sporting Goods Manufacturers Association were identified as project facilitators. FIFA and the US Youth Soccer Association were listed as project supporters. FoulBall criticized the Partnership Agreement as an industry attempt 'to pre-empt legislation and truly independent monitoring' (ILRF, 1997: 1).

After the project launch, SCF began its field research in Sialkot. The major purpose of the four-week study was to provide SCF and other organizations with a reliable baseline before introducing social protection programmes to assist children displaced from football stitching. SCF decided to participate in the partnership because it was concerned that 'emotive responses in the past have caused more harm than good' with banned child labourers often 'forced to take on harmful, less well-paid work, including prostitution.' SCF wanted to insure that 'sustainable solutions' would be developed to help overcome poverty, a root cause of child labour (SCF, 1997a: 1). In particular, SCF was worried about the loss of family income as a result of the decision to eliminate the use of child stitchers. This explains why SCF remains opposed to blanket bans on child labour. On a more strategic level, SCF's motivation for participating in the Pakistan project was

> to use [its] experience of child labour programmes elsewhere in a constructive partnership with the private sector – a new experience for [SCF] … [SCF] also saw this as an opportunity to link work at the micro level – in Sialkot – with macro level lobbying and advocacy on corporate social responsibility, [an area of increasing involvement] in the UK. (Marcus, 1997: 2–3).

Between March and April 1997, the ILO undertook a mission to Pakistan in its capacity as lead agency on the project. One of the major ILO tasks was to finalize the Partners' Operational Framework. The only major change to the original terms of reference concerned the issue of independent third-party monitoring in the Prevention and Monitoring Programme. In response to concerns expressed by SCCI about third-party monitoring, the partners have agreed to designate the ILO as external monitor. SCCI was mainly concerned that the expense involved in hiring a commercial auditor would be excessive for local manufacturers to bear. SCCI also felt that the ILO had the capacity and experience to fulfil the role. In particular, SCCI pointed to recent ILO monitoring and verification experience in Bangladesh. Since 1995 the ILO has been working with the Government of Bangladesh, UNICEF, and the Bangladesh Garment Manufacturers and Exporters Association (BGMEA) to remove under-age children from BGMEA factories and to place them in appropriate education programmes.

The Partners' Operational Framework was agreed in late June 1997. In addition to providing operational definitions, immediate objectives, long-term goals and specific project elements, the framework outlines the proposed roles of the on-the-ground partners. Furthermore, it specifies the implementation guidelines and successor arrangements for sustainability.

The overall project is being managed by the Project Coordinating Committee with representation from SCCI, ILO, UNICEF and SCF. Project partner representatives on the ground have formed the Sialkot Implementation Team to facilitate coordination between the two general programme areas and individual components within these programmes. SCCI, ILO and participating local manufacturers are implementing the Prevention and Monitoring Programme. As noted above, ILO is responsible for external monitoring and verification, whereas local manufacturers carry out internal monitoring. SCCI is expected to communicate progress achieved to its members and also to raise awareness of their roles and responsibilities in the prevention of child labour. ILO, UNICEF, SCCI, SCF, PBM, and BLCC are implementing the Social Protection Programme. The Board of the Pakistani organization PBM has made a commitment to assume responsibility for the continuation of the programme upon its estimated completion date in 1999.

By December 1997 the project was under way and SCF had formed a partnership with the National Rural Support Programme, a Pakistani NGO that will implement related social mobilization activities and a credit and savings scheme. In order to protect women's jobs and family incomes, SCF is organizing groups of women stitchers into units that will be inspected by ILO-trained child labour monitors, and has also initiated a social monitoring component to provide detailed tracking of the impact of the overall programme on local families and communities (Marcus, 1997).

More hurdles ahead

The project partners have made substantial financial and in-kind commitments to date. For organizations such as ILO and SCF, there are important questions about their capacity to respond to demands for similar partnerships in other industrial sectors around the world. This raises concerns about both the sustainability and replicability of such elaborate and ambitious monitoring and verification schemes, not to mention the vital social protection programmes. There are also questions about the capacity of the Pakistan partners to provide the necessary financial support for the long-term needs of the project and its beneficiaries. For local communities and industries dependent upon the preferences of global consumers, such projects bring hope for the future but leave many socio-economic and political issues unresolved. Many Pakistanis continue to challenge anti-child labour campaigns by suggesting that their underlying aim is to destroy foreign competition and protect Northern jobs. There is nevertheless a feeling among some members of the Pakistani middle class that global child labour standards are needed and that intellectual arguments to the contrary should be challenged (Marcus, 1997).

The most important lesson for other industry sectors appears to be the fundamental importance of corporate transparency and a willingness to accept independent monitoring. The credibility of the Pakistan partnership depends upon ongoing NGO support, both in the North and in Pakistan. The active role of the ILO in the monitoring programme also offers hope that United Nations agencies may be able to assume new governance roles as arbiters of global corporate standards. SCF's leadership on the ground and its advocacy work suggest that Northern-based development NGOs can play a significant role in promoting global corporate responsibility for sustainable development.

Meanwhile, various companies within the sporting goods industry continue to face the scrutiny of civil society everywhere. Despite its support for the Pakistan initiative, Nike remains a major target of protest. When in mid-1997 former United

States ambassador to the United Nations Andrew Young reviewed Nike factories in China, Indonesia and Vietnam in mid-1997 on behalf of Good Works International, his findings were mixed. Young found no evidence of 'systematic abuse or mistreatment of workers', yet he discovered that most workers knew little about their rights or Nike's code of conduct (quoted in Himelstein, 1997: 44). Furthermore, he called on the company to introduce a comprehensive third-party independent monitoring system because of the prevalence of absentee factory owners and limited Nike on-site supervisors. Although some of Young's recommendations echo the demands of many campaign groups, the response of company critics has not been positive. Global Exchange called the report 'meaningless' as it avoided any consideration of wages, 'what may be the most important concern of Nike's foreign workers' (*ibid.*).

In late 1997 FoulBall's Web site claimed that Nike and other industry players continue to demonstrate 'foot dragging, deliberate confusion and no strong leadership' in Pakistan and elsewhere. FoulBall suggested that 'only the potential for a World Cup boycott [in 1998] seems to be seriously getting the attention of the industry' (ILRF, 1997: 2). At the same time, action also depends upon the on-the-ground leadership of the Pakistani industry. SCF's Rachel Marcus (1997) argues that long-term success will depend upon local ownership.

Despite some forward movement on the child labour issue in the Pakistan soccer ball industry, the bottom line for many critics is that Northern-based sporting goods companies continue to promote double standards. Whether one is talking about EHS standards in the workplace or wider environmental impacts, companies such as Nike continue to source goods from the South that are often produced under conditions that would be unacceptable and often illegal in Northern countries. The end result is that people and their environments are often inadequately protected, particularly in the South. Pakistani families who depend upon their children's income, however, remain concerned about the consequences of eliminating child labour altogether. In the words of a father of child stitchers: 'It is not good for children to work, but if they don't, how shall we live?' (quoted in SCF, 1997b: 26).

Towards an Understanding of Business—NGO Relations

One of the goals of this chapter is to examine the changing nature of business–NGO relations in relation to sustainable development. It is hoped that this will promote new thinking about the future role of corporations in the sustainable development of the South. As noted earlier, research on the specific topic of business–NGO relations has until recently been limited. The literatures on environmental management, civil society, conflict theory, public–private partnerships and inter-organizational collaboration all offer important insights of relevance to this discussion. Many social scientists continue to see conflict and confrontational tactics as an essential driving force for changing the unsustainable nature of global industrial society (Lach, 1996; Manes, 1990).

Increasingly, however, less radical methods associated with various forms of partnership are being employed by NGOs. Although the idea of partnership has a long history in the world of business, there has been limited theoretical development to date specifically related to business–NGO partnerships. Social science researchers have examined public–private or social partnerships in the UK and USA (Waddock, 1988; Mackintosh, 1992; Bailey, 1994). Others have looked at the general field of inter-organizational collaboration (Gray, 1989; Gray and Wood,

1991; Wood and Gray, 1991). In terms of broader societal issues, Riane Eisler envisions 'a new integrated partnership politics that factors in matters that have been largely ignored in most analyses of how to move to a humane future' (1996: 565).

Some of this work provides useful general theoretical models of partnership without, as we have said, addressing the specific area of business–NGO partnerships. To redress this gap, a small but growing body of action-oriented, generally non-academic research on business–NGO environmental partnerships has begun to emerge in recent years, on the basis of which different partnership typologies can be identified (McKinsey and Co., 1992; Long and Arnold, 1995; SustainAbility, 1996). Our own work (Murphy and Bendell, 1997) has identified three models of business–NGO partnership where NGOs attempt to influence business policy or operational issues:

- *Process-oriented partnerships* involve NGOs with internal company management processes in some way. They often focus on broad issues such as environmental policies, eco-efficiency strategies or improving the performance of suppliers;

- *Project-oriented partnerships* focus on discrete projects to achieve objectives with significant implications for core business practice. They differ from process partnerships, as the relationship does not necessarily involve NGOs with internal management decisions;

- *Product-oriented partnerships* involve NGOs in specific product development and/or endorsement. The difference between these partnerships and process-oriented initiatives is that they do not involve the NGO with internal company management decisions. Unlike project-oriented partnerships, they focus on delivering improvements in products or product sales.

No one framework can fully explain the diversity of business–NGO relations on sustainable development. Most, if not all, of the typologies are very North-centric and fail to consider the contingent relationship between conflict and partnership. They also appear to be more concerned with the nature of the relationships and the benefits accruing to the partners than with considering the extent to which business–NGO relationships affect the inter-organizational problem domain of sustainable development. In this regard there are related questions about the extent to which business–NGO partnerships actually embody sustainable development principles. Furthermore, most of the research to date fails to explore the wider implications of closer and more collaborative business–NGO relationships, namely for democracy, governance, regulation and global social change.

Researchers such as Donna Wood and Barbara Gray (1991) argue for a comprehensive theory of collaboration. However, it should be remembered that 'partnerships are highly contextually specific ... [and] must be developed within the political and organizational culture of specific localities' (Stewart and Snape, 1996: 5). The more specific area of business–NGO partnerships for sustainable development embodies a wide range of industrial sectors, NGO types, geographical contexts, political cultures and organizational forms. Given this diversity, it seems unlikely that any one model of collaboration would be an adequate, let alone appropriate, analytical tool. Instead we offer some general characteristics of business–NGO collaboration which for the most part appear to be shared by all three case studies. These characteristics are presented as preconditions, interactive processes and outcomes.

Preconditions

It is important to understand the factors that give rise to partnerships, namely the preconditions that motivate organizations to seek out partners or to accept offers to collaborate (Gray and Wood, 1991). These may include external and/or internal issues unique to one organization or shared by the partners. The specific origins of the formal partnerships and other collaborative forms of business relations in each of the case studies are obviously unique. Below we offer a preliminary list of partnership preconditions that emerge from the case studies and other research. It is not exhaustive and should not be seen as a partnership formula.

- Emergence of sustainable development as a new – albeit contested – global–local problem domain where both business and NGOs are relevant stakeholders;
- Perceived and actual decline in the effectiveness of state regulation and global governance related to the enforcement of environmental and labour standards;
- Acknowledgement on the part of NGOs of the increasing political and economic power of global corporations as agents of unsustainable development and as potentially positive agents of socio-economic and environmental change;
- Proliferation of North–South 'double standards' in corporate social and environmental policies and programmes;
- Impact of different forms of sustained, often widespread NGO campaigning, including direct action, consumer awareness and information dissemination via new technologies, upon corporate reputation, market position and business responses to sustainable development;
- Recognition by beleaguered companies of the growing power and legitimacy of NGOs as agents of social change and potential partners to help solve business problems;
- Need for more inclusive and accountable models of society, governance, problem solving, standards setting, regulation, community development, etcetera.

Interactive processes

Another aspect of understanding the business–NGO partnership phenomenon is to consider the various interactive processes that take place as part of the development and implementation of such initiatives in different contexts. These may include interactions within the organizational boundaries of the partnership concerned as well as external influences. The following list is not a definitive checklist for the business–NGO partnership process, but rather initial perceptions based upon the case studies and other relevant material.

- Capacity and willingness of partners to cope with the diverse perspectives and paradoxical goals from the outset and throughout the process;
- Commitment of partners to principles of shared responsibility, symbiosis and joint ownership;
- Articulation of honest and realistic expectations by partners;
- Development of a flexible structure consistent with the purpose and functioning of the partnership;
- Organizational commitment of business partner(s) to change unsustainable practices through specific policies, concrete actions and ongoing support for the partnership;
- Ability of NGO partner to maintain organizational independence and integrity;
- Ongoing pressure from other NGOs and activists related to the problem domain;

- Capability of business and NGO partner(s) to respond appropriately to such ongoing pressure;
- Capacity to broaden partnership scope and participation in some cases to include relevant United Nations and governmental agencies (for example, Pakistan);
- Ongoing tensions between businesses and NGOs about the potentials and limits of partnership in different geographical, political, social and cultural contexts.

Outcomes and consequences

A third general way of understanding business–NGO partnership is to consider their outcomes and consequences. Gray and Wood suggest that partnership outcomes can be identified by considering 'whether problems were solved ... whose problems were solved ... whether shared norms were achieved' and whether the partnership survived (1991: 18). Another way of reviewing partnerships would be to consider some of the wider implications of closer and more collaborative business–NGO relationships. Given that most of the examples cited are still evolving and the newness of this specific area of study, the following list of partnership outcomes offers a tentative picture of an emerging phenomenon:

- Partnering NGOs are gaining greater credibility as important resources for both business and society;
- Some partnering businesses are being recognized for their more proactive approaches to social and environmental matters;
- Other NGO and consumer pressure on partnering businesses and/or industry sectors does not necessarily end and is often maintained;
- Shared norms are emerging around the general idea of sustainable development although it remains a contested and controversial problem domain;
- Many specific problem areas addressed by business–NGO partnerships remain complex and multi-faceted, and therefore require ongoing dialogue and negotiation in order to identify medium- and long-term solutions.

Seen from a wider perspective, business–NGO partnerships constitute part of a changing global political and economic context which is giving rise to new models of corporate accountability and stakeholder engagement. This context is characterized by a number of international developments, including the globalization of business, trade and finance; advances in communications technologies; and a growth in the number of NGOs and the scope of their activities. Many would argue that this context also includes unacceptable yet deepening levels of environmental degradation and human poverty. The perceived and actual decline in the role of the state in the face of globalization raises additional concerns about governance and regulatory gaps nationally and globally. We should remember that stories of NGO-driven corporate environmentalism are fresh straws of hope in a rotten haystack of unaccountable and irresponsible global capitalism. The unsustainable reality for billions of people on earth today nonetheless compels us to clasp at these straws of hope as potential catalysts for more sustainable and equitable world futures. This is our reason for venturing a new theory of corporate environmentalism based upon civil regulation, which we turn to in the following chapter.

Notes

1 Alongside business–NGO confrontation, various NGOs have accepted corporate donations for specific projects or causes. While some writers have characterized these activities as 'partnerships' (Forrester, 1990; Waddock, 1988), others have tended to view them primarily as corporate sponsorship agreements (Murphy and Bendell, 1997). Recent research suggests that greater attention is being given to the mutual benefits for business and NGOs of these agreements (Waddell, 1998).

2 This case study is based in part on previously published material (Bendell and Sullivan, 1996; Murphy 1996; Murphy and Bendell, 1997).

3 Interview with D. F. Murphy, November 1994.

4 Interview with D. F. Murphy, November 1994.

5 This case study is based upon research conducted by D. F. Murphy for the New Academy of Business.

6 These are 1995 figures based upon an average crude oil price of $17.24 a barrel.

7 The precautionary principle upholds the validity of taking action to protect the environment even in situations where scientific evidence regarding the cause and effects of environmental degradation is inconclusive.

8 This case study is based on material published in a paper on corporate social responsibility prepared for the ILO's Conditions of Work and Welfare Facilities Branch (Murphy, 1997a).

9 Pakistan is a signatory to three of six ILO conventions related to child labour: No. 59 on Minimum Age (Industry), No. 29 on Forced Labour and No. 105 on the Abolition of Forced Labour (ILO, 1996).

10 Informal sector, home-based hand stitching is 'notoriously hard to unionize' which may explain why many labour groups have campaigned against the use of child labour in soccer ball manufacturing (Marcus 1997: 1).

References

Associated Press (1995), 'Battled Child Labour Boy, 12, Murdered', *The Toronto Star*, 19 April.

Bailey, N. (1994), 'Towards a Research Agenda for Public–Private Partnerships in the 1990s', *Local Economy*, 8 (4) (February), 292–306.

BBC Online (1999), 'Business: The Company File – Shell to Invest $8.5 bn in Africa', published 8 February 1998 at 13:54 GMT, http://bbc.co.uk/hi/english/business/

Bendell, J. and F. Sullivan (1996), 'Sleeping with the Enemy? Business–Environmentalist Partnerships for Sustainable Development: The Case of the WWF 1995 Group', in R. Aspinwall and J. Smith (eds.), *Environmentalist and Business Partnerships: A Sustainable Model?*, The White Horse Press, Cambridge.

Bendell, J. and D. Warner (1996), 'If You Can't Beat 'em, Join 'em: The Costs and Benefits of Collaborating with the Environmental Movement', in *Proceedings of the Business Strategy and the Environment Conference 1996*, ERP, Leeds.

Browne, J. (1997), Climate Change Speech, delivered at Stanford University, California, 19 May.

Business Week (1997), 'The Business Week Global 1000', 7 July, pp. 55–92.

CEP (1995), *Child Labor: The Cutting Edge of Human Rights*, research report, Council on Economic Priorities (CEP), New York.

Colchester, M. (1997), *Social Aspects of Certification,* a report on the first meeting of the FSC Social Working Group (San Pedro, Brazil, 25–26 April 1997), Forest Peoples Programme, Moreton-in-Marsh, England.

Collingsworth, T. (1997), 'Child Labour in the Global Economy', *Foreign Policy in Focus*, 2 (46) (October), 1–3.

Collinson, H. (ed.) (1996), *Green Guerrillas: Environmental Conflicts and Initiatives in Latin America and the Caribbean,* Latin American Bureau, London.

CONCAWE (1996), *CONCAWE Review*, 5 (1) (April).

Corry, S. (1993), 'Harvest Moonshine Taking You for a Ride: A Critique of the Rainforest

Harvest Its Theory and Practice', a discussion paper, Survival International, London.

Dore, E. (1996), 'Capitalism and Ecological Crisis: Legacy of the 1980s', in H. Collinson (ed.), *Green Guerrillas: Environmental Conflicts and Initiatives in Latin America and the Caribbean*, Latin American Bureau, London.

Eisler, R. (1996), 'Creating Partnership Futures', *Futures*, 28 (6/7) (August/September), 563–6.

Erskine, H. (1971), 'The Polls: Pollution and Industry', *Public Opinion Quarterly*, 36 (2), 263–80.

FoE–UK (1991), 'Friends of the Earth Brings DIY Stores into Line', Press Release, 11 December 1991, FoE–UK, London.

FoE–UK (1992), 'Timber Agreement under Fire', *Earth Matters*, 17 (Winter), 5, FoE–UK, London.

Forrester, S. (1990), *Business and Environmental Groups: A Natural Partnership?* Directory of Social Change, London.

Goodall, A. (1994), 'You Can Be Sure of Shell', *New Internationalist* (June), 26–7.

Gray, B. (1989), *Collaborating: Finding Common Ground for Multiparty Problems*, Jossey-Bass, San Francisco.

Gray, B. and D. Wood (1991), 'Collaborative Alliances: Moving from Practice to Theory', *Journal of Applied Behavioral Science*, 27 (1), 3–22.

Greenpeace International (1994), *Shell-Shocked: The Environmental and Social Costs of Living with Shell in Nigeria*, Greenpeace International, Amsterdam.

Hall, A. (1996), 'Did Chico Mendes Die in Vain? Brazilian Rubber Tappers in the 1990s', in H. Collinson (ed.), *Green Guerrillas: Environmental Conflicts and Initiatives in Latin America and the Caribbean*, Latin American Bureau, London.

Han Hoog, I. (1993), 'Reflections of a Founding Father', *CONCAWE Review*, 2 (2) (October), 4–5.

Harris, P. G. (1996), *Letter to WWF*, 19 April, Timber Trade Federation, London.

Harvey, P. (1997), personal communication, 30 November, International Labor Rights Fund, Washington DC.

Hecht, S. and A. Cockburn (1990), *The Fate of the Forest: Developers, Destroyers and Defenders of the Amazon*, Penguin, London.

Herkströter, C. A. J. (1996), 'Dealing with Contradictory Expectations – The Dilemmas Facing Multinationals', speech by the President of Royal Dutch Petroleum Company in Amsterdam, 11 October, Shell International, The Hague.

Hilowitz, J. (1997), 'Social Labelling to Combat Child Labour: Some Considerations', *International Labour Review*, 136 (2) (Summer), 215–32.

Himelstein, L. (1997), 'Nike Hasn't Scrubbed Its Image Yet', *Business Week*, 7 July, p. 44.

Humphreys, D. (1997), *Forest Politics: The Evolution of International Cooperation*, Earthscan, London.

ILO (1996), *Child Labour: Targeting the Intolerable*, ILO, Geneva.

—— (1997a), *Combating the Most Intolerable Forms of Child Labour: A Global Challenge*, report to the Amsterdam Child Labour Conference (26 and 27 February 1997), ILO, Geneva, January.

—— (1997b), 'Child Labour: How the Challenge Is Being Met', *International Labour Review*, 136 (2) (Summer), 233–57.

ILRF (1997), *Soccer Balls: Inflated with Hot Air?*, International Labor Rights Fund (ILRF), Washington DC.

Ito, M. and M. Loftus (1997), 'Cutting and Dealing: Asian Loggers Target the World's Remaining Rain Forests', *US News and World Report*, 10 March.

Johnston, B. R. (ed.) (1997), *Life and Death Matters: Human Rights and the Environment at the end of the Millennium*, AltaMira Press, California.

Lach, D. (1996), 'Introduction: Environmental Conflict', *Sociological Perspectives*, 39 (2), 211–17.

Long, F. J. and M. B. Arnold (1995), *The Power of Environmental Partnerships*, Dryden Press, Fort Worth, Texas.

Mackintosh, M. (1992), 'Partnership: Issues of Policy and Negotiation', *Local Economy*, 7 (3) (November), 210–24.

McKinsey and Co. (1992), *Building Successful Environmental Partnerships: A Guide for Prospective Partners for the President's Commission on Environmental Quality*, McKinsey and Co., New York.

Manes, C. (1990), *Green Rage*, Little, Brown and Company, Boston.

Marcus, R. (1997), personal communication with D. F. Murphy, 8 December, SCF, London.

MOSOP (1992), *Ogoni Bill of Rights*, Saros International, Port Harcourt, Nigeria.

Murphy, D. F. (1996), 'In the Company of Partners – Businesses, NGOs and Sustainable Development: Towards a Global Perspective', in R. Aspinwall and J. Smith (eds.), *Environmentalist and Business Partnerships: A Sustainable Model?*, The White Horse Press, Cambridge.

—— (1997a), 'Multi-enterprise Schemes for Corporate Social Responsibility', unpublished background paper, ILO, Geneva.

—— (1997b), 'Voluntary Codes of Conduct and Forests', policy brief prepared for the IUCN in relation to the United Nations Intergovernmental Panel on Forests, IUCN, Gland, Switzerland.

Murphy, D. F. and J. Bendell (1997), *In the Company of Partners: Business, Environmental Groups and Sustainable Development Post-Rio*, The Policy Press, Bristol.

Nando.net and Associated Press (1996), *Labor Controversy Tempers Nike's Big Day*, 17 September, Nando.net and Associated Press.

Newell, P. (1997a), 'A Changing Landscape of Diplomatic Conflict: The Politics of Climate Change Post-Rio', in F. Dodds (ed.), *The Way Forward: Beyond Agenda 21*, Earthscan, London.

—— (1997b), 'The International Politics of Global Warming: A Non-Governmental Account', unpublished PhD thesis, Keele University, Staffordshire, UK.

NGO Task Force on Business and Industry (1997), *Minding Our Business: The Role of Corporate Accountability in Sustainable Development*, an independent assessment submitted to the United Nations Commission on Sustainable Development, prepared by J. Barber, Integrative Strategies Forum, NGO Task Force on Business and Industry, Washington DC.

Repetto, R. and M. Gillis (1988), *Public Policies and the Misuse of Forest Resources*, Cambridge University Press, Cambridge.

Revkin, A. (1990), *The Burning Season: The Murder of Chico Mendes and the Fight for the Amazon Rain Forest*, Collins, London.

Roddick, A. (1995), 'Shell Should Speak Out to Help the Ogoni', *Financial Times*, 1 November.

Ross, I. (1997), 'New Ethics Code Is Just a Start', *The Globe and Mail*, 9 September, p. B17.

Rowell, A. (1995), 'Oil, Shell and Nigeria: Ken Saro-Wiwa Calls for a Boycott', *The Ecologist*, 25 (6) (November/December), 210–13.

—— (1996a), *Green Backlash: Global Subversion of the Environment Movement*, Routledge, London.

—— (1996b), 'Sleeping with the Enemy', *The Village Voice*, 23 January 1996.

Royal Dutch Shell Group (1969), 'Policy on Environmental Conservation', *Quality: The Bulletin of the Shell Committee for Environmental Conservation*, 1 (December), 1.

SCF (1997a), *A Labour of Necessity*, Save the Children (SCF), London.

—— (1997b), *Stitching Footballs: Voices of Children*, SCF, London.

Serrill, M. S. (1997), 'Ghosts of the Forest', *Time*, 150 (17A) (November Special Issue), 50–5.

Shell International (1995), 'Shell in Nigeria', briefing note, Shell International, London, December.

—— (1997), 'How Shell Does Business', www.shell.com, Shell International, Amsterdam.

Shell–UK (1995), *Brent Spar,* internal newsletter produced by Barkers Trident Communications on behalf of Shell UK Ltd, London.

Shrivastava, P. (1987), *Bhopal: Anatomy of a Crisis*, Ballinger, Cambridge, Mass.

Stea, D., S. Elguea and C. P. Bustillo (1997), 'Environment, Development and Indigenous Revolution in Chiapas', in B. R. Johnston (ed.), *Life and Death Matters: Human Rights and the Environment at the end of the Millennium,* AltaMiraPress, California.

Stewart, M and D. Snape (1996), 'Keeping up the Momentum: Partnership Working in Bristol and the West', an unpublished study for The Bristol Chamber of Commerce and Initiative.

SustainAbility (1996), *Strange Attractor: Business–ENGO Partnership. Strategic Review of BP's Relationships with Environmental Non-governmental Organisations*, summary of findings, July, SustainAbility, London.

The Economist (1998a), 'The Camisea Shock', *The Economist*, 4 April 1998.

—— (1998b), 'Seismic Shock from Camisea' *The Economist*, 25 July 1998.

Tippee, B. (ed.) (1997), *International Petroleum Encyclopaedia*, Penwell Publishing, Tulsa, Oklahoma.

UNICEF (1997), *State of the World's Children Report 1997*, Oxford University Press, Oxford.

United Nations (1997), πWWF/The World Bank, Press Release No. 97, 25 June, United Nations, New York.

UNPO (1995), *Ogoni: Report of the UNPO Mission to Investigate the Situation of the Ogoni of Nigeria February 17–26, 1995*, prepared by Richard Boele, Unrepresented Nations and Peoples Organisation (UNPO), The Hague.

Waddell, S. (1998), 'Market–Civil Society Partnership Formation: A Status Report on Activity, Strategies and Tools', *IDR Reports*, 13 (5), Institute for Development Research, Boston.

Waddock, S. (1988), 'Building Successful Social Partnerships', *Sloan Management Review* (Summer), 17–23.

Wadsworth, J. (1996), *Study on Markets and Market Segments for Certified Timber and Timber Products – ITTC(XX)/7 11 April 1996*, ITTO, Manila.

WBCSD (1996), *Towards a Sustainable Paper Cycle*, summary report of a study on the pulp and paper industry by IIED, commissioned by the World Business Council for Sustainable Development (WBCSD).

WFSGI (1996), *The Way Forward,* proceedings of the Conference on Human Rights (Verbier, Switzerland, 3 November 1995), Brassey's Sports for the Committee on Ethics and Fair Trade, World Federation of the Sporting Goods Industry (WFSGI), London.

Wood, D. and B. Gray (1991), 'Toward a Comprehensive Theory of Collaboration', *Journal of Applied Behavioral Science, 27* (2), 139–62.

10

Towards Civil Regulation

NGOs and the Politics
of Corporate Environmentalism

JEM BENDELL and DAVID F. MURPHY

(related) Countries   F23 452
M14 458
K32 013

Introduction

What is corporate environmentalism, *really*? What can it offer the many people in less industrialized countries, today and tomorrow, who seek secure and sustainable livelihoods? Is the idea of growing business responsibility for the environment of developing countries our common future, or our shared fallacy? In this book various perspectives on the extent, character and potential of corporate environmentalism have been presented. Some of the authors have stressed that it is largely a public relations exercise or 'greenwash', so that companies can continue to plunder the planet. Others have insisted that it is a real and rational business response to ecological constraints and market opportunities. The 'rational business response' argument suggests that corporate self-regulation is an adequate strategy for sustainability. The 'greenwash' argument demands greater legal compliance from business if environmental degradation is to be reversed. These diametrically opposed analyses have generated much heated debate on the issues of sustainable development, corporate regulation and global governance.

In contrast, the changing business response to NGOs, which we described in the previous chapter, cannot be explained adequately by either side of this debate. Corporations are increasingly being compelled to take action by civil society, not by government. These phenomena are examples of neither self-compliance nor legal compliance, and the evidence we have presented contributes neither to the 'rational business response' argument nor the 'greenwash' argument. However, it is important to remember that the instances of NGO-driven business responsibility for sustainable development are limited in both number and geographical scope. As in nearly all cases the force for change has come from well-financed Northern NGOs, the potential role of NGO-driven corporate environmentalism in the South is currently unclear.

This chapter investigates the potential for the wider replication of NGO-driven corporate environmentalism in developing countries. This is done by placing the initiatives described in Chapter 9 within the context of global processes, including the globalization of business, trade and finance, and advances in communications technologies. This leads us to develop a theory of how corporations are regulated for social and environmental goals in a globalizing economy and to chart appropriate corporate, NGO and governmental strategies.

Our argument is this. First, corporate responsibility for environmental protection is a political process. This is not to dismiss the commercial win–win arguments for environmental management, which are now well-established. Instead, we point out that many environmental management initiatives go beyond eco-efficiencies and tackle issues where financial outlay does not generate immediate returns. Second, civil society organizations are increasingly important actors in determining the political-economic context within which business must operate. These very diverse organizations, called NGOs, are linking globally through communications technology, and are able to generate ethical responses from consumers. Third, the emergence of consumer politics and the growth of these NGOs is allowing a new model of regulation to develop. Whereas the 'rational business response' and 'greenwash' analyses suggest policies of either self-compliance or legal compliance respectively, our analysis leads us to describe the phenomenon of 'civil compliance' – or what we will call *civil regulation*.

The Political Dimensions of Corporate Environmentalism

The Gramscian concept of hegemony is one theoretical framework which can be used to analyse the politics of corporate environmentalism. Antonio Gramsci (1988) argued that in most societies there is a coalition of groups that dominate social, political and economic expression. This coalition of business, government, professional and intellectual elites is interested in protecting the *status quo* and is therefore constantly managing and incorporating opposition into its 'hegemonic control'. Accordingly, if levels of environmental degradation become socially unacceptable and engender civil protest, then industry and other hegemonic groups must respond to maintain confidence in the current political-economic system.

Employing this framework, David Levy (1997) argues that most environmental management is an exercise in political, not environmental, sustainability. Levy draws upon evidence that much environmental management cannot be explained on a purely financial basis. Rather, environmental initiatives, projects and codes of conduct go further than narrow eco-efficiencies and therefore have a strong stakeholder relations – or political – element. This is environmental management as corporate responsibility. For example, environmental consultants at McKinsey and Co. believe 'win–win situations … are very rare and will likely be overshadowed by the total cost of a company's environmental program' (Walley and Whitehead, 1994: 46). In addition, research in a Northern context shows that corporate environmentalism is primarily motivated by regulatory and public pressure rather than opportunities for financial savings, competitive advantage, or green premiums (Ashford, 1993; Dillon and Fischer, 1992; Rappaport and Flaherty, 1992).

The industry response to tropical deforestation, described in Chapter 9, demonstrates a political motivation for corporate environmentalism. Although there is a strong business case for ensuring future supplies of timber, and therefore the conservation of productive forests, the commercial pressures posed by NGOs, such as boycotts, were more immediate and therefore more significant. Similarly, developments in the oil industry suggest that the political motivation for environmental management is becoming more widely recognized by company managers. Since the Brent Spar and Nigeria episodes, Shell's President wants the company to replace its 'technological arrogance' with a more cooperative approach, which recognizes that environmental issues are 'social and political dilemmas' with 'a range of possible answers' (Herkströter, 1996: 9). Similarly the chairman of BP now believes that society's concern about global warming provides enough justification for action even though there may be ongoing scientific disagreements about its causes and consequences (Browne, 1997). Whereas in the past a faith in science and certainty governed business decisions, the emerging approach of senior management in oil, timber and other international companies is to put people in the centre of the debate and therefore acknowledge the political nature of corporate environmentalism.

This political dimension of environmental management is reflected in the emerging emphasis on stakeholder management and the concept of social capital. The theory of stakeholder management says that companies can only succeed if they pay attention to all those who affect or are affected by the company's operations. This includes customers, staff, shareholders, suppliers, interest groups, local communities and regulators. Depending on the scale and impact of the business, even the entire population of Planet Earth may be seen as stakeholders in a company (Wheeler and Sillanpaa, 1997).

Whether it is the primary purpose of a business to satisfy its stakeholders or only to do this in order to maintain dividends for shareholders is widely disputed. Supporters of the former position generally recognize the importance of social capital – a valuation put on the business benefits of stakeholder management such as trust and motivation. Francis Fukuyama (1995) believes the economic value of trust is considerable and should be valued in the same way as other capital assets. Social capital is therefore a valuation of the ability of people in groups and organizations to work together for common purposes.

Many individuals involved in the business–NGO partnerships which we described earlier champion stakeholder consultation as a sound way of finding socially acceptable solutions to sustainable development issues and, therefore, of protecting social capital. Senior managers from wood-product retailers have committed their companies to meeting targets and implementing policies largely defined by WWF–UK. Executives in both Shell and BP have sought political and technical advice from many of their critics in their efforts to revise company policies and operational guidelines.

Many of the participants in business–NGO partnerships are known to the authors personally, and we can say that a fresh sense of purpose and optimism surrounds their partnership activities. However, stepping back from the specific initiatives, some commentators voice a concern about the political implications of what is occurring. From the Gramscian perspective mentioned earlier, Levy (1997) argues that the political nature of corporate environmentalism is worrying. The concern is that political expediency rather than environmental necessity determines environmental management. This produces a business-first attitude to environmental and social problems, which often undermines more fundamental approaches to environmental sustainability: '[Corporate environmentalism] can be understood as an integrated response on the practical and ideological levels that serves to deflect more radical challenges to the hegemonic coalition' (Levy 1997: 127).

The deflection of more radical approaches to environmental management is an issue that is addressed by Richard Welford (see Chapter 6 above and Welford, 1997). 'Ecomodernism', he argues, is becoming the dominant industry discourse on the environment, and it treats the environment as another technological problem to be overcome in the pursuit of progress. To the ecomodernist, pollution is an economic opportunity for prevention and clean-up technologies and certainly not an indication of fundamental problems with the current economic system.

Levy and Welford may take different approaches but arrive at the same conclusion – that corporate environmentalism embodies a strong political element. Levy believes environmental management to be an overtly political process as most companies actively go beyond eco-efficiency and deal with community and stakeholder issues. Welford believes environmental management's narrow focus on eco-efficiency marginalizes more comprehensive and ambitious sustainability management approaches.

We agree that environmental management is becoming a more political process, but not only because of business attempts at better stakeholder relations or because more radical discourses are being undermined. We believe that civil society organizations are also playing significant roles in promoting environmental and social management (Murphy and Bendell, 1997). The evidence of anti-logging, anti-oil and anti-child labour protests, presented in Chapter 9, illustrates that NGOs are increasingly setting the political agenda which business must work within. The challenge is therefore to seize the opportunities afforded by corporate environmental politics, not lament its existence. The next section describes the ways in which NGOs are playing this increasingly political role.

NGOs and the Politics of Pressure in a Globalizing Economy

The increasing size, notoriety and apparent uncontrollability of transnational corporations (TNCs), coupled with the spread of information technology, is leading to a new NGO-driven politics of pressure. In recent years these organizations, in both the North and South, have focused increasingly on the activities of TNCs and the sensitivities of consumers to ethical concerns. This development is the result of a number of factors, which we describe below.

The first dynamic is the emergence of the global economy and the perceived decline in the role of the nation state. The 1990s have seen the rapid development of global money markets. Private investment in the developing world spiralled from US$44 billion in 1990 to over US$167 billion in 1995 (World Bank, 1996). During the same period, official development assistance (ODA) fell slightly to a total of US$59 billion by 1995 (OECD DAC, 1996). Today private money is influencing the levels of environmental protection in the South as much as, if not more than, ODA.

> From an environmental perspective, how the hundreds of billions of private capital are spent matters far more than how the few billion dollars of official assistance devoted to environmental investments gets dispensed. (Esty and Gentry, 1997: 2)

The globalization of trade and finance may be proceeding apace but the globalization of governance is not. As capital and industry become increasingly large and mobile, the power of many national governments to set their own policy agenda has weakened (Korten, 1995; Camilleri and Falk, 1992). In a global market, if a TNC does not favour the policies of a particular government, it may choose to locate elsewhere, particularly if the country in question has a relatively small internal market. These types of investment decisions by TNCs are increasingly important as they control 33 per cent of the world's productive assets (UNRISD, 1995). If the international money markets anticipate a withdrawal by a number of TNCs, then confidence in a country's economic performance and therefore its currency may decline, leading to an economic downturn. Consequently governments have been involved in a process of competitive deregulation.

The second dynamic relates to the role that some major corporations are beginning to assume in the psyche of people in developed and developing countries. With global expansion, certain brands have become well known throughout the world. A brand image is an aggregate of the thoughts customers or investors associate with a particular company symbol, from a product logo to a stock market listing. Brand image has become so important that changes to it can have significant effects on company profitability or value. Environmental and social issues hold both positive and negative potentials for companies with global brand images. Meanwhile, many NGOs carry public opinion with them on environmental and social issues, which means they have the ability to affect corporate brand image in these areas.

A third dynamic is the development in telecommunications and information technology. The types of protests described in Chapter 9 remind us that information dissemination is crucial in allowing the development of NGO pressure politics. Global access to computers, fax machines, modems, satellite communications, solar-powered battery packs and hand-held video cameras has provided many civil society groups with greater knowledge, voice and power. Although the vast majority of the world's poor and powerless do not have direct access to information technology, growing numbers of NGOs and activist groups do. The flow of information around the world during political uprisings and following the disappearances or murders of notable campaigners lends added political weight to these events. 'Thanks to cyber-space, absolute control over information access is no longer possible' and atrocities can no longer be covered up easily (Johnston, 1997: 336). Gramsci (1988) argued that 'hegemonic power' is maintained as much by manufacturing consent through the media as it is by coercion or force. Absolute control over information is one of the keys to controlling thought and behaviour, as information influences and shapes cultural belief systems and legitimizes political authority. From this perspective, the communications revolution is fundamental to the power of civil society.

In the North, the lack of government capacity and will to effect change coupled with the iconic nature of major corporations and the communications revolution is providing NGOs with added reason to focus on corporate practice. This development in strategy is part of 'third wave environmentalism' for environmental NGOs and the social market movement for development NGOs (Murphy and Bendell, 1997). In the South, NGOs have also begun to focus on the market. There are similar reasons for this change in focus. First, in many countries progress through lobbying their own governments has been difficult, whether they are democratic or not. The pressures of foreign debt and structural adjustment programmes often limit the scope of governments to act on ethical issues such as environmental protection and fair pay. Second, intergovernmental agencies have been slow to act, dis-illusioning groups in the South in the same way as is happening in the North. Third, Northern NGOs have begun to reach out to Southern groups and involve them in new market-oriented campaigns. For example, the World Development Movement in the United Kingdom often sponsors and organizes visits by Southern campaigners. These initiatives are facilitated by the communications technologies mentioned above.

Focusing on corporations and the market is also natural to many Southern campaigners. Many are fighting for economic justice as well as environmental justice and have identified the activities of certain corporations as the problem from the outset. The MOSOP campaign against Shell in Nigeria is one example of a Southern movement that linked environmental degradation, economic hardship and social exclusion as negative outcomes of irresponsible business behaviour. This presentation allowed the campaign to appeal to activists, as well as Shell's customers and investors, in Europe. The focus on markets is also illustrated by the international campaign of the Tupinikim and Guarani. Fearing that the Brazilian government will be swayed by the financial pressures and opportunities associated with a decision on Aracruz Cellulose access to indigenous lands, the Indians have appealed to European markets for support.

Given increasing concern with and ability to affect market behaviour, civil society organizations have developed a number of tools to change corporate policy. This is leading to new forms of market-oriented activity by NGOs, activist and community groups. Consequently there is now a wider spectrum of relations between companies and NGOs, from direct action protest to dialogue and partnership. One of the best known market-oriented NGO tactics is the corporate boycott. Boycotts of sports goods companies such as Nike, timber retailers such as B & Q and oil companies such as Shell have prompted them to take seriously the ethical concerns of the public. The growing NGO support for ethical investment, in which investments are screened against social and environmental criteria, is also a form of systematic boycotting of 'unethical' company shares. Although these tactics have worldwide implications, they do not appear to be a viable option for NGOs in countries where consumer and investment power is less influential.

A second confrontational tactic of NGOs is direct action protest, where groups deliberately sabotage the commercial operations of a company. In the South, the forest peoples of the Oriente in Ecuador have on numerous occasions blocked the building of new roads by the oil company ARCO (Collinson, 1996). In the North, activist attendance at annual shareholder meetings to demonstrate or table controversial motions is another form of direct action protest, which has affected companies such as Shell.

A third tactic is collaboration, as evidenced in the partnership initiatives, described in Chapter 9, in the timber, oil and sports goods industries. Similar partnerships are developing in other industry sectors, relating to other social or environmental problems. In 1996 WWF–International launched a partnership with Unilever Corporation, the world's largest buyer of frozen fish, to create economic incentives within the seafood industry for sustainable fishing throughout the world. The new Marine Stewardship Council (MSC) is the result of their endeavours. The Fairtrade Foundation, a coalition of international development, consumer and fair trade organizations, has launched a pilot project to work with British companies to develop codes of practice to guide relationships with their Southern suppliers. These partnerships differ from previous collaborations based on corporate charity, as the NGOs are helping business with internal operational issues. NGOs are increasingly involved in the development of systems which imply civil regulation; these include multi-stakeholder-agreed and independently verified codes of conduct for ethical business practice, such as the Forest Stewardship Council (FSC) system.

With a variety of campaigning tools at their disposal, NGOs – North and South – are creating a new politics of pressure to which business must respond. In her review of the state of the environment and human rights at the end of the millennium, Barbara Rose Johnston concludes that:

> Perhaps the strongest evidence of progressive political change is found in the informal 'civic organization' sector, where the ability to organize, communicate, create networks, and form coalitions has meant the emergence of a political force whose power and impact cannot be overstated. (1997: 332)

The emergence of this new political force demands more analysis in order to understand the true extent of its power and impact. A comparison with the characteristics of political movements in the past may throw some light on the subject.

From Producer Politics to Consumer Politics

It is widely understood that worker unrest with factory owners and other capitalists in most Northern industrialized countries at the turn of the last century led to the establishment and legal protection of trade unions and a democratic political force for workers. This was an incorporation of worker demands that served to head off the kind of revolutions against capitalism that occurred in some other countries. Critics of capitalism argued for the development of a 'producer politics' where workers unite in order to control capitalist access to labour. The social democracies that emerged from this period embodied the notion that capitalism worked best if there was a counterbalancing force to capitalists through strong government and trade unions: capitalists needed the workers while workers, it was argued, needed the capitalists.

This social democratic system has led to, or coincided with, a huge expansion of many economies during the twentieth century. At the close of the century this balance has been lost. Governments pursuing neoliberal policies have largely rejected the social democratic model, internally by rolling back the state and externally by promoting international free trade. Trade union power and influence have also declined. The result is that global business does not have an effective counter-balancing force of globally organized producers. Increasingly the offer of the lowest pay and working conditions wins the capitalist investment.

Meanwhile, in most Northern countries, work has changed. People are changing jobs more quickly than before. Family members no longer do what their parents did. Personal identity is not determined so much by one's work but increasingly by how one spends one's money and spare time. Thus the most recent political issues of our time are leading to different outcomes. In Western industrialized countries, environmental concern has not led to workers uniting to demand better corporate performance; instead, consumers do so. Whereas the establishment of trade unions and powerful political parties incorporated the workers' movement, the establishment of NGOs has incorporated the environmental movement. Usually supported by financial donations and voluntary labour, NGOs are the organizational expression of 'consumer politics'.

Whereas producer politics gained its power through controlling access to labour, consumer politics gains its power through controlling access to customers. Corporate boycotts and direct action protests are the confrontational outcomes of consumer politics, in contrast to the strikes and lock-outs of producer politics. Business–NGO partnerships are the cooperative tools of consumer politics, in contrast to the business–union deals of producer politics. Whether consumer politics can exert the same counterbalancing force as producer politics did in the past is still open to question. Business needs both workers and consumers. Consumers and workers both need business. The power of the worker resulted in a dialogue between employer and worker organizations. It seems that the power of the consumer will result in a dialogue between business and NGOs (consumer and environmental groups).

The scope for genuine environmental dialogue comes down to power and influence. Certain groups of consumers (and their advocates) do not have the same power as other consumers. Consumer power is directly related to spending power. In consumer politics it is one dollar one vote, not one person one vote. This poses major problems for people with little, or no, consumer power: citizens of Southern countries have far less of this political power than their counterparts in the North. At first sight, this suggests that there are fundamental constraints on the ability of consumer politics – and therefore civil regulation – to ensure business responsibility for environmental protection in the South.

However, we must remember that, with producer politics, power is not gained by an individual's worth as a worker but through collective action and collective bargaining. Thus cooperation and camaraderie between civil society in the North (especially consumers) and in the South (including producers) may be able to deliver the necessary counterbalance to international business and create a favourable socio-economic environment for sustainable development. We return to this point later.

Legal Compliance or Self-Compliance? Beyond the Dilemma

In the face of increasingly powerful consumer politics in most Northern countries, many companies are beginning to introduce new environmental and social policies for their operations in Southern countries. These initiatives range from codes of conduct and certification schemes to purchasing policies and partnerships. As noted earlier, Shell has added support for human rights and sustainable development to its Statement of General Business Principles. BP is collaborating with a group of British development NGOs to improve its social and environmental performance in Colombia. Wood product retailers throughout Western Europe and North America are committing themselves to sourcing only from FSC-certified forests. Leading sporting goods companies are working to eliminate the use of child labour in the production of soccer balls in Pakistan. Many other examples of new corporate environmental and social policies affecting the South can be found in other industrial sectors, including chemicals, clothing and food production.

Many would characterize these changes as evidence of the self-compliance agenda – a second-stage business response to sustainable development which is currently the dominant paradigm of environmental management. Self-compliance is championed as a way of promoting sustainable development by allowing flexibility in addressing environmental issues and by creating incentives for environmental innovations (WBCSD, 1997). However, self-compliance is criticized by both environmentalists and academics for not going far enough and for being used by industry as a means of discouraging new environmental legislation (Welford, 1997; FoE–UK, 1995). The United Nations Research Institute for Social Development (UNRISD) has also voiced these concerns, contending that 'international business cannot be expected to author their own regulation: this is the job of good governance' (UNRISD, 1995: 154 and 19).

We do not believe that all corporate environmental initiatives which are not demanded by governments are 'voluntary'. Certainly, some of the impetus for the changes is coming from the business community itself, through organizations such as the World Business Council for Sustainable Development (WBCSD) and the International Chamber of Commerce. Key individuals within companies are also playing instrumental roles in the change process. However, we believe it is the catalytic roles of Northern and Southern NGOs as business provocateurs and partners that are driving these changes.

Northern NGOs are playing major roles in challenging the environmental and social impacts of Northern-based businesses operating in the South. Greenpeace International has been one of the leading NGOs in the worldwide campaign against Shell's activities in Nigeria. Key Northern catalysts for public awareness of the destruction of tropical forests included: Rainforest Action Groups in the United Kingdom, USA and Australia, Friends of the Earth groups in the United Kingdom and Netherlands, and numerous other grassroots campaign groups throughout Western Europe. On the partnership front, WWF–International, with numerous national affiliates, has been the lead collaborator with business on forest-product certification and labelling. Likewise, SCF-UK and Oxfam-UK have been the first development NGOs to embrace partnership with sporting goods manufacturers and clothing retailers respectively.

The process of 'civilizing' global corporations also depends upon the active participation of Southern NGOs. On both social and environmental fronts, Southern NGOs have raised global awareness through their activism and networking. Only when rain forest protests by Southern trade unions and NGOs encountered a violent backlash during the 1980s did the deforestation issue gain greater prominence in the international political arena. The work of the Tupinikim and Guarani and the subsequent media attention in Norway shows the power of Southern activists to transform local struggles for land rights and conservation in the South into tangible consumer and political issues in the North.

Our argument is that these initiatives represent the emergence of a new form of regulation for international corporations which might be called civil regulation. Civil regulation occurs where organizations of civil society, such as NGOs, set the standards for business behaviour. Companies must then choose to adopt or not to adopt these standards. For those that adopt the standards a number of commercial and non-commercial benefits become available (credible marketing, staff motivation, etcetera). Those companies that choose not to adopt these standards can expect to come up against the confrontational tactics of consumer politics as deployed by civil society (boycotts or direct action, for example), with deleterious effects on company sales, costs and social capital. Whereas government fines for pollution violations now rarely affect company value, consumer politics brings greater financial risks. Although governments may have the purported monopoly on force – and therefore the 'final say' – in reality the ability of civil society organizations to regulate business behaviour through financial carrots and sticks is rapidly becoming more powerful.

In our discussion of the politics of corporate environmentalism in the previous chapter, our intention was to question the current stand-off between those who argue that environmental management is a rational business response and those who argue that it is only greenwash. In putting forward a theory of civil regulation, we aim to move the debate on effective corporate policy responses to sustainable development from the current self-compliance versus legal compliance dilemma to something more empowering. We believe that conceiving of corporate environmentalism as a political process – and seeing the changing relations between businesses and NGOs as the emergence of civil regulation – offers new policy opportunities for businesses, NGOs and governments, which may vary depending on whether they are based in the industrialized North or less-industrialized South. In the following sections of this chapter we turn to these policy options.

The Case for Civil Regulation

The fact that partnerships between businesses and NGOs are increasing rapidly is evidence in itself that there are strong commercial and campaigning reasons for civil regulation. In the following section we describe some of the benefits and some of the problems for participating businesses and NGOs, North and South.

The corporate rationale for civil regulation

We believe there is a strong business case for welcoming the emergence of civil regulation. Many managers, campaigners or governmental officials following social and environmental issues in the world today would recognize that there is a global race to the bottom of environmental and social regulation. While profitability may rise in the short term as a result of lax regulation, this is not a stable social climate for business in the longer term. Civil unrest in the South can be understood as a reaction to the inadequacy of the state and to corporate malfeasance.

Individual companies cannot respond to this emerging social and environmental crisis alone. To do so, for example, by unilaterally pulling out of a gas development project in Peru, might affect investor confidence in the competitiveness of the company. If companies collaborate to improve environmental and social standards, they may succeed in creating a more favourable business climate in the long term. To achieve this, business requires an external force which can push reluctant companies forward. In the twenty-first century it does not appear that governments will have sufficient capacity to play this role. Instead, intergovernmental bodies and civil society organizations must take on greater responsibility for maintaining a level playing field. This is the business case for new global governance mechanisms and, consequently, civil regulation.

Managers are beginning to recognize this need for an external force to drive all companies towards improved environmental and social management. For example, BP's Chris Marsden has said that if Greenpeace didn't exist, BP would need to invent it, and that overall 'there is a major part to be played by NGOs, interest groups, local communities and public sector bodies in helping companies to make their best possible contribution to the well-being of society as well as to their shareholders' (Marsden, 1997, personal communication). This 'help' can take the form of protest or partnership.

Given that the costs of confrontation are so high, especially when boycotts are involved, a number of companies are seeking constructive engagement with NGOs. There are many reasons why partnerships with NGOs are becoming an increasingly popular strategy for companies in the North. Understanding these reasons may give some indication of whether there will be new opportunities for partnership in the South. The reasons for working with Northern NGOs broadly relate to environmental public relations, eco-efficiency and organizational learning. We cover each in turn.

For reasons of marketing, recruitment, employee motivation and risk management (preventing store boycotts and protecting share prices), it is prudent to cultivate the public impression of a socially and environmentally responsible business in a society with established consumer politics. The need for credibility is one factor. A study by the Investor Responsibility Research Centre (IRRC) for the Global Environmental Management Initiative (GEMI), *Environmental Reporting and Third Party Statements*, outlines how environmental reports and claims by companies continue to suffer from a credibility gap in the eyes of a variety of stakeholders

(SustainAbility, NEF and UNEP, 1996). 'Faced with this credibility challenge, active dialogue and stakeholder partnerships assume unprecedented importance' (*ibid.*: 21).

Northern retailers of products from Southern countries are particularly in need of credible information to reassure consumers. Credibility comes from independent standards and assessment. Government or NGO involvement is therefore required. The case study of retailers of tropical timber products presented in Chapter 9 illustrates this point clearly. Companies such as B & Q faced a crisis of credibility over their environmental performance as consumers became aware of both rain forest destruction and the early attempts at greenwash by a number of retailers. Neither the British nor the Dutch government was able to provide suitable policy alternatives to empower retailers to respond to consumer concerns.

By working with NGOs, some companies are generating a level of interest in their environmental policies which hitherto has been experienced only by the likes of the eco-conscious Body Shop. The experience of many companies in the WWF–UK 1995 Group was that partnership with one NGO helped to reduce the attention of other NGOs. This has not been the experience of BP, which continues to face direct action from Greenpeace even while it engages development NGOs on other fronts. For the most part, however, collaboration with NGOs helps business to promote an environmentally responsible public image.

In addition to these benefits there are the more 'non-political' benefits which should not be overlooked. Financial and natural resource savings – or eco-efficiencies – can be achieved through partnership with NGOs. Companies in the 1995 Group saved on expensive consultancy fees by working with WWF–UK. With complex supply chains and often strained buyer–supplier relations, DIY retailers have benefited (and continue to benefit) greatly from WWF–UK's free advice in implementing their forest product sourcing and certification programmes. Similarly various sporting goods companies and their trade association WFSGI are learning from child welfare and labour standards experts with SCF–UK and ILO. Despite its ongoing problems with Greenpeace in the United Kingdom, BP is no doubt gaining a much needed critical perspective on its role in Colombia via the Interagency Group of British NGOs.

The Shell case, referred to earlier, reminds us that huge TNCs with a variety of subsidiaries have a major internal governance challenge. Newly adopted or revised policies relating to environmental protection, stakeholder management and social capital will take time to be implemented at the operational level. The global network of NGOs may be able to help by introducing managers of subsidiaries to new ideas and ways of working. This brings us to another important benefit of partnership for participating businesses which relates to organizational learning. If profit-making organizations are to meet growing social and environmental demands, they will need to undergo profound organizational change. Corporate strategies need to consider fundamental questions such as 'Who really needs this product?' and 'Will the community be healthy and prosperous enough to produce and to buy our products in the future?' In order to address such concerns, business needs to work with other sectors of society. A collaborative approach to solving the social and environmental problems caused by business may be the most progressive and relevant organizational learning strategy of all. By embracing partnership strategies, business and NGOs have the potential to define the future of private enterprise.

For companies based in the South, the benefits of partnership and proactive support for civil regulation are less clear. Further research is needed on the potential benefits of working collaboratively with local community groups, national and international NGOs. In addition, research could focus on the success of privately owned companies as opposed to worker cooperatives founded upon partnership principles. In the absence of this research, we can only speculate on the potential benefits for Southern companies.

First, there is a very real possibility that governments faced with illegal enterprise will license more foreign companies to exploit national resources. This is already happening in Latin America where, faced with illegal logging and mining, governments are turning to international corporations to exploit resources and police the concessions licensed to them. The governments concerned anticipate that these corporations will have better environmental management policies than national companies – due in part to pressure from northern NGOs. Southern companies may, nevertheless, be better placed to understand local communities and to develop more appropriate sustainability management policies than their Northern counterparts.

Second, growing numbers of Southern companies export to Northern countries. With increased market awareness in the North about the social and environmental performance of Southern suppliers, there are new commercial threats and opportunities. If Southern suppliers fail to adopt environmental management policies or to improve factory conditions, for example, they may lose major contracts. On the other hand, if Southern companies work with local and international NGOs on improving performance they may secure longer-term contracts and higher or more stable prices.

Third, by collaborating with NGOs, companies may be able to access new sources of finance. The recent commitment of the World Bank to lend millions of dollars to forestry companies that seek independent certification suggests that in the future sources of finance may be tied to demonstrable sustainable development management policies. Partnerships with civil society are a way of proving this commitment.

Fourth, local communities have a lot to offer global and national business. Local resources, both human and natural, are essential ingredients in a long-term commercial strategy. Companies have much to gain by encouraging the active participation of local people as company employees, suppliers, sub-contractors, customers and other beneficiaries. Despite the limited development of consumer politics in the South, there are also considerable business benefits in maintaining good community relations. To earn a reputation as a good corporate citizen, companies are expected to provide financial and material assistance to community development projects. As the experience of Shell in Ogoniland aptly illustrates, poor corporate community relations can lead local people and activist groups to obstruct and sabotage business activities.

It would be unwise to give the impression that the emergence of civil regulation provides only opportunities for the companies who respond positively. However, the business pitfalls with civil regulation are less easy to identify at present. The main problem for management in adopting a principle of complying with civil society is that it is difficult to know what the full implications may be. Business may find itself restricted by the often commercially unaware nature of campaigning groups, as illustrated by certain companies' frustration with the slow, cumbersome nature of the FSC decision-making process. Major soccer brands such as Umbro and Mitre and their Pakistani suppliers may eventually become impatient with the potentially bureaucratic nature of the monitoring and verification programme, particularly if it becomes too expensive and difficult to implement.

One of the major problems facing business is that NGOs have very different campaign strategies and priorities. As the impetus for civil regulation grows, no doubt competing or contradictory schemes will emerge from a growing list of potential NGO partners. Even if the end result is a long list of schemes on different themes, difficult choices lie ahead. Company X may find itself fully complying with Scheme A, while failing to making the grade on Scheme B. A related problem is that some civil regulation schemes may make uncompromising demands which prove to be incompatible with the commercial objectives of most companies.

Even if a company manages to collaborate successfully with NGOs, it risks being undercut by other companies that are not pursuing the same management agenda. The benefits of civil regulation will only be realized if NGOs and activist groups are able to organize, obstruct and protest when a company fails to perform. In political systems where civil liberties are not ensured, companies can silence their critics and externalize more costs than companies pursuing civil regulation strategies. In practice, the same is often the case with regulation. Companies which choose to obey the law while other companies evade it may face a commercial disadvantage. In some contexts and countries it makes better commercial sense to pay a small fine in order to realize a larger financial gain. However, in principle, legislation applies to all companies whereas civil regulation remains voluntary and seems unlikely to achieve universal commitment.

The NGO rationale for civil regulation

In outlining civil regulation as a new system of regulation, we do not mean to imply that there is a universal awareness of this system by campaigners working for NGOs with business-oriented campaigns. Unfortunately there is little appreciation of how the confrontational and collaborative campaigns of NGOs on a diverse set of single issues, North and South, are together providing a new context for international trade. With the increasing power and diversifying roles of NGOs there is a need for campaigners to acknowledge the links between confrontation and collaboration, between environment and development and between North and South.

Despite the rise of global NGO networks since Rio, there remains a surprising lack of understanding between the Northern environmental movement and local communities in the South. Many initiatives by Northern NGOs have been unable to overcome the environment–development or North–South divide. Northern conservation groups are still accused of ignoring indigenous people's needs; one example of this is the establishment of national parks which have expelled people from their former homelands (Anderson, 1988). The FSC, for example, was founded with the aim of promoting socially beneficial forest management. Four years after its formation, however, membership by development NGOs and trade unions is almost non-existent, with Northern environmental groups continuing to dominate. In addition, Southern representation has yet to exceed 25 per cent of the total membership. Conversely, many Northern-based development NGOs, working on a variety of different issues and in different countries, have not yet fully integrated environmental issues into their work.

The absence of a holistic NGO vision of sustainable development may restrict the pursuit of a comprehensive strategy for greater corporate responsibility. This should be of particular concern to environmental groups in the North: 'Making the environmental movement something more than a dim reflection of developed country environmental concerns will only happen once the immediate impact of environmental degradation on peoples' daily lives is addressed' (Kaimowitz, 1996: 31).

For civil regulation to become a powerful progressive force for environmental sustainability and social justice, different NGOs pursuing different campaigning tactics must maintain their links. Those involved in business partnerships should seek transparency with the wider NGO movement. As noted in Chapter 9, civil regulation requires confrontation as well as cooperation. Grassroots action will remain important in pushing business towards greater responsibility for environmental protection and social development. Protest is crucial for the empowerment of civil society, for stopping malpractice by alerting governments and citizens, and for reforming business towards sustainability by promoting the adoption of more effective environmental and social policies.

Partnerships are also crucial for effective civil regulation, particularly where they lead to systems of multi-stakeholder and independently verified codes of responsible business practice. This is how NGOs can help harness consumer support for environmental goals. Despite its many limitations, a more sustainable form of consumerism represents one way in which individuals can express their concern for the environment and promote positive change. By becoming involved in the development of consumer information systems and eco-labelling, we believe NGOs have the potential to restore consumer confidence in environmentally preferable products and hence the consumer's sense of agency. This may help to politicize the market in favour of sustainability goals and ensure that consumer concern is translated into substantial social and environmental improvements. As noted earlier, NGOs can also play a validating role for voluntary initiatives, thereby lending them added credibility and the necessary 'bite' to deliver more substantial change in business behaviour.

Dialogue and partnership with business is also a catalyst for the greater environmental education of society. Business managers, who may never previously have engaged constructively with sustainability issues, are now doing so. Given their global reach and commercial power, many corporations can reach far more people than an individual NGO. By promoting their environmental policies to customers and staff, they are teaching many people more about the role of business in solving environmental and social problems. In addition, the demonstration of workable partnership solutions can be an effective means of encouraging governments to pursue innovative policy alternatives. This need for new models is essential, given the apparent reluctance and/or inability of governments to introduce new and stronger environmental laws or to ensure compliance with existing legislation.

Business–NGO partnerships concerned with core business practices are a new phenomenon, one with which most NGOs are unfamiliar. Therefore partnerships with business present a number of strategic problems for NGOs. In the various forest-related partnerships outlined earlier, almost no attempt has been made to develop systems to evaluate the partnership's direct contribution to the achievement of specific environmental goals. Today the main quantitative analyses of an NGO's success are based upon membership levels and the extent of media coverage. Third-wave environmentalists need new ways to judge performance. Indicators such as 'the percentage reduction in waste per dollar spent' or 'the acres of forest saved per dollar invested' are required if we are truly to know the full costs and benefits of business partnerships for participating NGOs.

Some of these concerns appear to be addressed within other initiatives. Although it is too early to evaluate the Pakistan soccer ball partnership, the project's plans include both monitoring and verification of industry compliance and a wide range of social protection activities for children, their families and local communities. SCF–UK appears to have been instrumental in ensuring that the project will not just phase out child labour, but meet important social development needs as well.

This leads to another concern with business–NGO partnerships – the opportunity costs. With an increasing amount of time and finance spent on working with business, other means of achieving environmental and social goals, such as litigation or strengthening government capacity, may be compromised. In addition, media work may focus increasingly on the general public's role as green or ethical consumers rather than on the commitment of citizens to conservation, social justice and sustainable communities.

Then there is the question of independence. A concern of NGOs is the danger of being co-opted by business to improve the image of the company selling a certified and labelled product endorsed, directly or indirectly, by the NGO. There is a concern that single-issue partnerships may prevent NGOs from publicly criticizing their business partners on other social or environmental matters. In the case study on the sporting goods industry, described in the previous chapter, SCF–UK rejected invitations by the industry to become involved in a labelling scheme as it did not want to endorse a company's 'child-free' soccer balls while the same company continues to sell other unethical products. This example reflects a widely held belief on the part of many NGOs and activists that tools such as certification and labelling are too incremental and fail to address the underlying causes of social injustice and environmental degradation.

The Potential of Civil Regulation for the South

Much of the evidence provided for the emergence of civil regulation as a driver of corporate responsibility for environmental protection in the South involves Northern NGOs and transnational business. Although many of the corporate responses to environmental issues have occurred as a result of protest by groups and communities in the South, the role of Northern NGOs in facilitating civil regulation has been key. We have argued that in most cases it is consumer politics in Northern industrialized markets which compels companies to take action. Therefore one must question the potential for civil regulation to be replicated in different countries, particularly for businesses involved in domestic or international trade where the market does not feature well-developed consumer politics.

There are some signs that consumer politics is beginning to penetrate parts of the non-Western world. A joint Chile/Japan project to educate Japanese consumers about the problems with the woodchip trade is one example. Another is the growth of national eco-labelling schemes in Taiwan, Japan and South Korea. These examples suggest that some progress is being made in building consumer and corporate awareness in these key markets. However, there is much evidence to the contrary. In the case of forestry, Northern business support for the FSC has not stopped Asian companies with poor management practices from increasing their logging activities in tropical forests. The growing demand for timber in the emerging economies does not appear to be matched by growing consumer politics. Even as Northern-based companies in other sectors develop higher social and environmental standards for their operations in the South, their Asian or Latin American competitors are likely to continue to cut corners when supplying Southern markets. This means that civil regulation, as expressed through certification and labelling schemes, may merely serve to shift international trading patterns and have little effect on environmental protection or sustainable development in the South.

Despite the limited extent of consumer politics, Southern NGOs are beginning to become involved directly in civil regulation schemes (rather than contributing, through protest and conflict, to civil regulation administered by Northern NGOs). The case of Shell approaching the Peruvian NGO Red Ambiental Peruana (RAP) to monitor its operations in the Camisea region suggests that the civil regulation model is beginning to emerge in the South. At the same time, however, many other NGOs, activist groups and indigenous peoples' organizations continue to challenge Shell's activities in Nigeria and Peru. More research is needed on the capacity and desire of Southern NGOs to take on such monitoring roles.

More research on business response to citizen action in the South is also necessary. Charles Reilly's review of Latin American NGOs notes 'complex sets of national and international relationships' but offers no examples of formal business–NGO collaboration (1995: 248). However, Brian Loveman suggests that 'environmentally focused NGOs' in Chile are more likely to 'make demands upon government and nongovernmental actors (e.g. business) as a lobby ... or interest group' (1995: 126).

Throughout much of the South, many differences still remain between the commitment and capacity of national as opposed to global business on environmental matters. A 1995 survey on public perceptions of economic reforms conducted by the Consumer Unity and Trust Society in India and Nepal 'came across a universal opinion, notwithstanding Bhopal, that TNCs are better at environmental management than domestic entrepreneurs, because of their track record and circumstances at home' (Mehta, 1997, personal communication).

This seems logical, given our argument that much of the impetus for corporate environmentalism comes from the growing strength of civil society and consumer politics in the North. Where there is limited demand for environmental responsibility in the home nation, companies are more likely to continue to behave irresponsibly. It could be said that the forest communities of Papua New Guinea and other South Pacific countries are suffering the consequences of limited environmental awareness and consumer politics in Malaysia, Indonesia and Japan.

Meanwhile, most Southern NGOs continue to have little or no experience of cooperative relations with big business, either national or global. There is also little evidence in the literature of Southern business embracing civil society as allies. Mutual prejudices will take time to overcome. Nicanor Perlas, co-chair for civil society on the Philippine Council for Sustainable Development, explains that

> The thawing of the lines between business and civil society is fairly recent. Bridges are still being built. Trust is still being developed. Common policy agendas are still being nurtured. It may be sometime before actual partnerships emerge. (Perlas, 1997, personal communication)

In a similar vein, Miguel de Oliveira and Rajesh Tandon believe that 'in the countries of the South, NGOs ... have so far had little contact with the emerging initiatives of corporate philanthropy' (1994: 3). As and when Southern businesses expand their efforts in the areas of corporate community involvement and environmental protection, Southern NGOs and base groups may find themselves in the company of new partners.

In addition to developing collaborative relations with industry, civil society needs to perform its watchdog role competently. However, the ability to organize, take direct action and speak loudly and freely is seldom protected by government. In many countries, governments actively undermine NGO efforts to take on these roles:

> The recent murders of green activists in Honduras, Colombia and even Costa Rica (a country which prides itself on its environmental awareness) are reminders that

environmental campaigns can strike at the heart of political and corporate power. (Collinson, 1996: 1)

Without the ability to wield the 'stick', southern NGOs and communities will not be able to realize the benefits of civil regulation. Helen Collinson argues that the main failure here is the inability of governments to exercise responsible force:

> One reason why Latin American environmental campaigners are more vulnerable than their fellow activists in Europe or North America is that Latin America's democratic and judicial institutions are still weak and protesters often have limited recourse to the law. (1996: 1)

This reminds us that NGOs do not have the same power as governments, as they do not have a universal monopoly on the use of force. They do not have the ability to impose fines or other penalties. The power of NGOs lies in the use of the marketplace to boycott a company's products, affect its staff morale or investor confidence. This market power is usually limited to societies with well-organized consumer politics. It also depends on the ability of NGOs to communicate their message effectively to consumers and this usually requires substantial resources. Where NGOs do not have sufficient financial and communications resources, they may be constrained in their capacity to use the 'stick' of consumer boycotts or mobilizing dissent. This may not be only a matter of limited access to information technology. Unlike many large Northern NGOs, most Southern NGOs do not have the in-house public relations capacity to challenge slick corporate PR campaigns, such as Burson-Marsteller's efforts to undermine the indigenous peoples' campaign against Aracruz Cellulose.

It appears, then, that for Southern NGOs to become active in civil regulation they need to be linked with supportive NGOs in countries with developed consumer politics. The Shell Nigeria example also reminds us that Southern campaigning on its own is not always effective in changing corporate practices. Protests by local Delta communities against the operations of Shell began in the late 1980s. Shell's responsibility for the plight of the Ogoni became an issue for consumer politics in the North much later. Global civil society alliances backed up by activist companies and attentive media are also key determinants of effective NGO campaigning and civil regulation.

The need for North–South alliances between NGOs is an indication of the democratic deficit Southern civil society currently faces with civil regulation mechanisms. The cases examined in the previous chapter demonstrate that the power to regulate corporate activity in the South resides in the North. To influence the behaviour of global corporations or their subsidiaries, Southern civil society must make contact with Northern civil society in order to project Southern grievances and alternatives. Many Southern NGO campaigners argue that Northern NGOs impose solutions on them, demonstrating an approach which could be described as ethical imperialism. In order to overcome this problem, Southern NGO participation in policy development must be facilitated. This poses a logistical and financial challenge that many Northern NGOs appear reluctant to meet. However, as the civil regulation agenda develops, more questions will be asked of Northern NGOs relating to their legitimacy in negotiating on behalf of developing country communities: unlike pandas and whales, people can speak for themselves. Therefore NGOs seeking greater legitimacy for collaborative business campaigns will require greater Southern civil society input in the future.

Despite the many concerns about the limits of civil regulation outlined above, this new policy instrument holds some promise for reducing the social and ecological footprint of Northern economies on the rest of the world. Other complementary measures will no doubt be needed to regulate companies in the future, particularly those based in the South. Although many political battles may lie ahead, particularly in multilateral bodies such as the WTO, the ILO and the United Nations Commission on Sustainable Development, there is growing recognition of the need for a wider range of regulatory tools to monitor corporate performance on social and environmental matters.

Governmental Policy Frameworks for Civil Regulation

As mentioned earlier, governments are finding it difficult to provide a regulatory function in a global economy. The declining desire and capacity of the state to regulate, police and enforce is well illustrated in the case of deforestation. Against a history of land disputes and illegal logging, in 1997 both the Brazilian and Venezuelan governments announced that they would privatize forests in order to conserve them. The assumption is that major international corporations have greater resources than governments to police forest management in their concessions. There are concerns that the governments may not be able to regulate such companies effectively. It seems likely that the 'regulatory' power of NGOs will be required to ensure that irresponsible forest management is not taking place. In this section, we consider the role of governments in civil regulation and the need for supportive policy frameworks at the national and international levels.

Government as facilitator

There is a range of opinion on the role of government in promoting greater business responsibility for environmental protection in the South. As the role of NGOs in greening business is closely related to the inability of governments to regulate effectively on environmental and social matters, a number of NGOs may be tempted to ignore what government has to offer. The go-it-alone attitude can be found in the new fourth-generation NGO strategies, which include a focus on building capacity in the NGO sector for facilitating sustainable development (Korten, 1990). The broad NGO coalition now arguing against an international forest convention for reasons roughly summarized as 'it would be a distraction' is one example of this new thinking in civil society. Many of their partners in industry believe that the role of legislation is a limited one and that market-based mechanisms should prevail. However, a number of managers of companies involved in business–NGO partnerships do not believe that partnerships and voluntary initiatives should replace flexible and efficient legislation.

We believe that governments and intergovernmental bodies should actively promote global social and environmental responsibility in the business sector. To begin with, governments could support the ability of their citizens to promote civil regulation. This could be achieved by strengthening civil society through protecting the ability of people to organize, to speak freely, to protest and to suggest alternatives. Much of the violence against those campaigning for land rights or against particular development projects can be linked to the activities of companies or entrepreneurs. Many governments are equally culpable in the repression of environmental and social activists in the South: the violence of the Nigerian regime against the Ogoni is one example.

The problem appears to be that governments are seeking economic development in very narrow terms. The big and modern is valued more than the small and the appropriate. The environment is seen as something to be dominated rather than worked with. Consequently environmental issues are seen as a barrier to economic progress, a view which can be challenged on many fronts.

A fresh approach would see governments recognizing environmental challenges as opportunities for economic success. Given the growing power of civil society in the North, there are increasing opportunities for Southern governments to lever new funds to help exporters access new markets, and to work in partnership with foreign companies to promote cost-effective resource management. Southern entrepreneurs who recognize the social and environmental demands of Northern markets and adjust their strategies accordingly may be able to achieve greater success. Governments can support such efforts by obtaining additional financial resources for commercial projects that support sustainable development. One example is the partnership between WWF–International and the World Bank, which aims to provide millions of dollars of credit for timber projects that are independently certified as well-managed.

Southern governments could also assist their national companies to access new markets. There is a widely held belief that the Northern green consumer is only a niche market. However, green consumerism is not dictating the size of the green market. Instead it is the buying power of corporations, adjusting to the pressures and opportunities of consumer politics, that provide the real opportunity. For example, about 25 per cent of the British and 50 per cent of the Dutch timber markets are not niche markets. To help Cameroon companies supply this growing market, the Cameroon Ministry of Forestry is now working with the European Commission and environmental NGOs.

Furthermore, governments could work in partnership with foreign companies to promote cost-effective resource management. Faced with huge costs to enforce environmental regulations in remote areas, granting natural resource concessions to companies that meet independently monitored environmental and social standards could prove an effective tool for sustainable development. Currently this strategy is being frowned upon by many campaigners and commentators: however, if the standards used were to be developed in consultation with a variety of stakeholders, including local communities, then this strategy might be widely welcomed. New systems of globally applicable, stakeholder-negotiated and independently monitored environmental, social or ethical standards for business offer Southern governments new economic opportunities and regulatory mechanisms.

Towards global private regulation

The FSC is perhaps the best current model of a civil regulation organization. It sets global multi-stakeholder standards for forest management, based on a democratic decision-making process. Compliance with these civil standards is then independently monitored, similar to the way in which compliance with legal standards is measured. One of the possible problems with this model is that the business pays the civil regulation bills. This could compromise the independence of the regulator. To combat that possibility, accreditation is used. The actual monitoring and certification is performed by companies or organizations (certification bodies) who are paid for the regulatory service. These certification bodies are then accredited by the FSC to ensure that they uphold its standards and criteria. Whereas the certification bodies might be vulnerable to compromised independence, the accreditation process ensures the credibility of the system.

The standard-setting process is paid for by donations from governments, companies, trust funds and so forth. Companies pay for the actual certifications and eventually pass on the costs to the end consumer. In this way, companies or individuals pay for the regulation of a particular product when they buy that product. Independent certification of business against stakeholder-defined sustainability standards represents a privatization of the regulatory function of government, while protecting the democratic participation of citizens. We believe that this system could become the new regulatory framework for business in a global economy. We call it *global private regulation*.

Other policy options and obstacles

As we mentioned above, Southern governments have the opportunity to invite global corporations to invest with the proviso that their operations are independently certified against standards set by a variety of national and international stakeholders. For the government this is free regulation; and it offers the potential for international trade to promote sustainable and equitable future incomes. Northern governments should also promote this process as it allows for further politicization of the market and therefore the effective translation of consumer politics into beneficial social change.

However, the option of developing countries welcoming foreign direct investment (FDI) on the condition that it meet civil regulation standards appears threatened by the possibility of a Multilateral Agreement on Investment (MAI), of the type which was being drafted within the OECD until negotiations broke down in 1998. It aimed at smoothing the international rules governing foreign direct investment. As we described earlier, foreign direct investment (FDI) is now a critical determinant in development. Many NGOs were concerned that the OECD initiative would rule against the use of environmental conditions on FDI (Coates, 1997, personal communication). Other analysts believe that an investment agreement could, in principle, strengthen the ability of governments to place environmental conditions on FDI, and even propose a code of conduct for companies investing in developing countries (Esty and Gentry, 1997). Developing countries that sign such an an agreement in order to attract greater inward investment may therefore be prevented from facilitating sustainable development through a fresh approach of partnership with business and civil society. Our hope is that if a global investment agreement is eventually negotiated, it should contain an exemption so that signatory governments can require investing companies to meet globally recognized environmental and social standards.

The concern with how the MAI would affect government policies for sustainable development reminds us of the importance of intergovernmental agreements. No matter how effective corporate environmentalism, civil regulation or global private regulation could prove to be, international cooperation and mechanisms of global governance are urgently required. United Nations agencies could provide these mechanisms. The Pakistan case, referred to in Chapter 9, suggests a new activist role for United Nations agencies in the area of civil regulation. A revitalized UNEP may be able to assume the kind of monitoring and verification role currently being undertaken by the ILO in the Pakistan child labour project. As part of the United Nations Secretary-General's plans for United Nations reform, there is promise of future action to 'develop new measures' to reorganize and strengthen UNEP. Kofi Annan wants UNEP to reaffirm its role as 'the environmental agency of the world community' and promises to ensure that it has the 'status, strength and access to resources' needed to fulfil this task (Cohen, 1997, personal communication). In Annan's own words: 'Without good governance – without the rule of law, predictable administration, legitimate power, and responsive regulation – no amount of funding, no amount of charity will set us on the path to prosperity' (Annan, 1997).

Although we have argued that both government and intergovernmental agencies do have a role to play in a changed global economy, this role is not widely recognized. At the same time, the role of consumer politics, civil regulation and global private regulation in facilitating the contribution of the business sector to sustainable development is largely overlooked. Companies and governments are wary of NGOs, while activists remain wary of managing directors and politicians. Many Southern government ministers see calls for the inclusion of environmental or labour standards in trade and investment agreements as attempts at protectionism by Northern countries, rather than as opportunities for sustainable development. Negotiations towards a free trade area of the Americas is one example, where trade ministers of certain Latin American countries have stalled attempts by Costa Rica to discuss environmental standards and trade. Southern ministers still view weak environmental and social standards as a competitive advantage. Until this changes, the potential for civil regulation in the South will not be realized. One country that is seeking the opportunities afforded by sustainable development is the Philippines:

> Philippine Agenda 21 is the country's blueprint for sustainable development. It holds great promise for 'another' development. PA21 clearly defines the parameters for the involvement of FDI in the Philippine economy. The Philippines has realized, at least some segments of the Philippine bureaucracy, that if it does not clearly define its own vision, it will be defined from the outside by ODA and FDI. The real test will come when we clearly specify ... investment parameters connected to productivity, profitability, equity and sustainability, among others. Then we will see if FDI will be willing to work under these new parameters, and not simply flow where the labor is cheap, or the resources plentiful and unregulated. (Perlas, 1997, personal communication)

The behaviour of FDI in the Philippines over the coming years will indicate whether corporate environmentalism extends to accepting the will of the people – and acting on it.

Conclusion

In this chapter we have argued that:

- Corporate environmentalism is a political phenomenon;
- Through the politics of both pressure and engagement, NGOs are creating the new agenda for business, as much as companies are themselves;
- The political power of NGOs is not a passing fad but an expression of a new form of consumer politics which is the result of social, economic and cultural change;
- By describing a continuum of protest and partnership relations between business and NGOs we can observe a new form of regulation for global business, called civil regulation;
- Civil regulation organizations like the FSC and MSC will probably be replicated in other industrial sectors and come to be known as systems of global private regulation;

- These developments rely on the sensitivities of Northern markets, and may not be transferable to countries or regions where consumer-driven market pressure is not as prevalent;
- For the civil regulation agenda to develop in the South, and for Northern NGOs to maintain legitimacy when promoting corporate responsibility in developing countries, there must be stronger alliances between Northern and Southern NGOs;
- Changes in the global economy mean that governments need to assume a greater role as leaders and facilitators, but they are in danger of negotiating that role away through trade and investment agreements such as the MAI;
- The uncertainty that surrounds the issue of corporate environmentalism suggests we need greater international collaboration in this area.

At the close of the twentieth century the jury is still out on the role of such initiatives and indeed of business itself in the sustainable development process. It could even be said that the jury is still hearing the evidence for and against. Those who wish to prosecute business can present a catalogue of environmental disasters, human rights abuses, worker health and safety violations, and so on. Those who wish to defend the role of partnership can present an admittedly growing array of policy statements, environmental and social projects, civil regulation schemes and other fledgling initiatives. What this chapter shows is that we cannot deliver a verdict at this time and there is a need to collect more evidence for a fair trial. Eventually we may find that 'business' and 'partnership' should not be the only ones on trial but instead a cadre of company managers, government officials, United Nations experts, NGO campaigners, voters and consumers, who individually and collectively could be doing much more to promote a more sustainable and equitable future.

References

Anderson, D. and R. Grove (1987), *Conservation in Africa: People, Politics and Practice*, Cambridge University Press, Cambridge.

Annan, K. (1997), Statement by Secretary-General Kofi Annan to the opening meeting of the International Conference on Governance for Sustainable Growth and Equity, at United Nations Headquarters (New York, 28 July 1997), Press Release SG/SM/6291 DEV/2166.

Ashford, N. A. (1993), 'Understanding Technological Responses of Industrial Firms to Environmental Problems: Implications for Government Policy', in K. Fischer and J. Schot (eds.), *Environmental Strategies for Industry*, Island Press, Washington DC.

Browne, J. (1997), 'Climate Change' speech delivered at Stanford University, California, 19 May, www.edf.org.

Camilleri, J. A. and J. Falk (1992), *The End of Sovereignty: Politics of a Shrinking and Fragmenting World*, E. Elgar, Aldershot, Hants.

Coates, Barry (1997), personal communication with Jem Bendell, June, World Development Movement, London.

Cohen, J. (1997), personal communication with D. F. Murphy, 4 September, UNA–USA, New York.

Collinson, H. (ed.) (1996), *Green Guerrillas: Environmental Conflicts and Initiatives in Latin America and the Caribbean*, Latin American Bureau, London.

de Oliveira, M. D. and R. Tandon (eds.) (1994), *Citizens: Strengthening Global Civil Society*, CIVICUS, Washington, DC.

Dillon, P. S. and K. Fischer (1992), *Environmental Management in Corporations: Methods and Motivations*, Center for Environmental Management, Tufts University, Medford, Mass.

Esty, D. C. and B. S. Gentry (1997), *Foreign Investment, Globalization and the Environment,* Yale Centre for Environmental Law and Policy, New Haven, Conn.

FoE–UK (1995), *A Superficial Attraction: The Voluntary Approach and Sustainable Development,* FoE–UK, London.

Fukuyama, F. (1995), *Trust: The Social Virtues and the Creation of Prosperity,* Free Press, New York.

Gramsci, A. (1988), *An Antonio Gramsci Reader* (D. Forgacs, ed.), Schocken, New York.

Herkströter, C. A. J. (1996), 'Dealing with Contradictory Expectations – The Dilemmas Facing Multinationals', speech by the President of Royal Dutch Petroleum Company in Amsterdam, 11 October, Shell International, The Hague.

Johnston, B. R. (ed.) (1997), *Life and Death Matters: Human Rights and the Environment at the End of the Millennium,* AltaMira Press, California.

Kaimowitz, D. (1996), 'Social Pressure for Environmental Reform in Latin America', in H. Collinson (ed.), *Green Guerrillas: Environmental Conflicts and Initiatives in Latin America and the Caribbean,* Latin American Bureau, London.

Korten, D. (1990), *Getting to the 21st Century,* Kumarian Press, Hartford, Conn.

—— (1995), *When Corporations Rule the World,* Earthscan, London.

Levy, D. L. (1997), 'Environmental Management as Political Sustainability', *Organisation and Environment,* 10 (2), 126–47.

Loveman, B. (1995), 'Chilean NGOs: Forging a Role in the Transition to Democracy', in C. A. Reilly (ed.), *New Paths to Democratic Development in Latin America: The Rise of NGO-Municipal Collaboration,* Lynne Rienner, London.

Marsden, Chris (1997), personal communication with Jem Bendell, July, BP Corporate Citizenship Unit, London.

Mehta, Pradeep (1997), personal communication with Jem Bendell, June, Consumer Unity and Trust Society, India.

Murphy, D. F. and J. Bendell (1997), *In the Company of Partners: Business, Environmental Groups and Sustainable Development post-Rio,* The Policy Press, Bristol.

OECD Development Assistance Committee (1996), News Release, SG/COM/NEW (96)64, 11 June.

Perlas, N. (1997), personal communication with Jem Bendell, June, Phillipine Council for Sustainable Development, Manila.

Rappaport, A. and M. F. Flaherty (1992), *Corporate Responses to Environmental Challenges,* Quorum, New York.

Reilly, C. A., (ed.) (1995), *New Paths to Democratic Development in Latin America: The Rise of NGO-Municipal Collaboration,* Lynne Rienner, London.

SustainAbility, NEF and UNEP (1996), *Engaging Stakeholders,* SustainAbility, London.

UNRISD (1995), *States of Disarray: The Social Effects of Globalization,* UNRISD, Geneva.

Walley, N. and B. Whitehead (1994), 'It's Not Easy Being Green', in *Harvard Business Review* (May–June), 46–52.

WBCSD (1997), *Signals for Change,* WBCSD, Geneva.

Welford, R. (1997), *Hijacking Environmentalism: Corporate Responses to Sustainable Development,* Earthscan, London.

Wheeler, D. and M. Sillanpaa (1997), *The Stakeholder Corporation,* Pitman, London.

World Bank (1996), *World Debt Tables 1996,* World Bank, Washington DC.

WWF–International (1996), *Marine Stewardship Council Newsletter,* No. 1, WWF–International, Godalming.

Corporate Environmentalism in the South

Assessing the Limits and Prospects

PETER UTTING

Introduction

The preceding chapters have presented varying perspectives on the greening of business in developing countries. On balance, what do they tell us about its present-day reality and future prospects? This concluding chapter begins by summarizing some of the concerns which have been raised regarding the scope and substance of 'corporate environmentalism'. It then highlights briefly certain aspects related to regulatory frameworks, policy instruments, partnerships and pressures that may serve to promote corporate environmental responsibility, and considers whether there are forces in place that might promote a pattern of corporate environmentalism that is conducive to sustainable development.

By focusing on the political and structural underpinnings of corporate environmentalism, it is argued that certain developments may be prompting some companies, in both the North and South, to adopt improvements in environmental management systems. Increased corporate responsiveness to environmental concerns can be expected given the way in which power in democratic and 'civil' societies is contested and the nature of restructuring which is taking place in global production networks and industrial organization. Corporate environmentalism, within this context, is seen as more than an opportunistic response to so-called 'win–win' situations or a reactive response to civil society and regulatory pressures. Rather, certain political, institutional, technological and economic conditions have coalesced in the era of globalization to favour a more proactive response, particularly among transnational corporations (TNCs). It is argued, however, that this process is very uneven and contradictory. It is restricted to just a few techno-logical and managerial innovations, product sectors and countries, and remains highly questionable from the broader perspective of sustainable development.

The Limits to Corporate Greening

The overall picture which emerges from the preceding chapters is one of incipient progress in terms of a range of initiatives associated with improved environmental management, including the adoption of cleaner technology, codes of conduct, environmental policies, certification, audits and reporting. It is easy, however, to be lulled into a false sense of optimism by examples of company X doing this and company Y doing that. As several authors have suggested, there remain serious quantitative and qualitative limits to corporate environmentalism in developing countries. Various concerns have emerged, notably the piecemeal nature of the innovations and reforms; the inflated claims associated with corporate responsibility; and the assertion that the dominant strategy or model of economic growth continues to be that of 'business as usual'.

Even taking the case of countries where we might expect more progress, the situation is not particularly inspiring. From Costa Rica – a country which has gained international recognition for initiatives associated with environmental protection – Pratt and Fintel (Chapter 2) report that only one third of large companies have an environmental policy. Internationally, it is clear that an increasing number of companies and business and industry associations have developed codes of conduct and guiding principles but the proportion of companies adopting them is still relatively small in most countries. A recent OECD inventory listed 233 codes of conduct (OECD, 1999).[1] This figure pales beside the fact that there are, according to UNCTAD, some 60,000 TNCs in the world (UNCTAD, 1999).

If the adoption of codes still has a long way to go, their substance and implementation may leave even more to be desired. One analysis of the content of 145 codes which deal with environmental aspects (Gordon and Miyake, 2000), reveals that specific commitments related to aspects of environmental stewardship are only cited by a relatively small percentage of codes (generally between a fifth and a third). The two most frequently cited commitments were somewhat obvious or vague, namely 'comply with laws' (67 per cent of codes) and 'openness to community concerns' (40 per cent). In contrast, the two least cited commitments related to more concrete aspects, namely 'measurable objectives' (17.9 per cent) and 'transfer of technology' (9.2 per cent).[2]

Codes very often remain at the level of lofty principles and well-intentioned policy statements that are not effectively implemented (Kolk *et al.*, 1999). An UNCTAD review of the guidelines set by 26 world industry associations for their member firms found that 'most ... do not ask the signatories to commit to the principles or activities they recommend ... [and] only a handful require any kind of compliance by members' (UNCTAD, 1996: 7). Employees and consumers are often unaware of the existence of company codes, and firms frequently fail to specify the nature of sanctions for non-compliance (Jeffcott and Yanz, 2000). Where workers know that a code exists, they often lack the education necessary to understand specific provisions, and have not received relevant training. Where they are aware of abuses, they may not know how to channel their grievances. Of particular concern is the fact that effective company self-assessment or independent verification of compliance with codes is rarely practised (Dommen, 1999; ILO, 1999; UNCTAD, 1996).

Another area in which progress has been evident but weak is environmental reporting. A 1994 study by UNEP of 100 'pioneering companies' found that the reports of two thirds of the firms (64 per cent) ranged from 'green glossies' to annual reports that were more text than figures. Only 5 per cent contained meaningful performance data, while none amounted to 'sustainable development reporting'.[3] 'Whatever companies may call their reports, and however many times they mention sustainable development in the text, very little work is being done in this area as yet'

(UNEP, 1994: 67). A follow-up study carried out in 1997, which also focused on 100 companies, noted important areas of progress with most of the surveyed companies providing some useful data (UNEP and SustainAbility, 1997). There was, however, 'little evidence ... of real efforts to develop and plot progress against sustainability indicators' and only one company had approached the highest category of reporting standards.

The incipient character of corporate management reform is also apparent in relation to environmental certification. In Mexico, where close integration with the US market and the existence of environmental commissions associated with NAFTA might be expected to encourage improved corporate environmental management, Barkin (Chapter 1) reports that only a handful of firms have qualified for ISO certification of environmental management systems.[4] This is one of the most important international initiatives related to environmental certification. Between 1995 and the end of 1999, 14,106 certifications had been awarded world-wide. However, only 14 per cent of these were in developing countries, primarily in Asia. While the number of ISO 14000 certifications awarded annually is increasing in developing countries (they currently exist in 47 countries), only 733 new certifications were issued in 1999. This compares poorly with the ISO certifications related to quality management systems (ISO 9000), of which more than 22,000 were issued in developing countries in 1999 (ISO, 2000).

Before arriving at the conclusion that little has been done, it is important to remember that corporate environmentalism, particularly in developing countries, is a fairly recent phenomenon, having emerged, essentially, during the past decade. It may be unrealistic, therefore, to expect significant progress within such a short time frame. Given the fact that it is in its early days, it is perhaps more relevant to ask what sort of enabling environment is being established – in terms of policies, institutions, partnerships and pressures – that might encourage business to improve its environmental performance. We will return to this question later.

While progress to date has been somewhat limited, several authors have noted that corporate rhetoric often suggests that innovation and change have been impressive. The survey findings reported by Pratt and Fintel (Chapter 2) indicate that there is a fairly sharp gap between business rhetoric and practice in Costa Rica. This gap is also highlighted by Rodríguez and Camacho (Chapter 3) and Carrere (Chapter 4) who take to task two of the most publicized 'success stories' in the literature on corporate responsibility, namely the Costa Rican bioprospecting activities of the giant US pharmaceutical company, Merck & Co., and the Brazilian operations of the pulp and paper company, Aracruz Cellulose. Barkin (Chapter 1) also notes several cases of 'greenwash'[5] in Mexico.

In Central America, independent research and NGO monitoring has recently revealed other cases of inflated claims or double standards, in two of the industries – chemicals and forestry – commonly associated with initiatives in environmental management. Evaluating a high-profile project promoted by the international pesticide industry in Guatemala,[6] the International Union of Food and Agricultural Workers (IUF) found that although certain indicators of project performance looked impressive, there were some serious shortcomings in project design and implementation. On the positive side, a third of a million farmers, housewives, students and others had received training in pesticide use between 1991 and 1994, but training methods were found to be weak. More intensive, longer-term training, and consideration of more appropriate technologies associated, for example, with Integrated Pest Management were absent, as were participatory training methods.

Furthermore, waged agricultural workers – the bulk of pesticide users – were not included in the project, a fact which seriously undermined the claim of the pesticide industry that it aimed to extend product stewardship along the entire supplier–user chain. As training targeted primarily the farmer-customers of the pesticide companies, and ignored alternative methods of pest control, the industry was vulnerable to the charge that the project was an effective marketing strategy (Hurst, 1999). The concerns revealed through this type of inquiry highlight the value of independent evaluation and the need to include third-party verification in voluntary initiatives by business.

In the forestry industry, there are some signs of support for the principle of independent verification. But various doubts have arisen concerning the verification process. One problem concerns the gap between the image of forestry certification – as a process that is well under way – and the facts concerning certified areas. In Costa Rica, where the logging industry has supported the principle of promoting sustainable forestry through certification, only 25,000 hectares, managed by seven entities, have been certified (FSC, 1999). This represents 5 per cent of the approximately half a million hectares of forest outside protected areas.[7] When IIED published its extensive report on the world's pulp and paper industry in 1996, it noted that the nearly 6 million hectares of forests that had been certified accounted for just 0.5 per cent of global trade (IIED, 1996: 62). By early 1999 the area certified by FSC-accredited bodies had risen to 15 million hectares (one quarter of which were in developing countries) but this still represented less than 1 per cent of the world's forests outside protected areas.[8]

Another concern relates to the quality of the verification process. Even leaving aside the important criticisms of some environmentalists that what is being labelled 'sustainable logging' can still cause serious environmental damage (Colchester, 1990; World Rainforest Movement, 1999), other concerns have arisen. A study of a certified teak plantation company in Costa Rica, for example, revealed that its operations do not comply with several FSC principles and criteria. It notes, for example, the ongoing use of highly toxic pesticides, banned in many countries, and the dangerous way they were used by workers who hadn't received the necessary training and protective clothing. The study also notes that certain well-known international conservation NGOs were supporting false claims about the company's management practices and environmental and economic performance (Romeijn, 1999).

This study cautions against taking for granted the degree of autonomy of the verifiers, the rigour of their methods and substance of their benchmarks or goals. These need to be periodically scrutinized. As one activist/researcher turned independent verifier once confided to this author: 'Look at me. Having had to work so closely with CEOs, I'm beginning to look and sound like one. At some point a new generation of NGOs will probably have to come along to check on people like me'.

Another major criticism of environmental certification relates to the fact that what is evaluated is environmental management, not environmental performance:[9] 'does your company have an environmental policy?', not 'to what extent has your company reduced its emissions or use of energy?' The relationship between improved environmental management and performance is not always as apparent as one might think. As Levy has pointed out in a study of Northern TNCs with facilities in the United States, it may be 'surprisingly weak' (Levy, 1995: 57). Larger companies, in particular, were found to be strong on policy but weak on actual performance or outcomes.[10]

Perhaps the most inflated claim of all relates not to environmental protection *per se* but to the idea, often projected by companies, that they are promoting 'sustainable development'. Many companies, corporate foundations and business associations liberally apply the label 'sustainable development' to initiatives or activities that in practice amount to fairly minor interventions to improve environmental management systems or eco-efficiency. Despite its title, the WBCSD has, until recently, channelled its energies towards the promotion of eco-efficiency. Similarly, several UN–business partnerships that carry the sustainable development label focus narrowly on environmental or eco-efficiency aspects,[11] or even the formulation of investment laws in least-developed countries.[12]

Many companies focus narrowly on one particular aspect of corporate responsibility – for example, environmental protection – and ignore others such as labour standards. As Carrere points out (Chapter 4), some companies are claiming to promote sustainable development through initiatives associated with corporate environmentalism but they often ignore key social and political dimensions of the concept, such as empowerment or indigenous rights. In relation to environmental certification, some international trade unions are concerned that such instruments are legitimizing the activities of companies that continue to abuse certain basic rights. The International Federation of Building and Wood Workers (IFBWW) has called for the inclusion of additional social criteria related to ILO core labour standards in forest certification (Development and Cooperation, 1999: 31). Similarly, the IUF is highly critical of banana companies, like Chiquita Brands, that have adopted the ECO-OK label, which, *inter alia*, commits a company to reduce its applications of toxic pesticides. According to union organizations and officials, Chiquita not only continues to pursue environmentally damaging practices but also restricts basic rights associated with the freedom of association of workers in countries such as Costa Rica (personal communication with SITRAP official;[13] IUF, 1998).

As noted in the Introduction to this volume and by Welford (Chapter 6), the concept of sustainable development involves far more than environmental protection. Any strategy that merits the sustainable development label would need to be multi-faceted and demonstrate a degree of progress in areas of corporate policy and practice related not only to environmental and economic aspects but also, *inter alia*, to labour standards and community relations. Very few companies have attempted to adopt such a comprehensive strategy.

Apart from ignoring crucial dimensions of sustainable development, certain aspects of corporate environmentalism may actually reinforce the patterns of growth, industrial production, consumption and North–South relations that underpin 'unsustainable' development. The eco-efficiency approach, which has been championed by organizations such as the World Business Council for Sustainable Development, has been criticized for actually reinforcing the dominant growth model. According to Welford (Chapter 6) , eco-efficiency implies

> that solutions can be found which will allow the rich North to consume more and more whilst using fewer and fewer natural resources…. It adds an environmental dimension to the traditional growth path but does not allow that dimension to radically change the path. Perhaps more importantly, the ecomodernist trend has been subtly designed to reinforce the growth trend, justify the power of private capital, promote globalization and ignore the social dimensions of sustainable development.

Hawken *et al.* argue that

> narrowly focused eco-efficiency could be a disaster for the environment by overwhelming

resource savings with even larger growth in the production of the wrong products, produced by the wrong processes, from the wrong materials, in the wrong place, at the wrong scale, and delivered using the wrong business models. (Hawken *et al.* 1999: x)

Certain features of corporate environmentalism may work against development in other ways as well. In relation to specific tools such as eco-labelling, there is concern that it could harm developing countries by acting as a non-tariff barrier to trade (Markandya, 1997). According to Dawkins (1995: 5-6),

eco-labelling could exacerbate current global trends by which developing countries' share of international markets shrinks and, within all countries, small businesses' share of both national and international markets shrinks unless eco-labelling schemes are accompanied by aggressive affirmative policies to facilitate the participation of small firms and developing country exporters.

A study of the international horticultural sector (UNCTAD and SGS, 1998), suggests that more environmentally friendly forms of production could emerge. Achieving this, however, requires substantial investments, access to information and managerial expertise, which are beyond the reach of many smaller producers. The upshot 'is that supermarkets and importers are focusing on fewer, larger, better-organized and more sophisticated growers, processors and exporters'. Such a process tends to crowd out or restrict entry to smaller producers (UNCTAD and SGS, 1998: 7) although some niche markets – for example, for organically produced crops – are supplied by small farmers.

In relation to both corporate environmental and social responsibility, there are concerns that many firms (notably small and medium-sized enterprises) in developing countries will find it extremely difficult to raise standards. ISO certification, for example, can prove costly – generally between US$5,000 and US$20,000 for the first-time audit and consultation for establishing an environmental management system, assuming local auditors are available, plus an annual cost of $4,000 to $5,000. These costs will increase considerably if international auditors are used (Clapp, 1998).

Many firms find it difficult to comply with new standards being set by the transnational or large retailers they supply. A complaint of some suppliers in developing countries is that while higher standards are being imposed on them, the basic terms of their contracts – price paid, quantities delivered and delivery dates – remain as tight, if not tighter, than ever. In short they are being asked to do more with less. They also receive little managerial training and advice as to how to comply.[14] Presumably the notion of corporate responsibility in such contexts must extend beyond the elevation of standards to facilitating a supplier's ability to comply. Furthermore, compliance with the standards should not exacerbate some other feature of 'maldevelopment', for example, when attempts to ban child labour push the families affected further into poverty or the children themselves into more abusive forms of work (Mayne, 1999).

Initiatives associated with corporate environmentalism rarely encourage consumers to adopt very different consumption patterns that would significantly reduce environmental degradation. The IUF case study, referred to above, showed that in the field of chemical use and training, for example, attention was being focused on using conventional pesticides in less health-threatening ways, not on promoting alternative methods of pest control. More generally, the choice that consumers are offered tends to be between like products that vary only slightly in the degree to which they have an impact on the environment; consumers are not encouraged to reassess their lifestyles and patterns of consumption (West, 1995: 19). Similarly, when oil companies such as Shell go out of their way to promote 'multi-stakeholder' dialogues to discuss specific initiatives, the discussion is more likely to centre on how a particular project should be implemented than on whether it should go ahead (Rowell,1999).

Not seeing the forest for the trees

When assessing trends associated with corporate environmental responsibility it is important to be able to stand back from the anecdotes and case studies of 'best practice' or 'greenwash' and retain a sense of perspective regarding the bigger picture, that is, the broader trends associated with patterns of investment, industrial location, production processes and macro-economic policy. Several chapters in this volume remind us that we shouldn't lose sight of the forest for the trees by remaining fixated on specific events at the level of the firm. We need to step back and place what is happening in relation to corporate environmentalism in the broader context of trends in the national or world economy and political economy.

But here too the picture is very mixed. Several authors have highlighted different structural aspects which are constraining corporate responsibility. Carrere (Chapter 4) and Welford (Chapter 6) highlight the fundamental constraints on corporate environmental and social responsibility which derive from the logic of capitalist production and, in particular, the quest for profitability, which puts pressure on firms to cut or externalize costs and seek locations with weak labour and environmental regulations. Such pressures may well be escalating in the harshly competitive environment associated with economic globalization and liberalization. Through mergers and acquisitions, downsizing, outsourcing, the feminization and informalization of employment, and the lure of largely deregulated havens, such as Export Processing Zones, many corporations are shifting production to sites and systems with lower environmental and social standards.

In the case of the pulp industry in Brazil, Carrere suggests that this contradiction may be even more acute during the early phases of corporate activity, when companies attempt to obtain quick returns on large-scale investments by externalizing as many costs as possible. He shows how power structures reinforce this possibility. Not only did the large corporations he examines use political and economic power to obtain subsidies from government, they also had the coercive power of the state on their side when the externalities generated local opposition. Moreover, Carrere highlights another structural problem, that of scale. Even companies which are firmly committed to the goal of environmental responsibility and sustainable development are unlikely to realize these goals when the inherently large scale of their operations means that large-scale environmental impacts are inevitable. The choice, he argues, should not be between a very destructive and a less destructive corporation; we should also have the choice to promote an economic system based on smaller-scale enterprises more in tune with the local culture and the environment.

Barkin (Chapter 1) suggests that although many firms in Mexico are now taking steps to improve their environmental management systems, and institutions are emerging to facilitate this, the economic system as a whole in Mexico continues to demonstrate very perverse characteristics. Patterns of investment are such that polluting industries are expanding. Furthermore, trends in industrial location suggest that firms are being established or moving to areas of the country where planning and regulation are weak. As has been pointed out elsewhere, in relation to India, the process of competitive deregulation to attract investment not only involves countries but also regions or states within countries (Jha, 1999).

Pratt and Fintel (Chapter 2) reveal how institutional structures, associated in particular with macro-economic policy, constrain corporate environmental responsibility in Central America. Firms are less likely to adopt environmental improvements when, for example, the financial services sector imposes high interest rates and short lending terms. These can act as a disincentive to adopting the type of long-term business planning horizon which is often required for environmental management. Other policies of this sector, for example recommendations regarding the use of certain technical packages, may encourage agricultural producers to use outdated and environmentally damaging technologies. Similarly, the fiscal system discriminates against the importation and adoption of clean technology and under-values the use of natural resources.

These broader trends associated with the evolving nature of capitalist production, economic liberalization and macro-economic policy raise serious concerns for corporate environmentalism. But, as indicated in the Introduction to this volume, the proponents of ecological modernization generally argue that certain processes commonly associated with globalization may serve to facilitate some aspects of corporate environmentalism. Foreign direct investment and networks controlled by TNCs, for example, may act as conduits for the diffusion of cleaner technologies and improved environmental management systems; 'win–win' situations – where environmentally friendly business practices can also be good for profitability and competitiveness – are thought to be ubiquitous; and global civil society activism and networking is keeping TNCs in the spotlight and forcing the pace of environmental management reform. As Flaherty and Rappaport observe, 'companies may attempt to run but they can no longer hide' (1997). Later in this chapter we turn to the question of whether these contexts and 'drivers' of corporate environmentalism are likely to significantly improve the environmental performance of business in the South.

Promoting Corporate Environmentalism in Developing Countries

Best practice and replication

A central issue addressed in this volume concerns the question of how best to promote corporate environmentalism in developing countries. Much of the literature in this field is concerned with identifying 'best practices'. Once the knowledge of what works is available, it is often assumed that the technical and managerial innovations associated with best practices can be replicated in different countries.

Documenting and disseminating information on what has worked for one company or country is of course important, particularly in a relatively new field. Many CEOs and company managers are willing to take steps to improve their environmental record but are uncertain of what to do.[15] 'Best practice' information can assist them in this regard. It has been observed that TNCs and large companies, in particular, may be in a good position to take advantage of such information given the scope for knowledge and technology transfer and intra-firm learning within their structures, which derives partly from sophisticated networks of communication (Levy, 1995: 63).

There are, however, some serious problems with the 'best practice' approach. First, it can be fairly short-sighted. It is common, for example, to focus narrowly on one particular practice and conveniently ignore other aspects of corporate policy and behaviour which have negative environmental or social implications. Furthermore, as seen earlier, the benefits attributed to a particular best practice are often exaggerated, and the fact that best practices may quickly unravel as circumstances change is often ignored. Second, the analysis of the factors underpinning best practice can be very limited in the sense that technical, managerial and financial aspects tend to be emphasized while certain key institutional and political aspects are often ignored. Third, best practice literature often recycles the same cases which are relatively few in number. Several of these concerns are highlighted in the critical assessment which Rodríguez and Camacho (Chapter 3) and Carrere (Chapter 4) undertake of two of the classic cases in the best practice literature.

Other concerns also emerge in relation to the issue of the replication of best practices. It is often assumed that what needs to be done is to transfer to the South technology, management systems and policies that are perceived to be successful in the richer industrialized countries. Sometimes this transfer might take place from one developing country to another. The chapters by Hanks (Chapter 8) and Rodríguez and Camacho (Chapter 3) introduce a note of caution regarding the issue of replication.

In his analysis of the potential of negotiated agreements and their adoption in South Africa, Hanks concludes that a number of benefits could derive from such policies. But he also identifies some of the limits to replication in what are very different institutional contexts of developing countries. He argues that co-regulation tends to work best when there is a high level of environmental awareness in both government and industry, mutual trust between the various parties, high-quality information flows, political independence of relevant state authorities from industry, and some threat of punitive state sanctions as well as peer, community and consumer pressures. At least some of these conditions are often lacking in developing countries.

Rodríguez and Camacho also refer to the issue of replication in their analysis of the Merck–INBio agreement, which has been hailed as a 'model' in the field of bioprospecting. They show how this model developed in a context which is probably not found in too many countries. Costa Rica, for example, has an extensive system of reasonably well-administered protected areas which are extremely rich in biodiversity, a fairly strong research and scientific community and infrastructure, and large NGOs such as INBio which have a reasonably strong bargaining position. Their analysis questions whether this model can be easily reproduced in other countries.

Government regulation and social pressures

The proponents of corporate self-regulation and ecological modernization generally suggest that there are a number of sound business reasons why companies adopt measures to improve environmental management, notably the potential for cost reduction and the possibility of gaining competitive advantage and market share. But enlightened self-interest appears to confront serious limits both in terms of its diffusion throughout the business community and its ability to translate into mean-ingful changes in corporate environmental performance. For this reason several of the preceding chapters have looked at the types of regulatory regimes and social pressures that promote corporate environmental responsibility. More specifically they have looked at how governments and NGOs should interact with the business community.

Authors of some of the preceding chapters who have worked in or closely with business and business associations have highlighted the need for pragmatism and dialogue. They suggest that firms are limited in what they can take on at any one time in terms of environmental and social responsibility. While there may be much goodwill among corporate executives, many remain unconvinced of the need for major change and lack the necessary know-how regarding how to improve environmental management systems in a cost-effective way. Accordingly, feasible priorities and targets need to be set and practical information and training are also essential. Hanks (Chapter 8) argues that in many situations it makes sense to adopt an incremental approach, focusing initially on more obvious 'win–win' solutions where environmental management can also have a positive spin-off in terms of profits, company image and market share.

It has also been argued, however, that corporate environmental and social responsibility must ultimately derive from a political process. Whether governments and corporations act to promote sustainable development is not simply a technical issue of know-how, resource availability, 'win–win' situations or even greater environmental awareness on the part of key decision makers. All of the above may contribute to generating the political will needed for reform, but political will also stems from a social process involving power struggles between different actors and stakeholders. In this context, the emergence of 'consumer power', the capacity of environmental and human rights NGOs and international NGO networks to organize and mobilize, trade union pressures and the role of certain national and multilateral institutions calling for stricter environmental standards constitutes a political context that is essential for promoting corporate environmental responsibility. This mix of regulatory and social pressures clearly goes beyond the 'new model' of pollution control in developing countries proposed by organizations like the World Bank (World Bank, 2000) and based on market-based instruments, voluntary initiatives and 'informal regulation'.

Much of the discussion of these issues has centred on the role of policy and partnership initiatives involving certain forms of 'co-regulation'. Various authors see these as potentially more constructive than attempts either by governments to police the business community or by companies to regulate themselves. Two forms of co-regulation have been highlighted. The first, explored by Hanks (Chapter 8), involves 'negotiated agreements' between government and business associations to promote, for example, emissions control, recycling, environmental impact assessments, eco-audits and reporting. The second, examined by Bendell and Murphy (Chapters 9 and 10), involves 'civil regulation', through which NGOs and other civil society groups and organizations exert pressure on business via various forms of confrontation and collaboration. Business–NGO partnerships have expanded rapidly during the past decade, providing a mechanism through which NGOs can exert influence and provide advice and technical assistance, as well as specific services associated with auditing, reporting, certification and monitoring.

While several authors in this volume stress the importance of co-regulation, they are also aware of its limits, particularly in the developing world. In many such countries, consumer power and public environmental awareness may be relatively weak, state regulatory authorities may lack independence as well as human and financial resources, business may not be obliged to disclose basic information, and NGOs may be relatively few in number or lack the capacity to monitor corporate activities. Bendell and Murphy also point out that civil regulation has mainly been driven by Northern NGOs, whose legitimacy and capacity to promote corporate environmentalism in the South is likely to be compromised unless there is a stronger input from Southern civil society organizations.

Another concern prompted by the civil regulation model is that it revolves increasingly around partnerships between business and NGOs which provide services (such as certification, audits, advice on technology or management systems). Such relationships may not only compromise the autonomy and critical edge of NGOs but also lead to a failure to question such fundamentals of unsustainable development as certain patterns of economic growth and consumption or inegalitarian structures of power and income distribution. In view of these and other concerns, Hansen (Chapter 7) emphasizes the ongoing and prominent role that international and government regulation and policy should play in promoting corporate environmental responsibility: setting minimum industry-wide standards, providing incentives and support services for improving environmental management systems, and ensuring public disclosure and freedom of information. Pratt and Fintel (Chapter 2) and Welford (Chapter 6) also stress the importance of fiscal reforms to reduce or eliminate certain types of subsidies that underpin environmentally destructive resource management practices and consumption patterns. While some of the discussion has emphasized the poor performance of many governments in establishing appropriate policy frameworks and enforcing basic environmental laws, it is also apparent from corporate surveys that government regulation is one of the main drivers of improvements in corporate environmental management (see Hanks, Chapter 8; Hansen, 1999; Rappaport and Flaherty, 1990). It has been noted that, whether enforced or not, government regulations can have a powerful symbolic value – the mere presence or threat of regulations appears to act as a powerful trigger of corporate environmental responsibility (UNRISD/UNA, 1998).[16]

Research from other parts of the world also casts doubts on the assumption, commonly held by proponents of ecological modernization, that environmental management reform can derive primarily from corporate self-regulation and voluntary initiatives as opposed to mandatory regulations. In their analysis of Malaysia and Singapore, Perry and Singh (Chapter 5) point out the limitations of voluntary initiatives and suggest that, for the present, such initiatives cannot be seen as an effective substitute for government regulation. Referring elsewhere to specific market-based instruments and voluntary initiatives in East Asia such as environmental taxes, life cycle assessment, ISO 14001 and environmental reporting, they argue that

> each of these alternatives has shortcomings that do not reduce the need to pursue environmental improvement through traditional methods.... Many of the problems alleged to limit the effectiveness of command and control regulation in East Asia are also present within market-based and voluntary initiatives and these approaches suffer other limitations as well. (Perry and Singh, forthcoming)

Others have pointed to a potentially dangerous trade-off between voluntary initiatives and government regulation. In Argentina and Mexico, for example, governments have come under pressure from business to relax environmental regulations for those firms that have obtained ISO 14000 certification (Clapp, 1998: 310). Such forms of 'regulatory relief' could weaken rather than strengthen the regulatory framework (*ibid.*).

Political and Structural Determinants

Focusing on a few case studies of 'best practices' or 'greenwash' is often the methodology used to construct an empirical case for corporate environmentalism as either a meaningful new departure or a sham. What is disturbing about much of the literature in this field is the tendency to generalize about corporate behaviour and trends across very different product sectors and local and national contexts. The 'best practice' or 'win–win' literature tends to imply that the lead which has been taken by a few companies will almost inevitably be followed by others, once information flows improve and the right combination of carrots and sticks emerges. The greenwash literature suggests that business is fundamentally resistant to change along the lines needed to forge a new relationship to the environment. If it changes, it does so reactively and reluctantly, primarily under civil society or government pressure (Greer and Bruno, 1996).

Part of the problem with these two camps is the tendency to generalize from a few anecdotes and case studies, and/or from some notion of the innate logic of capitalist production which is perceived as either conducive or inimical to improvements in environmental management. Just taking the case of TNCs and their affiliates, let alone the many other firms which exist, the urge to generalize seems somewhat unusual, knowing that there are approximately half a million TNC affiliates operating in what are often extremely varied sectoral, national and local settings.[17]

A key question that needs to be asked is not so much whether business is innately amenable or resistant to change, but whether or not there are forces in place which might promote a pattern of corporate environmentalism which is less destructive of the environment and conducive to sustainable development. To answer this question, it is useful to refer to two bodies of theory related to power and corporate strategy in the context of globalization. In contrast to certain strands of ecological modernization theory, which tend to highlight the technological and managerial drivers of corporate environmentalism, this analysis suggests that it has important political and structural underpinnings.

The politics of corporate environmentalism

In the preceding chapter, Bendell and Murphy asked: 'What is corporate environmentalism, *really*?' Citing Levy (1997), they argue that it is less about efficiency, profits and competitive advantage or concern for the environment than it is about politics. Referring to Gramsci's concept of 'hegemony',[18] they argue that corporate elites seek to accommodate threats to their dominance which derive from civil society organizations and movements as well as regulatory institutions.

The correlation of social forces, then, is a crucial determinant of whether or not business will respond to social and environmental issues. The considerable growth of civil society organizations, networks and movements concerned with issues of corporate responsibility and accountability suggests that business is being forced to change. What Broad and Cavanagh (1999) call the 'corporate accountability movement' is targeting both specific corporations – for example, Nestlé, Shell, Nike, Philip Morris, Monsanto, Rio Tinto and Gap – and specific types or sectors of industry with a heavy presence or impact in developing countries, such as apparel, chemicals, footwear, mining, toys, and the *maquila* factories.

In the struggle for hegemony, then, elites must take on board some of the concerns and values of a broader range of social groups or, in contemporary parlance, 'stakeholders'. But the corporate response shouldn't be seen simply as a reaction to pressure and the threat of regulation. Gramsci's analysis of power reveals that the struggle for hegemony is also a pro-active cultural phenomenon whereby dominant groups seek to secure their position by not only accommodating oppositional values but also exercising moral, cultural and intellectual leadership (Bennett, 1986). They do this partly through the institutions of civil society – by building up a system of alliances through which the interests of a broader range of social groups are represented (Utting, 1992).[19]

What is often ignored in the analysis of the role of civil society in development is that when civil society is constituted and expands, that is, when individuals associate and organize in 'private' or 'voluntary' institutions, it becomes not only a force for change 'from below' but also 'from above'. Elite groups can themselves form 'voluntary' organizations or seek to work closely with others through various forms of collaboration and partnership. This leadership role is very apparent in the field of corporate environmental responsibility and, more specifically, in the eco-efficiency model actively promoted by business associations such as the World Business Council for Sustainable Development. It is also apparent in the way organizations such as the International Standardization Organization (ISO) and global corporations are increasingly influencing policy making at the international level related to environmental and development issues (Krut and Gleckman, 1998; Dawkins, 1995) and entering into partnerships with the United Nations system. The latest manifestation of this partnership approach is the Global Compact, formally launched in July 2000 with the support of 44 corporations, five business associations and nine labour and civil society organizations.

At various historical junctures big business has not only responded to pressure but also taken the lead in terms of institutional reform. In this respect it is useful to examine the wave of 'corporate social responsibility', associated with certain firms and industries early in this century. The idea that corporations were responsible for more than just the financial 'bottom line', gained in prominence in the United States when big industrialists such as Ford and Carnegie not only engaged in corporate charity but also took some steps to improve the conditions of workers. This was a period when certain sectors of big business restructured both the way they organized production and marketing, and the nature of their relations with various stakeholders. Gramsci referred to this dual phenomenon of technological and social change as 'Fordism':[20] new methods of organizing industrial production (for example, the assembly line) were combined with new relations with workers (higher wages, lower hours, education programmes), consumers (through advertising and credit) and the communities where companies were located. Transforming such relations was crucial in overcoming certain social limits to growth, related for example to absenteeism, sickness, strikes, social unrest, mistrust of big business and weak consumer demand (partly linked to low wages). As Clarke points out, the new production system, based on the interdependence of tasks, was highly vulnerable to breakdown if any one task was interrupted (1992: 19). A healthy and motivated workforce could partially reduce this vulnerability.

Backing this process of change were certain forms of state intervention which promoted social reforms and sought to curb the powers of big business through anti-trust legislation. But corporate social responsibility at this time confronted serious limits and remained very restricted in terms of the nature of the reforms as well as the industrial sectors and countries involved. The process of scaling up and deepening corporate social responsibility would require the strengthening of trade unions and the institution of collective bargaining. Indeed, it could be argued that it required a more fundamental change in the correlation of social forces, which included the weakening of big business. It was not until this occurred – notably in Europe and Japan after the Second World War – and the 'welfare state' had emerged (Gallin, 1999), that features associated with corporate social responsibility became much more generalized in the industrialized countries. However, the weakness of the labour movement and the welfare state in many developing countries, as well as the nature of the international division of labour and industrial organization, imposed limits on the spread of corporate social responsibility in much of the South.

As this example demonstrates, corporate social responsibility made sense in the context of changes which were taking place in the way certain sectors of business were being reorganized technologically and institutionally. But its scaling up depended also on a political process involving various forms of workers' resistance,[21] civil society activism, regulatory pressures and broader changes in the correlation of social forces. When analysing the drivers of corporate responsibility – whether social or environmental – it is important to bear in mind both the structural and political determinants of change. As Jessop, citing Gramsci, points out, the outcomes of struggle 'must also be congruent with the changing technical and material conditions for capitalist accumulation' (Jessop, 1990: 191). A combination of trends and circumstances, therefore, coalesced to produce a shift in the social relations which characterized certain industrial sectors.

Contemporary trends associated with the greening of business appear to exhibit certain parallels with corporate social responsibility. Like the latter, corporate environmentalism makes sense both as a political strategy or response to social pressures, and in the context of changing patterns of industrial organization. And like the early experience of corporate social responsibility, its scaling up confronts serious limits. Social movements demanding corporate accountability and corporate environmental responsibility have gathered force, particularly in the past decade. As Murphy and Bendell point out (Chapter 9) 'through the politics of both pressure and engagement, NGOs are creating the new agenda for business, as much as companies themselves'. Civil society groups and movements, however, are often limited in their capacity to exert pressure, particularly on a sustained basis. Of the many issues associated with corporate irresponsibility that activist groups are concerned with at any one point in time, only a few can be addressed with sufficient momentum and force to make a large corporation pause, take notice and respond in some shape or form. There is also the strategic problem of knowing where to intervene in the system and with which actors to engage and ally. Considerable effort can be wasted by intervening in the wrong places. The analysis of global commodity chains reveals the presence of multiple actors in any product sector, some of which are far more powerful and capable than others in terms of being able to influence the process of environmental management reform (von Moltke *et al.*, 1998). The example of the NGO campaign to reduce the production and consumption of tropical timber not sourced from sustainably managed forests suggests that, for many years, attempts to influence logging companies, consumers and governments had limited effect. It was not until a very small group of European wood-product retailers was targeted that things started to happen, given their strategic location in the chain and ability to exert pressures both downstream and upstream, on producers and consumers respectively.[22]

Social pressures that partly drive corporate environmentalism can also be accommodated and deflated through 'incorporation' or co-option. Several forms of business–NGO partnership may have the effect of diluting activist pressures (Currah, 1999). Many NGOs and activists have shifted tactics, reducing or abandoning more confrontational forms of activism and cooperating with business to provide technical assistance and services. There are concerns that closer NGO relations with business are being driven as much, if not more, by funding rather than political considerations, and that they may involve a trade-off with the political pressures that are a crucial driver of corporate responsibility (Currah, 1999).

The organization and mobilization of grassroots groups and reform-oriented NGOs in much of the South are often constrained by what might be called the priorities of everyday life and survival, as well as the lack of resources for organizing and the denial of human rights such as freedom of association and information. In addition, as Bendell and Murphy point out (Chapter 9), the global civil regulation agenda is being shaped primarily by Northern NGOs, many of which lack both an integrated vision of environmental and development issues and the legitimacy to lobby and negotiate on behalf of Southern groups and communities.

In view of limitations such as these, which affect the role of the NGO sector as an agent of change, it is important for NGOs to construct alliances with other sectors of civil society, in particular trade unions. Historically, some of the major gains in the development of responsible capitalism have been the result of trade union pressure and agreements reached through collective bargaining. The environmental movement needs to enlist the firm support of the labour movement.

Globalization has thrown up major new challenges and opportunities for the labour movement. In the words of one former leader, if new trade union structures are needed to deal with the growing power of TNCs and international forces, so also are alliances with other sectors of civil society, in order to build a broad-based social movement that can shape the path of development more effectively (Gallin, 1999). In countries such as South Africa, Korea and Brazil there are signs that some union organizations are working more closely with community and other groups to build such a movement (Gallin, 1999). There are still, however, numerous tensions that restrict the possibility of building such a broad-based movement.

To assess the scope for corporate environmentalism in today's world it is important to examine not only the politics of environmentalism and the strength of civil society activism, but also whether changing forms of production and investment facilitate or hinder the greening of business. When certain trends associated with globalization and contemporary patterns of production and industrial organization are analysed, there emerges a structural explanation for corporate responsiveness to environmental issues and related stakeholder concerns. However, as with the early experience of corporate social responsibility, the response by big business has been extremely partial and uneven.

Contemporary structural change

There are several drivers of corporate environmentalism associated with globalization and the way firms are responding to compete both nationally and internationally. As noted in the Introduction to this book and by Welford (Chapter 6), many companies are using improvements in environmental management as a strategy to gain competitiveness. Some writers have argued that in a context where global competition is reducing the scope for differentiating products in the marketplace on the basis of price and quality, so-called lead companies are attempting to maintain or gain competitive advantage through other product or company features associated with environmental and social responsibility (Flaherty and Rappaport, 1997).

A key question which needs to be asked is not only whether instruments associated with the greening of business are congruent with the strategy of individual firms to gain competitive advantage, and possibly reduce costs, but whether they have a structural basis in terms of the changes that are occurring in the international division of labour, global production networks and in patterns of industrial organization and FDI. While there is much debate about the nature of contemporary changes in the global economic system, certain structural developments appear to be conducive to corporate environmental responsibility and eco-efficiency in some sectors. Such developments relate to so-called 'flexible specialization',[23] 'global commodity chains' (Gereffi *et al.*, 1994), export orientation, and what has been referred to as 'the thicker institutional network of international production including subcontracting, joint ventures and strategic alliances' (Kozul-Wright and Rowthorn, 1998: 6). Various aspects associated with these models seem particularly relevant for explaining why some firms are adopting certain features of corporate environmentalism.

In a context where flexibility and innovation have become particularly important for competitiveness in certain sectors (Porter and van der Linde, 1995), companies are not only attempting to respond to new market opportunities which derive from more segmented demand and discriminating buyers in the North (Gereffi, 1994: 218), but are actively trying to create and expand such markets (Hirst and Zeitlin, 1991).[24] Markets for environmental goods and services are highly relevant in this regard, including, for example, eco-labelled products, organically produced foods, biological food products (grown using fewer chemicals), recycling-friendly packaging, nature or ecotourism, environmental auditing and certification services, and cleaner technology. Trends associated with flexibility and innovation also have important technological implications. The development of cleaner technology, for example, is to some extent facilitated by the mindset, skills and other resources associated with the active process of technological innovation which characterizes the flexible specialization model.

Models of industrial organization associated with flexible specialization and global commodity chains also require different relations between firms as well as between firms and their stakeholders. With the shift towards specialization and the production of customized products, as well as the increased sourcing of manu-factured products from developing countries, Northern companies rely increasingly on networking and subcontracting. New relations based on cooperation and trust are to some extent a feature of such models (Hirst and Zeitland, 1991). Certain aspects of corporate environmentalism associated, for example, with certification, auditing and reporting are instruments that can play an important role in the development of collaborative relations between the numerous firms that make up a network or commodity chain.

The increasing global reach of many firms, new patterns of industrial organi-zation and the information technology revolution mean that companies today must interact with and be more responsive to the concerns and demands of a variety of different stakeholders (Wilson, 2000). The protection of company reputation and brand-name image has become a key managerial concern for firms in certain product sectors (Nelson, 1997). To minimize or avoid any tarnishing of reputations, some companies are not only attempting to respond to environmental concerns related to their business activities but are engaging new forms of risk management by trying to anticipate where the next problem or threat might come from, and take preventive action (Schwartz and Gibb, 1999).[25]

These patterns of industrial production and organization are extending to the South (Evans, 1998; Gereffi *et al.*, 1994). Gereffi shows how 'diversified industrializa-tion' is spreading to many developing countries with export-oriented development strategies (1994: 211). He identifies two ideal types of global commodity chains, both involving complex organizational forms in which a relatively small group of 'core corporations' manage to 'make sure all the pieces ... come together as an integrated whole' (*ibid.*: 218). So-called 'producer-driven commodity chains' –

characteristic of car, computer and electrical machinery manufacturing – are controlled by TNCs. They involve complex backward and forward linkages with considerable international subcontracting of components (*ibid*.: 216). 'Buyer-driven commodity chains' – characteristic of labour-intensive consumer goods industries – rely heavily on specification contracting, with independent companies in developing countries making finished goods (clothing, footwear, toys) according to specifications supplied by large retailers and brand-name companies (Nike, Reebok) in the North (*ibid*.: 216). Such models have some important implications for the analysis of corporate environmentalism in the South. They reveal not only the way in which certain manufacturing enterprises in developing countries are being drawn into production and marketing chains controlled by large Northern corporations but also how the smooth functioning of these chains requires attention to issues of stakeholder management and corporate social and environmental responsibility throughout the production chain.

Structural developments such as these suggest that the increasing attention to environmental issues on the part of large corporations in the North may filter down in some form to certain developing countries. This can take place in various ways, for example through the standards and specifications imposed by such corporations on affiliates and suppliers, through pressures they exert on national and international standard-setting and regulatory institutions, and also through the so-called 'demonstration' effect of TNC involvement in developing countries. As Wilkins observes, TNCs transfer more than capital, goods and personnel; they also 'carry ... with them a package of business attributes, including ... processes, marketing methods, trade names, skills, technology, and most important management' (1998: 95).

As developing countries open up their economies and become more export-oriented, domestic firms are having to respond to new pressures associated with consumer demand and regulations in the North. The survey findings presented by Pratt and Fintel (Chapter 2) show how leading firms in Costa Rica, which are producing for the export market, are more likely to have improved some aspects of their environmental management systems than those producing for the domestic market. Similarly, they note a strong 'parent company effect': firms, owned to a considerable extent by international capital, particularly those producing for the export market, had more environmental policies, plans and procedures than domestic firms, partly due to the need to comply with 'headquarter guidelines'. In their survey of foreign-owned TNCs in Singapore, Perry and Singh (Chapter 5) also identify compliance with standards set by corporate headquarters as the most important motivation for voluntary environmental initiatives by affiliates. Another survey of TNC affiliates in Asia suggests the presence of 'an internal regulatory structure within the TNC network' with some TNC headquarters having a 'hands on approach to environmental management at affiliates'. While TNC supplier and subcontractor environmental linkages were less developed, they were expected to be 'increasingly emphasized in the future' (Hansen, 1999: 26).

This influence is particularly evident in the field of environmental certification. Such instruments are becoming increasingly important in the context of contemporary models of global industrial organization, given the triple role they can perform. They can facilitate the construction of cooperative relations between firms in order to ensure certain standards; they serve to defend core corporations from risks associated with the exposure of bad environmental or social practice among affiliates and suppliers; and they can also protect niche markets from both free riders[26] and new entrants.

While the ISO 14000 environmental management certification system is of recent origin and is taking off slowly in developing countries, it is expected to expand fairly rapidly. According to UNCTAD, 'There is no question that ISO 14000 will have a major role in the standardization of corporate environmental management systems in TNCs and their affiliates and subcontractors and suppliers worldwide' (1996: 86).[27]

The growing importance of certification is apparent in the case of the horticulture sector in developing countries which is linked to the export market. In a context where fewer and fewer larger companies are controlling the horticultural trade, such firms are imposing stricter standards on suppliers. As a recent United Nations report observes, 'Led by the supermarket sector, extremely high standards and accountability are demanded of exporters and growers in terms of chemical usage [and] food hygiene standards...' (UNCTAD/SGS, 1998). But from the analysis in the report it is also clear that tools associated with quality and environmental certification and auditing are also important in the framework of new inter-firm relations based on cooperation and trust.

> Increasingly, importers, distributors and end users, especially in developed countries, are looking for sources of supply that will not 'simply trade products, but act as a partner in a strategic alliance, in order to ensure consistent, high quality, technical and environmentally safe products at competitive ... prices.'[28] ... In many ways, strategic alliance is an 'attitude of mind' rather than a physical action. The need to develop partnerships can be characterised by the recognition of the inter-linkages in the horticultural production, processing and distribution chain. Each 'player' in the chain must rely on the others if [it] is to operate efficiently. (UNCTAD/SGS, 1998: 77)

From the perspective of our analysis of both the drivers and scope of corporate environmentalism in the South, it is important to note two important qualifiers identified in the UNCTAD/SGS analysis, which apply also to several product sectors associated with the new international division of labour. The first is that strategic alliances in general, and instruments associated with certification in particular, are being promoted by TNCs or large retailers in the North not simply to develop more efficient procurement, production and marketing systems but also in response to both stricter food safety legislation in the rich industrialized countries[29] and changing consumer preferences and concerns associated with environmental and ethical issues (UNCTAD/SGS, 1998: 3–4). The second is that the process by which certain instruments of environmental management are 'disseminated' to the South through the networks controlled by TNCs and large retailers such as supermarkets, is very uneven. Only some product sectors, types of enterprise and developing countries are involved.

The above analysis of political and structural dimensions suggests that corporate environmentalism amounts to far more than a response to the 'win–win' opportunities and technological and managerial innovations emphasized by many proponents of ecological modernization theory. It is also apparent that corporate environmentalism is more than simply a 'greenwash' or 'accommodation' strategy, or a defensive reaction to civil society pressure. The political analysis indicates that social pressures are indeed a key driver of corporate environmentalism. But it also suggests that some elite groups in contemporary democratic societies not only respond to pressure; they may also take a leadership role by proactively addressing broader societal concerns. Furthermore, from the analysis of business restructuring in the context of globalization it emerges that certain features of corporate environmentalism may be conducive to the smooth functioning of contemporary production and marketing systems.

Perhaps what needs to be asked is not so much whether big business can take on board a green agenda but what sort of environmentalism is being espoused, and on what scale. The analysis of the political and structural underpinnings of corporate environmentalism indicates that it is likely to be a very uneven phenomenon in both sectoral and geographical terms. Developments associated with flexible specialization and global commodity chains affect some product sectors and countries far more than others. Furthermore, each commodity chain can assume very different characteristics in terms of the actors, market conditions and pressures which shape the possibilities of improvements in environmental management. This is brought out clearly in the analysis of four commodity chains carried out by von Moltke *et al.* (1998). Analysing the case of copper in Zambia, semi-conductors in the Philippines, cotton in Pakistan and ecotourism in Costa Rica, these authors show how the environmental response throughout the chain and the prospects for promoting sustainable development are likely to vary considerably, depending on such aspects as the distribution of power among different actors in the chain, their (related) ability to capture rents and finance environmental improvements,[30] the degree of integration and dispersion of the chain[31] and the type of environmental problem involved.[32]

This type of analysis provides a more nuanced perspective of the possibilities of environmental management reform in different sectors. It suggests that it is not enough simply to categorize developing economies in terms of two sectors with very different potentials for improving environmental management: a more modern export-oriented sector more prone to innovation and the adoption of cleaner technology versus a more polluting and less resource-efficient, domestic-oriented sector (Wehrmeyer and Mulugetta, 1999).

The assumption that export-led growth and the rapid increase in foreign direct investment in a number of developing countries, which has occurred since the 1980s, provide contexts conducive to corporate environmentalism in the South needs to be handled with care. As noted above, the capacity and willingness of firms to introduce environmental management reforms is likely to vary considerably by firm, sector and country. While doubts have been cast on the 'pollution havens hypothesis' (UNCTAD, 1999), which claims that firms will move to less developed countries to benefit from weaker environmental regulations, a recent WWF study provides evidence that 'certain resource and pollution intensive industries have a locational preference for areas of low environmental standards'. Furthermore, this report suggests that while policy competition to attract FDI may not produce an overt race to the bottom, it may have a 'chilling effect on regulation and its enforcement.... There are many examples where competition for FDI has been cited as a reason for not introducing new environmental regulations or taxes' (Mabey and McNally, 1999: 5).

Much of the debate about the environmental impact of FDI has also ignored issues of scale. A report from Latin America shows that the environmental situation has indeed deteriorated in those countries which have attracted most FDI. It points out that this is due not to a reorientation of the production structure towards more polluting industries but to the sheer growth of the export sector for manufactures (Schatan, 1999).

The above analysis suggests that corporate environmentalism in the South is likely to remain highly restrictive, in relation to both the actual content of environmentalism (scale and type of environmental management improvements and concrete impacts) and the contribution of corporate environmentalism to sustainable development. The minimalist agenda associated with improvements in environmental management may be partly due to various constraints which restrict the capacity of business to respond – constraints associated, for example, with lack of information and know-how, limited investment resources for clean technology and altering production processes, the relatively high costs of certification and auditing, the difficulties in quantifying the benefits of environmental management, the limited size of niche markets for certain environmental goods and services, organizational inertia or lack of incentives for innovation (Levy, 1997: 132–3; Porter and van der Linde, 1995: 127; Dawkins, 1995: 2). It is also due to the structural and political dimensions noted above. Just a few types of instruments or innovations might suffice to keep the system functioning smoothly. Also, the social pressures that partly drive corporate environmentalism can often be accommodated and deflated through partial responses, co-option or so-called 'institutional capture', which enables business interests to exert considerable influence over the decision-making processes of standard-setting and regulatory institutions.[33]

There is also the problem of 'Northern capture'. Some of the major voluntary initiatives associated with the promotion of corporate environmental responsibility in the South have been essentially designed by Northern actors. Business–NGO partnerships, which attempt to modify the way corporations operate in the South, involve primarily Northern NGOs. As Bendell and Murphy point out (Chapter 10), some Northern NGOs claim to speak on behalf of Southern interests, but fail to involve Southern NGOs effectively in their decision-making and consultation processes. Northern corporations, often acting through business and industry associations, are becoming increasingly influential in international decision making on environmental and social standards. There is considerable concern that the new forms of global environmental governance associated with hybrid private–public regimes (Clapp, 1998) or what Bendell and Murphy refer to as 'global private regulation', such as ISO 14000 are being dominated by Northern interests (Krut and Gleckman, 1998). As Clapp observes, we are witnessing a shift from a system of environmental governance which was based on state-based regimes such as international treaties and national government regulation, to one in which private economic actors are increasingly influential and decision making is taking place or originates in the richer industrialized countries. In such a context, 'developing countries may be losing some of their voice in this realm' (Clapp, 1998: 312). If some of the contradictions, noted above, between corporate environmentalism and development or sustainable development are to be resolved, it is important that the relevant decision-making processes are democratized.

The nature of the political process underpinning corporate management reform is also likely to result in piecemeal reforms. As indicated above, corporations are quite capable and increasingly adept at responding to certain concerns of environmentalists, consumers or development activists, in order to dim or deflect the spotlight on their activities. This can be seen in the recent strategies of certain large oil companies such as Shell and BP. It is often possible to do this through very selective management reforms, such as the introduction of a code of conduct, and/or through green advertising and multi-stakeholder dialogues. The chemical industry's Responsible Care programme has been somewhat successful in this regard.

In a report prepared for the World Summit for Social Development in 1995, UNRISD (1995) pointed out that international business cannot be expected to author its own regulation: 'this is the job of good governance' – a process in which multiple actors at local, national and international levels must intervene and take responsibility. Similarly, the 1998 *Human Development Report* suggests that the task of changing production technologies and consumption patterns in a way that is conducive to sustainable development will not be achieved by business or technological solutions alone. Also crucial are government policies and regulations, strong public action related to consumer education and the protection of consumer rights, the strengthening of international mechanisms and global instruments to tackle environmental issues, building stronger alliances among social movements, and community and civil society initiatives (UNDP, 1998).

In the absence of stronger forms of regulation and more concerted civil society pressure, the process of greening business in developing countries will remain lukewarm. TNCs and other 'core corporations' in global commodity chains, as well as business and industry associations, will continue to promote certain features of corporate environmentalism in developing countries. As we have seen, however, the initiatives involved are likely to constitute a fairly minimalist and uneven agenda which is fraught with contradictions. By facilitating the smooth functioning of production and marketing processes, enhancing competitiveness and diluting alternative agendas for change, such initiatives may be more conducive to economic growth and the legitimization of big business than sustainable development.

Notes

1 Another OECD study analysed 246 codes (Gordon and Miyake 2000).
2 In actual fact the least cited commitment (0 per cent) was that of adherence to the 'polluter pays' principle.
3 Sustainable development reporting is 'based on the extensive use of quantitative methods (such as life-cycle analysis and mass balances) and on strong links with industry-wide and national sustainable development reporting against pre-agreed targets' (UNEP, 1994: 8).
4 The so-called 14000 series of the International Organization for Standardization (ISO), which relates to standards for environmental management, established in 1996.
5 'Greenwash' refers to the attempt by corporations to hide the unpleasant environmental facts of their activities by adopting an environmental discourse or specific policies and practices that appear to be environment-friendly but which do little, if anything, to change the relationship of business to the environment. Instances of greenwash have been well documented: see, for example, Greer and Bruno (1996).
6 The international pesticide industry, jolted by the events and fall-out from the 1984 Bhopal disaster in India, has taken several important initiatives under its Responsible Care programme and the Safe Use projects in Guatemala, Kenya and Thailand.
7 Based on 1996 estimates of forest area and protected areas in *1999 World Development Indicators* (World Bank, 1999).
8 Based on data from FSC, 1999; FAO, 1997; and World Bank, 1998.
9 This criticism has been levelled, in particular, at ISO 14001 (Krut and Gleckman, 1998), and has emerged more generally in the literature on corporate social responsibility (Hopkins, 1997).
10 Levy suggests two possible explanations: the fact that larger firms have more power to resist the introduction of costly environmental investments; and bureaucratic inertia (Levy, 1997: 60).
11 A UN publication on cleaner technology transfer to developing countries, for example, is entitled *Business and the UN: Partners in Sustainable Development* (United Nations, 1999).
12 This was an activity encouraged by UNDP's partnership with big business, the Global Sustainable Development Facility, until its demise in 2000.
13 Communication with Doris Calvo, Head of Women's Section, SITRAP, April 1999.
14 I am grateful to Lin Wang, a consultant to the ILO, for these observations.
15 This point emerged during discussions at the UNRISD/UNA workshop on 'Business

Responsibility for Environmental Protection in Developing Countries', Heredia, Costa Rica, 22–24 September 1997.

16 This point was made by Harris Gleckman at the UNRISD/UNA workshop on 'Business Responsibility for Environmental Protection in Developing Countries', Heredia, Costa Rica, 22–24 September 1997.

17 The 1999 *World Investment Report* indicates that there were some 59,902 parent firms with 508,239 foreign affiliates (UNCTAD, 1998: 3) located primarily in developing and transitional economies.

18 This concept explains how the dominance of ruling groups in industrialized societies is increasingly achieved less on the basis of coercion and more through a broader representation of opposing values and interests (Laclau and Mouffe, 1985).

19 The contemporary phenomenon of 'partnerships' for development can, to some extent, be viewed from this perspective.

20 See Gramsci, 1971.

21 See Clarke, 1992: 20–1.

22 I am grateful to Jean-Paul Jeanrenaud at WWF–International for these observations.

23 Flexible specialization has been defined as 'the manufacture of a wide and changing array of customized products using flexible, general-purpose machinery and skilled, adaptable workers' (Hirst and Zeitlin, 1991: 2). It is to be distinguished from mass production, which involves 'the manufacture of standardized products in high volumes using special-purpose machinery and predominantly unskilled labour' (*ibid.*:2).

24 The rapid increase in advertising spending, particularly notable in Asia and Latin America during the past decade, partly reflects such efforts. Conservative estimates put global advertising spending at $435 billion per annum, with all forms of marketing estimated at nearer $1 trillion (UNDP, 1998: 63).

25 This point was stressed by several participants (notably those currently or previously connected with large oil companies) at an UNCTAD workshop on corporate social responsibility, attended by this author (20 May 1999).

26 For example, the Costa Rican Certification for Sustainable Tourism Programme, created by the Costa Rican Tourism Board (ICT), is an attempt to ensure that mass tourism – which takes advantage of the country's green image – will not damage the ecotourism market (von Moltke *et al.*, 1998: 261).

27 It is interesting to note that ISO 9000 certification related to quality management standards increased from nearly 28,000 to 226,000 certificates in just five years from January 1993 to December 1997 (ISO, 1998: 9).

28 No citation given.

29 The retail and processing sector, for example, must be able to trace the origins of their products and show 'due diligence' over the use of agrochemicals and in food hygiene standards (UNCTAD/SGS, 1998: 6).

30 It is observed in relation to some product chains that it is often larger (mainly Northern-based) companies higher up the chain which have this ability, rather than smaller downstream producers in developing countries. In the case of the ecotourism chain in Costa Rica, it was found that a significant proportion of revenues do accrue to local providers of goods and services (von Moltke, 1998: 20).

31 In the cotton chain, for example, it is observed that the presence of many small producers greatly complicates the flow of information and finances necessary for improved environmental management, whereas this is far easier in the more integrated semi-conductor chain (von Moltke, 1998: 22–3).

32 Waste issues related to industrial processes, for example, are often far more manageable than environmental problems related to natural resource extraction (von Moltke, 1998: 22).

33 In their analysis of eco-labelling and certification, various authors highlight the dangers which can arise when international institutions responsible for standard setting are unduly influenced by Northern business interests and lack the balanced participation necessary for effective policy making in the broader public interest (see, for example, Dawkins, 1995; Krut and Gleckman, 1998).

References

Bennett, T. (1986), 'Introduction: Popular Culture and "the Turn to Gramsci"', in T. Bennett, C. Mercer and J. Woollacott (eds.), *Popular Culture and Social Relations*, Open University Press, Milton Keynes.

Broad, R. and J. Cavanagh (1999), 'The Corporate Accountability Movement: Lessons and Opportunities', *The Fletcher Forum of World Affairs*, 23 (2) (Fall), 151–69.

Clapp, J. (1998), 'The Privatization of Global Environmental Governance: ISO 14000 and the Developing World', *Global Governance: A Review of Multilateralism and International Organizations*, 4 (3) (July–September), 295–316.

Clarke, S. (1992), 'What in the F...'s Name is Fordism', in N. Gilbert, R. Burrows and A. Pollert (eds.), *Fordism and Flexibility: Divisions and Change*, Macmillan, London.

Colchester, M. (1990), 'The International Tropical Timber Organization: Kill or Cure for the Rainforests?', *The Ecologist*, 20 (5), 166–73.

Currah, K. (1999), *Activating the Self-Correcting Mechanism of Civil Society*, mimeo, World Vision, Milton Keynes.

Dawkins, K. (1995), *Ecolabelling: Consumer's Right to Know or Restrictive Business Practice?*, mimeo, Institute for Agriculture and Trade Policy, Minneapolis.

Development and Cooperation (1999), 'Certification to Save the World's Forests', *D+C*, 2.

Dommen, E. (1999), 'Pertinence et limites des codes éthiques', *Reflets et perspectives de la vie économique*, 38 (3), 41–51.

Evans, P. (1998), 'Transnational Corporations and Third World States: From the Old Internationalization to the New', in Kozul-Wright and Rowthorn.

Flaherty, M. and A. Rappaport (1997), 'Corporate Environmentalism: From Rhetoric to Results', paper presented at UNRISD/UNA workshop 'Business Responsibility for Environmental Protection in Developing Countries', Heredia, Costa Rica, 22–24 September.

Forest Stewardship Council (FSC) (1999), www.fscoax.org

Freeman, R. (1984), *Strategic Management. A Stakeholder Approach*, Pitman, Boston.

Gallin, D. (1999), 'Organized Labour as a Global Social Force', paper presented at IR Workshop, Washington DC, 20 February 1999.

Gereffi, G. (1994), 'Capitalism, Development and Global Commodity Chains', in L. Sklair (ed.), *Capitalism and Development*, Routledge, London.

Gereffi, G., M. Korzeniewicz and R. Korzeniewicz (1994), 'Introduction: Global Commodity Chains', in Gereffi and Korzeniewicz (eds.), *Commodity Chains and Global Capitalism*, Greenwood Press, London.

Gordon, K. and M. Miyake (2000), *Deciphering Codes of Corporate Conduct: A Review of Their Contents*, Working Papers on International Investment, No. 99/2, OECD, Paris.

Gramsci, A. (1971), 'Americanism and Fordism', *Prison Notebooks*, Lawrence and Wishart, London.

Greer, J. and K. Bruno (1996), *Greenwash: The Reality Behind Corporate Environmentalism*, Third World Network, Penang.

Hansen, M. (1999), *Environmental Management in Transnational Corporations in Asia: Does Foreign Ownership Make a Difference? Preliminary Results of a Survey of Environmental Management Practices in 154 TNCs*, Occasional Paper, CBS/UNCTAD Cross Border Environmental Management Project, Copenhagen Business School, Copenhagen.

Hawken, P., A. Lovins and H. Lovins (1999), *Natural Capitalism: The Next Industrial Revolution*, Earthscan, London.

Hirst, P. and J. Zeitlin (1991), 'Flexible Specialisation versus Post-Fordism: Theory, Evidence and Policy Implications', *Economy and Society*, 20 (1) (February), 1–56.

Hopkins, M. (1997), 'Defining Indicators to Assess Socially Responsible Enterprises', *Futures*, 29 (7), 581–603.

Hurst, P. (1999), *IUF Case Study: The Global Pesticide Industry's 'Safe Use and Handling' Training Project in Guatemala*, International Union of Food and Agricultural Workers, Geneva.

IIED (1996), *Towards a Sustainable Paper Cycle*, IIED/WBCSD, London/Geneva.

ILO (1999), *Voluntary Initiatives Affecting Training and Education on Safety, Health and Environment in the Chemical Industries*, Sectoral Activities Programme, ILO, Geneva.

ISO (1998), *The ISO Survey of ISO 9000 and ISO 14000 Certificates: Seventh Cycle – 1997*, ISO, Geneva.

—— (2000), *The ISO Survey of ISO 9000 and ISO 14000 Certificates: Ninth Cycle – 1999*, (available on www.iso.ch).

IUF (1998), 'International Banana Conference Explores Routes "Towards a Sustainable Banana Economy"', *IUF News Bulletin*, 3–4, IUF, Geneva.

Jeffcott, B. and L. Yanz (2000), *Codes of Conduct, Government Regulation and Worker Organizing*, ETAG Discussion Paper No. 1, Toronto.

Jessop, B. (1990), 'Regulation Theories in Retrospect and Prospect', *Economy and Society*, 19 (2).

Jha, V. (1999), *Investment Liberalization and Environmental Protection: Conflicts and Compatibilities in the Case of India*, Occasional Paper, CBS/UNCTAD Cross Border Environmental Management Project, Copenhagen Business School, Copenhagen.

Kolk, A., R. van Tulder and C. Welters (1999), 'International Codes of Conduct and Corporate Social Responsibility: Can Transnational Corporations Regulate Themselves?', *Transnational Corporations*, 8 (1) (April), 143–80.

Kolodner, E. (1994), *Transnational Corporations: Impediments or Catalysts of Social Development?*, Occasional Paper No. 5, World Summit for Social Development, United Nations Research Institute for Social Development, Geneva.

Korten, D. (1995), *When Corporations Rule the World*, Kumarian Press, West Hartford, Conn.

Kozul-Wright, R. and B. Rowthorn (1998), 'Introduction: Transnational Corporations and the Global Economy', in R. Kozul-Wright and B. Rowthorn (eds.), *Transnational Corporations and the Global Economy*, Macmillan, London.

Krut, R. and H. Gleckman (1998), *ISO 14001: A Missed Opportunity for Sustainable Global Industrial Development*, Earthscan, London.

Laclau, E. and C. Mouffe (1985), *Hegemony and Socialist Strategy: Towards a Radical Democratic Politics*, Verso, London.

Levy, D. (1995), 'The Environmental Practices and Performance of Transnational Corporations', *Transnational Corporations*, 4 (1) (April), 44–67.

—— (1997), 'Environmental Management as Political Sustainability', *Organization and Environment*, 10 (2) (June), 126–47.

Mabey, N. and R. McNally (1999), *Foreign Direct Investment and the Environment: From Pollution Havens to Sustainable Development*, WWF–UK, London.

Markandya A. (1997), 'Eco-Labelling: An Introduction and Review', in S. Zarrilli, V. Jha and R. Vossenaar (eds.), *Eco-Labelling and International Trade*, Macmillan, London.

Mayne, R. (1999), 'Regulating TNCs: The Role of Voluntary and Governmental Approaches', in S. Picciotto and R. Mayne (eds.), *Regulating International Business: Beyond Liberalization*, Macmillan, London.

OECD (1999), *Codes of Corporate Conduct: An Inventory*, OECD, Paris.

Perry, M. and S. Singh (forthcoming), 'Environmental Policy in East Asia – The Importance of Regulation' in C. Briffett and J. Obbard (eds.), *Environmental Assessment in East Asia*.

Porter, M. and C. van der Linde (1995), 'Green and Competitive: Ending the Stalemate', *Harvard Business Review* (September–October).

Rappaport, A. and M. Flaherty (1990), *Corporate Responses to Environmental Challenges: Initiatives by Multinational Management*, Quorum, New York.

Romeijn, P. (1999), *Green Gold: On Variations of Truth in Plantation Forestry*, Treebook No. 2, Treemail Publishers, Heelsum, Netherlands.

Rowell, A. (1999), 'Greenwash Goes Legit', *Guardian*, 21 July, p. 5.

Schatan, C. (1999), *Contaminación industrial en los países latinoamericanos pre y post reformas económicas*, ECLAC, Santiago.

Schwartz, P. and B. Gibb (1999), *When Good Companies Do Bad Things: Responsibility and Risk in the Age of Globalization*, John Wiley, New York.

United Nations (1999), *Business and the UN: Partners in Sustainable Development*, United Nations, New York.

UNCTAD (1996), *Self-regulation of Environmental Management: An Analysis of Guidelines Set by World Industry Associations for their Member Firms*, UNCTAD, Geneva.

—— (1998) *World Investment Report 1998: Trends and Determinants*, United Nations, Geneva.

—— (1999) *World Investment Report: Foreign Direct Investment and the Challenge of Development*, United Nations, Geneva.

UNCTAD and Société générale de surveillance S.A. (SGS) (1998), *International Market Access Information: Horticultural Sector*, United Nations, Geneva.

UNDP (1998), 'Changing Today's Consumption Patterns for Tomorrow's Human Development', *Human Development Report 1998*, Oxford University Press, Oxford.

UNEP (1994), *Company Environmental Reporting: A Measure of the Progress of Business and Industry Towards Sustainable Development*, SustainAbility/UNEP Industry and Environment, London/Paris.

—— (1998), *Voluntary Initiatives*, Industry and Environment, 21 (1–2).

UNEP and SustainAbility (1997), *Engaging Stakeholders: The 1997 Benchmark Survey*, Sustain-Ability, London.

UNRISD (1995*)*, *States of Disarray: The Social Effects of Globalization*, UNRISD, Geneva, distributed by Earthscan, London.

UNRISD and Universidad Nacional (UNA) (1998), *Business Responsibility for Environmental Protection in Developing Countries: Report of the International Workshop, Heredia, Costa Rica, 22–24 September, 1997*, UNRISD, Geneva.

Utting, P. (1992), *Economic Reform and Third-World Socialism: A Political Economy of Food Policy in Post-Revolutionary Societies*, Macmillan, London.

von Moltke, K. *et al.* (1998), *Global Product Chains: Northern Consumers, Southern Producers and Sustainability*, Environment and Trade 15, United Nations Environment Programme.

Wehrmeyer, W. and Y. Mulugetta (1999), *Growing Pains: Environmental Management in Developing Countries*, Greenleaf Publishing, Sheffield.

West, K. (1995), 'Ecolabels: The Industrialization of Environmental Standards', *The Ecologist*, 25 (1) (January/February), 16–20.

Wilkins, M. (1998), 'Multinational Corporations: An Historical Account', in Kozul-Wright and Rowthorn.

Wilson, I. (2000), *The New Rules of Corporate Conduct: Rewriting the Social Charter*, Quorum Books, Westport, Conn.

World Rainforest Movement (1999), *Tree Plantations: Impacts and Struggles*, World Rainforest Movement, Montevideo.

Index